The

Texture

of

Memory

The Texture of Memory

Holocaust

Memorials

and Meaning

James E. Young

Yale University Press
New Haven and London

Published with assistance from the Lucius N. Littauer Foundation, the Ronald S. Lauder Foundation, and the Jacob and Clara Egit Foundation for Holocaust and Jewish Resistance Literature, Toronto, Canada, through the Histadrut Assistance Fund.

Front and back endpapers: Auschwitz-Birkenau in the early morning. Photographs by Adam Kaczkowski.

Set in Trump Medieval type by Tseng Information Systems, Inc., Durham, North Carolina. Printed in the United States of America by Thomson-Shore, Inc., Dexter, Michigan.

The photographs on pp. 130, 151, 248, 311, 315, and 318 are copyright 1993 by Ira Nowinski.

Library of Congress Cataloging-in-Publication Data
Young, James Edward.
The texture of memory : Holocaust memorials and meaning / James E. Young.
p.   cm.
Includes bibliographical references and index.
ISBN 0-300-05383-5 (cloth)
       0-300-05991-4 (pbk.)
1. Holocaust memorials—Europe.   2. Holocaust memorials—Israel.   3. Holocaust memorials—United States.   4. Holocaust, Jewish (1939–1945), in art.   5. Art, Modern—20th century.   6. Public art.   7. Holocaust, Jewish (1939–1945)—Museums.
I. Title.
D804.3.Y68   1993
940.53'18—dc20   92-40888 CIP

A catalogue record for this book is available from the British Library.

The paper in this book meets the guidelines for permanence and durability of the Committee on Production Guidelines for Book Longevity of the Council on Library Resources.

10 9 8 7 6 5 4 3 2

Contents

Preface

As I write, a chirp-chirp-chirping sound emanates from the heart of Berlin, echoing between old bullet-pocked buildings on one side, steel-and-glass towers on the other. It is the sound of the Berlin Wall falling, not in a dusty heap, but in little Day-Glo flecks and chunks, chipped away a piece at a time by hammer and chisel in the hands of memory-entrepreneurs. Almost all the original flowery graffiti art on the western side of the wall has long since been eaten away. But this does not deter the industrious miners of memory, who simply spray a new coat of graffiti colors onto the porous concrete before chipping it off. After wrangling over price, one can buy pieces of the wall, packaged in clear plastic bags, from a souvenir (that is, memory) stand nearby.

Thus has Berlin devoured what was once Germany's greatest, if unintended, monument to the Second World War: a jagged scar cutting through the heart of the nation's former capital, a Christo-esque intrusion into the landscape symbolizing a Germany riven in two, divided and conquered for its crimes against Europe and humanity. Breached in November 1989 for much the same reason it was erected in August 1961—to staunch the flood of East Germans to the West—the wall itself will soon be little more than a memory. Even as a "found" monument, its significance varied, depending on which side of the wall one lived. *Mauerkunst* (wall art) flourished on one side, fed by the gregarious, cocky attitudes of free people. Armed soldiers patrolled the blank-faced other side, guarding it as they would a national shrine, poised to shoot violators of the sacred space. When the Germans finally dismantle the last sections of the Berlin Wall, they will leave three pieces standing: reminders of the wall itself, monuments to a disappeared monument.

As I suggest in a section on German "countermonuments" to follow, the vanishing monument has begun to emblematize Germany's conflicted struggle with Holocaust memory. But in a more general vein, I also recall the rise and fall of the Berlin Wall to illustrate the broad conception of memorials that underpins this study. For the sites of memory are many and diverse, deliberate and accidental. They range from archives to museums, parades to moments of silence, memorial gardens to resistance monuments, ruins to commemorative fast days, national malls to a family's Jahrzeit candle. By necessity, even this cultural history of Holocaust memorials might be regarded as an extension of these spaces, part of the memory-work that animates them.

Though I began this study with an eye toward discovering the ways different nations and communities publicly marked the destruction of European Jewry during World War II, it soon became clear that the very definition of a "Holocaust memorial" depends on its shape and location. For national memory of what I might call the Shoah varies from land to land, political regime to regime. What was a Jewish catastrophe for me—the mass murder of nearly six million Jews, or two-thirds of European Jewry—was experienced and is now remembered as an entirely different order of disaster by Poles and Germans. Rather than defining a single "holocaust" at the outset, therefore, I will allow every site to suggest its own definition, each to be grasped in its local context. At the heart of such a project rests the assumption that memory of the Holocaust is finally as plural as the hundreds of diverse buildings and designs by which every nation and people house remembrance.

By bringing different formal qualities to bear on memory, every "memorial text" generates a different meaning in memory. Where the ghetto scribes recorded events on a day-to-day basis in the literary cloth of Yiddish and Hebrew, contemporary film and video frame a survivor's recollection in the seemingly immediate images of the present moment. Memorials and museums constructed to recall the Holocaust remember events according to the hue of national ideals, the cast of political dicta. On the day in Israel and the Diaspora dedicated to Holocaust remembrance—Yom Hashoah—memory is performed ritually as part of a national commemorative cycle. In this study of Holocaust memorials, I examine precisely how and why public memory of this era is being shaped by the memorials, museums, and days created to remember events.

Like other representations of events, the exhibitions at Holocaust museums can be approached as aesthetic, artistic creations. They juxtapose, narrate, and remember events according to the taste of their curators, the political needs and interests of their community, the temper of their time. Even those museums where the artifact is treated as holy object necessarily display collections in ways that suggest meaning and coherence. The order in which we view, for example, a rusty spoon, a political pamphlet, and a yellow star emplots these objects in a narrative matrix, in which one object is sequentially linked to the one preceding or following it. With this in mind, I also explore the kinds of meaning created in a handful of Holocaust museums, the principles around which museums organize their memory-telling. In this study, I address both the physical and metaphysical qualities of these memorial texts, their tactile and temporal dimensions: what I call "the texture of memory."

The number of monuments and memorial spaces in Europe, Israel, and America dedicated specifically to the mass murder and resistance of Jews during World War II now reaches into the thousands, with dozens more being proposed and erected every year. Over one hundred museums and other memorial institutions devoted to this period have also been built, with many more planned. Some of these memorials and museums occupy the former sites of destruction, while others are built at great remove from the killing fields. They are proposed and designed at both national and local levels in every European country, as well as in Israel and America, by states and communities, by survivors' groups and soldiers' organizations, by synagogues and churches, by families and individuals. In every nation's memorials and museums, a different Holocaust is remembered, often to conflicting political and religious ends.

In the pages that follow, however, I will neither survey the hundreds of Holocaust memorials around the world, nor offer a strictly aesthetic critique of the several dozen I examine. Nor is this work intended as either catalogue or guidebook to Holocaust memorial sites, except insofar as it leads readers toward a critical grasp of the memorial process at large. Rather than writing a comprehensive survey of these memorials, or attempting merely to cull the "good" monuments from the "bad," I have focused on a selected handful in ways that will suggest a larger critique of all such memorials.

For, as I hope to make clear, neither a purely formal nor a historicist approach accommodates the many other dimensions at play in public monuments. I suggest, rather, that the "art of public memory" encompasses not just these memorials' aesthetic contours, or their places in contemporary artistic discourse. It also includes the activity that brought them into being, the constant give and take between memorials and viewers, and finally the responses of viewers to their own world in light of a memorialized past—the consequences of memory.

In what might be called "biographies" of Holocaust memorial sites, I hope to reinvigorate otherwise amnesiac stone settings with a record of their own lives in the public mind, with our memory of their past, present, and future. All of which is meant to expand the texts of these memorials to include not only their conception and execution among historical realities, but also their current and changing lives, even their eventual destruction. This is to draw back into view the very process, the many complicated historical, political, and aesthetic axes, on which memory is being constructed. For neither memory nor intention is ever monolithic: each depends on the vast array of forces—material, aesthetic, spatial, ideological—converging in one memorial site. By reinvesting these memorials with the memory of their origins, I hope to highlight the process of public art over its often static result, the ever-changing life of the monument over its seemingly frozen face in the landscape.

With the veritable explosion of Holocaust monuments in recent years, this approach becomes ever easier to justify. For memory never stands still. As dozens more monuments appear every year, any simple survey of these memorial sites would soon become obsolete. Indeed, as new governments themselves rise and fall, the pace of change in these memorials accelerates all the more rapidly. These cultural histories of Holocaust memorials have been narrated between 1982 and 1991. In these years, many new monuments sprouted up, old ones were remade, and still others were demolished altogether. Each was contingent on its particular time and place, subject to political winds and economic environment. It was better, I felt, to provide a critical context for evaluating future monuments than to survey sites that no longer exist as described. As will become clear throughout this book, my aim has been both to reveal the many layers of meaning in these memorials and to examine the processes by which such monuments are understood.

Counting sites throughout Germany, Austria, Holland, France, Poland, Israel, and America, it seems likely that as many people now visit Holocaust memorials every year as died during the Holocaust itself. Year in and year out, millions of Holocaust "pilgrims" have stood in these sites to remember, each one taking away a different experience of that moment, a unique memory. The estimated number of visitors per year at some of the best-known memorial sites include: 750,000 at Auschwitz; 900,000 at Dachau; 600,000 at the Anne Frank House in Amsterdam; 300,000 at Majdanek; 1,250,000 at Yad Vashem in Jerusalem; 200,000 at Lohamei Hageta'ot in northern Israel. With the sheer numbers of visitors in mind, I have resisted the temptation to characterize an entire nation's memory or relationship to its past, or to draw general conclusions, for example, from the antiseptic character of Dachau or the weed-choked Jewish cemeteries in Poland.

Rather than allowing one or two memorials to stand for all memorials in a land, I have tried to assemble several, occasionally conflicting memorials, which taken together constitute a more textured national memory. For national memory comprises many, often competing recollections. As long as we continue to look only at the anti-Jewish context surrounding Poland's memorials, for example, we are going to neglect other legitimate, highly complex sets of assumptions undergirding memory there. This is not to minimize the anti-Jewish bias that continues to play a role in Poland's memorials, but to recognize it as only one of many contributing factors in the creation of any national remembrance. Better in this case to make room for the many layers and dimensions of national memory than to create a monolithic memory for every nation. I would rather preserve the complex texture of memory—its many inconsistencies, faces, and shapes—that sustains the difficulty of our memory-work, not its easy resolution.

Readers will also note that I have tried to avoid applying individual psychoneurotic jargon to the memory of national groups. One of the problems with ascribing psychoanalytic terms to the memory of groups is the consequent tendency to see all the different kinds of memory in terms of memory-conflict and strategies for denial. If memory of an event is repressed by an individual who lacks the context—either emotional or epistemological—to assimilate it, that is one thing. But to suggest that a society "represses" memory because it is not in its interest to remember, or because it is ashamed of this memory, is to lose sight of the many other social and political forces underpinning national memory. One might speak figuratively of Israel's early repression of traumatic memory too painful to bear, or of Germany's denial of crimes inconsistent with its self-idealization. But ultimately, I believe it will be more fruitful to examine the many other socially dynamic forces at play in the ways entire cultures, nations, and peoples publicly recall the Holocaust.

In fact, one of my aims is to break down the notion of any memorial's "collective memory" altogether. Instead, I prefer to examine "collected memory," the many discrete memories that are gathered into common memorial spaces and assigned common meaning. A society's memory, in this context, might be regarded as an aggregate collection of its members' many, often competing memories. If societies remember, it is only insofar as their institutions and rituals organize, shape, even inspire their constituents' memories. For a society's memory cannot exist outside of those people who do the remembering—even if such memory happens to be at the society's bidding, in its name.

For even though groups share socially constructed assumptions and values that organize memory into roughly similar patterns, individuals cannot share another's memory any more than they can share another's cortex. They share instead the forms of memory, even the meanings in memory generated by these forms, but an individual's memory remains hers alone. By maintaining a sense of collected memories, we remain aware of their disparate sources, of every individual's unique relation to a lived life, and of the ways our traditions and cultural forms continuously assign common meaning to disparate memories. It is the difference between unified memory and unified meaning for many different kinds of memory. We will not speak of the collective memory in these memorials, but of the collective meaning passed down from one generation to the next in our national traditions, rituals, and institutions.

In this context, readers may not be surprised to find the author's presence so often pronounced at the scene of memory. For in fact, detached reflection on these memorials is no more possible than it is desirable: there is no way around the author's eye. Insofar as I stand within the perimeter of these memorial spaces, I become part of their performance, whether I like it or not. In describing these sites in narrative, I have unavoidably transformed plastic and graphic media into literary texts: how I critically evaluate these memorials and what conclusions I draw from them depend very much on how I have represented them—both to myself and to the reader. By calling attention to the ways I have presented these monuments, I remind readers that they are dependent on my wordy depiction, on my own selective memory. This is not to discredit my observations, but to warn readers against taking my narrative reconstructions of monuments any more naturally than they would the monument's own reconstruction of events.

By extension, I become part of others' experience as well as part of what I describe here. As I leave the space and others enter, memory in the monument changes accordingly. I make this clear to illustrate every visitor's place in the memorial performance—and to remind readers that without having visited these sites, they are dependent on my descriptions of them. Ultimately, this is also to recognize the integral part visitors play in the memorial text: how and what we remember in the company of a monument depends very much on who we are, why we care to remember, and how we see. When I incorporate other visitors' responses into my descriptions, I acknowledge that in my sharing the memorial space with them, their responses become part of my experience, part of the total memorial text. By extension, the texts of memory here include not only the author's personal responses, but this narrative as well: hence the openly impressionistic cast of some of these descriptions. In the end, I have attempted to write a cultural history of these memorials that acknowledges the author's central place in its telling.

All of which is to suggest the fundamentally interactive, dialogical quality of every memorial space. For public memory and its meanings depend not just on the forms and figures in the monument itself, but on the viewer's response to the monument, how it is used politically and religiously in the community, who sees it under what circumstances, how its figures enter other media and are recast in new surroundings. As will become clear, memorials by themselves remain inert and amnesiac, dependent on visitors for whatever memory they finally produce.

Having posited the visitor's essential role in the memorial space, it would be hypocritical for me to write about any site I have not visited. Fortunately for the reader, this does not mean that I include the stories of every Holocaust memorial I ever tracked down—only that I have visited all of those related here, sometimes for a few hours, sometimes for several days, even weeks. This is not to suggest that all monuments omitted here went unvisited by the author. Lengthy sections on Dutch, French, Hungarian, and Czechoslovak memorials were, in fact, also written for this study but excluded for reasons of space. In time, these sections will appear in some other form, either on their own or as part of a revised and enlarged edition of this book.

In a few instances, the exclusion of a nation's monuments reflects historical circumstances beyond my control. Two scheduled trips to the former Soviet Union, for example, had to be canceled at the last moment when borders were closed to the Baltic states. Hundreds of unofficial memorials that Jewish families erected to mark the killing fields in the forests outside Riga and Vilna stand in sharp contrast to their state-inspired counterpart at Babi Yar. Photographs deposited in Yad Vashem's archives by recently arrived Soviet immigrants capture dozens of the region's "family memorials": simple wooden tablets nailed to a tree or a small pile of stones, often surrounded by the victims' kin dressed in their Sunday clothes. The book of Soviet Holocaust memorials remains to be written. Likewise, the dozens of memorials in South America and South Africa, as well as in Yugoslavia and Romania, unvisited by the author will also merit our critical reflection.

The structure of this book will be clear from the outset. The Introduction defines the idea of the monument and my critical approach to it; it also raises, without entirely resolving, the difficult issues of appraising and evaluating the memorials. The rest of the book radiates outward from the memorials located at the killing sites to those built in the new, far-flung homelands of victim-rememberers. What is theoretically described in the Introduction is thus enacted in the narrative and pictorial memorial-tellings that follow.

Even though this book addresses Holocaust memorials in particular, it is meant to serve also as a broad critique of the memorialization process at large. As such, it should not only add an important dimension to Holocaust studies, but also heighten critical awareness of all memorials, of the potential uses and abuses of officially cast memory, and ultimately of the contemporary consequences that past events hold for us in their memorial representations.

Acknowledgments

As I look back over the thousands of miles I have traveled and the hundreds of sites I have visited in writing this book, my memories tend to play tricks on me. For what often comes to mind first are the long, lonely hours spent racing along a German autobahn toward places like Bergen-Belsen, as fast as the prisoners there would have dreamed of escaping; or poking my way through the Polish country-side, behind horse-drawn carts, spending a day to find the remnants of a vanished Jewish cemetery; or getting off the number 18 bus at Har Hazikkaron in Jerusa-lem for a slow, heat-baked walk to Yad Vashem. But in fact, these memories tend to be exaggerated, even romanticized slightly, during the genuinely lonely time one spends writing about them.

For, like the memorials themselves, the core of my work is animated by the people who made it possible: the scholars who taught me how to think about memory, the historians who made the past present, the survivors who gave voice to otherwise silent stones, the archivists and heads of institutions who opened their memory-houses to me, the friends and family who were always there to listen when I returned. In the acknowledgments that follow, I attempt to recall (however inadequately) the dozens of people who have shared their time and knowledge with me, whose humane generosity has counterpointed so starkly the depravity they helped me to remember.

In many cases, my most cherished friends have also been my teachers: Geoffrey Hartman has taught me by example and by firm editorial hand that in writing lucidly, we humanize our scholarship and thus show why we do it in the first place. Others with whom I have spent long and late hours lost in memory-reflection include Froma Zeitlin, Susan Shapiro, and Aharon Appelfeld, whose learning, experiences, and friendships inspire and humble me. For reading and responding so generously and honestly to parts of my book, I shall remain indebted to Sidra and Yaron Ezrahi, Paul Mann, Natalie Zemon Davis, Saul Friedländer, Romy Golan, Detlef Hoffmann, Andreas Huyssen, Karen Remmler, Antony Lerman, Jonathan Webber, Anthony Rudolf, Emily Bilski, and Gabriel Motzkin. Other friends whose love and counsel have nourished these pages over the years include Friedrich and Erika Suhrbier, Wiebke Suhrbier, Clive and Fran Sinclair, Murray Baumgarten, Dan and Elly Wolf, Alfred and Miriam Wolf, Anita Norich, and Pamela Lubbell.

Between 1981 and 1991, I made annual visits to Germany and Poland to visit the memorial sites, to gather materials and take photographs. In every country, I was assisted by local scholars, archivists, survivors, and friends, without whose time and hospitality this book would not have been possible. For sharing their profound knowledge, resources, and insights, for opening their homes to me, I thank from the bottom of my heart Jochen Spielmann, Gary Smith and Christiane Schütz, Robin Ostow and Y. Michal Bodemann, Annegret Ehmann and Tomas Lutz in Berlin; Karl Weber and Ralf Busch in Hamburg; Horst Hoheisel in Kassel; Barbara Distel, Detlef and Maria Hoffmann in Munich. None of my work in Poland would have been possible without the excellent translations and research, the generous hospitality of Tamara Slusarska; nor without the years of thought and writing, the dear friendship, of Monika and Stanislaw Krajewski in Warsaw.

Having lived in New York City since 1980 and spent almost three years in Jerusalem (in 1981–83 and 1988–89), I found myself no less dependent on friends and scholars in Israel and America for their expertise and guidance into otherwise familiar memorial terrain. Irit Salmon, curator of the Art Museum, and Yitzhak Mais, director of the Historical Museum, at Yad Vashem were extremely generous in their time and insights into Israel's national Holocaust memorial, as were Elly Dlin and Shalmi Bar-mor over the years. Alisah Schiller and Alisa Scheck at Beit Terezin on Kibbutz Givat Haim-Ichud were very helpful in guiding me through the archives there, as well as through the history of the museum itself. The combined wisdom and friendship of T. Carmi and Lilach Peled kept all my work in Israel in perspective.

The former director of the YIVO Institute for Jewish Research in New York, Samuel Norich, and the head archivist there, Marek Web, gave generously of their knowledge and of the institute's immense resources. Michael Berenbaum, project director of the U.S. Holocaust Memorial Museum in Washington, D.C., graciously shared both the museum's plans and his own insights into them with me, as did the director of the Heroes' and Martyrs' Memorial Museum in Los Angeles, Michael Nutkiewicz. Also helpful in Los Angeles were Gerald Margolis, director of the Simon Wiesenthal Center, and Joseph Young, sculptor of the Holocaust monument in Pan Pacific Park. In San Francisco, the director of the Holocaust Center of Northern California, Joel Neuberg, was generous with his time and resources, as was Rabbi Doug Kahn, head of the Jewish Community Relations Council. Elsewhere in America, I found the organizers of other local monuments and community leaders equally generous with their insights into the memorial making process: Fred Steiniger in Tucson; Mark Jacobs and Frieda Soble in Dallas; Helen Ginsburg and Michael Allen, director of the Holocaust Awareness Institute in Denver.

Due to considerations of space, I have had to cut sections of this book I wrote on the memorials in Holland, France, and Czechoslovakia—all of which will appear later in some other form. In the meantime, however, I owe tremendous debts to Dienke Hondius and Jan Erik Dubbelman at the Anne Frank House in Amsterdam for their nuanced expertise on national memory in Holland; to Annette Wieviorka for her profound work on the Shoah and memory in France; to Jochen Gerz and Esther Shalev-Gerz for opening up their own memorial-making process with me in Paris; and to Toman and Libuše Brod, as well as to Peter Brod and Daša Najbrtova, for their guided memory tours in both Terezin and Prague, their dear friendship and learned insights into the politics of Czech memory.

Very little of this writing could have taken place without the crucial assistance of several fellowships and grants, or without the cooperation of my academic colleagues. I am eternally indebted to the John Simon Guggenheim Memorial Foundation for its fellowship in 1989 and specifically to the foundation's president, Joel Conarroe, for his warm and constant encouragement. To the Yad Hanadiv/ Barecha Foundation in Jerusalem, I owe profound thanks for the fellowship that made my year in Jerusalem both possible and so pleasant. For the generous research and publication grants awarded me by the Lucius N. Littauer Foundation, I am extremely grateful; and for administering these grants so gracefully, as well as for encouraging me with an unending flow of new materials and clippings on memorials, I thank Programs Officer Pamela Brumberg. Yale University Press and I are grateful to the Jacob and Clara Egit Foundation in Toronto for sponsoring the publication grant awarded this book by the Histadrut (Labor Federation) in Tel Aviv. Finally, in this context, I must thank all my colleagues at the University of Massachusetts, Amherst, for their warm encouragement; specifically, Murray

Schwartz, former dean of Arts and Sciences, and Robert Bagg, former chair of the English Department, deserve praise for their generous support in the forms of leaves of absence, travel grants, and a flexible teaching schedule.

Parts of this book have appeared as articles in a number of journals and collected volumes. Though I do not need permission to reprint any of this material, I would like nevertheless to thank the editors of these journals and collected volumes for their encouragement and editorial suggestions: Natalie Zemon Davis and Randolph Starn at *Representations*; W. J. T. Mitchell at *Critical Inquiry*; Barbara Rose at the *Journal of Art*; Saul Friedländer, Dan Diner, and Geulie Arad at *History and Memory*; Anthony Lerman, coeditor of *Survey of Jewish Affairs* (Blackwell); Peter Hayes, editor of *Lessons and Legacies* (Northwestern University Press); and Geoffrey Hartman, editor of *The Shapes of Memory* (Blackwell). I would also like to thank Yale University Press for its early encouragement of this project, Senior Editor Jonathan Brent for his consummately professional hand in guiding it to completion, and Harry Haskell for his editorial vigilance.

From the beginning, I have had to recognize the importance of photographs in telling these memorials' histories. In no instance have I relied on photographs alone; I have not written about any site that I have not visited personally. But neither is this merely a photographic survey of all sites I have visited. Instead, I have selected images that both illustrate my memorial-telling and add to its texture. Where possible, therefore, I have drawn primarily from photographs I have taken myself. But some of the best images have been generously contributed by four brilliantly accomplished professional photographers: Monika Krajewska, Ira Nowinski, Donald Woodman, and Adam Kaczkowski. The book owes an unanswerable debt to them all.

Even with all these wonderful people, this writing would not have been possible without the unconditional love and support of my family. Though geographically removed, my parents, sister, and brother were at my mind's side every step of this long memory-tour; whether or not they knew it at the time, many of my first notes were jotted to them. My wife of near endless patience, Lori Friedman, did not always have the luxury of this distance. To her, therefore, my profound debt of gratitude comes mixed with an apology: for her love, for all she has taught me about contemporary art, and for teaching me how to see, I will thank her every day of my life. At the same time, I'm sorry for having turned every promised holiday into yet another memorial-hunt, for turning so many moments of joy into mourning. To our wedding Ketuba, I would like to add one more clause: a real vacation, if not from memory itself, then at least from the ubiquitous sites of memory.

Introduction   The Texture

of Memory

> Forgetting the extermination is part of the
> extermination itself.
> —Jean Baudrillard
>
> No one can become what he cannot find in his
> memories.
> —Jean Améry
>
> So this story will not finish with some tomb
> to be visited in pious memory. For the smoke
> that rises from crematoria obeys physical laws
> like any other: the particles come together and
> disperse according to the wind, which propels
> them. The only pilgrimage, dear reader, would
> be to look sadly at a stormy sky now and then.
> —André Schwarz-Bart

The further events of World War II recede into time, the more prominent its memorials become. As the period of Holocaust is shaped in the survivors' diaries and memoirs, in their children's films and novels, public memory of this time is being molded in a proliferating number of memorial images and spaces. Depending on where and by whom these memorials are constructed, these sites remember the past according to a variety of national myths, ideals, and political needs. Some recall war dead, others resistance, and still others mass murder. All reflect both the past experiences and current lives of their communities, as well as the state's memory of itself. At a more specific level, these memorials also reflect the temper of the memory-artists' time, their place in aesthetic discourse, their media and materials.

Memory is never shaped in a vacuum; the motives of memory are never pure. Both the reasons given for Holocaust memorials and the kinds of memory they generate are as various as the sites themselves. Some are built in response to traditional Jewish injunctions to remember, others according to a government's need to explain a nation's past to itself. Where the aim of some memorials is to educate the next generation and to inculcate in it a sense of shared experience and destiny, other memorials are conceived as expiations of guilt or as self-aggrandizement. Still others are intended to attract tourists. In addition to traditional Jewish memorial iconography, every state has its own institutional forms of remembrance. As a result, Holocaust memorials inevitably mix national and Jewish figures, political and religious imagery.

In Germany, for example, memorials to this time recall Jews by their absence, German victims by their political resistance. In Poland, countless memorials in former death camps and across the countryside commemorate the whole of Polish destruction through the figure of its murdered Jewish part. In Israel, martyrs and heroes are remembered side by side, both redeemed by the birth of the state. As the shape Holocaust memory takes in Europe and Israel is determined by political, aesthetic, and religious coordinates, that in America is guided no less by distinctly American ideals and experiences—such as liberty, pluralism, and immigration.

By themselves, monuments are of little value, mere stones in the landscape. But as part of a nation's rites or the objects of a people's national pilgrimage, they are invested with national soul and memory. For traditionally, the state-sponsored memory of a national past aims to affirm the righteousness of a nation's birth, even its divine election. The matrix of a nation's monuments emplots the story of ennobling events, of triumphs over barbarism, and recalls the martyrdom of those who gave their lives in the struggle for national existence—who, in the martyrological refrain, died so that a country might live. In assuming the idealized forms and meanings assigned this era by the state, memorials tend to concretize particular historical interpretations. They suggest themselves as indigenous, even geological outcroppings in a national landscape; in time, such idealized memory grows as natural to the eye as the landscape in which it stands. Indeed, for memorials to do otherwise would be to undermine the very foundations of national legitimacy, of the state's seemingly natural right to exist.

The relationship between a state and its memorials is not one-sided, however. On the one hand, official agencies are in position to shape memory explicitly as they see fit, memory that best serves a national interest. On the other hand, once created, memorials take on lives of their own, often stubbornly resistant to the state's original intentions. In some cases, memorials created in the image of a state's ideals actually turn around to recast these ideals in the memorial's own image. New generations visit memorials under new circumstances and invest them with new meanings. The result is an evolution in the memorial's significance, generated in the new times and company in which it finds itself.

The capacity for change in memorials has not always been so apparent, however. For, traditionally, the monument has been defined as that which by its seemingly land-anchored permanence could also guarantee the permanence of a particular idea or memory attached to it. In this conception, the monument would remain essentially impervious to time and change, a perpetual witness-relic to a person, event, or epoch. Hence, the first monuments mentioned in the Bible: a small pillar and a witness heap of stones *(gal-ed)* gathered to mark the agreement between Laban and Jacob (Gen. 31:45–48); the matzevah (tombstone) Jacob erected on Rachel's grave (Gen. 35:20). In both cases, the monuments would suggest themselves as everlasting remnant-witnesses by which subsequent generations would remember past events and people.

At this point, a clarification of terms may be in order. Many presume that "memorials" recall only past deaths or tragic events and provide places to mourn, while "monuments" remain essentially celebratory markers of triumphs and heroic individuals. In this vein, Arthur Danto has written that "we erect monuments so that we shall always remember and build memorials so that we shall never forget. Thus, we have the Washington Monument but the Lincoln Memorial. Monuments commemorate the memorable and embody the myths of beginnings. Memorials ritualize remembrance and mark the reality of ends. . . . Monuments make heroes and triumphs, victories and conquests, perpetually present and part of life. The memorial is a special precinct, extruded from life, a segregated enclave where we honor the dead. With monuments, we honor ourselves."[1]

But in fact, the traditional monument (the tombstone) can also be used as a mourning site for lost loved ones, just as memorials have marked past victories. A statue can be a monument to heroism and a memorial to tragic loss; an obelisk can memorialize a nation's birth and monumentalize leaders fallen before their prime. Insofar as the same object can perform both functions, there may be nothing intrinsic to historical markers that makes them either a monument or a memorial.

In this study, therefore, I prefer to distinguish a memorial from a monument only in a broader, more generic sense: there are memorial books, memorial activities, memorial days, memorial festivals, and memorial sculptures. Some of these are mournful, some celebratory: but all are memorials in a larger sense. Monuments, on the other hand, will refer here to a subset of memorials: the material objects, sculptures, and installations used to memorialize a person or thing. For the purposes of this book, I treat all memory-sites as memorials, the plastic objects within these sites as monuments. A memorial may be a day, a conference, or a space, but it need not be a monument. A monument, on the other hand, is always a kind of memorial.

In the last century, the very idea of the memorial-monument and its place in modern culture has grown no less contentious than its definition. Indeed, the traditional assumption of the monument's timelessness has nearly relegated it as a form to the margins of modern discourse. For once it was recognized that monuments necessarily mediate memory, even as they seek to inspire it, they came to be regarded as displacements of the memory they were supposed to embody. Even worse, by insisting that its memory was as fixed as its place in the landscape, the monument seemed to ignore the essential mutability in all cultural artifacts. "What is the use to the modern man of this 'monumental' contemplation of the past?" Nietzsche asked. "Monumental" was, after all, Nietzsche's disdainful epithet for any version of history calling itself permanent and ever-lasting, a petrified history that buried the living.[2]

A few years later, Lewis Mumford echoed Nietzsche's scorn for the monumental when he pronounced the death of the monument insofar as it seemed hopelessly incompatible with his sense of modern architectural forms. "The notion of a modern monument is veritably a contradiction in terms," he wrote. "If it is a monument, it is not modern, and if it is modern, it cannot be a monument."[3] In Mumford's view, the monument defied the very essence of modern urban civilization: the capacity for renewal and rejuvenation. Where modern architecture invites the perpetuation of life itself, encourages renewal and change, and scorns the illusion of permanence, Mumford wrote, "Stone gives a false sense of continuity, and a deceptive assurance of life" (p. 434).

Instead of changing and adapting to its environment, the monument remained static, a mummification of ancient, probably forgotten ideals. Instead of placing their faith in the powers of biological regeneration, fixing their images in their children, the eminent and powerful had traditionally sought in their vanity a petrified immortality. In Mumford's words, "They write their boasts upon tombstones; they incorporate their deeds in obelisks; they place their hopes of remembrance in solid stones joined to other solid stones, dedicated to their subjects or their heirs forever, forgetful of the fact that stones that are deserted by the living are even more helpless than life that remains unprotected and preserved by stones" (p. 434). Indeed, after his mentor Patrick Geddes, Mumford suggests that it was usually the shakiest of regimes that installed the least movable monuments, a compensation for having accomplished nothing worthier by which to be remembered.

More recently, the late German historian Martin Broszat has suggested that in their references to the fascist era, monuments may not remember events so much as bury them altogether beneath layers of national myths and explanations.[4] As cultural reifications, in this view, monuments reduce or, in Broszat's words, "coarsen" historical understanding as much as they generate it. In another vein, art historian Rosalind Krauss finds that the modernist period produces monuments unable to refer to anything beyond themselves as pure marker or base.[5] After Krauss, we might ask, in fact, whether an abstract, self-referential monument can ever commemorate events outside of itself. Or must it motion endlessly to its own gesture to the past, a commemoration of its essence as dislocated sign, forever trying to remember events it never actually saw?

Still others have argued that rather than embodying memory, the monument displaces it altogether, supplanting a community's memory-work with its own material form. "The less memory is experienced from the inside," Pierre Nora warns, "the more it exists through its exterior scaffolding and outward signs."[6] If the obverse of this is true as well, then perhaps the more memory comes to rest in its exteriorized forms, the less it is experienced internally. In this age of mass memory production and consumption, in fact, there seems to be an inverse proportion between the memorialization of the past and its contemplation and study. For once we assign monumental form to memory, we have to some degree divested ourselves of the obligation to remember. In shouldering the memory-work, monuments may relieve viewers of their memory burden.

As Nora concludes, "Memory has been wholly absorbed by its meticulous reconstruction. Its new vocation is to record: delegating to the *lieu de mémoire* the responsibility of remembering, it sheds its signs upon depositing them there, as a snake sheds its skin" (p. 13). As a result, the memorial operation remains self-contained and detached from our daily lives. Under the illusion that our memorial edifices will always be there to remind us, we take leave of them and return only at our convenience. To the extent that we encourage monuments to do our memory-work for us, we become that much more forgetful. In effect, the initial impulse to memorialize events like the Holocaust may actually spring from an opposite and equal desire to forget them.

Added to this is a contemporary skepticism of the supposedly common values all bring to public spaces, one of the reasons for the uprising against so much public art. "In the absence of shared belief and even common interests," John Hallmark Neff writes, "it should not be surprising that so much of the well-intentioned art acquired for public spaces has failed—failed as art and as art for a civic site."[7] That is, Neff suggests, without a set of shared expectations, beliefs, or interests, artists and their prospective public audience have no grounds for engagement, no common cultural language in which they might even argue their respective views.

But this formulation may overlook one of the basic functions of all "public art": to create shared spaces that lend a common spatial frame to otherwise disparate experiences and understanding. Rather than presuming a common set of ideals, the public monument attempts to create an architectonic ideal by which even competing memories may be figured. In this light, Neff's observation might be modified: in the absence of shared beliefs or common interests, art in public spaces may force an otherwise fragmented populace to frame diverse values and ideals in common spaces. By creating common spaces for memory, monuments propagate the illusion of common memory.

As in any state's official use of commemorative spaces, this function of monuments is clear most of all to the governments themselves. Though the utopian vision may hold that monuments are unnecessary as reminders when all can remember for themselves, Maurice Halbwachs has argued persuasively that it is primarily through membership in religious, national, or class groups that people are able to acquire and then recall their memories at all.[8] That is, both the reasons for memory and the forms memory takes are always socially mandated, part of a socializing system whereby fellow citizens gain common history through the vicarious memory of their forbears' experiences. If part of the state's aim, therefore, is to create a sense of shared values and ideals, then it will also be the state's aim to create the sense of common memory, as foundation for a unified polis. Public memorials, national days of commemoration, and shared calendars thus all work to create common loci around which national identity is forged.

To the extent that all societies depend on the assumption of shared experience and memory for the very basis of their common relations, a society's institutions are automatically geared toward creating a shared memory—or at least the illusion of it. By creating the sense of a shared past, such institutions as national memorial days, for example, foster the sense of a common present and future, even a sense of shared national destiny. In this way, memorials provide the sites where groups of people gather to create a common past for themselves, places where they tell the constitutive narratives, their "shared" stories of the past. They become communities precisely by having shared (if only vicariously) the experiences of their neighbors. At some point, it may even be the activity of remembering together that becomes the shared memory; once ritualized, remembering together becomes an event in itself that is to be shared and remembered.

The Site of Memory

In keeping with the bookish, iconoclastic side of Jewish tradition, the first "memorials" to the Holocaust period came not in stone, glass, or steel—but in narrative. The Yizkor Bikher—memorial books—remembered both the lives and destruction of European Jewish communities according to the most ancient of Jewish memorial media: words on paper. For a murdered people without graves, without even corpses to inter, these memorial books often came to serve as symbolic tombstones: "The memorial book which will immortalize the memories of our relatives and friends, the Jews of Pshaytsk, will also serve as a substitute grave. Whenever we pick up the book we will feel we are standing next to their grave, because even that the murderers denied them."[9]

The scribes hoped that, when read, the Yizkor Bikher would turn the site of reading into memorial space. In need of cathartic ceremony, in response to what has been called "the missing gravestone syndrome," survivors thus created interior spaces, imagined grave sites, as the first sites for memory.[10] Only later were physical spaces created. While the function of place in mnemonic memory has been well examined, starting with Cicero, and re-examined through the brilliant studies of Yates and others, the reciprocal exchange between a monument and its space is still too little studied. For a monument necessarily transforms an otherwise benign site into part of its content, even as it is absorbed into the site and made part of a larger locale. This tension between site and memorial can be relieved by a seemingly natural extension of site by monument, or it can be aggravated by a perceived incongruity between site and monument. It is better in the view of many contemporary monument makers, in fact, to provoke the landscape with an obtrusive monument than to create a form so pleasingly balanced that it—and memory—recede into the landscape (and oblivion) altogether.

Taken further, a monument becomes a point of reference amid other parts of the landscape, one node among others in a topographical matrix that orients the remember and creates meaning in both the land and our recollections. For like narrative, which automatically locates events in linear sequence, the memorial also brings events into some cognitive order. In this sense, any memorial marker in the landscape, no matter how alien to its surroundings, is still perceived in the midst of its geography, in some relation to the other landmarks nearby.

A stainless steel obelisk situated in an empty field, for example, generates different meanings from that situated in a neighborhood shopping mall. Instead of being the only thing standing, it is one of several towers, barely noticed, surrounded by large buildings. American monuments, in particular, are placed often to maximize opportunities for symbolic meaning: the U.S. Holocaust Memorial Museum on the Mall in Washington, D.C., necessarily resonates to other nearby national monuments. The Museum of Jewish Heritage: A Living Memorial to the Holocaust, planned for the Battery in New York, will form part of an immigrant triad, with Ellis Island and the Statue of Liberty in sight. Likewise, the Liberation monument in Liberty Park in Jersey City, New Jersey, echoes the ideals and theme of the Statue of Liberty on the skyline in the background. A new Holocaust memorial in Boston, whatever shape it finally takes, will derive further American meaning from its place on the "Freedom Trail."

The Art of the Monument

In every case, Holocaust memorials reflect not only national and communal remembrance, or their geographical locations, but also the memorial designer's own time and place. For, like their generational counterparts in literature and music, most of the contemporary artists commissioned to design memorials remain answerable to both art and memory. In a hypothetical marker they designed for the Anne Frank House in Amsterdam, for example, the Starn twins have overlaid sepia-tinted automat photographs of Anne onto an enlarged page of her diary. Instead of segmenting these photographs, they have left them intact in two series of three, placed side by side, almost twinlike. The diary page, Frank's last, is dated and so recalls the dates of a tombstone, her epitaph self-inscribed.

Hans Haacke, as he has done so effectively with the icons of big business, resurrected a Nazi memorial in Graz, Austria, in order to remind all of the site's complicitous past. In *Bezugspunkte 38/88*, a city-wide installation, the artist duplicated the Nazis' draping of the town's patron saint in swastika-emblazoned banners in order to turn the image of Nazism against itself.[11] Haacke's "point of reference" was itself turned inside-out when neo-Nazis torched the monument, an act which the artist then incorporated into the text of the memorial by adding the inscription: "On the night of 9 November 1938, all synagogues in Austria were looted, destroyed, and set on fire. And during the night of 2 November 1988, this memorial was destroyed by a fire bomb."[12]

In an installation entitled *Memorial*, Christian Boltanski has likewise extended his earlier work, mixing fuzzy photographs, light bulbs, and wires to recall a Jewish day school, the instruments of memory, and the resulting difficulty of memory. Sol Lewitt's black cube set in the square of a former palace in Münster recalled both the absent Jews of the city and his own geometrical forms—before the monument itself was dismantled by town authorities. When commissioned to create a monument for San Francisco, George Segal turned reflexively to his white plaster figures, using an Israeli survivor as his primary model. In fact, as Albert Elsen reminds us, for many contemporary artists, the needs of art, not the public or memory, come first.[13] For artists working in an era of abstract expressionism, earthworks, and conceptual art, and for architects answerable to postmodern and deconstructivist design, the perceived public audience is often none other than themselves.

While contemporary designs are welcomed by the artists and architects, critics and curators, however, they often run up against a wall not only of public bewilderment but also of survivor outrage. For many survivors believe that the searing reality of their experiences demands as literal a memorial expression as possible. "We weren't tortured and our families weren't murdered in the abstract," the survivors complain, "it was real." In reference to his Warsaw Ghetto Monument, for example, the sculptor Nathan Rapoport once asked plaintively, "Could I have made a rock with a hole in it and said, 'Voilà! The heroism of the Jewish people'?" Probably not. All of which raises the question of the dual roles of public and memory in public art: for, as becomes clear, not every work of public art is a monument, not every memorial a work of public art.

Though not a historical monument, Richard Serra's *Tilted Arc* and its removal from the government plaza in New York exemplify the dilemma. On the one hand, *Tilted Arc* was scrupulously true to its maker's vision, his material, his time and place. At the same time, however, it was precisely the work's integrity and brilliance that alienated the very public it was intended for. *Tilted Arc* could not have it both ways: it could not please a community of artists who almost unanimously supported it and lay viewers disturbed by what they perceived as a violation of their public space. The conundrum remains: how is the artist going to be answerable both to his discourse and to public taste at the same time? How is she to balance the needs of a lay public against the occasionally obscure sensibilities of contemporary art—all of which depend on civic administrative approval?

Nor is this dilemma particularly new. For, as Elsen has also noted, modern and avant-garde sculptors between the wars in Europe were rarely invited to commemorate either the victories or losses, battles or war-dead of World War I.[14] The reluctance on the part of donors and government sponsors to commission abstract memorials, in particular, seems to have stemmed from two parallel impulses in the public and state. War-related memorials were perceived generally as intended to valorize the suffering in such a way as to justify it historically. This aim was best accomplished by recalling traditional heroic icons in order to invest memory of a recent war with past pride and loyalties, which would also explain the recent war in ways visible and seemingly self-evident to the public. In both cases, figurative imagery seemed best to naturalize the state's memorial messages. It was clear to those in position to memorialize World War I that the primary aim of modern sculptors after the war was to repudiate and lament—not to affirm—both the historical realities and the archaic values seeming to have spawned them.

Not that many of the modern sculptors would have shown much interest in such projects to begin with. At what was regarded as the nadir of European civilization, artists and monument makers vociferously resisted traditional mimetic and heroic evocations of events, contending that any such remembrance would elevate and mythologize events. In their view, yet another classically proportioned Prometheus would have falsely glorified and thereby affirmed the horrible suffering they were called upon to commemorate. In the minds of many graphic and literary artists of the time, this would have been tantamount to betraying not only their experience of the Great War, but also the new reasons for art's existence after the war: to challenge the world's realities and the conventions encouraging them. If figurative statuary were demanded of them, then only antiheroic figures would do, as exemplified in the pathetic heroes of Wilhelm Lehmbrück's *Fallen Man* and *Seated Youth* (1917). As true to the artists' interwar vision as these works may have been, however, neither public nor state seemed ready to abide memorial edifices built on foundations of doubt instead of valor. The pathetic hero was thus condemned by emerging totalitarian regimes in Germany and Russia as defeatist for seeming to embody all that was worth forgetting—not remembering—in the war.

In addition to the ways abstraction was thought to ameliorate a work's sense of mimetic witness, it also seemed to frustrate the memorial's capacity as locus for shared self-image and commonly held ideals. In its hermetic and personal vision, abstraction encourages private visions in viewers, which would defeat the communal and collective aims of public memorials. On the one hand, the specificity of realistic figuration would seem to thwart multiple messages, while abstract sculpture could accommodate as many meanings as could be projected onto it. But in fact, it is almost always a figurative monument like the Warsaw Ghetto Memorial that serves as point of departure for political performances. It is as if figurative sculpture were needed to engage viewers with likenesses of people, to evoke an empathic link between viewer and monument that might then be marshaled into particular meaning.

The fundamental dilemma facing contemporary monument makers is thus two-sided and recalls that facing prospective witnesses in any medium: first, how does one refer to events in a medium doomed to refer only to itself? And second, if the aim is to remember—that is, to refer to—a specific person, defeat, or victory, how can it be done abstractly? For many who survived solely to testify to the Holocaust, memory and testimony are one: witness for these survivors entails the most literal transmission possible of what they saw and experienced. Since few survivors would regard themselves as witness to form alone, as became clear in the art recovered from the ghettos and camps, even artists of the avant-garde redefined their aesthetic task as testimonial realists.[15] What has come to be regarded as "documentary" art and literature seemed to them the only mode in which evidence or witness could be delivered. But as historians and literary critics have come to accept the impulse in writers to testify in narrative, even as they look beyond witness to the kinds of knowledge created in such writing, so might critical viewers of Holocaust memorials accept the parallel impulse in Holocaust memorial makers to testify through literal figuration—before turning to the ways that public memory is organized in such figures.[16]

In referring to the general condition of the world, an inner state of mind, broken trust in humankind, or even art's inability to represent the real, abstract forms still offer artists the widest possible variety of expression. Maya Lin's succinctly abstract Vietnam Veterans Memorial, for example, commemorates the nation's ambivalence toward the Vietnam War and its veterans in ways altogether unavailable in figuration.[17] Instead of merely condemning the figurative mode as archaic and out of touch, however, we might acknowledge the need in public audiences for figuration, even as we recall the constructed nature of figurative iconography. In this way, we can keep monumental figuration from naturalizing itself, from putting a finish on its significance.

The Consequences of Memory: An Alternative Critique

Public art in general, and Holocaust memorials in particular, tend to beg traditional art historical inquiry. Most discussions of Holocaust memorial spaces ignore the essentially public dimension of their performance, remaining either formally aestheticist or almost piously historical. So while it is true that a sculptor like Nathan Rapoport will never be regarded by art historians as highly as his contemporaries Jacques Lipchitz and Henry Moore, neither can his work be dismissed solely on the basis of its popular appeal. Unabashedly figurative, heroic, and referential, his work seems to be doomed critically by precisely those qualities—public accessibility and historical referentiality—that make it monumental. But in fact, it may be just this public appeal that finally constitutes the monument's aesthetic performance—and that leads such memorials to demand public and historical disclosure, even as they condemn themselves to critical obscurity. Instead of stopping at formal questions, or at issues of historical referentiality, we must go on to ask how memorial representations of history may finally weave themselves into the course of ongoing events.

While questions of high and low art may well continue to inform the discussion surrounding Holocaust monuments, they must not dictate the critical discussion any longer. Instead, we might keep in mind the reductive—occasionally vulgar—excesses in popular memorial representations, even as we qualify our definitions of kitsch and challenge its usefulness as a critical category for the discussion of public monuments. Rather than patronizing mass tastes, we must recognize that public taste carries weight and that certain conventional forms in avowedly public art may eventually have consequences for public memory—whether or not we think they should. This is to acknowledge the unfashionable, often archaic aspects of so many Holocaust memorials, even as we look beyond them. It is also to recognize that public art like this demands additional critical criteria if the lives and meanings of such works are to be sustained—and not oppressed—by art historical discourse.

For there is a difference between avowedly public art—exemplified by public monuments like these—and art produced almost exclusively for the art world, its critics, other artists, and galleries, which has yet to be properly recognized. People do not come to Holocaust memorials because they are new, cutting-edge, or fashionable; as the critics are quick to note, most of these memorials are none of these. Where contemporary art is produced as self- or medium-reflexive, public Holocaust monuments are produced specifically to be historically referential, to lead viewers beyond themselves to an understanding or evocation of events. As *public* monuments, these memorials generally avoid referring hermetically to the processes that brought them into being. Where contemporary art invites viewers and critics to contemplate its own materiality, or its relationship to other works before and after itself, the aim of memorials is not to call attention to their own presence so much as to past events *because* they are no longer present. In this sense, Holocaust memorials attempt to point immediately beyond themselves.

In their fusion of public art and popular culture, historical memory and political consequences, therefore, these monuments demand an alternative critique that goes beyond questions of high and low art, tastefulness and vulgarity. Rather than merely identifying the movements and forms on which public memory is borne, or asking whether or not these monuments reflect past history accurately or fashionably, we turn to the many ways this art suggests itself as a basis for political and social action. That is, we might ask not only how the monument maker's era and training shaped memory at the time, and how the monument reflects past history, but, most important, what role the monument plays in current history.

We might now concern ourselves less with whether this is good or bad art, and more with what the consequences of public memorial art are for the people. This is to propose that, like any public art space, Holocaust memorials are neither benign nor irrelevant, but suggest themselves as the basis for political and communal action. With apologies to Peter Bürger, I would like to propose a reworking of what he has called the "functional analysis of art," adapted to examine the social effects of public memorial spaces.[18] My aim is to explore not just the relations between people and their monuments, but the consequences of these relations in historical time.

Whereas some art historians have traditionally dismissed such approaches to art as anthropological, social, or psychological, others have opened their inquiry to include larger issues of the sociology of art: public memorials in this case are exemplary of an artwork's social life, its life in society's mind. As Marianne Doezema has suggested, there is much more to the monument's performance than its mere style or school of design. "The public monument," she writes, "has a responsibility apart from its qualities as a work of art. It is not only the private expression of an individual artist; it is also a work of art created for the public, and therefore can and should be evaluated in terms of its capacity to generate human reactions."[19] To my mind, such reaction refers not just to an emotional affect, but to the actual consequences for people in their monuments. The question is not, How are people moved by these memorials? but rather, To what end have they been moved, to what historical conclusions, to what understanding and actions in their own lives? This is to suggest that we cannot separate the monument from its public life, that the social function of such art *is* its aesthetic performance.

"There is nothing in this world as invisible as a monument," Robert Musil once wrote. "They are no doubt erected to be seen—indeed, to attract attention. But at the same time they are impregnated with something that repels attention."[20] This "something" is the essential stiffness monuments share with all other images: as a likeness necessarily vitrifies its otherwise dynamic referent, a monument turns pliant memory to stone. And it is this "finish" that repels our attention, that makes a monument invisible. It is as if a monument's life in the communal mind grows as hard and polished as its exterior form, its significance as fixed as its place in the landscape. For monuments at rest like this—in stasis—seem to present themselves as eternal parts of the landscape, as naturally arranged as nearby trees or rock formations.

As an inert piece of stone, the monument keeps its own past a tightly held secret, gesturing away from its own history to the events and meanings we bring to it in our visits. Precisely because monuments seem to remember everything but their own past, their own creation, my critical aim will be to reinvest the monument with our memory of its coming into being. None of this is intended to fix the monument's meaning in time, which would effectively embalm it. Instead, I hope to reinvigorate this monument with the memory of its acquired past, to vivify memory of events by writing into it our memory of the monument's origins.

By returning to the memorial some memory of its own genesis, we remind ourselves of the memorial's essential fragility, its dependence on others for its life; that it was made by human hands in human times and places, that it is no more a natural piece of the landscape than we are. For, unlike words on a page, memorial icons seem literally to embody ideas, to invite viewers to mistake material presence and weight for immutable permanence. If, in its glazed exteriority, we never really see the monument, I shall attempt to crack its eidetic veneer, to loosen meaning, to make visible the activity of memory in monuments. It is my hope that such a critique may save our *icons* of remembrance from hardening into *idols* of remembrance.[21]

For too often a community's monuments assume the polished, finished veneer of a death mask, unreflective of current memory, unresponsive to contemporary issues. Instead of enshrining an already enshrined memory, the present study might provide a uniquely instructive glimpse of the monument's inner life— the tempestuous social, political, and aesthetic forces—normally hidden by a monument's taciturn exterior. By drawing back into view the memorial-making process, we invigorate the very idea of the monument, thereby reminding all such cultural artifacts of their coming into being, their essential constructedness.

To this end, I enlarge the life and texture of Holocaust memorials to include: the times and places in which they were conceived; their literal construction amid historical and political realities; their finished forms in public spaces; their places in the constellation of national memory; and their ever-evolving lives in the minds of their communities and of the Jewish people over time. With these dimensions in mind, we look not only at the ways individual monuments create and reinforce particular memory of the Holocaust period, but also at the ways events re-enter political life shaped by monuments. Taken together, these stages comprise a genuine activity of memory, by which artifacts of ages past are invigorated by the present moment, even as they condition our understanding of the world around us.

On a more general level, we might ask of all memorials what meanings are generated when the temporal realm is converted to material form, when time collapses into space, a trope by which it is then measured and grasped. How do memorials emplot time and memory? How do they impose borders on time, a facade on memory? What is the relationship of time to place, place to memory, memory to time? Finally, two fundamentally interrelated questions: How does a particular place shape our memory of a particular time? And how does this memory of a past time shape our understanding of the present moment?

Through this attention to the activity of memorialization, we might also remind ourselves that public memory is constructed, that understanding of events depends on memory's construction, and that there are worldly consequences in the kinds of historical understanding generated by monuments. Instead of allowing the past to rigidify in its monumental forms, we would vivify memory through the memory-work itself—whereby events, their recollection, and the role monuments play in our lives remain animate, never completed. In this light, we find that the performance of Holocaust memorials depends not on some measured distance between history and its monumental representations, but on the conflation of private and public memory, in the memorial activity by which minds reflecting on the past inevitably precipitate in the present historical moment.

It is not enough to ask whether or not our memorials remember the Holocaust, or even how they remember it. We should also ask to what ends we have remembered. That is, how do we respond to the current moment in light of our remembered past? This is to recognize that the shape of memory cannot be divorced from the actions taken in its behalf, and that memory without consequences contains the seeds of its own destruction. For were we passively to remark only the contours of these memorials, were we to leave unexplored their genesis and remain unchanged by the recollective act, it could be said that we have not remembered at all.

Part I

Germany:

The Ambiguity

of Memory

Introduction

As part of Germany's "Skulptur Projekte 87," the American geometric minimalist Sol Lewitt installed a large cube of black stones smack in the middle of the plaza in front of the Münster Palace and dedicated it to "the missing Jews of Münster." It sat like an abandoned coffin amid soaring mock-baroque facades and gas lamps, a black blight squatting in the center of a sunny and graceful university square. In time, the *Black Form* was covered by graffiti and political slogans, which further heightened the contrast between it and its elegant surroundings. Chauffeurs for university administrators complained that it left them no room to turn their limousines around after dropping off their charges; other citizens objected to the way it spoiled the aesthetic integrity of an expensive new plaza. Despite angry protests by the installation curator and anguished pleas from the artist, a jackhammer crew from the university demolished the *Black Form* in March 1988. An absent people would now be commemorated by an absent monument.

Memory of the monument remained strong in the community's mind, however. Eight months later, during commemorations of Kristallnacht, the city council asked the artist to reconstruct what they called a new "wall-work." Still faithful to his geometric medium, Lewitt agreed to remake his *Black Form*, a bleak reminder, he said, that without Jewish children in town, the monument would mark the end of generations. Within days, the threat of its reappearance reignited the debate over how to commemorate the Holocaust without seeming to violate contemporary spaces. A seminar was planned, with philosophers and art historians invited to reflect on the nexus between "seeing and thinking." Only the Green party dissented from the process, not because its members weren't in sympathy with the monument, but because they feared that the controversy, meetings, aesthetic debates, and bureaucratic wrangling had all but displaced study of the period itself.

Perhaps no single emblem better represents the conflicted, self-abnegating motives for memory in Germany today than the vanishing monument. On the one hand, no one takes their

Sol Lewitt's *Black Form Dedicated to the Missing Jews*, Münster, Germany, 1987. It was demolished that year and rebuilt in a slightly larger format in Hamburg's Altona district, 1989. Photo: Courtesy of the Landesmuseum für Kunst und Kultur Geschichte, Münster.

Sol Lewitt's "Black Form" in its new home in front of the Town Hall in Hamburg-Altona, 1989. Photo: James E. Young

memorials more seriously than the Germans. Competitions are held almost monthly across the "Fatherland" for new memorials against war and fascism, or for peace; or to mark a site of destruction, deportation, or a missing synagogue; or to remember a lost Jewish community. Students devote their summers to concentration camp archaeology at Neuengamme, excavating artifacts from another, crueler age. Or they take up hammer and nails to rebuild a synagogue in Essen, or to build a monument at the site of Dachau's former satellite camp at Landsberg. Brigades of young Germans once again report dutifully to Auschwitz, where they repair delapidated exhibition halls, tend shrubs around the barracks, and hoe weeds from the no-man's-land between formerly electrified fences. No less industrious than the generations preceding them, German teenagers now work as hard at constructing memorials as their parents did in rebuilding the country after the war, as their grandparents did in building the Third Reich itself.

Nonetheless, Holocaust memorial-work in Germany today remains a tortured, self-reflective, even paralyzing preoccupation. Every monument, at every turn, is endlessly scrutinized, explicated, and debated. Artistic, ethical, and historical questions occupy design juries to an extent unknown in other countries. In a Sisyphian replay, memory is strenuously rolled nearly to the top of consciousness only to clatter back down in arguments and political bickering, whence it starts all over again. Germany's ongoing memorial-work simultaneously displaces and constitutes the object of memory. Though some, like the Greens, might see such absorption in the process of memorial building as an evasion of memory, it may also be true that the surest engagement with memory lies in its perpetual irresolution. In fact, the best German memorial to the Fascist era and its victims may not be a single memorial at all—but simply the never-to-be-resolved debate over which kind of memory to preserve, how to do it, in whose name, and to what end.

Given the state-sponsored monument's traditional function as self-aggrandizing locus for national memory, the ambiguity of German memory comes as no surprise. After all, while the victors of history have long erected monuments to their triumphs and victims have built memorials to their martyrdom, only rarely does a nation call upon itself to remember the victims of crimes it has perpetrated. Where are the national monuments to the genocide of American Indians, to the millions of Africans enslaved and murdered, to the Russian kulaks and peasants starved to death by the millions? They barely exist.[1]

What then of Germany, a nation justly forced to remember the suffering and devastation it once caused in the name of its people? How does a state incorporate its crimes against others into its national memorial landscape? How does a state recite, much less commemorate, the litany of its misdeeds, making them part of its reason for being? Under what memorial aegis, whose rules, does a nation remember its own barbarity? Where is the tradition for memorial mea culpa, when combined remembrance and self-indictment seem so hopelessly at odds? Unlike state-sponsored memorials built by victimized nations and peoples to themselves in Poland and Israel, those in Germany are necessarily those of the persecutor remembering its victims. In the face of this necessary breach in the conventional "memorial code," it is little wonder that German national memory remains so torn and convoluted: it is that of a nation tortured by its conflicted desire to build a new and just state on the bedrock memory of its horrendous crimes.

Germany's struggle with memory of its Nazi past is reflected in nearly every aspect of its national being: from its deliberations over the government's return to Berlin to its ambivalence over a single national holiday; from the meticulously conceived museums on the former sites of concentration camps to a new generation of artists' repudiation of monumental forms, still redolent of Nazi art. On the former site of Hamburg's greatest synagogue at

Bornplatz, Margrit Kahl has assembled an intricate mosaic tracing the complex lines of the synagogue's roof construction: a palimpsest for a building and community that no longer exist. Norbert Radermacher bathes a guilty landscape in Berlin's Neukölln neighborhood with the inscribed light of its past. Alfred Hrdlicka began (but never finished) a "countermonument" in Hamburg to neutralize an indestructible Nazi monument nearby. In a suburb of Hamburg, Jochen and Esther Gerz have erected a black pillar against fascism and for peace that is designed to disappear altogether over time. The very heart of Berlin, former site of the Gestapo headquarters, remains a great, gaping wound as politicians, artists, and various committees forever debate the most appropriate memorial.

Even the search for a "national day," a day intended to unify Germans in memorial reflections on their past, churns up more angst than pride. While some in Germany would pinpoint the moment of their national rebirth at *Null-Stunde* (Zero Hour) on 8 May 1945, many others are loath to turn the day of their unconditional capitulation into a national holiday. A few have suggested 20 July, the day in 1944 of the Wehrmacht officers' unsuccessful attempt on Hitler's life; but again, this would have commemorated an attempted coup of German leaders against their own in wartime, a patriotic contradiction. As became all too clear, in fact, any day finally chosen would have to compete with the only day on the calendar to have acquired truly national proportions over the course of the twentieth century in Germany: an antiday, the unspoken holiday around which great events continue to cluster in spite of itself—November 9.

On this day in 1918, Kaiser Wilhelm II abdicated his throne, marking the beginning of the Weimar Republic. With this day of the Reich's dissolution in mind, Adolf Hitler attempted to anoint himself leader on 9 November 1923 in his failed Munich beerhall putsch. In partial homage to that event, Kristallnacht was launched on the eve of 9 November 1938. During the war itself, the Nazi leadership saved its victory speeches for 9 November, as if to blot out Hitler's earlier ignominy. And, as if mystically drawn by the great negative gravity of this day fifty years after Germany invaded Poland, Germans broke through the Berlin Wall on 9 November 1989, leading to the reunification of their country less than a year later. If there were ever a single national day around which practically all of Germany's twentieth-century history might be organized, this is it.

Precisely because of its terrible load, of course, the ninth of November will remain only a phantom national day. Germany's national day has been set for 3 October, after the day in 1990 when East and West Germany (symbolizing

East and West Europe) officially became one nation again. It will be a new day, unencumbered by the past, to commemorate yet another beginning, which will turn the period between 1945 and 1989 into a gestatory interregnum, a rehabilitative sentence served before Germany could be reborn again, whole. At the first parliamentary meeting of the reunified Germany, on 3 October 1990, Chancellor Helmut Kohl called a moment's silence to remember all the victims of events leading up to and issuing from Germany's division: the victims of nazism, communism, and the Berlin Wall. On the one hand, this moment reminded Germans that they had internalized remembrance of the Holocaust to such a degree that it had become, in Dan Diner's words, the actual—if unwritten—constitution of the Federal Republic.[2] At the same time, however, by uniting memory of its own martyrs with those it once victimized, making all victims the center of its first nationally shared memorial moment, Germany also attempted a qualified return to more traditional patterns of national remembrance, to what has been called a normalization of the past.[3]

For a nation's impulse to memorialize its own crimes is difficult to sustain and is almost always imposed as a certain kind of penance from without. When memory and penance are linked, however, what happens when the greatest burden of penance—Germany's division—

is removed? It is likely that without the wall as a punitive reminder, Germany will become a little more like other nations: its national institutions will recall primarily its own martyrs and triumphs. These include civilian victims of Allied bombings, dutiful soldiers killed on the front, and members of the wartime resistance to Hitler. One wonders whether the whole new Germany will become more like its former western part, forever trying to overcome memory. Or whether the new Germany will become a little more like the former eastern sector, absorbed in the future, having already officially mastered the past. Finally, even Germany's nearly obsessive preoccupation with memory itself may be partly displaced by the reunification process, submerged by its sheer costs. As was the case immediately after the war, the arts of memory, monuments, and museums may even seem a little luxurious in the face of national reconstruction.

Chapter 1

The Countermonument:

Memory against

Itself in Germany

Away with the monuments!
—Friedrich Nietzsche

For a new generation of artists in Germany today, the question is not whether to remember or to forget the Holocaust. Rather, given the tortuous complexity of their nation's relation to its past, they wonder whether the monument itself is more an impediment than an incitement to public memory. Perhaps the most stunning and inflammatory response to Germany's memorial conundrum is the rise of its countermonuments: brazen, painfully self-conscious memorial spaces conceived to challenge the very premises of their being.

Ethically certain of their duty to remember, but aesthetically skeptical of the assumptions underpinning traditional memorial forms, a new generation of contemporary artists and monument makers in Germany is probing the limits of both their artistic media and the very notion of a memorial. They are heirs to a double-edged postwar legacy: a deep distrust of monumental forms in light of their systematic exploitation by the Nazis, and a profound desire to distinguish their generation from that of the killers through memory.[1]

At home in an era of earthworks, conceptual and self-destructive art, these young artists explore both the necessity of memory and their incapacity to recall events they never experienced directly. To their minds, neither literal nor figurative references suggesting anything more than their own abstract link to the Holocaust will suffice. Instead of seeking to capture the memory of events, therefore, they remember only their own relationship to events, the great gulf of time between themselves and the Holocaust.

For German artists and sculptors like Jochen Gerz, Norbert Radermacher, and Horst Hoheisel, the possibility that memory of events so grave might be reduced to exhibitions of public craftsmanship or cheap pathos remains intolerable. They contemptuously reject the traditional forms and reasons for public memorial art, those spaces that either console viewers or redeem such tragic events, or indulge in a facile kind of *Wiedergutmachung* or purport to mend the memory of a murdered people. Instead of searing memory into public consciousness, they fear, conventional memorials seal memory off from awareness altogether. For these artists, such an evasion would be the ultimate abuse of art, whose primary function to their minds is to jar viewers from complacency, to challenge and denaturalize the viewers' assumptions. In the following case studies of four contemporary countermonuments, we explore the process whereby artists renegotiate the tenets of their memory-work, whereby monuments are born resisting the very possibility of their birth.

The Gerzes' Countermonument

To some extent, this new generation of artists in Germany may only be enacting a critique of memory-places already formulated by cultural and art historians long skeptical of the memorial's traditional function. As if in response to the seemingly generic liabilities of monuments, conceptual artists Jochen and Esther Gerz have designed what they call a *Gegen-Denkmal* (countermonument). It was built at the city of Hamburg's invitation to create a "Monument against Fascism, War, and Violence—and for Peace and Human Rights." The artists' first concern was how to commemorate such worthy sentiments without ameliorating memory altogether. That is, how would their monument emplace such memory without usurping the community's will to remember? Their second concern was how to build an antifascist monument without resorting to what they regarded as the fascist tendencies in all monuments. "What we did not want," Jochen Gerz declared, "was an enormous pedestal with something on it presuming to tell people what they ought to think."[2]

To their minds, the didactic logic of monuments, their demagogical rigidity, recalled too closely traits they associated with fascism itself. Their monument against fascism, therefore, would amount to a monument against itself: against the traditionally didactic function of monuments, against their tendency to displace the past they would have us contemplate—and finally, against the authoritarian propensity in all art that reduces viewers to passive spectators.

The artists decided that theirs would be a self-abnegating monument, literally self-effacing. So when Hamburg offered them a sun-dappled park setting, they rejected it in favor of what they termed a "normal, uglyish place." Their counter-

Harburg's
*Monument
against
Fascism,*
designed by
Jochen Gerz and
Esther Shalev-
Gerz, shortly
after its
unveiling in
1986, before its
first sinking.
Photo:
Courtesy of
Hamburg's
Kulturbehörde.

monument would not be refuge in memory, tucked away from the hard edges of urban life, but one more eyesore among others on a blighted cityscape. They chose the commercial center of Harburg, a somewhat dingy suburb of Hamburg, located thirty minutes from the city center by subway across the river, just beyond a dioxin dump, populated with a mix of Turkish guest-workers and blue-collar German families. Set in a pedestrian shopping mall, their countermonument would rise sullenly amid red brick and glass shop windows: package-laden shoppers could like it or hate it, but they could not avoid it.

Unveiled in 1986, this twelve-meter-high, one-meter-square pillar is made of hollow aluminum, plated with a thin layer of soft, dark lead. A temporary inscription near its base reads—and thereby creates constituencies in—German, French, English, Russian, Hebrew, Arabic, and Turkish: "We invite the citizens of Harburg, and visitors to the town, to add their names here to ours. In doing so, we commit ourselves to remain vigilant. As more and more names cover this 12 meter tall lead column, it will gradually be lowered into the ground. One day it will have disappeared completely, and the site of the Harburg monument against fascism will be empty. In the end, it is only we ourselves who can rise up against injustice." A steel-pointed stylus, with which to score the soft lead, is attached at each corner by a length of cable. As one-and-a-half-meter sections are covered with memorial graffiti, the monument is lowered into the ground, into a chamber as deep as the column is high. The more actively visitors participate, the faster they cover each section with their names, the sooner the monument will disappear. After several lowerings over the course of four or five years, nothing will be left but the top surface of the monument, which will be covered with a burial stone inscribed to "Harburg's Monument against Fascism." In effect, the vanishing monument will have returned the burden of memory to visitors: one day, the only thing left standing here will be the memory-tourist, forced to rise and to remember for himself.

With audacious simplicity, the countermonument thus flouts any number of cherished memorial conventions: its aim is not to console but to provoke; not to remain fixed but to change; not to be everlasting but to disappear; not to be ignored by passersby but to demand interaction; not to remain pristine but to invite its own violation and desanctification; not to accept graciously the burden of memory but to throw it back at the town's feet. By defining itself in opposition to the traditional memorial's task, the countermonument illustrates concisely the possibilities and limitations of all memorials everywhere. In this way, it functions as a valuable "counterindex" to the ways time, memory, and current history intersect at any memorial site.

A local citizen
adds her name
to Harburg's
*Monument
against
Fascism*. Photo:
James E. Young

How better to remember forever a vanished people than by the perpetually unfinished, ever-vanishing monument? As if in mocking homage to national forebears who planned the Holocaust as a self-consuming set of events—that is,
intended to destroy all traces of itself, all memory of its victims—the Gerzes have
designed a self-consuming memorial that leaves behind only the rememberer and
the memory of a memorial. As the self-destroying sculpture of Jean Tinguely
and others challenged the very notion of sculpture, the vanishing monument
similarly challenges the idea of monumentality and its implied corollary, permanence. But while self-effacing sculpture and monuments share a few of the same
aesthetic and political motivations, each also has its own reasons for vanishing.
Artists like Tinguely created self-destroying sculpture in order to preempt the
work's automatic commodification by a voracious art market. They hoped such
works would thereby remain purely public and, by vanishing, would leave the
public in a position to examine itself as part of the piece's performance. "The
viewer, in effect, [becomes] the subject of the work," as Douglas Crimp has observed. Or, in Michael North's elaboration of this principle, "the public *becomes*
the sculpture."[3]

A photographic record of the Harburg monument's disappearance is included with invitations to each of the ceremonial sinkings. Photo: Courtesy of Jochen Gerz and Esther Shalev-Gerz.

10. Oktober 1986
Einweihung

1. September 1987
1. Absenkung

23. Oktober 1988
2. Absenkung

The Gerzes' countermonument takes this insight several steps further. "Art, in its conspicuousness, in its recognizability, is an indication of failure," Jochen Gerz has said. "If it were truly consumed, no longer visible or conspicuous, if there were only a few manifestations of art left, it would actually be where it belongs—that is, within the people for whom it was created."[4] The countermonument is direct heir to Gerz's ambivalence toward art's objecthood. For him, it seems, once the art object stimulates in the viewer a particular complex of ideas, emotions, and responses which then come to exist in the viewer independently of further contact with the piece of art, it can wither away, its task accomplished. By extension, once the monument moves its viewers to memory, it also becomes unnecessary and so may disappear. As a result, Gerz suggests, "we will one day reach the point where anti-Fascist memorials will no longer be necessary, when vigilance will be kept alive by the invisible pictures of remembrance" (p. 47). "Invisible pictures," in this case, would correspond to our internalized images of the memorial itself, now locked into the mind's eye as a source of perpetual memory. All that remains, then, is the memory of the monument, an afterimage projected onto the landscape by the rememberer. The best monument, in Gerz's view, may be no monument at all, but only the memory of an absent monument.

The Gerzes are highly regarded in Europe as poets and photographers, and as conceptual and performance artists. In fact, much of their conceptual art conflates photographs and poetry, overlaying image with word. In their performances, they aspire simultaneously to be "the painter, medium, paintbrush, and not just witness to a work."[5] In their countermonument, the artists have at-

6. September 1989
3. Absenkung

22. Februar 1990
4. Absenkung

4. Dezember 1990
5. Absenkung

27. September 1991
6. Absenkung

tempted a "performative piece" that initiates a dynamic relationship between artists, work, and viewer, in which none emerges singularly dominant. In its egalitarian conception, the countermonument would not just commemorate the antifascist impulse but enact it, breaking down the hierarchical relationship between art object and its audience. By inviting its own violation, the monument humbles itself in the eyes of beholders accustomed to maintaining a respectful, decorous distance. It forces viewers to desanctify the memorial, demystify it, and become its equal. The countermonument denaturalizes what the Gerzes feel is an artificial distance between artist and public generated by the holy glorification of art. Ultimately, such a monument undermines its own authority by inviting and then incorporating the *autho*rity of passersby.

In fact, in this exchange between artist, art object, and viewer, the sense of a single authority, a single signatory, dissolves altogether: that the work was never really self-possessing and autonomous is now made palpable to viewers. The artist provides the screen, passersby add their names and graffiti to it, which causes the artist to sink the monument into the ground and open up space for a fresh exchange. It is a progressive relationship, which eventually consumes itself, leaving only the unobjectified memory of such an exchange. In its abstract form, this monument claims not to prescribe—the artists might say, dictate—a specific object of memory. Rather, it more passively accommodates all memory and response, as the blank-sided obelisk always has. It remains the obligation of passersby to enter into the art: it makes artist-rememberers and self-memorializers out of every signatory. By inviting viewers to commemorate themselves, the countermonument reminds them that to some extent all any monument can do is provide a trace of its makers, not of the memory itself.

The Gerzes' monument is an intentional visual pun: as the monument would rise up symbolically against fascism before disappearing, it calls upon us to rise up literally in its stead. It reminds us that all monuments can ever do is rise up symbolically against injustice, that the practical outcome of any artist's hard work is dissipated in its symbolic gesture. The Gerzes suggest that it is precisely the impotence of this symbolic stand that they abhor in art, the invitation to vicarious resistance, the sublimation of response in a fossilized object. In contrast, they hope that the countermonument will incite viewers, move them beyond vicarious response to the actual, beyond symbolic gesture to action.

From the beginning, the artists had intended this monument to torment—not reassure—its neighbors. They have likened it, for example, to a great black knife in the back of Germany, slowly being plunged in, each thrust solemnly commemorated by the community, a self-mutilation, a kind of topographical hara-kiri.[6] The countermonument objectifies for the artists not only the Germans' secret desire that all these monuments just hurry up and disappear, but also the urge to strike back at such memory, to sever it from the national body like a wounded limb. In particular, the Gerzes take mischievous, gleeful delight in the spectacle of a German city's ritual burial of an antifascist monument on which it has spent $144,000—enough, in the words of Hamburg's disgruntled mayor, to repave ninety-seven yards of autobahn. Indeed, the fanfare and celebration of its 1986 unveiling are repeated in all subsequent lowerings, each attended by eager city politicians, invited dignitaries, and local media. That so many Germans would turn out in such good faith to cheer the destruction of a monument against fascism exemplifies, in the artists' eyes, the essential paradox in any people's attempt to commemorate its own misdeeds.

At every sinking, the artists attempt to divine a little more of the local reaction. "What kind of monument disappears?" some citizens demand to know. "Is it art when we write all over it?" ask teenagers. At one point, the Gerzes went from shop to shop to gather impressions, which varied from satisfaction at the attention it had generated in the commercial district to less encouraging responses. "They ought to blow it up," said one person. Another chimed in, "It's not so bad as far as chimneys go, but there ought to be some smoke coming out of it."[7] The Gerzes found that even resentment is a form of memory.

In their original conception, the Gerzes had hoped for row upon row of neatly inscribed names, a visual echo of the war memorials of another age. This black column of self-inscribed names might thus remind all visitors of their own mor-

Graffiti on Harburg's *Monument against Fascism*. Photo: Courtesy of Jochen Gerz and Esther Shalev-Gerz.

tality, not to mention the monument's. Execution did not follow design, however, and even the artists were taken aback by what they found after a couple of months: an illegible scribble of names scratched over names, all covered over in a spaghetti scrawl, what Jochen likened to a painting by Mark Tobey. People had come at night to scrape over all the names, even to pry the lead plating off the base. There were hearts with "Jurgen liebt Kirsten" written inside, stars of David, and funny faces daubed in paint and marker pen. Inevitably, swastikas also began to appear: how better to remember what happened than by the Nazis' own sign? After all, Jochen insists, "a swastika is also a signature." In fact, when city authorities warned of the possibility of vandalism, the Gerzes had replied, "Why not give that phenomenon free rein and allow the monument to document the social temperament in that way?"[8]

The town's citizens were not as philosophical, however, and began to condemn the monument as a trap for graffiti. It was almost as if the monument taunted visitors in its ugliness. But what repels critics is not clear. Is it the monument's unsightly form or the grotesque sentiments it captures and then reflects back to the community? As a social mirror, it becomes doubly troubling in that it reminds the community of what happened then and, even worse, how they now respond to the memory of this past. To those members of the community who deplore the

Harburg's
vanishing
*Monument
against
Fascism*, almost
gone. Photo:
James E. Young.

ease with which this work is violated, the local newspaper answered succinctly: "The filth brings us closer to the truth than would any list of well-meaning signatures. The inscriptions, a conglomerate of approval, hatred, anger and stupidity, are like a fingerprint of our city applied to the column."[9] The countermonument accomplishes what all monuments must: it reflects back to the people—and thus codifies—their own memorial projections and preoccupations.

Its irreverence notwithstanding, the memorial quality to most graffiti is legendary: we know Kilroy was here, that he existed, by the inscribed trace he left behind. As wall and subway graffiti came to be valued as aesthetic expressions of protest, however, they were also appropriated commercially by galleries and museums, which absorbed them as a way of naturalizing—hence neutralizing— them. (How else does one violate a graffiti-covered wall? By cleaning it?) In its gestures to both graffiti artists and to the Mauerkunst of the Berlin Wall, the countermonument points guiltily at its own official appropriation of guerrilla art, even as it redeems itself in its eventual self-destruction.

In addition to demonstrating the impulse toward self-memorialization and the violation of public space, some of these graffiti also betray the more repressed xenophobia of current visitors. Inscriptions like "Ausländer raus" (Foreigners, get out) echo an antipathy toward more recent national "guests," as well as the defiling of Jewish cemeteries and other memorials in Germany. By retaining these words, the countermonument acknowledges that all monuments ultimately make such emendations part of their memorial texts. That is, the monument records the response of today's visitors for the benefit of tomorrow's, thus reminding all of their shared responsibility in that the recorded responses of previous visitors at a memorial site become part of one's own memory.

Finally, part of the community's mixed reaction to the countermonument may also have been its discomfort with this monument's very liveliness. Like other forms of art, the monument is most benign when static: there when you face it, gone when you turn your back. But when it begins to come to life, to grow, shrink, or change form, the monument may become threatening. No longer at the mercy of the viewer's will, it seems to have a will of its own, to beckon us at inopportune moments. Such monuments become a little like Frankenstein's monster, a golem out of the maker's control.

Hrdlicka's Countermonument

If the Gerzes' countermonument aims to contest the authoritarian tenets its makers perceive in all monuments, another countermonument situated in the center of Hamburg attempts to neutralize the fascist charge in a Nazi-built monument still standing nearby. This seemingly indestructible military monument by Richard Kuohl was erected by the Nazis in 1936 near the entrance to Hamburg's wondrous Botanical Garden at the Dammtor. A massive cube of granite blocks, it is encircled by a frieze of marching German soldiers, four abreast in profile relief. In Gothic script typical of the Third Reich, the monument is dedicated to the memory of soldiers from Hamburg's Second Hanseatic Infantry Regiment number 76 who fell in the 1870–71 war and in the First World War.

Despite its militaristic tenor and Nazi origin, the monument might have remained undisturbed had it not been for a line of poetry by Heinrich Lersch inscribed on one side: "Deutschland muss leben, auch wenn wir sterben mussen" (Germany must live, even if we have to die). In the midst of the surrounding devastation after the war (this monument was practically the only edifice left standing in the Dammtor after the bombing), this verse had taken on a mockingly hollow ring in 1945, a perceived affront to the dead of all wars.

As antiwar sentiment rose over the years, Kuohl's monument came under siege by demonstrators, who smeared it with paint and took hammer and chisel to its stone reliefs. It has incited full-fledged rock-and-bottle riots between skinheads and police, as other police and antiwar marchers battled in the streets nearby. At the same time, veterans of the Second Hanseatic Infantry Regiment number 76 continued to honor their fallen comrades at the monument's base, and the city continued to clean the monument and repair its vandalized facade. At one point, Radio Bremen invited listeners to turn out en masse and swaddle the monument in rags, blankets, and linen—à la Christo. All the networks covered this live "TV happening," to the great concern of local Christian Democratic Union politicians and veterans groups still attempting to protect the monument from its public. Eventually, the city gave up cleaning the monument, caught between its popular rejection as a glorification of war and the veterans' need for a place to honor their comrades. Having withstood the Allies' bombs, the monument also defeated the townspeople's own attempts to demolish it.

This memorial stone had become, in the punning vernacular, a "Stein des Anstosses"—an annoyance, a stone of contention—that just wouldn't go away. "Move it to the Ohlsdorf Cemetery," some had suggested, where there were already monuments to the resistance, as well as to Hamburg victims of the bombings and camps. The Christian Democrats insisted that the monument stay put, unchanged, and be rededicated to the fallen soldiers of all wars. They then recommended that such a monument could always be balanced with a separate marker to the victims of the Nazis, to be erected at another, undetermined site. After months of debate, city authorities decided on a compromise: they would leave the Nazi monument in place and build a contemporary countermonument right next to it.

To this end, a jury was appointed, a competition called, and more than one hundred artists, sculptors, and architects responded with models and designs. A winning design was finally approved by the jury, but in its ironic literality, it met with broad resistance when time came to build it. Seemingly modeled after a 1934 cartoon by satirist A. Paul Weber, the design nearly mirrored the bas-relief image of the original monument; but instead of soldiers marching around the frieze, the new monument's soldiers marched downward, off to war in descending groups of four, one after the other, into the ground, an open grave.[10] Though appreciative of the proposal's sentiment, one of the artists on the jury, Austrian sculptor Alfred Hrdlicka, had also dissented. After further negotiations, he arranged to have himself invited to design the countermonument.

On 8 May 1985, the fourtieth anniversary of German capitulation, the first of four proposed pieces in Hrdlicka's "memorial environment" was unveiled. *The Hamburg Firestorm* is a seven-meter-long, five-meter-high wall of roughly cast bronze, symbolizing the charred timbers of a bombed-out city. Through gaping holes, we can still see the Nazi cube behind, the implied fifth part of this installation. An emaciated figure, either a bombing victim or a concentration camp survivor, sits leaning against the wall. Against the precise lines of soldiers marching, the artist counterpoints the ragged remains: now sharing the same space, the demonic order of fascism is chastened by its consequences.

At the same time, all the figures in this dialogue between memorials—including civilians, camp survivors, and soldiers—are now included in the memorial space. The war's makers may not be neutralized by the war's victims so much as added to the sum of war casualties. In this view, the victims of fascism include not only the innocents exterminated in killing centers, but also the more anonymous people killed in their beds during bombing raids, even soldiers killed on the battlefield. And then, reflecting the local anxiety that any future war might also begin on German soil, the artist reminds us in a pictorial panel mounted nearby that, in a sense, the next war has already begun: "I would like to point out that this is the place where World War III and its mass-killing of civilians was already rehearsed."[11]

In the second part of his installation, *The Image of Women*, Hrdlicka's narrative panel would remind visitors that war "is not only a matter for men, although the death of a hero is usually reserved for men." Ironically linking the Nazi-idealized heroine to the wracked and broken figure of a woman from the camps, the sculptor suggests the heroism of women through their antiheroic treatment. Still unbuilt, this section also proposes to represent the soldiers' suffering and death at the front, a stark contrast to the tightly marching soldiers on the cube. By personalizing the soldiers and removing them from the anonymous mass of the military, Hrdlicka suggests that an individual's suffering is no less if he suffers as part of a mass. Also as yet unbuilt, the planned fourth part is devoted to the persecution and killing of dissidents and resistance fighters. In an echo of the German Democratic Republic's own memorial code, Hrdlicka would thus tie current dissidence to past resistance, binding all together as collective victims of fascism.

To date, however, only half the work has been installed, with little prospect of its completion. The city has changed its mind. After installing the first two sections, Hrdlicka demanded more funds to finish a monument the city no longer wanted. Were it to remain incomplete, as many hope, it would still come to represent an especially German memorial concept: the perpetually unfinished monument. Memorial debate becomes a form of memorial activity, never resolved, forever in flux. In fact, from the beginning, Hrdlicka's countermonument aimed to create a perpetual-motion dialogue with the old one nearby, an argument, really, that could be won by neither side. For Hrdlicka, the memorial provocateur, an embroidered tablet, an urn of ashes, or wreaths somberly laid would just not suffice. Instead, it is precisely the dialectic between a monument and its public, the tension between it and its surroundings, that sustains memory and occludes complacency.

Radermacher's Disruption of Public Space

Not long before the citizens of Harburg bury their countermonument, another conceptual memorial will be "unveiled" in the Neukölln district of Berlin—the former site of a forced labor camp and one of Sachsenhausen's satellite camps. Though Norbert Radermacher's memorial will bear little formal resemblance to the Gerzes' countermonument, both its concept and spirit promise to make it a kindred soul. Like its Hamburg cousin, Radermacher's memorial also integrates written text and disappears. Unlike the permanently vanished column, however, Radermacher's memorial then reappears with the entry of every new passerby into its space.

In Radermacher's design, pedestrians strolling along the Sonnenallee, next to the sportsground (former site of the KZ-Aussenlager [satellite concentration camp]), trip a light-beam trigger, which in turn flicks on a high-intensity slide projection of a written text relating the historical details of the site's now invisible past. In the artist's words, "The lettering from this text is beamed first onto the crowns of the trees, where one can see the text but cannot quite read it. Slowly, it moves down to the wire fence [surrounding the sportsground and perimeter of the former camp] until the words become more clear and legible. The text is then projected onto the sidewalk, where we can read it quite clearly. It remains for one minute before slowly fading out."[12] In effect, by overlaying the nearby trees, houses, fence, and pavement in this way, the beam literally bathes an otherwise forgetful site in the light of its own past—a spotlight from which neither the site nor pedestrians can hide.

As innovative as it is, no installation could also be truer to the artist's previous work. For years, Radermacher has made public spaces his primary canvas, creating installation texts in the minimal disruption of public spaces. His aim has not been to remake these spaces, but to add to them in ways that cause the public to see and experience them anew. In the most unlikely settings, he installs small, unexpected objects that disrupt space, but remain so unobtrusive as to be almost absorbed by their surroundings: a white, foot-high stone obelisk beneath an overpass in Berlin; a round, cakelike stone under another bridge in Düsseldorf; small seashells affixed to the stone balustrade of a Parisian cathedral. A palm-sized, square mirror attached to a long brick wall reflects sky and trees in Paris; a small concrete gyro-compass lies on its side, lost amid the cobblestones of an immense square in Düsseldorf.[13] Each of these causes pedestrians to pause, if only momentarily, on realizing they have accidentally entered an artist's installation, a space they had previously regarded as banal. What is it? they ask. Who made it? And why is it here? Radermacher delights in such questions, of course, and knows that by their public nature, these installations are irreproducible in the museum or gallery—thereby resisting their commercialization as well.

Like the Gerzes' monument, the memorial installation at Neukölln is meant to be ever-changing. According to Radermacher, the total message of his memorial text will never repeat itself: various times of the day, climates, seasons, and bystanders will ensure that no two showings are exactly alike. By day, the landscape will appear to be speckled with text, while by night distinct words will assume the very shapes of the objects over which they are draped. In a night rain, the droplet-filled air will become the medium for a message that cannot be washed away. Once the landscape has been overlaid with its memorial inscription, it retains an afterimage in visitors' minds—and is therefore never innocent of memory again.

In addition, Radermacher has invited schoolchildren to continue researching the history of the area before adding their own slide texts to his. By integrating the children's messages, the artist hopes to illustrate both the capacity in his memorial to absorb new meanings in new times, and the essentially participatory nature of all memorials. In effect, Radermacher would remind us that all such sites depend for their memory on the passersby who initiate it—however involuntarily. He also suggests that the site alone cannot remember, that it is the projection of memory by visitors into a space that makes it a memorial. The site catches visitors unaware but is no longer passive: it intrudes itself into the pedestrians' thoughts. Of course, such memory can also be avoided by simply crossing the street or ducking under the light-beam trigger. But even this would be a memorial act of sorts, if only in opposition. For to avoid the memorial here, we would first have to conjure the memory to be avoided: that is, we would have to remember what it is we want to forget.

Until the installation of this mechanism sometime in 1992—a memory implant, as it were—there will be no sign that this site was ever anything other than what it appears to be: a sportsground and empty lot. The particular slice of history to be projected begins in 1941, when the German branch of the National Cash Register Company, an American firm, bought the property at 181–89 Sonnenallee as part of its wartime expansion. Having waxed and waned during the First World War, the Depression, and the era of inflation, business at NCR began to boom in 1941 with the addition of its munitions plant at Neukölln. The company built a factory at one end of the site and barracks for slave labor at the other end, called NCR Colony, one of dozens of forced-labor camps in Berlin alone.

Between 1942 and 1944, the number of foreign (mostly female) slave laborers from Poland, the Soviet Union, and France fluctuated between 400 and 863. In August 1944, the barracks were cleared to house some 500 Jewish women from the Lódź Ghetto. They had been transported to Auschwitz during the early summer of 1944, to Sachsenhausen that fall, and thence to Neukölln. From September 1944 to April 1945, the Neukölln barracks were thus turned into one of Sachsenhausen's many satellite camps. Bombings forced the women into shelters during much of the early spring of 1945, and as the Red Army approached in April, the SS shipped them back to Sachsenhausen, whence they were transported to Ravensbrück, the women's concentration camp. In the last days of the war, most of this group was taken by train to Sweden in Aktion Bernadotte, a rescue operation supervised by the Swedish Red Cross. The rest of the women escaped from a forced march to Lübeck, along with other survivors of Ravensbrück.

By May 1945, little remained of either the camp or the NCR factory, which had been dismantled by the Red Army and shipped back to the Soviet Union. Over the next few years, the cash register factory was rebuilt and, despite its low priority among American investors, flourished for awhile during the 1950s, when it exported its machines around the world. By the 1960s, however, bad management led to its closing; the factory was demolished and a sportsground put into its cleared space. The three-meter fence now surrounding the sports field is said to be exactly as high as the one that once enclosed the forced-labor camp here— the lone physical reference to the site's past.

Other than the projected text, Radermacher prefers to leave the site unaltered, a reminder of absence and the effacement of memory—and of the deliberate effort it takes to remember. The site disruption, in this case, is the equivalent of a memorial inscription, reinvesting an otherwise unremarkable site with its altogether remarkable past. In fact, by leaving the site physically unaltered, the artist allows it to retain a facade of innocence only so that he might more forcefully betray its actual historical past. Radermacher's memorial thus reminds us that the history of this site also includes its own forgetfulness, its own memory lapse.

Hoheisel's "Negative-Form" Monument

When the city of Kassel invited artists to consider ways to rescue one of its destroyed historical monuments, the Aschrott-Brunnen (Aschrott Fountain) in City Hall Square, local artist Horst Hoheisel decided that neither a preservation of its remnants nor its mere reconstruction would do. For Hoheisel, even the fragment was a decorative lie, suggesting itself as the remnant of a destruction no one knew very much about. Its pure reconstruction would have been no less offensive: not only would self-congratulatory overtones of Wiedergutmachung betray an irreparable violence, but the artist feared that a reconstructed fountain would only encourage the public to forget what had happened to the original.

In the best tradition of the countermonument, therefore, Hoheisel proposed a "negative-form" monument to mark the original twelve-meter-high neo-Gothic pyramid fountain, surrounded by a reflecting pool in the main town square, in front of City Hall. Built in 1908, it was designed by the City Hall architect, Karl Roth, and funded by a Jewish entrepreneur from Kassel, Sigmund Aschrott. But as a gift from a Jew to the city, it was condemned by the Nazis as the "Jews' Fountain" and so demolished during the night of 8–9 April 1939 by Nazi activists, its pieces carted away by city work crews over the next few days. Within weeks, all but the sandstone base had been cleared away, leaving only a great, empty basin in the center of the square. Two years later, the first transport of 463 Kassel Jews departed from the Central Train Station to Riga, followed in the next year by another 3,000, all murdered. In 1943 the city filled the fountain's basin with soil and planted it over in flowers; local burghers then dubbed it "Aschrott's Grave."

During the growing prosperity of the 1960s, the town turned Aschrott's Grave back into a fountain, sans pyramid. But by then, only a few oldtimers could recall that its name had ever been Aschrott's anything. When asked what had happened to the original fountain, they replied that, to the best of their recollection, it had been destroyed by English bombers during the war. In response to this kind of fading memory, the Society for the Rescue of Historical Monuments proposed in 1984 that some form of the fountain and its history be restored—and that it recall all the founders of Kassel, especially Sigmund Aschrott.

On being awarded the project, Hoheisel described both the concept and form underlying his negative-form monument:

> I have designed the new fountain as a mirror image of the old one, sunk beneath the old place in order to rescue the history of this place as a wound and as an open question, to penetrate the consciousness of the Kassel citizens so that such things never happen again.

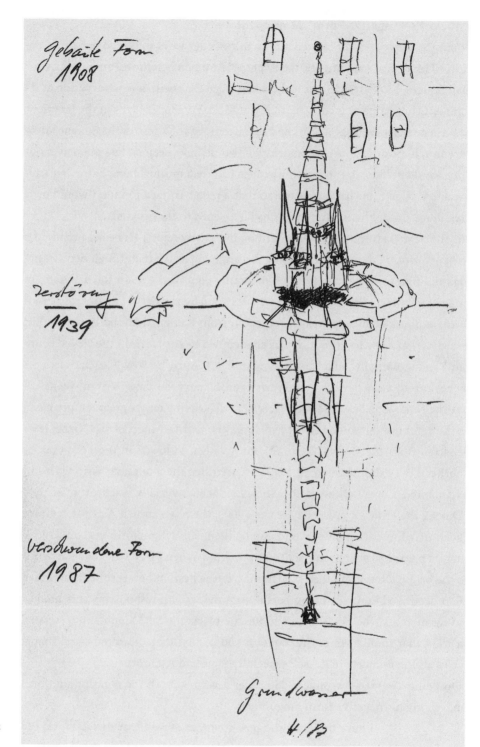

Artist Horst Hoheisel's preliminary sketch of his "negative-form monument," commemorating the Aschrott-Brunnen in Kassel. Photo: Courtesy Horst Hoheisel.

That's why I rebuilt the fountain sculpture as a hollow concrete form after the old plans and for a few weeks displayed it as a resurrected shape at City Hall Square before sinking it, mirror-like, twelve meters deep into the groundwater.

The pyramid will be turned into a funnel into whose darkness water runs down. From the "architektonischen Spielerei," as City Hall architect Karl Roth called his fountain, a hole emerges which deep down in the water creates an image reflecting back the entire shape of the fountain.[14]

How does one remember an absence? In this case, by reproducing it. Quite literally, the negative space of the absent monument will now constitute its phantom shape in the ground. The very absence of the monument will now be preserved in its precisely duplicated negative space. In this way, the monument's reconstruction remains as illusory as memory itself, a reflection on dark waters, a phantasmagoric play of light and image. Taken a step further, Hoheisel's inverted pyramid might also combine with the remembered shape of its predecessor to form the two interlocking triangles of the Jewish star—present only in the memory of its absence.[15]

In his conceptual formulations, Hoheisel invokes the play of darker associations, as well, linking the monument both to Kassel's Jewish past and to a traditional anti-Semitic libel. Coming into touch with the groundwater, the history of the Aschrott Fountain continues not over but under the city. As an emblem of the Holocaust, the history of the fountain becomes the subterranean history of the city. In Hoheisel's figure, the groundwater of German history may well be poisoned—not by the Jews, but by the Germans themselves in their murder of the Jews. By sinking his inverted pyramid into the depths in this way, Hoheisel means to tap this very history. "From the depth of the place," he says, "I have attempted to bring the history of the Aschrott Fountain back up to the surface."

Of course, none of this is immediately evident on a visit to City Hall Square in Kassel. During construction, before being lowered upside-down into the ground, the starkly white negative-form sat upright in the square, a ghostly reminder of the original monument. The site is now marked by a bronze tablet with the fountain's image and an inscription detailing the original fountain and why it was lost. As we enter the square, water fills narrow canals at our feet before rushing into a great underground hollow, which grows louder and louder until finally we stand over the Aschrott-Brunnen. Only the sound of gushing water suggests the depth of an otherwise invisible memorial, an inverted palimpsest that demands the visitor's reflection. Through an iron grate and thick glass windows, we peer into the depths. "With the running water," Hoheisel suggests, "our thoughts can

The negative-form monument to the Aschrott-Brunnen, phantomlike in its whiteness, before being inverted and lowered into the ground. Photo: Horst Hoheisel.

be drawn into the depths of history, and there perhaps we will encounter feelings of loss, of a disturbed place, of lost form."

In fact, as the only standing figures on this flat square, our thoughts rooted in the rushing fountain beneath our feet, we realize that we have become the memorial. "The sunken fountain is not the memorial at all," Hoheisel says. "It is only history turned into a pedestal, an invitation to passersby who stand upon it to search for the memorial in their own heads. For only there is the memorial to be found." Like the Gerzes in Hamburg and Radermacher in Berlin, Hoheisel has left nothing but the visitors themselves standing in remembrance, looking inward for memory.

On the surface, time and memory seem to operate to irreconcilable ends: where time might be described, in Aristotle's terms, as that which "disperses subsistence," memory can be regarded as recollective in its work, an operation that concentrates the past in the figurative space of a present moment.[16] The counter-monument would turn this over: it forces the memorial to disperse—not gather—memory, even as it gathers the literal effects of time in one place. In dissipating

itself over time, the countermonument would mimic time's own dispersion, become more like time than like memory. It would remind us that the very notion of linear time assumes memory of a past moment: time as the perpetually measured distance between this moment and the next, between this instant and a past remembered. In this sense, the countermonument asks us to recognize that time and memory are interdependent, in dialectical flux.

The material of a conventional monument is normally chosen to withstand the physical ravages of time, the assumption being that its memory will remain as everlasting as its form. But, as Mumford has already suggested, the actual consequence of a memorial's unyielding fixedness in space is also its death over time: an image created in one time and carried over into a new time suddenly appears archaic, strange, or irrelevant altogether. For in its linear progression, time drags old meaning into new contexts, estranging a monument's memory from both past and present, holding past truths up to ridicule in present moments. Time mocks the rigidity of monuments, the presumptuous claim that in its materiality a monument can be regarded as eternally true, a fixed star in the constellation of collective memory.

At the negative-form monument to the Aschrott-Brunnen in Kassel, the visitor is the monument. Photo: Horst Hoheisel.

By formalizing its impermanence and even celebrating its changing form over time and in space, the countermonument refutes this self-defeating premise. It seeks to stimulate memory no less than the traditional everlasting memorial, but by pointing explicitly at its own changing face, it remarks also the inevitable—even essential—evolution of memory itself over time. In its conceptual self-destruction, the countermonument refers not only to its own physical impermanence, but also to the contingency of all meaning and memory—especially that embodied in a form that insists on its eternal fixity.

By negating its form, however, the countermonument need not negate memory. And by challenging its premises for being, neither does it challenge the call for memory itself. Rather, it negates only the illusion of permanence traditionally fostered in the monument. For in calling attention to its own fleeting presence, the countermonument mocks the traditional monument's certainty of history: it scorns what Nietzsche called "antiquarian" and "monumental" history. In effect, it might even be said that the countermonument negates the very basis for these epithets' central trope: after the countermonument, the "monumental" need no longer be conceived merely as a figure for the stone-dead. By resisting its own reason for being, the countermonument paradoxically reinvigorates the very idea of the monument itself.

If the place of memory is "created by a play of memory and history," as Pierre Nora believes, then time may be the crucible for this interaction. Memory is thus sustained, not denied, by a sense of human temporality, deriving its nourishment from the very changes over time that would otherwise mock the static, "everlasting" memorial. Nora is most succinct here: "If we accept that the most fundamental purpose of the *lieu de mémoire* is to stop time, to block the work of forgetting, to establish a state of things, to immortalize death, to materialize the immaterial . . . all of this in order to capture a maximum of meaning in the fewest of signs, it is also clear that the *lieux de mémoire* only exist because of their capacity for metamorphosis, an endless recycling of their meaning and an unpredictable proliferation of their ramifications."[17]

Even so, the precise beauty of the countermonument may not lie merely in its capacity for change, nor in its capacity to challenge a society's reasons for either memory or its own configuration of memory. For in addition, the countermonument seeks its fulfillment in—not at cross-purposes with—historical time. It recognizes and affirms that the life of memory exists primarily in historical time: in the activity that brings monuments into being, in the ongoing exchange between people and their historical markers, and finally, in the concrete actions we take in light of a memorialized past.

Chapter 2   The Sites

of Destruction

Public memorialization of the war era began in Germany, as it did elsewhere, with every group remembering its own fate: as victims, heroes, or bystanders. Within days of their liberation, former concentration camp inmates at Dachau, Buchenwald, and Bergen-Belsen had fashioned makeshift memorial towers from the bric-à-brac of their dismantled prisons. Soviet, American, and British soldiers erected stone markers throughout Germany's battle-scarred landscape, inscribed to the memory of their fallen comrades. Jewish, Catholic, and Protestant clergy gathered around specially designated spaces to mourn their respective dead—and to begin organizing their return to life. Memory of terror at the hands of the Nazis both energized and constituted the very raison d'être for Social Democrats, Communists, and other formerly persecuted parties, whose memorial ceremonies and political rallies immediately after the war often became one and the same.

In Germany, these public commemorations were joined by hundreds, occasionally thousands, of nonvictims who attended for a variety of reasons. The first massive antifascist memorial demonstration in Germany, organized by a municipal coalition representing all the victims' groups, drew thirty-five thousand people to the Werner-Seelenbinder-Arena in Neukölln on 9 September 1945.[1] Some came to this "Commemorative Rally for the Victims of Fascist Terror" to mourn lost friends and family, others to express solidarity with the victims. Many came to cast their lot publicly with the new order, a few to repent their past complicity in the old. Still others, perhaps the majority, came because—with their cities in ruins, their families lost and maimed in bombings, their fathers and brothers

Thirty-five thousand Germans gather at the first postwar memorial rally for the "Victims of Fascist Terror" at the Werner-Seelenbinder Arena in Neukölln, Berlin, 9 September 1945. Photo: Courtesy of Berliner Festspiele.

killed on the front, and their country occupied—they, too, now regarded themselves as victims. Like other nations, Germany was still without a tradition to mandate the memory of those it had victimized; like that of other nations, German memory of this time would begin when its citizens remembered their own *as* victims—even as victims of themselves.

Plotzensee and the Memory of Resistance

To a great extent, this paradoxical ambiguity was an essential feature in the memorial legacy embodied in Berlin's first memorial, "To the Victims of the Hitler Dictatorship," set at the Plotzensee Prison. Though other nationals, mostly captured resistance fighters, were either hanged or guillotined here, most of the twenty-five hundred prisoners executed at Plotzensee were German political detainees. Once paired with foreign resistance fighters, these prisoners came to be regarded as part of the German resistance to Hitler. By an act of the Berlin senate in 1952, the prison was restored, an inscribed wall erected, and an urn with soil from the concentration camps placed near the courtyard entrance. A scroll buried beneath the memorial's foundation reads: "During the years of the Hitler dictatorship, from 1933 to 1945, hundreds of human beings were put to death by judicial murder on this spot. They died because they chose to fight against the dictatorship for human rights and political freedom. They included people from every walk of life and nearly every country. Through this memorial, Berlin honors those millions of victims of the Third Reich who, because of their political convictions, religious beliefs, or racial origins, were vilified, abused, deprived of their freedom, or murdered."[2]

Set in the very room of the executions, the shrine tends to submerge the great differences between victims beneath a welter of grisly detail, the horror of their deaths. The urn containing soil of the camps at the entrance links victims of the camps with other victims of Hitler's wrath, some of whom assisted in the mass murder of Jews. By dedicating the memorial to all of Hitler's victims, regardless of nationality, religion, or political convictions, the city defined victims of the Reich in the broadest possible terms, creating a common meaning for the murder of disparate millions. In the words and images of the resistance museum installed here, all had died for Germany. As the resistance had been victimized, all victims of the war might now be regarded as honorary members of the resistance.

In July 1953, Berlin added a second memorial to the resistance, this one dedicated specifically to the Wehrmacht officers executed for plotting to kill Hitler and his inner circle in July 1944. The conspirators' ambiguous legacy further exemplifies the Germans' memorial dilemma. They had heard General Alfred Jodl describe Germany's desperate military situation during a speech on 9 November 1943. In light of a series of strategic blunders by Hitler, and the imminent prospect of an Allied invasion, the officers seemed less concerned with bringing "human rights and political freedom" to the German people than with saving the homeland from military catastrophe. After aborted attempts on the day after Christmas 1943, and in February and June 1944, their self-designated leader, Claus von Stauffenberg, succeeded in planting a British briefcase bomb next to Hitler at a meeting on 20 July. A minute before it went off, someone moved the bomb slightly behind a massive wooden table leg while trying to get closer to the map they were all studying. Shielded from the full force of the explosion, Hitler was only maimed. Stauffenberg flew to Berlin expecting to head the Army's uprising against the Nazis. He landed only to find that Hitler had survived and that he himself was now a fugitive. The conspiracy quickly unraveled. Within hours, Stauffenberg and several of his accomplices were taken out behind the officers' headquarters on Bendlerstrasse and shot. By September, some two hundred other conspirators were tried and executed, eighty-nine of them at Plotzensee.[3]

On the site of the former "Bendler-Block," its street now renamed Stauffenbergstrasse, the city erected in 1953 a life-sized figure in bronze, naked, with his arms folded and his clenched fists trussed in front of him, standing determinedly atop a meter-high pedestal. By 1980, the square had been cobbled over and the statue moved to ground level, with an inscription on the wall nearby: "Here they died for Germany on 20 July 1944," followed by a list of the conspiring officers' names. But here, also, official memory countermands itself: Were Stauffenberg, Ludwig Beck, Friedrich Olbricht, Werner von Haeften, and Albrecht von Quirnheim heroes? Or were they just better Nazis than Hitler? Can they, as Nazis, be remembered as antifascists? Can they, as soldiers who attempted to assassinate their leader, be recalled as patriots? Stauffenberg had supported the annexation of Austria and Czechoslovakia, as well as Hitler's early conquests of Holland and France. It was only after the disastrous Barbarossa operation and massacre of civilians in the Soviet Union that he resolved to kill Hitler. That all of these officers had unreservedly backed Hitler's early conquests, and some—like Arthur Nebe— had even commanded mobile killing units in the East, remains unremarked in the newfound commonality created among victims here.

This ambiguity is heightened further in the convoluted definition of resistance in the guide to the memorial at Plotzensee: "Every year, on July 20, we remember those men and women who were involved in this attempt to rid Germany of Hitler and his regime. At the same time we remember all those, whatever their political or religious convictions, who resisted this evil force from 1933 to 1945. And we remember, too, the millions of nameless victims who were murdered and are forever linked with the dreadful names Auschwitz [and] Majdanek."[4]

Though German resistance is epitomized here in the attempt on Hitler's life, its circle gradually widens to embrace all others. Even the Jews who died in death camps are now honorary members of the group once committed to their destruction. "Not all of [the German resistance] saw their goal in a democratic society," the Plotzensee pamphlet concedes. "But over and above all their differences, they had one thing in common: the readiness to risk their lives for humanity, for freedom, justice, and peace." In a further ironic twist, it is not only political and Jewish victims who object to being lumped together with their mortal enemies. When the new museum to the resistance opened in 1989, Stauffenberg's own family protested his memory being thrown in with that of the Communists. All of which leaves the twentieth of July plotters stranded in a curious memorial netherworld.

Although the plot to kill Hitler was initially dismissed by the Allies as so much infighting among gangsters, it found a more sympathetic reception among the postwar occupation forces looking for ways to rally Germans around some anti-Nazi symbol. Both the Allies and the Germans seemed to recognize that memory of past triumph or victimization often serves to unify nations. This fact might explain a divided Germany's need for memory of a national resistance. Yet such memory can be anchored less in the historical past than in the present desire for unity. In an otherwise even-handed account of this confused legacy, historian Klemens von Klemperer accedes to just this rationale when he concludes that "the memory of [the plotters'] action, their commitment to freedom and human rights at the expense of their lives, should help endow German unification with meaning that goes beyond the enhancement of German power in Central Europe."[5] The question the Germans and all nations are left with is a vexing one: To what extent does any nation use memory of the past to unify itself at the expense of historical rectitude?

While nations have long used the memory of their triumphs and defeats to provide citizens with a seemingly shared legacy, few cultivate memorial traditions to recall their crimes against others. Insofar as such self-accusing centers of memory would seem to divide, not unify, the population, Germany's early and later creation of traditional, even redemptory reasons for memory becomes understandable. But over time Germany has shown that a negative memorial legacy can be sustained as well, even cultivated as a basis for national identity. Such memory serves as a negative infrastructure against which the state judges its present actions: memory of past crimes committed in its name now determines what Germany may no longer be or do. In this light, antimemory of the Holocaust in Germany may be as much a part of the new Germany's self-idealization as all the memory of its heroes and victims put together.

Memorializing the Concentration Camps

Because there were no killing centers per se in Germany and so few non-Jewish Germans were interned in the death camps, the mass murder of Jews has entered German memory as more a figurative than a literal experience. In fact, had it not been for the massive, last-ditch evacuations of Jewish prisoners from death camps in Poland, who died by the tens of thousands at the end of their forced marches back into Germany, the mass murder might have remained a foreign phenomenon altogether. German experience of the prisoners' plight in the camps was limited largely to either helping Jewish neighbors or watching quietly as they disappeared, guarding the camps or being forced by Allied soldiers to march through them after liberation. As a result, what we call Holocaust memorials in Germany tend to be highly stylized when remembering the Jews and oriented toward all victims of fascism when remembering the Germans.

Particularly in former West Germany, where single-minded rebuilding has largely effaced remnants of the war era, the camps are often recalled primarily through the literal image of their names. At the subway station at Wittenbergplatz in Berlin, for example, a simple, unadorned metal sign stands with the names of camps printed in high-visibility yellow on black slats. It reads, "Orte des Schreckens, die wir niemals vergessen dürfen" (Places of terror that we should never

"Places of terror
that we should
never forget."
Memorial
signpost erected
in front of the
Wittenbergplatz
subway station
in Berlin.
Photo:
James E. Young.

forget), followed by a list: Auschwitz, Stutthof, Maidanék, Treblinka, Theresienstadt, Buchenwald, Dachau, Sachsenhausen, Ravensbrück, Bergen-Belsen. Five of
the camps are German, four Polish, one Czech. They are in no special order, other
than that the German camps are listed last. Standing amid bustling shoppers and
commuters, stop signs and neon lights, with no arrows pointing in the camps'
directions, the signpost leads us only to itself.

In German communities removed from the camps, memorial references remain
as oblique or direct as their specific experiences were. The memorials to the victims of the *Cap-Arcona* catastrophe, in particular, exemplify how a community
refracts memory through its own, necessarily blinkered experiences—with little

reference to details lying immediately outside its ken. Tucked into a glen at the end of a farm road between Neustadt and Pelzerhaken on the Baltic coast, a small graveyard with two stones and a large wooden cross marks the final resting place of "621 of the 7000 victims of the Thielbek and Cap-Arcona catastrophe of 3 May 1945." From the narrative of events and diagrams inscribed on a nearby tablet, we learn that the *SS Cap-Arcona* and *Thielbek* were two of three converted cruise liners carrying thousands of former prisoners from KZ-Neuengamme into the Baltic Sea, where, we are told, the *Cap-Arcona* was strafed and bombed by Royal Air Force warplanes. According to local villagers, bodies clad in striped uniforms washed onto the pristine beaches near Neustadt and Timmendorf for months afterwards and were immediately buried by townspeople to prevent the spread of disease.

From the tablet and cross alone, however, it is not clear whether the "catastrophe" of the *SS Cap-Arcona* lay in the massacre of innocents by the RAF (which had reportedly mistaken the ships for troop transports) or in the horrible irony of the camp survivors' ultimate fate. The detailed narrative makes no mention of where the prisoners had been before Neuengamme (a political camp near Hamburg), how they came to be gathered in Lübeck Bay, where they were going, or why the RAF bombed the ships. The result is a memorial to seven thousand defenseless prisoners killed by the British. That many had survived the death marches from Auschwitz, that most were Jews, and that all were being hastily evacuated from concentration camps in northern Germany to somewhere, anywhere, away from German soil is not recalled here. These details were not among the experiences of the memorial makers—townspeople who had witnessed the bombings, found their shores littered with bodies, and then buried the dead.[6]

Eventually, several other monuments to the catastrophe of the *SS Cap-Arcona* appeared at other points along Lübeck Bay, in Neustadt, Niendorf, Timmendorfer Strand, Haffkrug, Sierksdorf, and Gromitz. Those sponsored by international committees of former political prisoners from Neuengamme reflect their experience and understanding of events no less than those erected early on by nearby villagers. As political prisoners, they grasped all victims of the Reich as such. At Timmendorfer Strand, for example, the memorial tablet reads: "Here rest 810 political prisoners from 16 nations, who found their death on the Cap-Arcona in Neustadter Bay, 3 May 1945." Similarly, at the Jewish Cemetery in Neustadt, nearly one hundred Jewish victims of the catastrophe are buried under a memorial to "the men and women of Jewish faith who died under the evil oppression of Nazi Germany. Those buried in this place died in Neustadt after the day of liberation, 3 May 1945."[7] In both cases, victims are remembered according to the experiences and identity of the rememberers.

Memorials in the Camps

For Germans who experienced both the economic boom during Hitler's Reich and the destruction of their cities during the war, who knew both total military victory and unconditional surrender, memory of this time encompasses much more than the images of liberated concentration camp prisoners by which the era has so often been epitomized in America and England. Indeed, the piles of corpses in German camps ironically seemed to reflect back to many Germans their own total devastation, the masses of dead in German cities and on the front. At first, the Germans' only nexus of identification with Jewish victims lay in the destruction they now seemed to share, not in that which they had wrought in Hitler's name.

For many Jews liberated at Bergen-Belsen, Buchenwald, and Dachau, however, their last moments of degradation often came to stand, too, for all that had happened before: the anti-Semitic laws, deportations, ghettos, camps, and murdered families. Whereas only these final images remain in the minds of American, English, and Soviet soldiers, or in the minds of surrounding townspeople, survivors recall an entirely different order of experience. As a result, memory at the former sites of concentration camps in Germany remains divided between that of Germans and non-Germans, political and racial internees, persecutors and victims. Only gradually has the German notion of *Weltkrieg* (world war) or *Hitlerzeit* (the era of Hitler) evolved to include the victims' sense of *KZ-Zeit* (the era of the camps) or "Holocaust."

The German experience at Bergen-Belsen, for example, was not one of dying, but of burying the dead: the memorial here was thus conceived early on as a great burial ground, its monuments recalling those of a cemetery. Except for what is shown in a tastefully refurbished documentation center of stone and glass, little of what transpired specifically at Bergen-Belsen is reflected in the outdoor memorial space. Instead, as if harking back to the grisly film footage by which Bergen-Belsen is most commonly recalled, the principal motif is the prisoners' deaths and mass graves. Grouped in rows of burial mounds, each grave is marked by a small stone-and-mortar facade, inscribed with the number of dead it contains: "Here rest 5,000 dead," or 2,000 dead, or 1,000 dead. Amid the mounds and scattered individual tombstones inscribed in Hebrew, Jewish memory is condensed in a four-meter stone-block marker, etched in English and Hebrew, dedicated by the British Army in November 1945. Between 1945 and 1949, the rest of the camp was cleared away by the British Military Government, which then erected a thirty-meter-high, white marble-and-granite obelisk to all the anonymous dead, placed before a free-standing wall of inscriptions. In 1952, responsibility for the memorial passed from British hands to the West German state of Lower Saxony,

One of the
many burial
mounds
covering the
mass graves at
Bergen-Belsen.
Photo:
James E. Young.

ISRAEL AND THE WORLD SHALL REMEMBER
THIRTY THOUSAND JEWS
EXTERMINATED IN THE CONCENTRATION CAMP
OF BERGEN-BELSEN
AT THE HANDS OF THE MURDEROUS NAZIS

EARTH CONCEAL NOT THE BLOOD
SHED ON THEE!

FIRST ANNIVERSARY OF LIBERATION
15th APRIL 1946
(14th NISSAN 5706)

CENTRAL JEWISH COMMITTEE
BRITISH ZONE

Mourners
reading the
Kaddish prayer
for the dead at
the base of the
Jewish
memorial at
Bergen-Belsen.
Photo:
James E. Young.

which has administered the memorial to this day.

Though often visited by members of the Bergen-Belsen survivors' association and British servicemen from the nearby air base, the memorial at Bergen-Belsen remained relatively obscure until 1985. Not long before leaving on his controversial wreath-laying trip to Bitburg in May 1985, President Ronald Reagan added Bergen-Belsen to his itinerary—a crude attempt to balance the respects he would pay at the graves of Waffen-SS with the memory of their victims. By flying from Bergen-Belsen to Bitburg, he fostered the absurd notion that, in his words, "those young men [buried at Bitburg] are victims of Nazism . . . just as surely as the victims in the concentration camps." In his speech at Bergen-Belsen, Reagan compounded his disgrace by claiming that a letter from a young American Jewish girl asking him not to go to Bitburg had actually approved of his visit.[8]

Reagan had drawn what seemed to be "natural" conclusions from the memorials at Bitburg. Because Waffen-SS and Wehrmacht soldiers lie together in a patch of land designated to commemorate Germany's war dead, the different roles they may have played in the war are subsumed in the general memory of their common fate. United now with countrymen they may have spurned during the war and with forebears from the First World War, some of whom—if Jews—would have been considered their enemies, the SS soldiers buried at Bitburg have not only been absorbed into the greater continuum of all Germans who ever fell for their homeland, but have also come to represent the universal victims of war.

Ironically, as Helmut Sonnenfeldt has already pointed out, it may have been the Americans' early postwar attempts to de-Nazify the dead at such cemeteries that led to this crisis in the first place. Reflecting a common anxiety just after the war that separate graves for the Waffen-SS might become shrines for unreconstructed and neo-Nazis, the Americans often encouraged both the demolition of former Nazi meetingplaces and the mixed burial of Waffen-SS and Wehrmacht soldiers.[9] This policy has come back to haunt the Germans in two ways. First, with so few of the Nazis' own commemorative sites preserved as potential memorials, the Germans are often accused of destroying incriminating evidence of past atrocities. Second, the distinction between Waffen-SS and Wehrmacht becomes symbolically muddled during ceremonies like that at Bitburg, tarring the Wehrmacht of both past and present with the crimes of Hitler's shock troops.

All the while, a group of Americans, led by representatives of veterans', survivors', and Jewish religious organizations, sat in the rain outside the gates at Bergen-Belsen protesting Reagan's "desecration" of the memorial space. Images of Jewish demonstrators being carried away, however gently, by German police continue to haunt. Fifteen minutes after Reagan's helicopter had departed Bergen-Belsen for Bitburg, a group led by Menachem Rosensaft of the Children of Jewish

Holocaust Survivors entered the memorial site to reconsecrate it. By reciting the Kaddish and observing their own memorial silence, the group hoped to return dignity and sanctity to a site they regarded as blatantly defiled by political opportunism.

Shortly thereafter, a public footpath was laid to connect the Bergen-Belsen memorial to the Horsten Soviet Prisoner of War Cemetery, half a kilometer distant—thus relinking the site to its origin as Stalag 311, a POW camp for Soviet soldiers from 1940 to 1943. On this path "between cemeteries," visitors now have time to recall the intervening years, as well: April 1943, when the Germans converted Bergen-Belsen into a detention camp for several thousand Jews waiting in vain as possible exchange prisoners; December 1944, when its conversion to concentration camp was completed with the appointment of former Auschwitz-Birkenau commandant Josef Kramer, and thousands of prisoners from death camps in the East poured in.

Deathly quiet now except for the song of birds and roar of planes landing at the British Army camp next door, the land has covered itself modestly with shrubs and flowers. The surrounding forest acts as a natural barrier between Bergen-Belsen and the outer world. The only "camp" in sight is the military base, where the soldiers are occasionally taunted by anti-NATO protesters as the new "Lager-Commandants," tarred by their proximity to a camp they liberated more than forty years before.

The directors of the museum and memorial complex at former KZ-Neuengamme, just outside Hamburg, have taken their lesson from the Allied reeducation campaign after the war. They have instituted a summer work camp for international students on the grounds of the former concentration camp. As described by one of the lecturers, the twin objectives of the program are to teach today's youth about Germany's Nazi past, thus linking pedagogy and memory, and to foster greater understanding among the youth of different nations. Both aims are undertaken in the context of memorialization, which literally becomes a kind of *Denkmal-Arbeit,* or "memorial-work." Mindful, however, of the pernicious echo in the German word *Arbeitslager,* the project refers to itself instead by the more benign, international English term *work camp.*

Where mostly political prisoners of the camp were once worked to death in the brick factory as slaves, volunteers at Work Camp Neuengamme now labor as excavators of remembrance. The grounds of the concentration camp are mapped out, gridlike, the site of an archeological dig, where remnants of a dark past are unearthed and catalogued as evidence of Nazi atrocities. The instructors reassemble, teach, and memorialize events around such artifacts as nails, tools, and old shoes. If the archeological approach threatens to turn the camp into ancient history, this may be a consequence of all museums. For, as Theodor Adorno has warned, "the German word *museal* [museumlike] has unpleasant overtones. It describes objects to which the observer no longer has a vital relationship and which are in the process of dying."[10] By bringing the past into the present one rusty artifact at a time, these young archeologists of the Holocaust necessarily atomize events in order to reconstruct them.

Dachau: History of a Memorial

As the first concentration camp in Germany, and one of the country's later memorials, Dachau exemplifies how memorials can supplant the events they commemorate, even as they embody the gulf of time between past and present. Both Dachau's history and its reception in the public mind have come to characterize the promise and essential paradox of German memory of the camps on its soil. With so little visible evidence of its past, the memorial threatens to float atemporally above its own history. For in fact, in its twenty-year evolution from camp to memorial, Dachau accumulated other kinds of memory as well.

On 21 March 1933, in the wake of the elections when Hitler assigned himself dictatorial powers, Heinrich Himmler announced the opening of a concentration camp the next day near Dachau, just outside Munich. After refurbishing a number of abandoned stone huts of a former World War I munitions factory, the SS brought its first political prisoners in to construct barracks for five thousand inmates. On 15 August 1938, the new Dachau was completed. Between 1933 and 1942, in fact, Dachau gained a reputation among inmates as relatively luxurious: each prisoner was assigned his own bunk, a small cupboard, and stove. With its well-stocked library, long periods of leisure, sports programs, and such prominent detainees as the prime ministers of France (Léon Blum) and Hungary (Miklos Kallas) and the former chancellor of Austria (Kurt Schuschnigg), Dachau was recalled almost longingly by prisoners who were later shipped to labor and death camps.

Like other German concentration camps built between 1933 and 1938 (such as Buchenwald, Ravensbrück, and Sachsenhausen), Dachau housed primarily political opponents of the Reich from within Germany—Social Democrats, Communists, clergymen, prominent and obscure dissidents—and so created German victims. Of the survivors of Dachau still living in Germany, most are Christians, many of these clergymen. Even the Jews among these first concentration camp inmates were interned not as racial prisoners (though they were treated much more harshly for being Jews), but as political enemies of the Reich. Only on Kristallnacht (9 November 1938), when some twenty thousand Jews were rounded up off the streets and interned in camps like Dachau and Buchenwald, was a racial caste of prisoners created.

Many of these newly arrested Jews were later released, and while some of them emigrated, others returned home only to be rearrested and deported to death camps in the East a few years later. The Jewish political prisoners who remained in German camps were then assigned "mixed identities": red triangles combined with yellow ones to constitute a Jewish star. But unlike the German prisoners who remained behind, most of the Jews were deported to killing centers in Poland, once again leaving the German concentration camps home to political prisoners from Germany and, increasingly, elsewhere, as the Nazis occupied France, Holland, Belgium, Denmark, and Norway.

Though several thousand Soviet Army officers were executed at Dachau during the war, and there were mass slaughters of Jews at Buchenwald, the only extermination centers on German territory were Mauthausen and Hartheim Castle in Austria, with their operational gas chambers. But beginning in late 1943 and increasing through 1944 into 1945, as Soviet troops advanced in the East, the Germans evacuated masses of starved, disease-ravaged Jews from the death camps in Poland to Germany. Thus Dachau, while never a killing center per se, became a kind of death camp as it was inundated with open cattle cars of dead and dying prisoners.

With the sounds of U.S. Army guns nearby, the underground prisoners' association—the International Committee of Dachau—secreted two inmates out of the camp to guide the Americans to Dachau on their way to Munich. The day before the Americans arrived, a handful of Dachauers joined a few escapees in an attempt to force the SS out of the town, a minirevolt that was bloodily suppressed. When the Forty-second Division of the U.S. Army arrived on 29 April 1945, they found thirty thousand starving inmates at Dachau, many of them near death, and thousands of corpses piled in cattle cars parked on rail sidings near the camp—images that simultaneously seared Dachau into public consciousness and displaced the previous twelve years of its history.

Immediately after the war, the Americans turned Dachau into a military stockade, where they interned SS officers awaiting trial for war crimes. By converting the camp's administrative headquarters into a courthouse, the Americans literally housed these trials within the space of evidence itself. When the last of the SS had been convicted and sentenced in 1948, and the others had been released, the barracks were cleaned and prepared for an influx of thousands of German refugees expelled from the Sudetenland after the war. Within a few months, Dachau had been transformed from a German concentration camp to an American military stockade, and then into a sprawling refugee camp. Between 1948 and 1960,

some five thousand people lived there as new housing was being built for them. The barracks were divided into family huts, some of them turned into tobacco and newsstands, many sprouting television antennae.

Visiting Dachau in 1954, an English reporter found "raggedy children at play along the gutters; households of old women peer[ing] through blurred and broken window-panes." In stark contrast to the dilapidated barracks and their refuse-strewn walks, Terrence Prittie reported that "the crematorium stands in its own little park, perfectly preserved, with a well-kept two-acre garden around it and a single American sentry at the gate."[11] This was the "Garden of Remembrance," landscaped by the Americans and maintained by the Bavarian State, part of what was then called the "Dachau Detachment."

In another section of the camp, Americans had set up a gigantic food-processing center for U.S. troops stationed in Germany and Austria. Large trucks came and went all day long, while visitors were directed by a large billboard at the camp entrance to "the Memorial and the Crematorium." According to reporter Gaston Coblentz, the left side of this billboard also pointed the way to the postal ex-

The last German POWs, held by Americans, are released from Dachau with clothes and three days' rations, 30 June 1947. Photo: Courtesy of Dachau Museum Archives.

change, fire station, and bowling alley. The right side directed visitors to "laundry and dry cleaning, chapel, crematory and motor pool."[12]

It was the Americans who mounted the first graphic exhibit of atrocity photographs to remind locals of their neighborhood's past. They showed guards bludgeoning inmates, a prisoner being electrocuted on the camp's outer wire fence, and snarling SS guard dogs leaping at inmates. Local German civic leaders complained bitterly that the display was not only offensive to good taste but also damaging to international relations. So in early 1955 the Americans relented, shut down the exhibit, and posted a sign on the door: "Closed until further notice."

A little later that year, a group of former prisoners gathered at Dachau to commemorate the tenth anniversary of their liberation. Shocked to find the makeshift museum closed, and dispirited by the shambling remains of the barracks, the survivors pressed demands for a dignified memorial space where they might at least conduct ceremonies. Once again, this proposal met with fierce opposition in the local town council and other citizens' groups, some of whom claimed that the second, newer crematorium and unused gas chamber had been built by the

German children of refugees from the Sudetenland gather wood among the barracks at Dachau, their temporary home, ca. 1954. Photo: Courtesy of Dachau Museum Archives.

Americans themselves as anti-German propaganda. Others urged that the camp be razed altogether to eliminate a blight on their beautiful landscape. Frustrated by the town's balkiness, the former inmates angrily moved to reconstitute their former resistance organization, the International Dachau Committee, this time to resist forgetfulness itself. With the help of the Americans, they set up a small, provisional museum in the crematorium complex, just behind the barracks. Here they displayed photographs and artifacts, uniforms and brief narrative panels describing the camp's history.

A few years later, a visiting group of clergy and laymen from England found conditions in the former camp so appalling that they appealed to the Roman Catholic auxiliary bishop of Munich, Johann Neuhaeusler, to rectify the situation. Having spent four years as a prisoner at Dachau, the seventy-two-year-old bishop led efforts to erect a Catholic memorial chapel there in 1960. Given the predominantly Catholic make-up of the Bavarian population and the heavy losses suffered by the Catholic clergy at Dachau, it seemed fitting to local burghers that the first monument built on the grounds would be to Catholic victims.[13] On 5 August 1960, over fifty thousand people, mostly Bavarian Catholics, jammed the main street behind the barracks, while three thousand young Catholic men and a number of priests who had survived Dachau replicated Christ's passion, carrying a cross fifteen kilometers from a tent city near Munich to Dachau. After arriving at Dachau, the last station of the cross, Polish and German priests dedicated a "Monument of Atonement" to the "agony of Christ."

A rounded cylinder of unhewn stone, forty-one feet high and forty-five feet in diameter, the Catholic monument opens in the front to create a large, airy vestibule for prayer. The space is empty except for a large cross, and a gigantic crown of thorns is perched on top. This is clearly a "monument of atonement," whose meaning is made only partially clear in the altar's inscription: "To the honorable memory of the victims, for the atonement of the crimes, as a lesson for all visitors to the camp, for the peace of all nations." As part of his public dedication of the monument, the bishop specified what demanded atonement. He recalled Christ as a Jewish victim, elevating the deaths of Jews in Dachau to Calvary proportions. "Lord Jesus Christ, off-spring of David's house," he pleaded, "deliver our people from all enmity against the Jews. Atone for the murder of many millions of the people of Abraham, the destruction of so many synagogues. Put an end to the hatred between the Arabs and the Jews. Put an end to the hatred between the Boers and the natives, between the Frenchmen and the Algerians, between the Whites and the Negroes in North America. Deliver the White Race from presumption and arrogance."[14]

On the back of the monument, another plaque was mounted by Polish priests to remember their own, inscribed in Polish, French, German, and English: "Here in Dachau, every third victim was a Pole†; one of every two Polish priests was martyred†; their Holy memory is venerated by their fellow prisoners of the Polish clergy†." Four years later, a group of Carmelite nuns established a monastery just behind the memorial, accessible through one of the former guard towers. Unlike the Carmelite convent established later at Auschwitz, the monastery at Dachau has aroused little controversy, primarily because it was not regarded as an especially Jewish site, except insofar as it has come to symbolize the concentration camp system and its most extreme form of barbarism, the genocide of Jews.

By 1962, the International Dachau Committee was already making plans for the dedication of a central memorial here, scheduled to coincide with the twentieth anniversary of the liberation of the camp by the Forty-second Division of the U.S. Seventh Army (29 April 1945). Such a memorial would be, in the words of the committee, "a permanent reminder of the cooperation and comradeship that proved themselves unconquerable in the concentration camp despite all the efforts of the Nazis to the contrary."[15] This would not be a marker to mere horror but to the spirit of both those who survived and those who died, a way of uniting victims with survivors. By 1964, in preparation for the memorial, the last huts used by the refugees had been torn down and the entire site scrubbed from end to end. Two model barracks were reconstructed, symbolic concrete foundations laid to recall those destroyed, and the grounds covered over in white gravel.

A year after the dedication of the Dachau museum and memorial on 9 May 1965, a smoldering controversy between the American Army and the local museum staff flared into the open. Even though the army had moved its food-processing plant out of the immediate camp area, it had retained several of the most secure barracks as a military stockade—not for former SS this time, but for wayward American GIs. In what would become sorely needed administrative offices and archives, the army kept its jail house until 1968. "This is Eastman Barrack, not Camp Dachau," the head of military police insisted to an inquiring reporter in 1966. Instead of triangles, these prisoners wore an "S" on their sleeves, for "sentenced." Most were locked up for a few days for going AWOL, while more serious offenders spent up to six months in the stockade, some on a restricted diet of twenty-one hundred calories per day (bread, potatoes, and water). "In the summer," said one inmate to the reporter, "there's an awful stench here . . . that comes from the crematorium. I'm glad I won't be here for the smell."[16]

In the meantime, the memorial committee had invited four sculptors to submit designs for the international monument at the camp: Nandor Glid and Dusan

1933-1945

The memorial sculpture at Dachau by Nandor Glid, dedicated in 1968. Photo: Courtesy of Dachau Museum Archives.

Dzamonja of Yugoslavia, Herman Klug of West Germany, and Grizel Niven of Great Britain. They were to work toward expressions of three themes: spirit of resistance, suffering of the victims, and hope for a better future. The competition jury was comprised mostly of survivors and former inmates of Dachau, though for the purpose of fundraising, American liberators were also invited to join— making them honorary victims by virtue of having discovered Dachau. Additional funds for the monument came from the city councils of Munich, Dachau, and Paris and from the Luxembourg government.

In 1967, Glid, the son of Jews murdered in Auschwitz, was named winner of the competition. His design, devoted primarily to the suffering of the victims, reflected his past as both contemporary sculptor and orphan of the Holocaust: a forty-five-foot-long, black bronze grid of human forms enmeshed in barbed wire. Arms and legs stretch taut and thin like wire; hands and feet are represented in broken star clusters, like barbs. Torsos and heads jut out at excruciating angles, mouths wide open in silent cries—the sculptor's own, the victims', and now visitors'. The inscription on a stone wall beside the Glid monument makes explicit its aim to unify visitors in memory. In French, English, German, and Russian, it reads: "May the example of those who were exterminated here between 1933–1945 because they resisted Nazism help to unite the living for the defense of peace and freedom and in respect for their fellow man."

Though they may not have reflected these decorous sentiments, the unveiling ceremonies on 9 September 1968 did capture both past memory and the spirit of the "generation of 1968." Just as the Social Democratic mayor of Berlin, Klaus Schütz, arrived with military delegations from several NATO countries, a group of demonstrators burst into the former roll-call square, chanting and carrying red banners and signs reading "Today They Hold Memorials—Tomorrow They Hold Executions" and "Today They Incite Pogroms—Tomorrow the Final Solution." According to police, the demonstrators included members of the Socialist Student Federation and Socialist Workers' Youth, as well as a number of former camp inmates allied with them. Fights broke out between guests and demonstrators as the ushers tried to seize their banners. After speeches by dignitaries and wreath-laying ceremonies, the five thousand guests bowed their heads for a moment of silence in memory of those murdered at Dachau—broken seconds later by shouts of "NATO raus!" (NATO, get out).

Two years after the international memorial was dedicated and a year before Glid's monument was erected, a Jewish memorial chapel designed by Hermann Guttmann was consecrated, on 8 May 1967. Philip Shabekoff of the *New York Times* reported that German priests and bishops mixed with young Israeli girls in miniskirts and hoop earrings, American tourists with survivors and soldiers from the nearby bases, all interspersed with local Germans, some decked out in the traditional green costumes of the Bavarian peasant. When asked why they had come to open the Jewish memorial here, Shabekoff reported, few could give a clear answer. Only one middle-aged woman replied angrily, "No, I'm not Jewish. I came here because of the Germans who died in Dachau."[17] As is the case at any memorial, visitors will usually remember their own first.

The Jewish monument is a simple stone-and-mortar vault, entered by a descending path bordered on both sides by a pronged iron fence. The door to the chamber is barred by a barbed iron gate, with stars of David on either side. A shaft of light beams down from a round hole at the top: and we realize that we are standing in the pit of a furnace looking up through the chimney, a stylized white menorah rising from its lip like a wisp of smoke. Juxtaposed, the gates of the memorial and those of the nearby crematorium echo one another: a not-so-subtle reference to the death of the Jews, to extermination itself. At Dachau, the most German of camps, where proportionally few Jews died or were interned, the Jewish memo-

Crematorium oven at Dachau. Photo: Courtesy of Dachau Museum Archives.

The Jewish memorial at Dachau, designed by Hermann Guttmann in 1967, mirrors the shape of crematorium ovens. Photo: James E. Young.

rial does not reflect the small part of the Jewish catastrophe that took place here, but rather points to the deadlier killing centers in the East.

Over the years, Dachau's town council has begrudgingly come to accept the village's notoriety. Confronted with the most intractable of public relations dilemmas, authorities have put the best possible face on matters. In a slightly defensive, if well-intentioned, pamphlet issued by the Dachau tourist office, Mayor Lorenz Reitmeier greets visitors as "Dear Guests":

> You have come to Dachau to visit the memorial site in the former concentration camp. I should like to welcome you on behalf of the town of Dachau. Innumerable crimes were committed in the Dachau Concentration Camp. Like you, deeply moved, the citizens of the town of Dachau bow their heads before the victims of this camp.
>
> The horrors of the German concentration camps must never be repeated! After your visit, you will be horror-stricken. But we sincerely hope you will not transfer your indignation to the ancient, twelve-hundred-year-old Bavarian town of Dachau, which was not consulted when the concentration camp was built and whose citizens voted quite decisively against the rise of national socialism in 1933. The Dachau Concentration Camp is a part of the overall German responsibility for that time.
>
> I extend a cordial invitation to you to visit the old town of Dachau only a few kilometers from here. We would be happy to greet you within our walls and to welcome you as friends.[18]

The mayor's public relations conundrum may remain unsolvable: how to acknowledge that without the concentration camp, many visitors would not come to Dachau, while attempting to contain culpability for the crimes committed within the walls of the camp. Seemingly torn between his position as standard-bearer for civic pride and knowledge of the town's past, the mayor is in the perverse position of welcoming tourists to his town and apologizing for their having to come there in the first place.

On the facing page of the pamphlet, between glossy color photographs of natives in traditional costumes sitting amid half-empty steins of beer in a beer garden and a view of the valley and Alps from the local castle, a short paragraph tells us that "no visitor should miss the view from the Dachau Palace towards the distant foothills of the Alps. On the days when the 'Fohn' wind blows, you can see the Zugspsitze, the Wendelstein, and the entire Alpine chain 'directly on Dachau's front doorstep.' " The rest of the brochure chronicles the long history of the town, from its Celtic origins in 500 B.C.E. to the present day. In a section entitled "years of terror," the transformation of Dachau from a nearly abandoned armaments industry town to concentration camp reminds visitors of the small favors shown prisoners by locals during the war: a scrap of bread, a potato left on the curb. It briefly describes the "uprising" by locals and a group of escaped prisoners the day before the liberation of the camp, its bloody suppression, and the liberation itself: "The surviving prisoners cheered their liberators, and the town, too, could hope for a new and democratic start." In this memory, townspeople and survivors alike can share the joy of their common rebirth at what Germans call the Null-Stunde, or Zero Hour.

Today, according to museum director Barbara Distel, over nine hundred thousand visitors a year tour Dachau and its museum. Most are Germans, but hundreds of thousands come from abroad on a pilgrimage to what has become one of the most notorious tourist stops in Germany. What may not be apparent to most of the memory-tourists, however, is that Dachau's notoriety stems less from its having been one of the deadliest concentration camps (it was not) than from the widespread media coverage of its liberation, the on-site war trials, its proximity to Munich, and, the excellent museum and inviting memorial grounds themselves. The success of the memorial at Dachau has to some extent elevated it to highly symbolic proportions: as Auschwitz has come to symbolize the Holocaust for survivors of the death camps, Dachau has come to serve as a Holocaust icon in the eyes of Western tourists, taking on a life of its own in the culture of travel. In an ironic twist, its historical significance seems to have grown in direct proportion to the success of the memorial.

Dachau's clean, beautifully swept gravel walks, freshly painted barracks, and gleaming white walls now come to stand for all that opposed such order and aesthetic balance. Newly lacquered barracks walls are posted with placards warning visitors not to touch. Another sign on the way to the gas chambers tells us that the crematorium is open from 9 to 5. But in fact, this abstracted, aesthetisized lay-out may also be the most appropriate of all memorial forms, precisely in the ways it calls attention to the great gulf between its past and its present. Unlike the restored ruins of other sites, the memorial at Dachau does not ask visitors to confuse its orderly, sterile present with its sordid past. In its abstract references to what it once was, Dachau reminds visitors that their own memory of this time, dependent on sites like Dachau, is also necessarily abstract. They will never know these experiences, but only the well-groomed memorial itself. For younger students or less critically minded adult visitors, such fine distinctions might not be readily apparent. They have come to Dachau, after all, to "see what it was like." Being told that this is not what Dachau was like, but only what its

memorial is like, may leave some visitors bewildered as to why they have come at all.

Part of the solution may come in the fine guides and booklets provided by the museum to make this distinction clear. They trace the history of KZ-Dachau from beginning to end in order to illustrate the evolution of a site's "memory" over time. For in fact, such sites almost never transmit their own pasts. As German art historian Detlef Hoffmann reminds us, the concentration camp at Dachau did not appear overnight. First there were provisional fences and huts, then higher fences and barbed wire. Every citizen of Dachau watched the camp being constructed, as well as many Müncheners, who traditionally took Sunday excursions to Dachau and its castle.[19]

Hoffmann reported that on a visit to Dachau in 1961, he had to blaze his way through brush grown so high that it concealed the fences and outer moat. Twelve years of concentration camp history, he felt, had gone to ruin after the war. For Hoffmann, these twenty years following the liberation—when Dachau had become unmentionable, a haven for refugees, homeless, even winos living in aban-

The memorial grounds at Dachau, now swept clean save the symbolic foundations of barracks. Photo: James E. Young.

doned and overgrown huts—became as significant as the twelve years it was in operation. In Hoffmann's eyes, the townspeople, having once denied the camp's existence, had allowed nature to deny it again. He wondered what it must have been like for them to see the high brush chopped away to reveal the camp's—and their own—past again. Hoffmann's only regret was that in the memorial's sparkling renovation, the town's former repression had itself been lost to memory. In this sense, Hoffmann reminds us that part of the history in these memorials may also be the neglect of traces they might otherwise preserve, as well as their belated safekeeping.

Buchenwald: The Other Side of Memory

In western Germany, memory-work is often regarded as a punitive, if self-inflicted, penance for crimes of a past regime. But in its rush to rebuild after the war, the western sector not only absorbed itself in reconstruction but also effaced a number of remnants from the Nazi period. With the encouragement of its Allied occupiers, the Federal Republic strove to begin anew, to put its Nazi past behind. West Germans would regard Zero Hour, the point of absolute capitulation and destruction, as the beginning of time, which would now be measured in the ever-elapsing distance between the old order and new.

In East Germany, however, the Soviet occupiers ensured that as much of the debris of Germany's destruction as possible would remain visible for decades to come. On the one hand, what was officially regarded in the West as Germany's disastrous defeat was recalled in the East as East Germany's victory, its seeming self-liberation. At the behest of the Soviets, East Germans came to recall primarily the Communist victory over fascism, the great redemption of socialist martyrs in the founding of the German Democratic Republic (GDR). On the other hand, bullet-pocked facades, weedy no-man's land, even the destroyed Reichstag served to remind a vanquished nation precisely how it arrived at the present moment. Implicit in the devastation was a warning that it could be repeated at any time, that in fact the East Germans were now a subjugated nation.

From the end of the war to the present day, sites of persecution and resistance have been assiduously marked and preserved in the East. It was not only the Soviets who had an interest in preserving a few well-placed ruins, but also the German Communist party, politically vindicated by its ordeal under Nazi rule and now propped up by the Soviet Army. Because of their role during the war as Germany's only coherent resistance organization, the Communists could define themselves afterwards as the premier antifascist party, Hitler's first victim. If in the West wartime resistance is recalled largely in the images of the Wehrmacht officers' plot against Hitler or in the "white rose" students' campaign, in the East it has come to be symbolized primarily by the Communist party and the martyrdom of its leaders.

Having defined itself as an antifascist state, and thereby absolving itself of responsibility for fascist crimes, the GDR needed to take only a small step to commemorate itself as a victim-state, as well: since 1945, the second Sunday in September has been celebrated as a national remembrance day for the victims of fascism. From that time on, consummate service to East German society consisted simply in having been a martyr to fascism. Both resistance fighters and victims—and their children—were by law compensated with privileged housing, health and education, and pensions.[20] Under this provision, Jews were accorded special rights—but only as antifascists, never as Jews. In practice over the years, such benefits even accrued genealogically: the children of victims were also presumed to be antifascists, honorary members of the resistance by birthright.

In this sense, the national identity of the GDR was rooted in the political memory of the Nazis as an occupying power. This self-idealization was enacted to great effect in both the plastic monuments and museum narrative at Buchenwald, which, we are told, was not liberated by American soldiers, but was instead "selbst befreit," or self-liberated, by the camp underground, comprised mostly of German Communists. In this version, the American Army was officially regarded as another, interim occupier, before the Red Army came as true liberators. Of all the camps in Soviet-occupied Germany, only Buchenwald became a truly national East German memorial to the Nazi period.

Indeed, as both place and idea, Buchenwald played a fundamental, nearly mythological role in the GDR's self-conceptualization. First, as an internment center for young German Communists, the camp served as an enforced gathering site for debate and political formulation, a place where plans were drawn for the future and leaders were chosen to create the new order. As a remembered site, Buchenwald became a place in the mind, where character, courage, and communist identity were forged. It played such a formative part in young German Communists' coming of age that later visits were often characterized as returns to the very wellsprings of their being, the roots of their identity. As a site of suffering and resistance, as the seedbed of the German Communist party, Buchenwald became hallowed ground. Little wonder, then, that GDR officer cadets were awarded their bars at Buchenwald—where their political forebears had symbolically earned their own stripes as enemies of the Third Reich.

In some ways, the Nazis built a concentration camp at Buchenwald, just up the hill from Weimar, precisely because it already had a mythological past in the

German mind. When Himmler cynically designated Goethe's oak as the center of the camp he would begin in July 1937, he hoped to neutralize the memory of Goethe even as he invoked the philosopher's cultural authority. What better way to commemorate the obliteration of Weimar culture than to seal it in barbed wire, to turn it into its own prison? Indeed, Buchenwald was chosen as the center of the GDR's commemorative activity for some of the same reasons the Nazis chose to build a camp there in the first place: this stunningly beautiful region seemed in both cases to exemplify the cultural heart of Germany. As the nearby Ettersberg mountain range and city of Weimar would suggest the majesty of German culture, the charred and withered remains of Goethe's oak would symbolize the depths to which the culture had sunk.

By 1943, Buchenwald held seventeen thousand prisoners, mostly German Communists, Social Democrats, criminals, clergymen, and captured partisans. Because they comprised the largest group in Buchenwald and were already politically organized, the Communists and Social Democrats worked together to form an International Camp Committee, which gathered arms for revolt and organized acts of sabotage in the nearby weapons factories. At this point, Jews did not constitute a large part of the camp's population for the simple reason that they were being shipped directly to the killing centers in the East for immediate death. But when Jews were interned as political prisoners, they often survived as part of a political network. As a result, later German-Jewish remembrance of Buchenwald would retain many of the trappings of their political, not ethnic or religious, lives there.

In late 1943, however, the camp's composition began to change: a load of French prisoners arrived, followed by eight thousand Soviet POWs who were murdered almost immediately. The next year, as the death camps in the East were being abandoned, tens of thousands of half-dead Jews flooded in. Because they were segregated from the other prisoners—housed in what was called the "Little Camp"—Jews were neither protected by the International Committee nor recalled afterwards in the committee's memorials. As the Communists ran the prisoners' administration during the war, they also ran the administration of memory afterward: Buchenwald would remain a site of exclusively political martyrdom in their eyes.

Between 3 and 10 April 1945, the SS began a desperate evacuation of prisoners from Buchenwald, marching columns of thousands out of the camp before shooting them. Thousands of other prisoners, mostly Jews and the weakest of other groups selected by the International Committee, were stuffed into boxcars destined for Dachau. Instead, they roamed the Czech countryside aimlessly looking for unbombed track: nearly all the prisoners died of suffocation or starvation, entombed by their railway coffins. At noon on 11 April 1945, as the remaining twenty thousand prisoners were being herded into the Appelplatz (Roll Call Plaza) at Buchenwald, with the sounds of Gen. George S. Patton's approaching Fourth Armored Division guns in the air, the International Committee rose up furiously with machine guns and grenades, routing the handful of guards and SS soldiers who had not already fled. Three hours later, committee fighters stormed the gates of the camp and the remaining watchtower guards took to the woods. By the time Patton's troops arrived, the prisoners had hung a white flag from the entrance tower to signify their victory. These few moments of glory would literally be frozen in time: the hands of the Buchenwald camp clock were stilled at exactly 3:15. Today, they remain in this position, a visual reminder of Buchenwald's "self-liberation."

The first memorial at Buchenwald, aside from the remains of the camp itself, was a wooden obelisk erected by former prisoners ten days after their liberation, one of several temporary monuments built in the surrounding Weimar countryside. The first memorial tours of Buchenwald were conducted by American soldiers, who marched the citizens of Weimar through the camp to view the wretched conditions, to hear descriptions of their crimes, and often to bury the victims of their Reich—all of which forcibly created German memory of the victims. Three years later, however, the Americans were replaced by Soviet soldiers, and the wooden makeshift monuments had already begun to rot. So, on 9 April 1948, the prisoners' association began a vigorous campaign for an official memorial at Buchenwald. A year later the city of Weimar, the government of Thuringia, and former prisoners constructed a "grave of honor" in memory of Buchenwald's 239,000 inmates, of whom some 56,000 had died.

Within a few years, the organization of former prisoners—the Vereinegung der Verfolgten des Naziregimes (VVN), or Organization of Victims of the Nazi Regime—initiated a further plan for developing the camp as a museum. Not until 1951 was the Central Committee able to allocate money, and even then the museum was competing with housing for funds. Three years later, the local council of ministers approved a government proposal for constructing a separate memorial: all of which served to bring the memorial within the purview of the Party and state at a central level, as Eve Rosenhaft has observed. Indeed, by this time, the government's sense of itself was so intertwined with remembrance of the committee's past victimization that it dissolved the VVN in 1953 on the grounds that its aims were now official government policy. In its stead, the Committee of Antifascist Resistance Fighters was established, a move that substituted fighters as a figure for all victims.

The "Medal for Fighters against Fascism, 1933–45" would thus be awarded both to those who fought in the resistance and to those persecuted by the Nazi regime, provided "they retained their antifascist attitudes after 1945 and actively supported the development of the rule of the workers and peasants in the GDR."[21] No backsliders were allowed, only those who joined the Party. This defined antifascists as those who continued to support the Party and then restricted their number further still, when it was deemed that "the title 'Resistance Fighter' belongs only to those who acknowledge the leadership of the party of the working class, defend the unity of the Party, and do everything to build socialism in the GDR."

The aims of commemoration are even more explicitly stated in a later declaration that "every antifascist resistance fighter must be a socialist educator of our working people and youth. . . . Part of the socialist education of our people is the transmission of the lessons and experiences of the antifascist struggle." In these terms, neither victims nor fighters would be recognized as such outside their identification with the Party. All of which was mere groundwork for the official declaration on the Buchenwald memorial's opening in September 1958: "The resistance struggle against Hitler-fascism was organized and led by the working class and its parties."[22] The official museum guidebook further elaborates this theme, making explicit both the reasons for and object of remembrance.

Rather than paraphrasing the guidebooks, it seems preferable to let them speak for themselves. A section on "the system of concentration camps" opens: "From the very beginning, the proclaimed aims of the German fascists were the elimination of Marxism, revenge for the lost war and a brutal terror campaign against everyone who stood in their way. Their aims were congruent to those of big business which supported the Nazi movement generously. With their support the fascists came to power in 1933, and immediately began to crush the organized working class movement which was the main obstacle to their plans."[23] A couple of pages later, atop photographs of factory workers, piles of corpses, and a rail line, a chart traces the profits of I. G. Farben (still a large German company) from 1932 (48 million marks) to 1937 (231 million marks) to 1943 (822 million marks). The essay on the facing page concludes, "The millions big business had invested in Hitler were bearing rich fruit." As Peter Hayes and others have made clear, the ties between German industrialists and the Nazis were often strong and mutually beneficial. But it was apparent to East German visitors that these businesses continued to operate only in West Germany—which, by implication, had become a mere extension of the fascist state under another name.[24]

By the 1970s, the GDR had proclaimed itself the bastion of progressive traditions, leaving West Germany as a catch-all of reactionary forces. Memorials in this context served only one purpose: to generate and deepen socialist historical consciousness. In one of his addresses at Buchenwald, former Prime Minister Erich Honecker stated explicitly: "It remains a major task . . . to elaborate on our material dialectic idea of the world view and to represent it in its unity of scientific objectivity and revolutionary spirit. Very significant for the strengthening of the workers' socialist consciousness are the efforts for the further realization of the Marxist-Leninist image of history." By their nature, public memorials in East Germany would become iconographic lodestars of government policy, pieces of the landscape around which the principles enunciated by Honecker were organized and eventually naturalized. Accordingly, even the hard-working staff at the Buchenwald memorial defined its primary task as "the struggle against imperialism and its manifestations, for the respect and pride of the working class, their fight for which they have sacrificed so much."[25]

By recalling resistance only, the leaders of the GDR continued to ratify their own legitimacy as opponents to and victims of fascism. They remembered their role in defeating Hitler, thereby sustaining the notion that they were in no way accountable for his crimes. Though not incompatible with the memory of resistance, to mourn the victims of anti-Jewish terror was perceived as deflecting from the mission at hand: it was to identify with those who liberated the camps and not with the victims of tyranny. For, as victims of past tyranny, East Germans might have identified themselves a little too easily as victims of current tyranny, as well.

From its inception, therefore, the state museum and memorial at Buchenwald were not intended to mark the loss of life so much as to illustrate the glories of resistance—and to celebrate the socialist victory over fascism. To this end, any public art it commissioned would take the shape of victory, not martyrs', monuments.[26] As a result, the Buchenwald National Memorial, the most gargantuan complex of memorial sculpture and edifices located at any of the German camps, is striking for its largely triumphal scenes of uprising and self-liberation. In the sheer size of the sculpture and by virtue of the spectacular landscape, the state hoped to monumentalize beyond question its own reason for being, to create a site that would remember definitively the state's own birth.

The most prominent architects in the country were enlisted to enact a vision of great roads of blood and sacrifice leading to landscaped mountainsides, crowned by victory monuments overlooking the beautiful Ettersberg Valley. Fritz Cremer won the 1951 competition for a central monument, which he adapted by its 1958 dedication to include eleven bronze figures set before a 160-foot-tall belltower.

Fritz Cremer's memorial statuary at Buchenwald recalls the prisoners' uprising, their supposed self-liberation. Photo: James E. Young.

Revolt of the Prisoners consists of a spreading victory wedge of dignified, fighting figures unbent by their travails in the camps. All the figures, including a small boy at the left, stand tall, some with weapons, beckoning others to follow, hands upraised as they stride forward. Even the single falling figure in the front drops heroically to one knee, his clenched fists still held high. It is a monument to triumph and resistance, to triumph *in* resistance. When the bell sounds loudly throughout the valley on commemoration days, it is a liberty bell, rousing victory chimes, its surface lined not by stress fractures but by embossed strands of barbed wire.

Throughout the memorial at Buchenwald, martyrs are distinguished from the fighters both spatially and iconographically. Inside the camp itself, murdered Jews and Soviet POWs are remembered by smaller, more sepulchral stones spread out randomly over acres of the former barracks and crematoria. The German Socialist leader murdered at Buchenwald, Ernst Thaleman, is commemorated with a small bronze bust, set in the yard of the crematorium. Without the hundreds of barracks that once filled the space inside the gates, absence rules as motif. The ruins of the crematoria, empty fields, and stopped watchtower clock counterpoint the assertive presence of eighteen pylons with bowls flanking the "Street of Nations," seven granite cubes emblazoned with reliefs telling the camp's story, all running down a series of twenty-meter-wide stairs comprising the "Street of Freedom." Had the rest of the country been built as monumentally, as grandly and solidly, as the Buchenwald memorial complex, East Germany might indeed have projected itself as a model of the Socialist world.

With the fall of the Communist regime, however, more than just the edifices here are now mocked. Shortly after Germany's reunification, a Western reporter found the museum at Buchenwald closed, undergoing both physical and ideological renovation. "Dear Visitors," a sign read, "Be patient. Changes are being made." Even its most recent, meticulously reconceived exhibition, on tour in West Germany when reunification came, was now out of date. What had never been acknowledged before, it seems, was the memory nearby citizens had of the continuing terror at Buchenwald and other camps in the Soviet occupation zone.

On liberating some eleven concentration and POW camps in the East in 1945, the Soviet Army turned them immediately into internment camps for their own enemies, perceived and actual. Camps like Buchenwald and Sachsenhausen were filled with new German prisoners: former Nazi party officials, Waffen-SS, German POWs, and civilians deemed for whatever reason to be security risks. And then, according to the former Party newspaper *Neues Deutschland*, now published by the Social Democrats, after the rounding up of Nazi suspects, the Soviets began to intern Social Democrats who had refused to join the Communist party (into which their party had been merged) as well as Communist victims of Stalin's purges. Of some 130,000 Germans who passed through eleven Soviet-run camps, 50,000 died. While many, perhaps hundreds, of these were shot and thrown into mass graves, most of the dead probably succumbed to hunger, disease, and general neglect in the immediate postwar era of shortages and famine.

But in recalling the forgotten Soviet takeover of the Nazi camps at Buchenwald and other places, the new German government has created a new order of memorial as well. Now when Chancellor Helmut Kohl lays flowers at Buchenwald to the victims of Nazi terror, he saves a wreath for the six new memorial crosses commemorating the estimated eight to thirteen thousand Germans who died at Buchenwald during Stalin's reign. The accretion of memory at Buchenwald now includes Stalin's terror as well as Hitler's; it is becoming a place where Germans were victimized by both Nazis and Communists. With a little updating, Buchenwald may begin to serve as a national memorial for the new Germany, as well as it did for the GDR. With the introduction of further German victims into its memorial landscape, Germany's normalization proceeds apace.

Chapter 3   The Gestapo-Gelände:

Topography of

Unfinished Memory

As I suggested earlier, the best memorial to the fascist era and its victims in Germany today may not be a single memorial at all—but only the never-to-be-resolved debate over which kind of memory to preserve, how to do it, in whose name, and to what end. Imagine, for example, a series of annual competitions, whereby the proposed designs and jury's debate are exhibited in lieu of an installed winner. Visitors to such a memorial installation would be invited to submit their own evaluations of designs, which would in turn be added to the overall memorial text. Instead of a fixed figure for memory, the debate itself—perpetually unresolved amid ever-changing conditions—would be enshrined.

In fact, the seeds for such a memorial already exist in Berlin's painful, if instructive, attempt to reinvest the former site of the SS and Gestapo headquarters with memory of its dark past. The administrative heartland of the SS state—a magnificent complex of palatial buildings and museums—was gutted by Allied firebombs during the war and demolished by city planners afterward. Scraped clean but for a great weed-choked mountain of rubble, for many years the Gestapo-Gelände (Gestapo Terrain) recalled primarily the absence of memory, the destruction of telltale ruins, the nation's memorial struggle with itself. Now it serves as a veritable "tel," or hill of ruins, of memorial strata in the center of Berlin.

What was to become the Gestapo-Gelände had been a favorite district of Hitler and the Nazi party in Berlin well before he was appointed chancellor. Having long preferred the ornate and stately comforts of the Prinz-Albrecht Hotel for high-level meetings, the Nazi party moved the editorial offices of its newspaper,

Der Angriff (The assault), to nearby Wilhelmstrasse 106 in 1932. With Hitler's rise to power and the Nazis' need to coordinate state and party institutions, one security branch after another moved into the neighborhood, until the party and SS occupied virtually the entire district.

Beginning in May 1933, the newly created Secret State Police Office moved into the former School of Industrial Arts and Crafts at Prinz-Albrecht-Strasse 8. The Museum of Industrial Arts and Crafts next door at number 7 (now the Martin Gropius Bau) had been moved a few years earlier to another site in town, leaving only the arts library in the huge building. With its insatiable appetite for office and storage space, the Gestapo then occupied this building as well, dumping art books from the library into the courtyard to make way for its massive files. Early the next year, after being appointed head of the Gestapo, Heinrich Himmler transferred the administrative branches of the SS and SD from Munich to Berlin: he took the palatial Prinz-Albrecht Hotel for himself and the SS, and gave the Prinz-Albrecht-Palais to Reinhard Heydrich, head of the SD. Adolf Eichmann was to begin his career on Wilhelmstrasse, around the corner from the offices of Ernst Kaltenbrunner, Heinrich "Gestapo" Muller, and the Gestapo Prison. These were just a few of the seven thousand "bureaucrats" who came to work every day at these offices.

By 1939, when the Criminal Police, SS, and SD were all brought under one Main Office of Reich Security (the RHSA, or Reichssicherheitshauptamt), the area of stately buildings and museums surrounding the Prinz-Albrecht-Palais had become the "most feared address" in Berlin. Though operation centers had by 1943 spread out across Berlin, the area bordered by Prinz-Albrecht-Strasse and Anhalter-Strasse, Saarland- (now Stressenman-) Strasse and Wilhelm-Strasse, still served as the nerve center of the Nazis' security apparatus. Nearly all the major decisions and plans regarding the fate of Germany's "enemies"—racial, political, and social—were made here. If the theoretical principles of the Final Solution had been decided at the Wannsee Villa, the laborious practical means were formulated in these buildings: the organization of deportations, coordination of exterminations, analysis of and response to *Einsatzgruppen* (special killing commando units) reports. This was both home to "armchair" murderers and a base for the hands-on killers coming in to receive their orders.

The carpet bombing of Berlin begun by the Allies in November 1943 had begun to focus on the government sector by April and May 1944, when all the buildings in the Gestapo-Gelände were hit. While the main centers of the Prinz-Albrecht-Palais and Hotel were almost completely destroyed that May, other buildings, including the Martin Gropius Bau, were only gutted and still retained their basic structure. Hundreds died during these raids, including twenty concentration

American soldiers on patrol pass the main entrance of the former Gestapo headquarters on Prinz-Albrechtstrasse in Berlin, 1945. Photo: Courtesy of Berliner Festspiele.

camp prisoners from Sachsenhausen, who had been brought in to clear rubble from the area and were killed when the SS forced them to take cover in an exposed, shallow trench during a bombing. After the massive air raids of 3 February 1945 and the Red Army's artillery barrages during their final assault, mountains of rubble obscured the former map of Berlin—but the majority of buildings surrounding the Gestapo-Gelände still stood, if only as burned-out shells.

Immediately after the war, memory of the Gestapo-Gelände seemed as faceless and uninteresting to occupying troops as the armchair murderers who had once pushed pens there. Indifferent to the seat of Nazi terror, American and Soviet troops focused instead on the Reichstag building and Reich's Chancellery, symbol-laden scenes of Hitler's rise and fall. Berliners, too, showed little interest in either renovating these buildings or preserving their ruins. When neighbors ransacked the rubble, it was not for files or evidence, but for food, clothing, and fuel. It seems that only the Germans who had survived interrogation and beatings at the Gestapo headquarters—such as Bertolt Brecht, who made a widely publicized memorial visit in 1949—had any interest in preserving the remains. Other, similarly political manifestations of memory blossomed nearby: a streamer-festooned brick wall across the street from the actual site read: "Prinz-Albrecht-Strasse. Here was Himmler's headquarters of unrestrained murder. This ruin calls for Socialist unity."[1]

As the first memorial references to this site's murderous past had been born in political memory, so too would the site's eventual amnesia be politically inspired. For in this case, the reconstruction of West Germany as both physical and economic bulwark against the Soviet Union was, in Western eyes, a far higher priority than cultivating memory of the war. Not only were the Germans encouraged by the Western allies to begin their history again on 8 May 1945, but all signs of defeat itself would have to be effaced for rebuilding to commence.

In fact, many feared that if the ruins of the Gestapo-Gelände were left, they might even be readopted by former SS soldiers as a memorial not to what they had perpetrated, but to what they had lost. Better, in the eyes of municipal authorities, to wipe the topographical slate clean of past crimes and suffering before starting anew. As the Germans had been liberated from the Nazi scourge, the land itself would now be liberated from all traces of its past, from the burden of memory.

While the demolition of the Reich's Chancellery had generated massive international coverage, hardly anyone noticed when the bombed-out Prinz-Albrecht-Palais was dynamited on 27 and 28 April 1949. Even the local architectural historians were not informed until several days after the razing. By 1950, nothing remained of Gestapo or SS headquarters on Wilhelmstrasse but piles of rubble, which were eventually removed altogether. Under the sponsorship of the Federal Republic and the Berlin senate, an urban renewal contest—"Capital Berlin"—was launched in 1957. "The practical task of the contest," according to its announcement, "will be the rebuilding of Berlin's central part, so badly damaged during the war; its spiritual task will be to fashion the center in such a way that it will become a visible expression of Germany's capital and that of a modern metropolis."[2] New topographical landmarks would arise, foci of the new Berlin, in the new Germany. Even the relatively well preserved Museum of Ethnology on the corner of Prinz-Albrecht-Strasse and Saarland-Strasse, which had actually reopened for a time in the 1950s, was dynamited in 1963. The entire area, save the Martin Gropius Bau, had been turned into a gaping wasteland.

The split in Berlin's municipal administration at the end of 1948 marked the first stage of its division into Eastern and Western sectors. While Prinz-Albrecht-Strasse belonged to the Soviet sector, the buildings along its southern edge fell within the Kreuzberg district, administered by the Americans. As a result, the past role of this site in Nazi crimes was overwhelmed by its present role in the East-West conflict: memory itself had been divided and conquered by the new powers of the land. What had once been the heart of the city remained desolate and devastated, a buffer and possible flashpoint between the East and West.

The construction of the Berlin Wall in 1961 further marginalized the area. Although developers in the West saw it as a no-man's land and so ignored it during the reconstruction boom of the 1960s, the border zone preserved the ruins on both sides of the wall. With so much else destroyed and so few resources for reconstruction, East Berlin authorities could not afford to tear down buildings that still stood—and so reoccupied them as office buildings. Only the bullet-pocked facades reminded people on the street of what had happened there—and these were references to war itself, not to the terror of the Gestapo. On the west side of the wall, the border zone was hidden away out of public view. On top of mountains of rubble remaining from the demolition of the buildings in 1951, garbage and refuse from other demolition and construction sites were dumped and covered with layers of sand and soil. As the last trace of a repressed history, the Gestapo-Gelände itself was now geographically lost.

As is the wont of repressed memories, however, the site returned to public consciousness with an obsessive, ferocious vengeance—and has now become a controlling focal point for all German memory. The ruins lay dormant until 1978, when, during a convention in Berlin of environmentalists and anarchists self-described as "the Do-Nothing Congress," architectural historian Dieter Hoffman-Axthelm guided tours of the no-man's land. Pointing out its historical significance, he asked why these buildings—the most important and last remaining of the Schinkel school—had been demolished after the war, although several had not been totally destroyed by bombing.

In response, Berlin's International Exhibition of Construction and Design (IBA) moved to protect the terrain from plans to pave it over as a roadway. By 1980, several other organizations added their voices, demanding that the city erect a memorial in the border zone to the victims of fascism. Some, like the International League for the Rights of Man, wrote open letters to Berlin's Senator for Internal Affairs; others, like the Study Group of Persecuted Social Democrats, suggested themselves as arbiters of such memory.[3]

At about the same time, preparations were getting under way for Berlin's 750th anniversary celebration, which included plans for a national museum of German history. In an effort to deflect the Kreuzberg district's demands for a document center in the border zone, the only remaining building, the Martin Gropius Bau, was suggested as the future home of the museum. For the time being, it would serve as a temporary exhibition hall; its first installation, "Prussia: An Attempt at

Reappraisal," was scheduled to open in 1981. As a result, further attention spilled from the renovated Martin Gropius Bau onto the adjacent, still rubble-strewn terrain.

In 1982, Berlin's senate passed a motion by the Social Democrats to erect a memorial and announced a competition to be sponsored by Richard von Weizsäcker, then Lord Mayor of Berlin. The IBA was made executor of the contest and memorial. In his invitation to contestants, von Weizsäcker stressed the integral link between history and topography, between memory and urban development. "Reshaping the terrain where the Prinz-Albrecht-Palais formerly stood is one of the most important responsibilities our city faces," he wrote,

> both for reasons of history and urban development. For better or for worse, Berlin is the custodian of German history, which here has left worse scars than anywhere else.
>
> The terrain adjacent to the Martin Gropius Bau, which shall ultimately house a Museum of German History, contains invisible traces of a heavy historic legacy: invisible are the buildings from where the SS state operated its levers of terror. Visible is the Wall, cutting like a knife across the former Prinz-Albrecht-Strasse; and this we may well see as the nemesis of cynical power as it was practiced in this street during the National Socialist era.
>
> As we go about reconstructing this area, it will be our task to proceed with contemporary history in mind while also providing a place for contemplation. Yet at the same time we must not miss the opportunity to give the Kreuzberg district a terrain where life can unfold and leisure is possible.[4]

However well-intentioned, von Weizsäcker's invitation went on to suggest two nearly paralyzing conditions for memorial designers. The competition would strive to find a creative solution that "would reconcile the historical depth of the location with practical applications, such as the establishment of a park, playground, and exercise area."[5] The notion that the memorial was to be an all-purpose terrain for memory and recreation sparked still further debate: Was it to be a "memorial with a park attached" or a "park with a memorial in it"? And why was there no mention of a document house? How could anybody know what had happened there unless the city told them?

The 194 proposals submitted to the jury cut a wide swath through the fields of contemporary art and architecture, drawing on plastic, performance, conceptual, and architectural media. Some applicants suggested leaving the site as it was: a monument to historical denial. Others proposed reconstructing part of the buildings, erecting stylized, artificial ruins. Many designers took literally the call for a

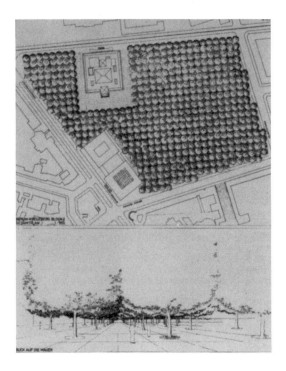

Drawing of the first-place entry in the competition for a memorial at the Gestapo-Gelände, by Jürgen Wenzel and Nikolaus Lang. The land would be sealed by iron plates and hidden from heaven's view by the leaves of chestnut trees, planted in neat rows. Photo: Courtesy of Berliner Festspiele.

"memorial park" and so proposed a variety of landscape formations including abstract pyramids, groves of trees, squares, transverse walks, and other land forms in the metaphorical shapes of swastikas, stars of David, or bomb craters.

In April 1984, the jury awarded first prize to the most radically innovative design, submitted by the Berlin landscape architect Jürgen Wenzel and the Bavarian artist Nikolaus Lang. They proposed to seal over the entire area with great plates of cast iron, broken only by round holes large enough for a tight and orderly grid of hundreds of chestnut trees. On several thousand of the plates, actual documents from the SS files would be emblazoned, precisely as they appeared in the originals: directives ordering the deportations of Jews, the wearing of the star; consignment notes; victims' letters and diaries. Instead of hiding bureaucratic evidence in archives, Wenzel and Lang would cast the documents in iron and display them for all to see. The raised lettering on these otherwise smooth plates would literally cause visitors "to stumble over their own history." This would be an iron-floored forest, a cold landscape, sealed against the possibility of anything ever growing here again.

The designers had taken their inspiration, they said, directly from their first guide to memory in the Gestapo-Gelände, Dieter Hoffman-Axthelm, who had remarked that even if landscape could not remain explicitly cursed, this area could never again be used for "normal" activities. Because the terrain had been deliberately scraped clean of all physical reminders of its past, the memorial should not pretend to be preserving remnants of the past; in fact, their design would also attempt to reflect efforts to eradicate the site's past. It would remain, in their words, an "Ungelände" (anti-site), its memory sealed over both to preserve memory of the past and to keep it from springing forth again.[6]

Objections to the design soon poured in. The jury stipulated that instead of sealing the whole terrain off in cast iron, patches should be covered in pebbles, to make the area more inviting for visitors. Outside critics took issue with other features: Wasn't this a little like one of Albert Speer's productions, columns of chestnut trees standing like rows of soldiers in a Prussian barracks square? Still others began to question all over again the fundamental need for another German memorial. After all, they said, Berlin had already marked many sites, including the Plotzensee Memorial and the one at Bendlerstrasse for those executed in connection with the plot on Hitler's life. Wenzel answered that there may have been other German monuments, but where could one go to remember the unrepresented victims: Jews, gypsies, homosexuals, Communists, Polish and Russian peasants? He proposed a complement to the installation in the form of an "Active Museum," to make explicit who the victims of the Gestapo and SS had been.[7] The debate itself was turning out to be far more instructive of memory than any memorial could ever have been.

Having failed to reach a consensus, the competition committee decided not to act on any of the submissions. In December 1984, Wenzel and Lang were notified that their design would not be installed after all. Because no further plans were contemplated, a group calling itself the "Active Museum of Fascism and Resistance in Berlin" issued a public appeal to join them in a commemorative dig on 8 May 1985, the anniversary of the Nazis' capitulation. In this "memorial operation," volunteers would symbolically excavate their nation's buried past by literally digging up the terrain in preparation for a "document house." Theirs would be a model of memorial activism, an unearthing of memory, all part of reinfusing an amnesiac site with memory of its blighted past.[8] In the event, the excavators found not only symbolic memory but actual ruins: the basement and kitchen areas of Gestapo headquarters. The competition, which had been based on a site without ruins, had now been rendered moot.

In 1987, a temporary exhibit on the history of the SS and police, appropriately entitled "The Topography of Terror" and incorporating the now excavated ruins, was mounted in the former administrative center of the SS state. The aim of this new center was to "accentuate the site's special historical significance, without eliminating the traces of post-war efforts to render history invisible and repressed."[9] In effect, by preserving the character of the site as an open wound,

Members of the "Active Museum" excavate memory at the site of the former Gestapo headquarters, 1985. Photo: Courtesy of Actives Museum Faschismus und Widerstand in Berlin e.V.

89

The Gestapo-Gelände

the exhibit would recall both memory of events and the city's past repression of memory.

Today, behind the Martin Gropius Bau and beyond the temporary documentation center, wooden stairs lead up the side of a steep hill—a tel of ruins—to a wooden observation deck. In the summer of 1990, when the last chunks of the Wall were toppled, one could see from this platform a panorama of Berlin: the graffiti-covered Wall bordering one side of the terrain, with dilapidated prewar buildings beyond the Wall on the East, modern high-rises on the West. City maps with landmarks are still posted on each side of the deck, orienting the visitor in light of the city's past.

The 750th anniversary celebrations have come and gone, the debate continues, and visitors continue to flock to the Gestapo-Gelände. Among the three hundred thousand who came to the exhibit in the first year was a young American serviceman. "Was this Hitler's bunker?" he asked, perhaps a little too enthusiastically. "No, it's over there," I said, pointing north and east. "This is only the former Gestapo headquarters." His face brightened and he studied the map carefully. Had he come as an admirer of Hitler's military machine, I wondered, or as a student of German history?

In this provisional memorial, the city of Berlin seems to recognize that perhaps there can be no more "final solutions" to any dilemma—especially memory of the last Final Solution. Indeed, were the competition itself to be extended indefi-

View of the Gestapo-Gelände (Gestapo Terrain), long a tel of rubble and recently excavated ruins of the Gestapo prison cellar, here laid with wreaths, 1986. Photo: Courtesy of Berliner Festspiele.

nitely, its proposals collected, displayed, and perpetually debated, the entire process might recommend itself as an exemplary, ever-expanding memorial text. For together, the proposed designs and the jury's responses, the city's reasons for the "memory park," and the public outcry over the winner constitute—however unintentionally—a dialectical model for memory of this time. The memorial here is comprised not by material space and ruins, but by memory-work itself. Left unresolved, the memorial project at the Gestapo-Gelände flourishes precisely because it contests memory—because it continues to challenge, exasperate, edify, and invite visitors into a dialogue between themselves and their past.

Chapter 4   Austria's

Ambivalent

Memory

> Waldheim wasn't a Nazi, only his horse was.
> —Fred Sinowatz

For the purposes of this study, Germany and Austria will be considered together, not because they are unambiguously linked, but because they share certain cultural traditions and historical memories, and thus more unites than divides them. This is neither to tar Germany with Austria's postwar indifference to the Holocaust, nor to assign equal blame to Austria for Germany's crimes. But in coming to Austria from Germany, we move from a painfully self-conscious memorial culture to one distinguished mostly by its ambivalence toward the recent past.

Although they traditionally present themselves as Hitler's first victims, the Austrians never had the audacity to formalize this boldly self-serving myth in stone. But with so few Jews left in Austria, there has never been much pressure to memorialize the country's role in the mass murder. Instead, a nervous decorum prevails, which until recently admitted little discussion. President Kurt Waldheim's silence about his wartime activities merely confirmed the national silence. The Austrians' seeming detachment from the Holocaust was not completely self-inspired, however: it was openly encouraged as part of an Allied agreement during the war. As "the first free country to fall victim to Hitlerite aggression," according to a carefully worded statement issued by American, Soviet, and British foreign ministers in 1943, Austria quietly accepted the mantle of martyrdom as its own. In order to ensure Austrian neutrality in the Cold War, neither the U.S. nor the Soviet Union wanted to label it a wartime belligerent.

John Bunzel has even called the 1955 "State Treaty" absolving Austria of any responsibility for the war that nation's founding myth. Though Bunzel maintains with some justification that the Allies used this formulation in 1943 to "stimulate Austrian resistance against the Third Reich," once so characterized, the Austrians themselves were loath to give up their exculpatory disclaimer.[1]

Because Austria was never held to account for its past, however, the sweeping away of signs of Austria's accession to Hitler along with the war rubble was not accompanied by the national soul-searching we find in Germany. If anything, Austria seems to share only the more dubious aspects of the two Germanys' reconstruction: like the Federal Republic, it concentrated so single-mindedly on rebuilding, on effacing all links with the past, that there seemed to be little time or inclination for commemorating the Nazi past; and like the GDR, Austria's official position that it was Hitler's first victim relieved Austrians of the obligation to recall the crimes of their own sons and daughters during the war.[2]

Almost immediately after the war, Austria was proclaimed "liberated" from the Nazi scourge and a full-scale de-Nazification program began—on both cultural and topographical levels. It was a little like a warm sun coming out from behind the clouds of war to dry a landscape soaked with Nazi emblems. Nazified street signs were torn down, their names changed back from Nazi to Hapsburg heroes. Destroyed by Allied bombing in May 1945 and then rebuilt afterward, even the cobblestone streets of Vienna were purged somehow of memory, seemingly unable to recall the public humiliation of Jews on these same stones after the 1938 Anschluss.

Few tell-tale signs of the war remain, aside from the monumental sculpture garden at the former camp at Mauthausen and scattered memorials erected by Jewish communities across the Austrian countryside, or by the U.S. Army to some of its own paratroopers pitchforked to death by Austrian farmers when they alighted near Graz. Partly, it seems, because of the confusion generated by official memory, and partly because of a reluctance to face their past, Austrians have been more content than most to let the Germans do the memorial dirty work—and they have strenuously resisted attempts to force memory on them from the outside. In the following stories of Austrian memory-sites at Mauthausen, Graz, and at the Albertinaplatz in Vienna, I hope to illustrate how this national ambivalence has found its monumental expression.

Mauthausen: The Pastoral Memorial

Within a matter of years after the war, most public memory of the Holocaust in Austria was concentrated in the monuments and museum at Mauthausen, the infamous quarry and camp nestled in the rolling green hills above a picturesque

Inside the
Mauthausen
concentration
camp memorial,
guard towers
and barbed wire
intact. Photo:
James E. Young.

village of the same name on the Danube. Though it was not technically an extermination camp, Mauthausen had some of the worst elements of all camps: a gas
chamber, crematorium, killing wall, and its notorious rock quarry that ground
prisoners down faster even than starvation and torture. Even prisoners at Auschwitz were said to have blanched at the prospect of transport to Mauthausen. Like
Germany's Dachau, Austria's Mauthausen has since been transformed from a
hellish scar on the landscape to a clean, beautifully maintained state memorial.
Its fine museum is housed in the original barracks and meticulously exhibits the
site's terrible past.

Hungarian tourists pose in front of their national monument, designed by Agamemnon Makrisy and Istvan Janaky in 1964, in Mauthausen's sculpture garden. Photo: James E. Young

By midday, the parking lot at the camp is filled with giant, gleaming tour buses from all parts of Europe. This was an international camp, after all, and it is now a repository for memorial sculpture representing the twenty national homes of prisoners. Overlooking idyllic farmlands, the sculpture garden is comprised of twenty different national memorials, which together suggest the essential plurality of memory, nation by nation. Despite the overarching sense that the prisoners died for their respective homelands, this theme is articulated in a number of disparate sculptural forms—abstract and figurative, heroic and pathetic. A free-standing black marble wall, adorned with photographs and mementos of Italian victims, is dedicated "to the name and memory of those Italians who suffered and died for human dignity." The Yugoslav memorial, by Nandor Glid and B. Storjanovic, consists of two white marble pillars and what seems to be an early study of Glid's Dachau sculpture. It is dedicated in Serbo-Croatian "to the victims of Mauthausen, 1941–1945, from a grateful Yugoslav nation." A heavy figurative sculpture of a grieving woman by a collective team led by the Buchenwald memorial designer, Fritz Cremer, is inscribed, "Your sons who fought and died here carried their belief in a true Germany into the future."

Like Dachau, the memorial at Mauthausen remembers primarily the criminals, POWs, and political prisoners who comprised most of its population. Since Jews

were usually sent straight to the death camps, from which they were occasionally transported to Mauthausen, the Jewish monument here is one of twenty national sculptures: an abstracted, seven-pronged menorah, crooked and branchlike, accompanied by a smaller sculpture of stylized Hebrew letters spelling *zachor* (remember) in the same sharp-pronged style. A stone on the path to the quarry, inscribed in German, reminds visitors that, unlike the criminals, Spanish republicans, or Soviet POWs, the Jews died here died solely for having been Jews.

The most prominent monument in the sculpture garden, to the Soviet POWs, was also one of the first ones built, in 1957. Though it is inscribed in Russian and German to "the victims of fascism, 1941–1945," a red star on the towering granite obelisk suggests precisely which victims are meant. Erected nine years after Nathan Rapoport's Ghetto Monument (the first major heroes' and martyrs' memorial in Europe) was unveiled in Warsaw, the Soviet memorial seems to have drawn almost directly from both the Ghetto Monument's statuary and its bas relief. A muscular young man in chains pulls forward from the obelisk wall of stone, dragging a slackened woman in his arms. In both posture and visage, he recalls Rapoport's Anielewicz, a fighter clenching a dagger, workerlike. This heroic figure is flanked on both sides by bas reliefs of men, women, and children carrying a fallen comrade lying draped on a funerary bier. In profile, the funeral procession

The monument to Jewish victims at Mauthausen, a menorah on the left and stylized Hebrew lettering on the right that spells *zachor* (remember), overlooks rolling farmland above this Austrian village on the Danube. Photo: James E. Young.

The former Soviet Union's monument to the victims of fascism at Mauthausen seems inspired partly by Nathan Rapoport's Warsaw Ghetto Monument. Photo: James E. Young.

at the right could almost have been imprinted directly from the exiles' procession on the reverse of the Ghetto Monument, both set against stone blocks. Ten figures (as opposed to Rapoport's twelve), including a young child posed identically to the child in the Ghetto monument, march forward, their eyes downcast. Precisely in the spot where an adolescent walks in Rapoport's work, a wreath appears in the Soviet version; an old woman in long scarf seems to be absorbed in the shroud covering the body in the Soviet memorial.

As the Ghetto Monument figured its Jewish heroes in proletarian, even classical, proportions, so too does the Soviet memorial here. The source of the woman's figure, however, is not so clear, since the Soviet dead at Mauthausen were almost exclusively soldiers and captured male children, of whom thousands died. Instead of the Torah scroll carried by a rabbi in Rapoport's monument, the mourners here carry a wreath; and instead of appealing to God (as did the rabbi), they march toward the heroic figure at center, the worker-fighter ideal (see the section below on the Warsaw Ghetto Monument).

Smaller memorials dot the path to the stone quarry, which retains much of its daunting terror: the infamous 186-step staircase of death serves as its own best monument. As a motif, these stone steps have been reproduced on a smaller scale in other places. Excruciatingly steep, they descend into what was called the "Wienergraben," or Viennese grave, where Mauthausen inmates were worked to death or crushed beneath the stones they were forced to carry up and down the steps. Both the prisoners thrown by guards and those who pitched themselves over the lip of the quarry into the lake a hundred feet below were known as "parachutists." A small sign in front of the quarry pool at the base of the sheer granite cliff asks visitors not to swim or picnic here.

Graz: *Bezugspunkte 38/88*

In its search for the most appropriate site for a Holocaust monument, the German city of Duren was stymied by the lamentable plethora of candidates. Which was best: the now empty lot where the town's synagogue once stood? The place of the Jews' deportation? The hospital where the mentally ill were killed? The district court that functioned as part of the Nazi administrative apparatus? Because a memorial at any one of these sites might have neglected other, equally significant aspects of Duren's fascist past, artist Ulrike Ruckriem placed ten three-meter-high stone blocks throughout the city at each spot, creating a network of memory, whereby each stone would implicate the other sites in a collectively guilty landscape.

Like mute and inert stone monuments, landscapes and cityscapes remain as amnesiac or as memory-laden as the people who live in their midst. As Ruckriem reinvested the Duren cityscape with memory of deeds committed there, and Norbert Radermacher overlaid an otherwise blank-faced landscape with memory of its past in Berlin's Neukölln neighborhood, Werner Fenz invited sixteen artists to remark the significance of Graz's own points of Nazi reference. The result was *Bezugspunkte 38/88* (Points of Reference), an outdoor public exhibition for the annual Styrian Autumn festival in 1988, using the entire city as installation space. These were not to be monumental works, however, decoratively placed in historical sites. In the curator's words, "'Points of Reference' would like to avoid spectacular, artistic decorations of the city; it considers public space not as a museum without walls but as an intellectual space of action." This "space of action" is three-dimensional and exists in the movement between the artist,

The staircase of
death at
Mauthausen
rises out of the
stone quarry.
Photo:
James E. Young.

The quarry at
Mauthausen
and
"Parachutists'
Leap" above.
Photo: Donald
Woodman.

the physical space, and the memory of time uniting them. Instead of prescribing any particular aesthetic, therefore, Fenz looked for an argument, a challenge to the site, to the people who are part of it. In Fenz's words again, "The work of art results from confronting this environment."[3]

A few of the "points of reference" chosen for installation were already marked with some sign of their Nazi past, while others remained clean of all past traces. But in fact, neither Graz nor the "points of reference" within it were actually chosen by the curator, so much as by the Germans themselves during their occupation: the police station they had turned into Gestapo headquarters; the city hall taken over by their bureaucrats; the public squares where the Nazis had held massive rallies. The exhibition began by calling attention to Graz's general history, challenging its more benign self-remembrances. Each point would now be made to refer to something beyond its immediate self, to its past and what it once stood for.

As originally conceived, the show was to have fourteen reference points, representing the stations of the cross. In this scheme, the suffering of martyrs would have been clearly plotted in the figure of Christ's passion—leading in turn to a redemptory understanding of the victims. The Jews might have been perceived as having died so that Austria might live. In the end, there were so many submissions that two more sites were added. Only the sixteen sites themselves might now be redeemed, not by martyrs but by the memory of martyrs.

Sculptors, painters, and conceptual artists were invited to participate, all melding their respective media to the site's special significance. At a spot in front of the Technical University, Norbert Radermacher turned to his disruption of public spaces, placing four glowing letters—R-E-D-E (speech)—each atop a phone booth, to attract attention to the problem of whether sites could ever communicate anything at all. On several corners, Jochen Gerz mounted photographic plays on words—photos of schmaltzy lederhosen advertisements turned upside down, printed with "Der Grazer heute" (The Grazer today) and "Anschluss ist gestern" (The Anschluss is yesterday), alienating the site and passersby from both present and past. For his part, Peter Baren stopped the town clock at half past five for twenty-five days by hanging a dummy human form from the big hand. Time is stopped: is it an omen? A desire to stop time, even to turn back the clock? Without the sense of advancing time constantly intruding between ourselves and past events, our return to the sites of history suggests a return to events themselves.

All the installations succeeded in provoking both site and public to memory, but none more so than Hans Haacke's resurrection of a Nazi monument in the city center. Not long after Hitler had appreciatively honored Graz as the "city of the

The original
Nazi
monument in
Graz, Austria,
proclaiming,
"And you were
victorious after
all," 25 July
1938. Photo:
Courtesy of
Landesmuseum
Joanneum,
Graz.

Column of the
Virgin Mary,
which was
covered first by
the Nazi
monument in
1938 and then
again by artist
Hans Haacke in
his memorial
replication of
the Nazi
monument in
1988. Photo:
Courtesy of
Hans Haacke.

people's insurrection," the Germans covered over one of the town's oldest Catholic monuments—a column to the Virgin Mary—with red cloth, emblazoned with the swastika. In a reference to the annexation of Austria, which followed a failed Austrian Nazi putsch four years earlier, the Germans congratulated themselves with the inscription: "Und Ihr habt doch gesiegt" (And you were victorious after all). A great celebration was held at the square, filled with fifteen thousand parading Nazis. As he had done so effectively with his prior subversions of corporate emblems, Haacke again draped the Mariensaule in Nazi colors, swastikas and all, turning the image of Nazism against itself. By adding a further inscription in Gothic script to "the vanquished of Styria," the artist seems to have created a Nazi memorial honoring its own victims: "300 gypsies killed, 2,500 Jews killed, 8,000 political prisoners killed or died in detention, 9,000 civilians killed in the war, 12,000 missing, 27,900 soldiers killed."

While working on the project, Haacke carefully gauged the townspeople's reactions, fully aware that their early responses were also part of the work's performance. "As soon as the obelisk was covered with the red drapery carrying the inscriptions and the Nazi eagle and it became clear why the statue of the Virgin had been encased, there was a commotion at the site," Haacke has written.

> Throngs of people gathered and engaged in heated debate over whether, after fifty years, one should stir up the Nazi past again. Some of the opposition was clearly motivated by anti-Semitic sentiments. While most people of retirement age were incensed, local television also showed several passionate supporters of the idea that they must confront and come to terms with their ugly past. Among them was an old woman commenting, while the camera was rolling, "I wonder why these people are so upset. They must feel guilty." The reaction of those who, due to their age, could not have been implicated in the Nazi period, was very mixed, ranging from hostility, indifference, and incomprehension to enthusiastic approval of the Styrian Autumn project."[4]

For weeks, people continued to mill about the monument, arguments flared, supporters held vigils, dissidents threatened the work. A guard was even posted—but to no avail. Just a week before the end of the exhibition, arsonists fire bombed the cloth-covered obelisk, destroying most of the red fabric and severely damaging the statue of the Virgin inside. As Haacke had sought to turn the Nazis' emblem against itself, another kind of countermonument, his "point of reference," was itself now turned inside-out. An outpouring of sympathy followed, and headlines dubbed the *Mahnmal* (memorial) a *Schandmal*—a pun for "monument of shame." Because these events too had become part of the installation,

Hans Haacke's "point of reference" after it was firebombed by neo-Nazis, 2 November 1988. Photo: Angelika Gradwohl. Courtesy of Hans Haacke.

Haacke incorporated them into the text of the memorial by adding the inscription: "On the night of 9 November 1938, all synagogues in Austria were looted, destroyed, and set on fire. And during the night of 2 November 1988, this memorial was destroyed by a fire bomb." For the artist, events and their memory had come full circle: what began with the destruction of synagogues (that is, sites of memory) was followed by the destruction of the "people of memory" and resumed with the destruction of sites commemorating both.

Though these public installations were not intended as memorials, when artworks of any kind are placed at such "points of reference," they inevitably refer to something beyond themselves. By creating an exchange among themselves, their sites, and the history of their sites, such works make palpable memory itself, now formalized in their presence. Art placed at these sites suddenly becomes more than a public, decorative art, a distraction from the significance of place. At the moment reference is made to specific events—even if it remains implied—such art becomes memorial art: it reminds the site of its own past, even as it reminds people in these sites that time moves on, that only places remain, oblivious to time and its significance. "Only when art confronts the public space as such can it become effective within it," Fenz has written.[5] This might be construed two ways: art confronting a space with its own invisible past, or an artwork that creates a tension between itself and the space it inhabits. The successful monument might be regarded as one that accomplishes both.

The Street-washing Jew at Albertinaplatz

Neither Mauthausen, with its serene sculpture garden, nor the cutting-edge "reference points" installed in Graz could have catalyzed Austrian memory of its war-past as provocatively as Alfred Hrdlicka's *Monument against War and Fascism*, set in central Vienna's Albertinaplatz. The fiery controversy surrounding what has come to be known as Hrdlicka's "street-washing Jew monument" serves as an object lesson in how memorials provide a public stage for the working through of a community's deepest memorial anxieties and political preoccupations. A memorial like this also suggests the sheer futility in divorcing a monument's supposed "artistic worth" from its political and historical significance, a forced separation that ultimately denies such an installation its essential function as a focus of public discourse.

Regarded as one of Austria's greatest living artists, Hrdlicka revels in both his notoriety as troublemaker and his fame as an artist, often using one to inflame the other. Some Austrians remember him for having stolen through the night streets of Vienna in 1938 with his father and uncle, both Communists, to hand out anti-Nazi pamphlets. Others regard him as an unreconstructed Stalinist, astonishingly adept at alienating just about every political and artistic faction. For example, Hrdlicka once called Kassel's Dokumenta (a major contemporary art fair) the "Nazi Congress of Fine Arts." He dismissed German dealers as the "Blockwarte of modern art," referring to the prisoners who served as concentration camp barracks wardens, and the artwork itself as "museum refuse."[6] At the same time, as a sculptor of public monuments, he is well known for his monument to Friedrich Engels in Wupperthal, his "crucifixion group" monument in Salzburg to the Austrian police who resisted the Nazis, his portrait bust of Karl Renner, the first president of Austria's second republic, and his unfinished "countermonument" in Hamburg. But it is for the "street-washing Jew" of the Albertinaplatz that Hrdlicka's own memory will ultimately be reviled or kept sacred—or both.

Planning for an antifascist monument in Vienna began in 1972, at least partly at the urging of Hrdlicka, who had proposed a monument to Viennese Auschwitz victims. Ironically, however, after seeing the artist's preliminary sketch of the monument, local survivors objected to what they felt was an overly literal conception, and asked for something more symbolic. In 1978, city authorities sanctioned a limited competition for such a monument to be set in front of St. Stephen's Cathedral. Hrdlicka's proposal consisted of two parts: a street-washing Jew and a figurative relief depicting the stoning of St. Stephen, thereby linking the city's martyred patron saint with its martyred Jews. Two planned additions would also remember, he hoped, the suppression of workers by the Fascist regime and the suffering of civilians in a war imposed on the world by Hitler, who, after all, was an Austrian.

Community response was swift and skeptical. The local newspaper, *Die Presse*, warned against scandalizing the local population with such a pairing, and the mayor suggested installing Hrdlicka's piece at Morzinplatz, former site of the Gestapo headquarters in Vienna. The staunchly right-wing Austrian People's party (OVP) concurred. Rather than tainting the very heart of their beloved city with unwanted memory, they said, why not locate the monument at the source of Nazi atrocities?

But Hrdlicka had already set his heart on yet another site: the triangular patch of lawn at the Albertinaplatz, next to the State Opera and the Sacher Cafe, in front of the two-hundred-year-old Albertina Museum, in the very center of Vienna. When warned that this site was not available for such an installation, Hrdlicka threatened to withdraw his proposal altogether and sniffed, "I don't make mobile monuments."[7] For the artist had found support for his choice of Albertinaplatz in then Culture Minister Helmut Zilk, who would later, as mayor, permit him to use the plaza. Both Hrdlicka and Zilk saw that the site was ideal, not only in its geographic centrality but in the several layers of historical memory repressed and buried there. They recalled that the Albertinaplatz, though innocuous-looking, had long been haunted by grim memories for historically minded Viennese.

For the artist-provocateur, only an Albertinaplatz monument would recall to citizens that the very heart of Vienna had already been poisoned—both by historical events and by what he regarded as the generic tendency among the Viennese to bury their past without a trace. Hrdlicka remembered that on the night of 12 March 1945, nearly two hundred Viennese huddled in a bomb shelter below the Philipshof, a royal house at the Albertinaplatz, had been buried alive when the building collapsed during one of the last American bombing raids of the war. Neighbors are still haunted by the memory of the knocks and cries of victims trapped in the cavernous cellar, signaling for help. For them, Hrdlicka's monument would function as a gravestone for those entombed below.

The city's decision not to disinter the bombing victims for a proper burial scandalized Viennese in 1945, and again when the site was covered over with sod and shrubs. Citizens were scandalized yet again when the city considered turning the subterranean caverns into an underground parking lot. Though attention was focused on the bombing and the authorities' subsequent refusal to disinter the victims, Hrdlicka seems to have grasped that the civic trauma may have stemmed from the denial of a still older memory associated with the Albertinaplatz, which had bordered a Jewish cemetery in medieval times. Some Viennese believe that the authorities feared unearthing not just the remains of the bombing raid victims but also the charred bones of Jews who had been burned at the stake in a pogrom at that site on the very same day, 12 March, in 1421.

After five years of haggling, Vienna's city council, on 30 September 1983, voted unanimously to proceed with Hrdlicka's memorial, now redesigned. All unanimity vanished, however, with Hrdlicka's exuberant part in the anti-Waldheim campaign, three years later, culminating in the notorious "wooden-horse incident" during Waldheim's presidential inauguration. In response to conservatives who contended that Waldheim's service in an SS cavalry unit didn't make him a Nazi, Austrian chancellor Fred Sinowatz remarked sarcastically, "Waldheim wasn't a Nazi, only his horse was." With this witticism ringing in their ears, a group of some four hundred artists, writers, and intellectuals who had come together under the name "New Austria" suddenly began to show up at Waldheim rallies with great papier-mâché horses. The crowning prank came when Hrdlicka gleefully fashioned a giant wooden horse for Waldheim's inauguration in 1987, resplendent in the colors and cap of a Nazi Storm Trooper. On the day of the inauguration, the horse was wheeled into Stephensplatz, saddled with loudspeakers blaring protests recorded by some of Austria's most prominent writers. Instead of Greek soldiers, the horse disgorged Hrdlicka himself, who promptly delivered a speech to the nation on Waldheim and his Nazi past.

The crowd at Stephensplatz roared with delight, but the conservative People's party never forgave Hrdlicka and moved immediately to have him barred from all public ceremonies. From then on, Waldheim's past would be linked to Hrdlicka's monument, which the President reportedly could see directly from his apartment in the Hofburg. Overnight, the antifascist monument had become a partisan issue. The far right demanded that Waldheim cancel Hrdlicka's recent nomination to a professorship at the Art Academy. The conservative leader of the city-center district recommended that André Heller, a popular decorative artist, be appointed to design a new monument. Science Minister Hans Tuppy proposed

a moratorium on any new construction in the downtown area in order to stop the monument's installation. The tabloid newspaper *Kronen Zeitung* declared that the Stalinist Hrdlicka was the last person to preach antifascism to the Austrians.[8]

Libel followed calumny for the next year until the Social Democratic party, led by Mayor Zilk, pushed through construction of Hrdlicka's monument at the Albertinaplatz, though polls showed that only 31 percent of the population was in favor of it. On the night of 24 November 1988, a thousand people gathered in the freezing rain to unveil the city's only "monument against war and fascism." In addition to the Chancellor of the Republic, Franz Vranitzky, and Mayor Zilk, hundreds of representatives from socialist and resistance groups turned out, as well as Catholic, Protestant, and Jewish clergy who led prayers for the dead.

Conspicuous by their absence were Foreign Minister Alois Mock and other leaders of the People's party. Police, who had stood guard around the site all day to discourage threatened demonstrations by neo-Nazis, scuffled only with young leftist protesters who tried to unfurl a banner declaring that "the Führer left, but his disciples stayed." Long after the last politician had gone home, small groups of citizens lingered, arguing over the monument, its meaning, and the time it

Alfred Hrdlicka's *Monument against War and Fascism* at the Albertinaplatz in Vienna. Photo: James E. Young.

commemorated. The next day, teachers brought their classes by the dozens, using the sculptures as a text for that day's lessons. Many wondered how long the police would need to guard the site against the paint and chisels of vandals.

Paved with granite blocks from the quarry at Mauthausen, the triangular Albertinaplatz is bordered on one side by a large neobaroque apartment building, and on the other two sides by busy streets lined with cafes and horse-drawn transoms awaiting their tourist charges. Pedestrians pass through it on their way to the nearby shopping district. An equestrian sculpture of Archduke Albrecht stands atop a neobaroque platform on the Albertina Museum, which has overlooked the square since 1899. Absent now is the Mozart monument erected in 1906 and moved to the Burggarten during World War II. Among the local landmarks are the Sacher Cafe and two other well-known coffeehouses, the Braunerhof, where local literati gather, and the Hawelka, haunt of German tourists and often of Hrdlicka himself.

The five-piece monument begins, according to the artist, with the "gate of violence," an opening between two square columns of granite quarried at Mauthausen. The columns are composed of concentration camp victims on one side and "soldier-dead" on the other. Though the soldiers are remembered, their legacy remains corrupted in the artist's eye. Hrdlicka dedicates their side of the gate to what he calls the "Hinterlands Front," where "cowards mass-murdered women and children behind the front lines of battle" in order not to be sent to real fighting on the front. Mass murder cannot be dismissed as a war crime, Hrdlicka concludes. Naked, half-formed skeletal figures, some huddled, others with hands bound behind, claw their way out of a slab of marble perched atop one of the two columns; a sculpted hypodermic needle protrudes, columnlike, on one side, referring to the deadly phenol injections administered by Nazi doctors in the camps. The tortured forms seem to mock the classical polish of the marble. While the human figures appear to represent concentration camp inmates, Viennese have also described them as the buried victims of the bombing raid. In this view, the antiwar monument collapses both sets of victims into war-victims.

Walking through the gate, we come face to face with the street-washing Jew, prostrate on hands and knees. From a distance, the bronze sculpture is not easily identifiable as a human form: it sits rather Sphynx-like, its hands and brushes set upon the stones like lion's paws. Even on a closer look, the figure is so roughly cut that only the bearded head, yarmulke on top, and the hands and brush are clearly defined. Occasionally, elderly shoppers carrying bags stop to rest in the Albertinaplatz, taking a seat on the back of the Jew on their way home.

After the Anschluss, local Jews were marched through the streets of Vienna to scrub anti-Nazi scrawlings from the cobblestones and buildings. Forced to their

The "street-washing Jew" in Hrdlicka's monument on the Albertinaplatz, Vienna. Photo: James E. Young.

Hrdlicka's "street-washing Jew" also served as a park bench for weary shoppers. Later, a barbed-wire crown of thorns was added to discourage this practice. Photo: James E. Young.

knees, they scoured the stones with their bare hands, shirts, coats, and even toothbrushes. By prompting contemporary Viennese who stand around the figure to recall the photographs of other citizens laughing at the plight of their Jewish neighbors, Hrdlicka would accuse both generations of being bystanders.

When asked to whom he would dedicate the "street-washing Jew," Hrdlicka replied, "To the Viennese soul"—a cynical reference to Viennese indifference. "The Viennese always behaved as if they were ignorant of what was happening to the Jews, but it was the Viennese after all who forced the Jews to wash the street with toothbrushes. . . . A mass murder of such great proportions necessarily demands a great mass of murderers. To those masses of murderers I dedicate the street-washing Jew. It doesn't matter whether they ordered the mass murder from their desks or turned the gas on themselves, or whether they only looked away."[9] In the same interview, Hrdlicka also suggested that because his monument was public, it could not be dedicated to any specific group. "It affects all those who look at it or experience it. I intended to provoke all kinds of thoughts with this memorial—that's why it has five parts."

Depending on one's vantage point, the crawling Jew could be praying Moslem-fashion or kneeling at the foot of a stone sculpture. One of Hrdlicka's Jewish friends objected to depicting a Jew on hands and knees, as if kneeling in obeisance to the granite figures before him. The artist answered that just as Christ has been remembered in the icon of his greatest humiliation, the Jews of Vienna might also be recalled in the image of their humiliation at the hands of local Viennese. "If the Jews do not like my idea of taking humiliation as a symbol [of their suffering], I am sorry for them," Hrdlicka said. "Humiliation has been for Christians a symbol of resistance, something we should learn from the Christians. One cannot always refer to Auschwitz, for it started with the washing of the streets."[10] In a city studded with Christian crosses on buildings, in parks, and in squares, Hrdlicka has created another icon: this time of the Jews' humiliation at the feet of the laughing Viennese. Ironically, the sculpture's Christian trappings were reinforced when the city placed a string of barbed wire in a circle on the Jew's back—a crown of thorns—to keep passersby from sitting on it.

According to Hrdlicka, the fourth piece, "Orpheus Entering Hades," is meant to remind viewers of the last days of those buried alive in the bombing of the Philipshof.[11] In this reference, too, the Viennese stand ironically accused: for as Orpheus descended into Hades in search of his beloved Eurydice, the Viennese did not descend into the cellar of Philipshof to rescue their trapped countrymen. In a more playful vein, Hrdlicka also suggests that Orpheus, the music lover, represents a greeting to the State Opera, the Albertina Museum, and the nearby theater. In other conversations, he has suggested that the "descent of Orpheus" was dedicated specifically to all the Nazis' victims in Austria.

The final section of Hrdlicka's installation is a thirty-foot-high stone fragment on which are inscribed parts of Austria's declaration of independence, dated 27 March 1945, only two weeks after the bombing. The text runs to the ragged edges of the stone, itself chastened by the dark-bronze street-washing Jew nearby. The stone could pass as either tombstone or broken obelisk, a shard or a disfigured fragment of the war, suggesting a state born of the war's detritus.

In fact, the total effect of the walk-in space reminds one of a ruin: fragmentary columns, pieces of statue, an open area created by the destruction of edifices that formerly stood nearby. The rough texture of stone not only captures the ever-incomplete sense of the sculpture, but, as John Czaplicka has noted, it also recalls the explicit violence of the artistic shaping of memory: the dynamiting of granite in the quarry, the hacking, chopping, and drilling, the hammer and chisel taken to its surfaces.[12] Hrdlicka's monument against war and fascism commemorates not only the history of the site and the trauma endured by a society calling these memories to public consciousness after so many years of denial, but also the artist's and public's preoccupations, both aesthetic and political.

Responses to the monument on its unveiling were as varied as the visitors themselves. Some asked whether this should be one of the primary images of Vienna that foreign tourists take home with them. *Die Presse* joined the *Jerusalem Post* in asking why the antifascist memorial made no mention at all of the Nazis. Others continued to focus on what they regarded as the "actual scandal" of an antifascist monument—its erection over the burial site of Viennese killed by American bombers.[13] Still others asked whether this memorial cynically equated the victimization of Jews and bombing victims.

Some wondered why it had taken forty-three years to build any kind of monument at all, and whether it was a gesture to memory or to a guilty conscience. Was it a nobly inspired mourning place, or only a gloss for foreign consumption? Is the aim of art merely to incite political consciousness? And since when does a republic commission one artist to remember such a complex past in the name of an entire nation? Horst Christoph even speculated that one day the military might incorporate this site into the national landscape and begin swearing its officers in here.[14]

Another writer, Robert Menasse, wanted to know why the last paragraph of the Austrian Declaration of Independence was omitted from the stone's inscription and why the face of the "street-washing Jew" bore such a striking resemblance to Karl Marx. The writer George Eisler responded that Marx had an entirely different hair-do. The figure was the humiliated but still dignified old rabbi of Vienna, Taglich, who is reported to have replied to the jeering mobs who forced him to scrub the street that he was merely "washing God's earth."[15] In every case, the visitors' preoccupations were given full vent in this walk-in space—and argued thoroughly afterward at the neighborhood coffee houses.

In still other ways, Hrdlicka's drawing on the well-known images of Jews washing the streets of Vienna also gestures both to the photo-painting of his contemporaries (such as Gerhard Richter) and to recent monuments modeled on well-known photographs (such as the Iwo Jima Memorial in Arlington National Cemetery in Virginia, designed by the Viennese artist Felix de Weldon and based on the Pulitzer Prize–winning photo of Marines re-enacting the planting of the flag on Iwo Jima during World War II). Hrdlicka seems to have combined photographs of Jews scrubbing the streets with the people's memory of these images. Perhaps, as Christoph suggested, Hrdlicka's real achievement was merely the unveiling of these sore feelings, repressed memories, anger, and controversy. Painfully and self-consciously wrought, his monument belongs wholly to those who want to remember without drawing too much attention to their memory-art. Instead of relieving past trauma, memory becomes its own trauma, perpetually deferred.

Part II Poland:

The Ruins of Memory

The day I was leaving Warsaw, while I was waiting for a taxi, suitcase in hand, a drunk was
standing twenty paces from me in front of a
plaque dedicated to the victims of Nazism. Stag-
gering, he stared at it intently, stubbornly, and
with the unction of a drunkard on the stage, he
waved his hat through the air to make the sign
of the cross. Then he fell across the sidewalk in
the posture of a man who has been shot. . . .
You see, I live in an odd country . . . where
drunken tourists are taken in buses to see the
sites of former exterminations. An odd country,
which never forgets its past, but which more
often than not does not understand it.
—Kazimierz Brandys

Introduction

Of Jewish life and death in Poland, only the fragments remain. Forty-five years after the Holocaust, a new generation has come to know a
millennium of Jewish civilization in Poland by
its absence and the rubble of its destruction:
dilapidated synagogues, uprooted and plowed-
under cemeteries, warehouses piled high with

religious artifacts, concentration camp ruins.
Whether suggested in the glimpse of a door-
jamb's missing *mezuzah* or a synagogue turned
into a granary, or in the growing number of
tombstone-fragment monuments in otherwise
abandoned Jewish cemeteries, absence and brokenness emerge as twin memorial motifs indigenous to a landscape of shattered *matzevoth*.

Like the Holocaust memorials of other lands,
those in Poland reflect both the past experiences and current lives of their communities, as
well as the state's memory of itself. In assuming
the idealized forms and meanings assigned to
this era by the state, these memorials tend to
concretize particular historical interpretations;
in time, such memory grows as natural to the
eye as the landscape in which it stands. But in
a land until recently shared by Poles and Jews,
such memorials also remain bitterly contested.
Before turning to the terribly complex inter-
penetration of Jewish and Polish memory of the
Holocaust, therefore, we might first consider a
particularly emblematic moment for the Poles.

Within days of the German invasion and occupation of Poland in September 1939, whole
Polish towns and communities were obliterated. Polish professionals and intelligentsia
were rounded up, imprisoned, and often executed—solely as Poles. The treatment of Poles
was so brutal at the outset of the war that many
of the especially desperate members of the intelligentsia actually donned the Jewish star as

a means of protection from the Nazis.[1] At this point, even the "special handling" of the Jews seemed preferable to summary deportation and execution. Later, when the Jews were singled out, non-Jewish Poles grasped the deportation and murder of Jews in light of their own recent suffering. In Polish eyes during and immediately after the war, before the full measure of the Jews' loss became clear, both groups seemed persecuted equally.

The significant place of national martyrdom in the histories and identities of both Poles and Jews further complicates the delicate memorial equation in Poland. For, ironically, Poland's identity as a nation perpetually under siege may actually compete with the Jews' traditional sense of themselves as the primary victims of history. As self-perceived "Christ among the nations," Poland has exalted its martyrdom to an extent that rivals the place of catastrophe in Jewish memory.[2] As Iwona Irwin-Zarecka makes clear, Polish romanticism extolled the memory of national martyrs so effectively as to turn it into a central pillar around which national identity would be built and defined. Not so unlike the Jews, Poland had become a nation whose destructions would occupy as central a role in national memory and identity as its relatively few triumphs.

Between 1939 and 1945, some 3.2 million of Poland's 3.5 million Jews were killed by the Nazis and their collaborators. With the mass exit of Poland's surviving Jewish remnant after the Kielce and other pogroms in 1946, Jewish memory also departed: memory of a thousand-year Jewish past, of good and bad relations with their Polish neighbors, of the Holocaust, and finally of Poland's own post-Holocaust pogroms. When Jewish Holocaust survivors next remembered, it was often among themselves in their new communities abroad—and among their new compatriots. It was not among the Poles, who were left alone with their own, now uncontested memory of events. This memory was not to be challenged again until the survivors returned to Poland years later as tourists with their children in tow. As a result, all remaining memory of this past was left in Polish hands and thus reflected a characteristically Polish grasp of events, Polish ambivalence, and eventually even a Polish need for a Jewish past.

"Memory is blind to all but the groups it binds," writes Pierre Nora. "History, on the other hand, belongs to everyone and to no one, whence its claim to universal authority."[3] That is, history is what happened; memory is the recollection that binds what happened to ourselves in the present. After Nora, we recognize that memorial spaces inevitably assume lives of their own, dependent on the attributes of those who visit or live in their midst. If the surrounding population is Polish and Christian, then so will be much of the memory here, whether we like it or not. Polish Catholics will remember as Polish Catholics, even when they remember Jewish victims. As Jews recall events in the figures of their tradition, so will Poles remember in the forms of their faith. The problem is not that Poles deliberately displace Jewish memory of the Holocaust with their own, but that in a country bereft of Jews, the memorials can do little but cultivate Polish memory. In this light, we realize that Auschwitz is but one of dozens of memorial sites dedicated to the martyrdom of "the Polish and other nations." It is part of a national landscape of suffering, one coordinate among others by which both Jews and Poles continue to grasp present lives in light of a remembered past.

In the chapters that follow, "Holocaust memory" in Poland will be examined along several of its monumental axes: the memorialized ruins in the former sites of death camps; the Jewish-made, Polish-used Warsaw Ghetto Monument in Warsaw; and the burgeoning number of broken tombstone monuments across Poland's countryside, often built by Poles for Jewish mourners. In fact, there is a renaissance of interest in Jewish life and death in Poland, a re-integration of Poland's lost Jews into the Polish national heritage. Whether motivated by a genuine sense of bereavement, or by mere political and economic expediency, memory of a Jewish past in Poland remains as tangled and shifting as relations between Jews and Poles have always been.

Chapter 5   The Rhetoric of Ruins:

The Memorial Camps

at Majdanek

and Auschwitz

When the killing stopped, only the sites remained, blood-soaked but otherwise mute. While in operation, the death camps and the destruction of people wrought in them were one and the same: sites and events were bound to each other in their contemporaneity. But with the passage of time, sites and events were gradually estranged. While the sites of killing remained ever-present, all too real in their physical setting, time subtly interposed itself between them and their past. Events that occurred in another time seemed increasingly to belong to another world altogether. Only a deliberate act of memory could reconnect them, reinfuse the sites with a sense of their historical past.

Nevertheless, the magic of ruins persists, a near mystical fascination with sites seemingly charged with the aura of past events, as if the molecules of the sites still vibrated with the memory of their history. Some people claim to intuit such a charge in places of "history," but usually this aura is apparent only to those who already know something of the site's past, or who suspect a site is somehow historical. As houses come to be "haunted" by the ghosts (memory, really) of their former occupants, the sites of destruction are haunted by the phantoms of past events, no longer visible, but only remembered.

By themselves, these crumbling sites of destruction lack what Nora has called "the will to remember." That is, without a people's intention to remember, the ruins remain little more than inert pieces of the landscape, unsuffused with the meanings and significance created in our visits to them. Without the will to remember, Nora suggests, the place of memory, "created in the play of memory and history . . . becomes indistinguishable from the place of history."[1] In concert with his suggestion, cited earlier, that such places of memory exist "only because of their capacity for metamorphosis," Nora's observations will cut two ways for our understanding of the "memorial camps" in Poland, such as Majdanek and Auschwitz.

On the one hand, we're reminded that it was the state's initial move to preserve these ruins—its will to remember—that turned sites of historical destruction into "places of memory." On the other hand, we find that these sites of memory begin to assume lives of their own, often as resistant to official memory as they are emblematic of it. In some cases, memorials created in the image of a state's ideals actually turn around to recast national ideals in the memorial's image. Later generations visit memorials under new circumstances and invest them with new meanings. The result is an evolution in the memorial's significance, generated in the new times and company in which it finds itself.

The very first Holocaust memorials anywhere were the places of destruction themselves. Liberated by the Red Army in July 1944, the intact remains of the concentration camp at Majdanek, just outside Lublin, were turned into the first memorial and museum of its kind. Early the next year, the Polish Committee of National Liberation conferred similar status on the ruins of Stutthof, the earliest camp in Poland, and on the gargantuan complex at Auschwitz-Birkenau, commonly regarded as the "epicenter" of the Holocaust. All these camps had been evacuated and abandoned, but not destroyed, by the Germans in their hasty retreat. When we recall that the Germans had rounded up 250 local Jews to build the camp at Auschwitz, we also realize that the memorial there was, in effect, built by the victims it would later commemorate.

One's first visit to the memorials at Majdanek and Auschwitz can come as a shock: not because of the bloody horror these places convey, but because of their unexpected, even unseemly beauty. Saplings planted along the perimeters of the camps, intended to screen the Germans' crimes from view, now sway and toss in the wind. Local farmers, shouldering scythes, lead their families through waist-deep fields to cut and gather grass into great sheaves. Beyond their pastoral facade, however, the memorials at Majdanek and Auschwitz are devastating in their impact: for they compel the visitor to accept the horrible fact that what they show is real. In both cases, the camps seem to have been preserved almost exactly as the Russians found them a half-century ago. Guard towers, barbed wire, barracks, and crematoria—mythologized elsewhere—here stand palpably intact. In contrast to memorials located away from the sites of destruction, the remnants here tend to collapse the distinction between themselves and what they evoke. In the rhetoric of their ruins, these memorial sites seem not merely to gesture

toward past events but to suggest themselves as fragments of events, inviting us to mistake the debris of history for history itself.

Majdanek

In the words of the guidebook of the State Museum at Majdanek, the aim of the memorial is threefold: to preserve the buildings as material evidence of the crimes committed here; to analyze the facts of these crimes; and to present analyzed facts to the public.[2] As becomes clear, however, the ruins here are material evidence not only of these crimes but also of a state's reasons for remembering them. Indeed, there is little reason for preserving the ruins outside of the meanings preservation imputes to them. At Majdanek, such objects thus "tell" the story of the camp's Soviet liberators, configured in a reflexively Marxist interpretation of the war and its victims. As a result, the Jewish victims of Majdanek are assimilated twice over: once to the memory of Polish national suffering, and again to a stridently economic critique of the camp blind to the ethnic identity of its victims. At Majdanek, where Jews accounted for more than four-fifths of the 350,000 murdered victims, the memorial recalls Jews primarily as part of other persecuted groups, including Poles, Communists, and Soviet POWs.

The barracks here have been converted to house individual exhibitions explicating the text of the preserved ruins. What the ruins remember here depends on

Groundskeeper at the concentration camp memorial at Majdanek, Poland. Photo: Donald Woodman.

accompanying inscriptions. As we enter the first barrack, devoted to an exhibition entitled "Hitlerism in the Years 1933–1942," we stop to read a large black wall panel with white print: "With the help of German industrialists, on January 30, 1933, Adolf Hitler became chancellor of the German Reich. The coming into power of the Fascists marked the beginning of a period of brutal and ruthless dictatorship. The arson of the Reichstag served as an excuse for granting the government extraordinary plenipotentiaries and for endowing Hitler with unlimited power. Mass persecution of Communists, Socialists, and Jews followed . . . ."[3] As handmaiden to German industrialists, Hitler merely did the dirty work of big business, and fascism was only a form of monopoly capitalism run amok. By extension, the camp itself is represented as a kind of factory, fueled by the blood of its worker-inmates. The barracks next door now function as exhibition storerooms, housing bins piled high with the victims' shoes, hats, and clothes—material evidence of the economic theft and plundering of victims by German Nazi industrialists, according to explanatory notes inside.

Subsumed once in an economic critique of the camp, the murder of Jews is submerged yet again in the national identities of victims in the next converted barracks housing an exhibition on the inmates. "Poles constituted the most numerous group and almost all of them were political prisoners," the guidebook tells us. "Jews and citizens of various states considered to be of Jewish descent constituted the next largest group. They were put into the camp for racial reasons. A large proportion of the camp population was represented by citizens of the Soviet Union, many of whom were war prisoners" (p. 13). This breakdown is literally correct: since Jews were most often killed within days of their arrival, they accounted for a relatively small percentage of living prisoners. But this also ignores the number of Polish Jews interned on both political and racial grounds, who are counted here as Poles only. In fact, the statistics tend to encourage this numerical exchange between Jews and Poles: of the nearly six million Jews who died in the Holocaust, three million were from Poland; of the six million Polish nationals who died in World War II, three million were Jews and three million non-Jews. The total number of Poles (including Jews) who died is the same as the total number of Jews who died in the Holocaust: six million. When we consider further that one out of every two Poles was either killed, wounded, or enslaved during the war, even the proportions of "national suffering" of these two groups grows similar.

All of which is reflected in the exhibition on mass killing at Majdanek, which begins with several panels devoted to the Jews' fate here and at other camps, describing the Jews as the first of many victims in the Nazis' genocidal plans. At the back of the hall, empty canisters of Zyklon-B gas are stacked grocery-style to the ceiling, surrounded by wall-sized enlargements of the German lists of murdered prisoners. Though the prisoners on these rolls are almost all designated by the Germans as Polish Jews, each exhibit wall panel is punctuated by a red triangle, denoting political—not racial—persecution. Having introduced the extermination process at Majdanek with its first victims, the Jews, the installation ends with a panel illustrating the potential extermination of the Poles. The Poles' averted genocide is thus framed by the actual massacre of Jews; as such, it is grasped as an extension of the Jewish Holocaust, even its last stage.

Given the Poles' own experiences during the war and their general self-recollection as the Germans' first national victims, the memorial exchange between Polish and Jewish figures becomes less surprising. In fact, the Poles may not be neglecting Jewish memory here at all, but only recalling the Jews' experiences through the images of their own remembered past. That the death camps were located on Polish soil suggests to the Poles not their national complicity, but their ultimate violation: it was one thing to be ravaged outside one's land, another to be occupied and enslaved at home. In this view, the killing centers in Poland were to have begun with the Jews and ended with the Poles. The mass murder of Jews becomes significant in Polish memory primarily as a memorial figure for the Poles' own devastation.

Not only do the relics of destruction comprise the core of museum exhibitions at the memorial camps, but these remnants are also integrated into the plastic monuments erected here—both as material elements and as stylistic motif. Monuments at Stutthof, Majdanek, and Auschwitz are cast in the images of seemingly natural formations, unsculpted relics of the landscape. To this end, the sculptor Wiktor Tolkin retained the barbed wire fence at Stutthof, but cut holes in it to signify both the liberation of the camp and its former reality as prison. At Majdanek, Tolkin proposed a monument in two parts: one a mausoleum holding the ashes of the victims, the other a gigantic, abstract form of almost prehistoric proportions.

Dedicated on 1 September 1969, the thirtieth anniversary of Germany's invasion of Poland, Tolkin's Majdanek memorial was selected from 130 submissions in a competition lasting from 1967 to 1968. In his design, the great weight of memory at Majdanek stands on a proportionally undersized base, which creates a sense of top-heaviness, even danger, for those standing beneath it. The sculptor has intended this effect, he says, not only as a symbolic reference to past danger, but also as a literal gesture to the hazards in memory itself, which can jeopardize our current sense of well-being. In fact, Polish officials were so concerned with the safety of rememberers that they proposed a railing along the outline of the sculpture's overhanging rock to keep people from standing beneath it. Pleased with this anxious response, Tolkin assured authorities that the memorial only looked dangerous: no fence was necessary.[4]

From the main road leading out of Lublin, we approach this monument through a "gate of hell" before descending into a symbolic valley of death. Sharp stones protrude on both sides as we climb out of the valley to the base of the monument. Standing beneath this stone, we gaze down upon an arrow-straight road, one mile long, open fields on the left, barracks on the right. In the distance, at the very end of the road, we can see a great dome covering the mausoleum of ashes and to its right a squat building with tall chimney: the crematorium and gas chamber complex. It takes nearly twenty minutes to walk this path, an enforced time of meditation, when our eyes remain fixed on the mausoleum and chimney looming ever larger into view.

Immediately after the camp's liberation, townspeople from Lublin gathered several tons of ash into a great pile near the crematorium, where it sat until Tolkin's monument was built to contain it. We go up a few steps to the edge of the mausoleum and look into a huge marble bowl, which is open, protected only by the dome top. The dome is supported by three pillars, allowing visitors to gaze upon this black mound of bone-flecked ash. In its allusion to the traditional Slavonic custom of burying the remains of cremated dead in urns, this monument enacts

Wiktor Tolkin's
monument at
Majdanek,
dedicated in
1969, conveys a
sense of
impending
danger. Photo:
James E. Young.

View through
the base of
Tolkin's
monument at
Majdanek
shows the gas
chamber and
crematorium
complex still
standing.
Photo:
James E. Young.

an essentially Polish burial of the victims. The inscription in Polish reads: "Let our fate be your warning." Anchored in the actual site, such memorials seem to draw their rhetorical authority from the very remnants of destruction.[5]

The Veneration of Ruins

Nor is the sanctification of ruins entirely foreign to Jewish tradition. At the Western Wall in Jerusalem, for example, we find that the artifacts of destruction have acquired a holiness unequaled in Jewish tradition. As the most sacred icon and memorial space in Judaism, the remnant Western Wall of the Second Temple recalls the destruction of the Temple through its own fragmentary link to the historical event. Though many would argue that the Western Wall is holy because of its link to the Temple and not because of its reference to the Temple's destruction, it is the Temple's destruction and subsequent dispersion that Jews have traditionally bewailed, not its building.

Remnants of our historical past have long come to stand for the whole of events: in the ruins of ancient cities, in the relics displayed in museums, even in the remains of our ancestors, we would recall entire civilizations with an eye toward understanding them. Too often, however, these remnants are mistaken for the events from which they have been torn: in coming to stand for the whole, a fragment is confused for it. Authentic historical artifacts are used not only to gesture toward the past, to move us toward its examination, but also to naturalize particular versions of the past. Pieces of charred brick, a broken bone seem to endow their arrangement in museums with the naturalness of their own forms. At such moments, we are invited to forget that memory itself is, after all, only a figurative reconstruction of the past, not its literal replication.

Modern memory may indeed be archival, as Nora suggests, relying entirely on the materiality of the trace. The fragment presents itself not only as natural knowledge, but as a piece of the event itself. At least part of our veneration of ruins and artifacts stems from the nineteenth-century belief that such objects embody the spirit of the people who made and used them. In this view, museum objects are not only remnants of the people they once belonged to, but also traces of the values, ideas, and character of the time. In the subsequent fetishization of artifacts by curators, and of ruins by the "memory-tourist," however, we risk mistaking the piece for the whole, the implied whole for unmediated history. Moreover, our veneration of a place leads to its consecration as holy site, sacred and transcendent in its significance.

As a result, museums, archives, and ruins may not house our memory-work so much as displace it with claims of material evidence and proof. Memory-work becomes unnecessary as long as the material fragment of events continues to function as witness-memorial. Are we delegating to the archivist the memory-work that is ours alone? Do we allow memorials to relieve us of the memory-burden we should be carrying? The archivists' traditional veneration of the trace is tied directly to their need for proof and evidence of a particular past. But in this they too often confuse proof that something existed with proof that it existed in a particular way, for seemingly self-evident reasons. When taken together with the viewers' emotional, intellectual, and ideological responses to these arranged artifacts, the museum's total text functions much as any other hand-crafted work of art. And while the museum's and viewers' intentions are important, beyond intention lie the actual consequences of such exhibitions: What has the viewer learned about a group of artifacts, about the history they represent? On exiting the museum, how do visitors grasp their own lives and surroundings anew in light of a memorialized past?[6]

The problem is not our uncritical belief in the notion that a spatial juxtaposition of artifacts can produce understanding (it does, it must). Rather, it is our uncritical belief in the particular kind of understanding produced, naturalized by the artifacts themselves, parts of a seemingly "natural order." In confusing these ruins for the events they now represent, we lose sight of the fact that they are framed for us by curators in particular times and places. This critique may be made of all museums, in fact, and it is not intended to discredit any given Holocaust museum. At the same time, however, we must continue to remind ourselves that the historical meanings we find in museums may not be proven by artifacts, so much as generated by their organization.

Auschwitz-Birkenau

At the end of April 1940, some six months after occupying Poland, the Germans reinforced and electrified the fences surrounding the Polish Army barracks in Oswiecim, a small half-Jewish town in Silesia, erected guard towers there, and so converted it into Konzentrationslager Auschwitz. Though some of the first gassings were carried out here, Auschwitz-I was intended initially as an internment camp for Polish political prisoners, and eventually for Russian POWs. Within the year, however, it was decided to expand the camp into separate labor and killing centers. For labor, the Germans built a subcamp, Buna, near the rubber and petrol works at Monowice. For their massive extermination center, the Nazis razed the Polish village of Brzezinka, three kilometers down the road from Auschwitz-I, and built a gigantic complex of barracks, gas chambers, crematoria, and burning pits—all fed by a rail spur diverted from the main line. Thus, what the Germans would call Birkenau was itself built on the site of a demolished village, its very foundation a bed of ruins. Over the next four years, some 1.6 million people (90 percent Jews) were murdered and burned at Birkenau, their ashes plowed into the soil, dumped into small ponds, and scattered into the nearby Vistula River.[7]

Late in November 1944, with the Red Army approaching, the Germans evacuated Auschwitz, leaving the sick and dying behind and forcing the rest on deadly marches west. After dynamiting gas chambers and crematoria and setting several dozen barracks alight, the Germans fled. The ruins, littered with dead and dying, were still smoldering when the first horse-mounted Red Army patrols arrived a few days later. To prevent the spread of disease, the Soviet soldiers burned down several of the barracks at Birkenau; others were dismantled by local Poles in search of building materials and firewood.

Prisoners' clothing on display inside a barracks building at Majdanek. Photo: Donald Woodman.

Prisoners' shoes piled in bins in the barracks at Majdanek. Photo: Donald Woodman.

Ruins of a gas chamber and crematorium complex at Auschwitz-Birkenau, dynamited by the Germans on their evacuation from the camp. Photo: Ira Nowinski.

In 1947, the Polish parliament declared that the rest of the camp would be "forever preserved as a memorial to the martyrdom of the Polish nation and other peoples."[8] Five years later, a group of survivors and relatives of victims organized the International Committee of Auschwitz, which would oversee the memorial project. Though most of its members were Jews, their identity as survivors was defined largely by their experiences as resistance fighters and as Socialists. From its conception, therefore, the memorial at Auschwitz assumed a decidedly internationalist cast. Unlike the barracks at Majdanek, the blocks at Auschwitz-I were converted into national pavilions, each with an exposition devoted to the national memory of a different country's citizens at Auschwitz. Here Belgians, Hungarians, Austrians, Jews, and others from nineteen countries were invited to remember their own. By collecting a composite memory of Auschwitz, these national pavilions preserve the essential diversity of memory here. On the other hand, Jews came to see in this pluralization of memory a splintering of Jewish suffering into so many national martyrdoms.

In fact, the Jewish pavilion was closed after the Six-Day War in 1967, at the height of the Polish government's anti-Jewish purges, ostensibly for renovations, and remained closed until 1978, when it was rededicated. In his address at the reopening, the Polish minister of culture, Janusz Wieczorek, gave consummate ex-

pression to the contemporary Polish understanding of Auschwitz reflected until very recently in its memorial:

Solitary visitor gazes on the barracks at Auschwitz-I. Photo: Donald Woodman.

> Distinguished Guest, here at the graveyard of Europe, at this necropolis of human hopes and inconceivable drama, one should keep silent . . . .
>
> But to keep silent also means to resign, yet our presence today proves we have not given up.
>
> We are richer with true facts discovered in the laboratories of scientists and statisticians examining the history of World War II, martyrology of states and nations condemned by [] Nazi Germany to political and biological extermination. Among those doomed, Jews and Poles rank in the first place. . . .
>
> In their studies, scientists and statisticians have almost completed calculating the millions of Jews and Poles who perished in that holocaust. Oswiecim, Treblinka, Chelmno, Plaszow, Belzec, Sobibor, Lodz, Bialystok, and the Warsaw Ghetto, and dozens of other places of "the Warta district" and "the General Gubernyia"—they are all stages of extermination, stations of the Cross of Polish Jews and Jews treacherously brought from

other countries of Europe. We know nearly everything about their gehenna [Calvary], the misery of Poles.[9]

In this address, Jews and Poles not only share first place in a hierarchy of victims, but, in equating political and biological extermination, Wieczorek suggests that all were to have shared the same fate, as well. Despite the overwhelming number of Jewish victims at the camps and ghettos listed here, the Polish names of these sites automatically lend Polish memory to them, creating distinctly Polish significance in the Jewish landscape of suffering. In coming to know "nearly everything about their [the Jews'] gehenna," the Poles would come to know their own past misery.

In addition to the national pavilions at Auschwitz-I, two blocks are devoted to historical chronologies of events leading to the camp. As was the case at Majdanek, however, what most visitors remember from trips to the Auschwitz museum are their few moments before the huge glass-encased bins of artifacts: floor to ceiling piles of prosthetic limbs, eyeglasses, toothbrushes, suitcases, and the shorn hair of women. With the earlier discussion of museological remnants in mind, we might ask, What precisely does the sight of concentration-camp artifacts awaken in viewers? Historical knowledge? A sense of evidence? Revulsion, grief, pity, fear? That visitors respond more directly to objects than to verbalized concepts is clear. But beyond affect, what does our knowledge of these objects— a bent spoon, children's shoes, crusty old striped uniforms—have to do with our knowledge of historical events?

More specifically, what do we understand of the killers and victims through their remains? In one way, all we see here can be construed as remnants of the killers and their deeds. The dynamited ruins of gas chambers at Birkenau, for example, recall not only the fact of the gas chambers, but also the German attempt to destroy evidence of this fact: a monument both to events and to the guilt of the killers. But, in a perversely ironic twist, these artifacts also force us to recall the victims as the Germans have remembered them to us: in the collected debris of a destroyed civilization.

For, by themselves, these remnants rise in a macabre dance of memorial ghosts. Armless sleeves, eyeless lenses, headless caps, footless shoes: victims are known only by their absence, by the moment of their destruction. In great loose piles, these remnants remind us not of the lives that once animated them, so much as of the brokenness of lives. For when the memory of a people and its past are reduced to the bits and rags of their belongings, memory of life itself is lost. What of the relationships and families sundered? What of the scholarship and education? The community and its traditions? Nowhere among this debris do we find traces of what bound these people together into a civilization, a nation, a culture.

Heaps of scattered artifacts belie the interconnectedness of lives that made these victims a people. The sum of these dismembered fragments can never approach the whole of what was lost.

That a murdered people remains known in Holocaust museums anywhere by their scattered belongings, and not by their spiritual works, that their lives should be recalled primarily through the images of their death, may be the ultimate travesty. These lives and the relationships between them are lost to the memory of ruins alone—and will be lost to subsequent generations who seek memory only in the rubble of the past. Indeed, by adopting such artifacts for their own memorial presentations, even the new museums in America and Europe risk perpetuating the very figures by which the killers themselves would have memorialized their Jewish victims.

The First Memorial Competition

In 1957, five years after its formation, the International Committee of Auschwitz launched a competition for a monument that would provide a specific locus

Great bins at Auschwitz-I hold the suitcases of victims, who were ordered to write their names and birthdates on them before their deportation to the camp. They appear now as self-inscribed epitaphs. Photo: Donald Woodman.

The rail
entrance to
Auschwitz-
Birkenau.
Photo: Donald
Woodman.

for official commemorations and ceremonies. Henry Moore was invited to chair
the competition, a choice lending great prestige and integrity to the formation
of a jury.[10] Reflecting its internationalist cast, the committee announced that the
competition would be open to all in every land—all, that is, except those who had
in any way collaborated with the killers. The winning monument would be situated at Birkenau, "where the rails end on which the transports from twenty-three
countries arrived," and would not alter in any way the remains of the camp.[11]

The jury first met in Auschwitz at the end of April 1958, to begin poring over the
426 designs submitted by artists and architects from thirty-six countries. Members considered both sculptural and architectonic designs, some representative
of contemporary cutting-edge work, others exemplary of early twentieth-century
modernism, and still others gesturing back to romantic and figurative forms
of the nineteenth century. Judging a competition in the midst of early abstract

expressionism and headed by the greatest contemporary material formalist in modern sculpture, the committee faced a difficult task indeed. How would they balance the needs of a lay public against the obscure sensibilities of contemporary art, knowing that the ultimate design would have to be approved by government authorities? It would not be easy, as Moore conceded, though the process proved to be remarkably prescient of subsequent competitions.

After selecting seven designs for the second stage of review, the jury invited the artists to visit Auschwitz, where they could acquaint themselves with the terrain and atmosphere, and further refine their conceptions. A few months later, in November 1958, the jury convened again, this time in Paris, where Moore announced their decision:

> The choice of a monument to commemorate Auschwitz has not been an easy task. Essentially, what has been attempted has been the creation—or, in the case of the jury, the choice—of a monument to crime and ugliness, to murder and to horror. The crime was of such stupendous proportions that any work of art must be on an appropriate scale. But, apart from this, is it in fact possible to create a work of art that can express the emotions engendered by Auschwitz?

> It is my conviction that a very great sculptor—a new Michelangelo or a new Rodin—might have achieved this. The odds against such a design turning up among the many maquettes submitted were always enormous. And none did. Nor were any of the purely architectural . . . projects fully satisfactory.

> There were, in the end, three projects, all of which were judged good, but none of which was considered entirely adequate. The jury considered that its primary task was not to award a prize, to decide which of these three was the best, but rather to ensure that the finest possible monument be built at Auschwitz.

> With this end in view, a unanimous decision was reached: the three best teams have been asked to submit, if possible in collaboration, but if necessary singly, a new project or new projects. A final judging will take place in 1959. The jury will meet again to decide whether one of these projects is worthy of its approval, and if so, which.[12]

In this extraordinary statement, Moore seems to concede that the project was doomed from the start, that none on the jury could imagine a winner, that, hypothetically, there might be no winner. The myriad of competing factors that would

Design for
memorial at
Birkenau by a
Polish team
including Oskar
Hansen, Jerzy
Jarnuszkiewicz,
Julian Palka,
Lechoslaw
Rosinski,
Edmund
Kupiecki, and
Tadeusz
Plasota. A black
swatch of stone
cuts the camp
in half,
outlining the
ruins of gas
chambers on
either side.
Photo:
Courtesy of the
State Museum
at Auschwitz.

paralyze future museums and competitions had nearly blocked the first such competition.

The greatest proposal in the opinion of the artists and architects on the jury was unacceptable to the survivors from the Auschwitz Committee. In a design that Moore called "exceptionally brilliant," a Polish team headed by Oskar Hansen proposed laying a seventy-meter-wide swatch of black stone slabs cutting diagonally from one end of the camp to the ruins of the largest crematorium at the other end. The path would have evoked a symbolic refutation of the camp's past reality, a black scar upon the face of this profaned earth, and a sealing over of the camp's landscape to ensure that nothing but memory would ever grow on the site.

Despite its brilliance, however, the design met resistance on three fronts. First, even though it would have left the rubble of the crematoria intact, in covering over nearly seventy thousand square meters of Birkenau and clearing out all the barracks in its path, it was not in keeping with the jury's rule against altering the ruins. Second, the survivors on the committee felt it was too diffused and abstract, without a focal point for commemorations; in addition, they felt that such an abstract remembrance was not in keeping with the literalness of their experiences. Finally, all agreed that it would simply cost too much to build and that, even if they could afford it, the materials for such a project might take years to acquire.

If Hansen's conception was regarded as too oblique in its focus, the runner-up design by Julio Lafuente's Italian team proved overly specific. Based on the figure of the death trains, it would have placed twenty-three stone blocks on the tracks leading to the gas chambers, to represent the sealed box cars bringing victims

Design for memorial at Birkenau by Julio Lafuente, Pietro Cascella, and Andrea Cascella, of Rome. Twenty-three trains of stone, linked by barbed-wire clasps, represent the twenty-three national homes of the victims at Auschwitz. Photo: Courtesy of the State Museum at Auschwitz.

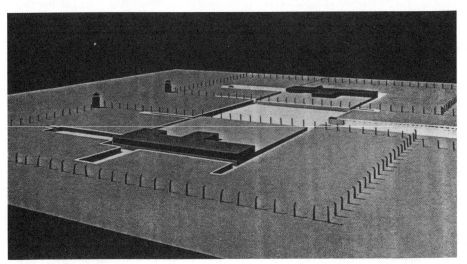

Design for memorial at Birkenau by finalists Maurizio Vitale, Giorgio Simoncini, Tommaso Valle, and Pericle Fazzini. A large cut-out groove leads to the end of the tracks. Photo: Courtesy of the State Museum at Auschwitz.

The final model for the memorial at Birkenau, designed by a team composed of members from the three winning teams, including Pietro Cascella, Jerzy Jarnuszkiewicz, Julian Palka, Giorgio Simoncini, Tommaso Valle, and Maurizio Vitale, 1967. Photo: Courtesy of the State Museum at Auschwitz.

from twenty-three different countries. These roughly hewn stone carriages were to be linked by claw-toothed couplings recalling barbed wire, their path blocked by a great stone barricade erected across the tracks. Though admired for its sculptural inspiration and internationalist approach, the motif of the trains was finally rejected as too narrow to recall the terrible range of suffering at Birkenau.

The third set of finalists, another Italian team led by Maurizio Vitale, combined figurative sculpture and abstract architecture. In their design, a gradually sloping, dug-out "road of death" ran alongside the unloading platform to a great rectangular basin cut into the ground between the two crematoria at the end of the line. A network of deep, square-edged canals surrounded the ruins on all sides, each leading back to the square, with its cluster of small sculpted figures in various defensive poses. Not only were the figures too slight to support their burden of memory, according to Moore, but like Hansen's project, this design would have destroyed too much of the camp itself.

Rather than submitting all-new designs, the three leading teams agreed to collaborate on one project. The result was a composite design, drawing from the most inspired elements in each of the early proposals: the Gate of Death at the camp's entrance would be symbolically barred; a paved path would run parallel to the tracks, alongside the barracks all the way to the end of the line; huge blocks of stone in the forms of boxcars or sarcophagi would be erected at the end of the tracks, next to the crematoria ruins; a narrow and deep passage would

then run toward a layered depression, over whose rim one could view ruins of the crematoria and the rest of the camp. The jury met in Rome in May 1959 to consider this synthesis and, after recommending several modifications, approved it a year later.

Together with representatives from the design teams and the plenipotentiary of the Polish Ministry of Culture and Art, Prof. Jan Zachwatowicz, a technical commission appointed to oversee the construction of the memorial convened in Paris in 1961. At this meeting the designers were informed that the approved proposal was no longer feasible: it would cost too much and displace too many newly restored camp buildings. After two more years of wrangling, representatives from the three teams formed a single group and submitted one last model, a drastically scaled-down version limited to the immediate area of the crematoria. The technical commission and government both accepted it, and construction began two years later.

What was unveiled on 16 May 1967 and what had been accepted were two different monuments, however. In its final proposed stage, the monument consisted of a row of blocklike sarcophagi, slightly elevated, and a stone tower of cubist figures. Although the memorial sculpture has been described as sarcophagal, it also suggested human forms: three abstract figures emerged from the stone.[13] In these vertically rectangular shapes rising to rounded blocks, one could see the cubist shadow lines of a torso with rounded head perched on top. In their number

Detail of the figures proposed in the final design for the memorial at Birkenau. Though initially erected, they were replaced just before unveiling by a black slab of marble with a single triangle commemorating all victims. Photo: Courtesy of the State Museum at Auschwitz.

and sizes, they resemble a human cluster: two parents and a child.

In fact, this version of the memorial was mounted in 1967, but it was not what was unveiled to the public a week later. For one week, the figures stood as workers cleaned the grounds in preparation for the official dedication. At the last minute, however, the carved stones were moved from their pedestal to the ground in front and replaced by a great polished square of black marble with a triangle in the middle. To this day, there has been no official explanation for this change, which we know about only through snapshots taken by workers during the installation.

Why did the technical committee substitute a triangle for these figures? Without forcing an overly tendentious argument, I would suggest that in their different sizes, the stones did not satisfactorily define the political character of the victims desired by the authorities. Although the triangle represents all the victims, it does so in the figure of specifically political inmates. By contrast, the different sizes of stones in the initial sculpture suggested children, who could not have been killed as political prisoners, but only as Jews. In 1967, the discerning critical eye of the authorities apparently caught this subtlety of meaning, which led them to replace human figures with a symbol of political suffering.

At Birkenau, memory would be a mix of ruins and sculpted art. Surrounded by a seemingly endless field of barracks chimneys and piles of dynamited crematoria, the blocklike sarcophagi marked the end of the rail line, the beginning of the death zone. In concert with the relics nearby, the monument remembered and provided material evidence for the simple message inscribed on twenty stone tablets in twenty different languages, including Yiddish and Hebrew: "Four million people suffered and died here at the hands of the Nazi murderers between the years 1940 and 1945."

With Poland's change in regime twenty-three years later, these inscriptions were removed from the tablets, memory's slate wiped clean. For, as Yehuda Bauer reminds us, citing the French Jewish historian, Georges Wellers, this figure is impossible. While historians agree that the exact number of people murdered here will never be known, they believe the most accurate count is closer to 1.6 million, of whom about 1.3 million were Jews. The remaining 300,000 victims were comprised of Polish Catholics, gypsies, and Russian POWs.[14] The figure of 4 million was as wrong as it was round, arrived at by a combination of the camp commandant's self-aggrandizing exaggerations, Polish perceptions of their great losses, and the Soviet occupiers' desire to create socialist martyrs. The inflated number may have diminished Stalin's own crimes, even as it created millions of Polish and Soviet martyrs at Auschwitz. Ironically, by assenting over the years to this unwarranted claim, Jewish visitors have unwittingly assisted in the Polish nationalization of Auschwitz-Birkenau.

Memorial as it was realized at Birkenau.
Photo: James E. Young.

Auschwitz and Its Memory Evolve

For most of those removed from the site, Auschwitz has come to exist primarily as symbol, its physical topography supplanted by historical significance. Little by little, time and memory have turned the ground into sacred space, seemingly inviolable. It has become a place of the mind, an abstraction, a haunted idea. For the Poles of Oswiecim, however, it is also home—and this small fact continues to bear directly on the shape of memory we find here. What happened at Auschwitz may also be memory for many townspeople here, but the rusting barbed wire, crumbling barracks, and bus loads of tourists constitute something more: daily realities by which current lives are navigated.

For neighboring farmers and villagers, time has turned the ruins at Birkenau not into memorial symbol or sacred space, but into landscape. They are a refuge where a few live and where others come to cut hay, rest, or play. Young lovers stroll among the rubble in search of a secluded glen to spread a picnic lunch. Children ride bicycles into shaded birch groves where other children once waited for death. Teenagers fish quietly on the bank of a little pond behind the crematoria, its shallows still white with human ash. They mean no harm. Our memory space

The memorial tablets at Birkenau, swept clean of inscriptions by the postcommunist regime, await new memory.
Photo: James E. Young.

is, after all, their city park and state preserve. Whether we like it or not, the local citizens have become part of our memory here, reinforcing our own prejudices perhaps, feeding our distrust.

For in fact, we must also recognize that this awful place remains sacred only in the great distance between it and ourselves, between its past and our present. The site retains its symbolic power over us partly because we don't live here, because we must make this pilgrimage to memory. For those who call Auschwitz their home, there may be no choice: every day and its small chores are framed not merely in the remembered image of this place, but in its hard reality. Life goes on. The Poles who live here know Auschwitz in the context of current lives, jobs, and family. It is part of a larger place called Polska. By contrast, we memory-tourists tend to see not only Auschwitz through the lens of its miserable past, but all of Poland through the image of Auschwitz itself.

Like all memorials, Auschwitz also functions as a performance space, a political stage. As we see in the familiar photograph of Helmut Kohl's visit to Auschwitz, it can serve as an ideal setting for pricking the Germans' conscience. After his visit, Kohl promised more than 2.2 billion dollars in aid to the new government. The *New York Times* headline confirmed the obvious: "Kohl Recalls Auschwitz and Agrees to Aid Poles." In a gesture aimed as much at disarming his critics at home as toward fostering remembrance, Kohl reminded us that every memory can have a political end.

Recently, Birkenau has been used as a more literal stage set for films such as *War and Remembrance* and *Triumph of the Spirit.* In a move recalling the common literary device of mixing actual documents into fictional narrative, the makers of these films incorporated the refurbished ruins into their own drama. The same rhetorical purpose was served: to heighten the emotional appeal of the story with the realia of actual events, to foster the illusion of authenticity. A fake gas chamber and crematorium complex built for *Triumph of the Spirit* stood for months after filming within meters of the ruins of real gas chambers and crematoria. From one angle at a slight distance, it struck me as an eerily realistic facsimile. But as I approached and noticed the peeling papier-mâché of chimneys and exposed rafters and two-by-fours propping up the back side of the building, confusion took over. The facade seemed to infect the rest of the ruins, to corrupt them with its fiction. The props threatened to turn all of Birkenau into a movie set, a theme park.

The Carmelite Convent at Auschwitz

Finally, we turn to the controversy surrounding the Carmelite convent at Auschwitz, a micro-study in the conflict between Jewish and Polish memory here. The

Kohl Ends Trip to Poland With a Visit to Auschwitz

Chancellor Helmut Kohl of West Germany was accompanied by Rabbi Menachem Joskowicz of Poland yesterday as he arrived for a wreath-laying ceremony for Nazi victims at the Auschwitz death camp. Mr. Kohl also signed an agreement to provide Poland with $2.2 billion in economic aid. Page A14.

After German chancellor Helmut Kohl's visit to Auschwitz in 1989, he signed an agreement providing Poland with 2.2 billion dollars in economic aid. Photo: Courtesy of Agence France-Presse.

history of this episode does not begin in 1984, when ten sisters of the Carmelite order moved into a building adjoining the camp complex. It can be traced back to an address delivered in 1971 by then Cardinal Karol Wojtyla at a beatification ceremony honoring Maximilien Kolbe, a rabidly anti-Semitic priest who died at Auschwitz after voluntarily exchanging himself for a Polish prisoner. "The Church of Poland," Wojtyla began, "since the beginning of the postwar period sees the necessity of such a site of sacrifice, of an altar and a sanctuary, precisely in Auschwitz. The beatification of Fr. Maximilien made this even more necessary. We are all convinced that in this site of his heroic immolation, a site which will always remain linked to the memory of this sacrifice, a church should be erected, as since the first centuries of Christianity churches have been created on the tombs of martyrs and saints."[15]

Eight years later, on 7 June 1979, Wojtyla returned to Auschwitz as Pope John Paul II to confirm the sanctification of this site as "the Golgotha of the contemporary world." In this image, he recalled the site of a million Jewish martyrs in the figure of one Jew crucified for the redemption of humankind: the martyrdom of Christ recapitulated in the mass murder of Jews. Later, he would extol the martyrdom of Edith Stein in similar terms. In his words, "She died as a daughter of Israel for the glorification of the Holy name of God and, at the same time, as sister Teresa Benedetta of the cross." That is, she died as both a Jew in the tradition of kiddush hashem and as a Polish Christian in the tradition of expiatory sacrifice. All of which makes Edith Stein the Catholic victim par excellence of Auschwitz, a Jewish martyr turned Christian saint. Having been condemned to Auschwitz as a Jew, Edith Stein was martyred as a Catholic.

According to Cardinal Macharski, the Carmelite sisters took the papal exhortations to heart and so, in the fall of 1984, moved into an unused building just outside the perimeter of the fence at Auschwitz-I to conduct lives of prayer in atonement for the crimes at Auschwitz and to honor the martyrs there. The convent occupies an old brick building that served as a theater for the Polish Army barracks before the war. During the operation of the camp, the SS converted the theater into a storehouse for canisters of Zyklon-B. Today, the building is tidy and refurbished inside: windows decorated with lace curtains look out onto a vegetable garden and rose bushes, all dominated by a twenty-four-foot wooden cross. It was not long before the entire site reverted again to its original calling as a theater—only this time for political and religious melodrama.

Within the year, a Belgian Catholic group launched a fundraising drive for the convent, which was established, in the words of their solicitations, not only to seek atonement for the sins committed there and to pray for the souls of the victims, but also "as a spiritual fortress and guarantee of the conversion of strayed brothers from our countries, as well as proof of our desire to erase outrages so often done to the Vicar of Christ [Pope Pius XII]." This last point caught the eye of Jewish groups in Europe, whose protests led to its elision from further mailings. But now the convent had the attention of Jewish survivors and leaders, who began to wonder what a convent was doing there in the first place. In a series of meetings arranged by Theo Klein, a leader of French Jewry and president of the European region of the World Jewish Congress, and the archbishop of Paris, Cardinal Jean-Marie Lustiger (a Jewish convert to Catholicism), Jewish and Polish Catholic delegations agreed to move the convent from the grounds of the camp to an interfaith Center for Information, Education, Encounter, and Prayer to be built nearby. This agreement was signed on 22 February 1987 in Geneva and was to be implemented within two years.

Under terms of the agreement, the main Polish signatory, Cardinal Macharski, was to keep Jewish leaders apprised of the new center's progress and the relocation of the nuns. When, after several inquiries, Klein had received no reply from Macharski, he began to worry that something was amiss—and for good reason. On his return to Poland, the cardinal had run into stiff opposition. Although he had grasped the international ramifications of the convent, the sisters and local Catholic officials could not see what harm they were doing. "Our people get annoyed at these protests," one villager said. "What right do they have? People here are glad the nuns are there, that someone prays." The problem lay not only in convincing the local faithful to accept the Geneva agreement, but also in acquiring an alternative site for the convent. It would have to be bought, and with Western currency no less. As one local villager observed, "In the West it takes two years to build the Eiffel Tower. But this is Poland." How long do you think it will take then? he was asked. "A generation, twenty-five years, at least."[16]

Without a will to move the convent, the Poles found no way to raise the money for a new building and interfaith center. Macharski asked for and received a six-month extension from Jewish leaders in Europe, who were fully aware of the delicate and painful discussions under way between Catholics in and out of Poland. Albert Decourtay, archbishop of Lyon, even arranged for a delegation of French and Belgian Carmelite nuns to spend two weeks at the Auschwitz convent to explain to their sisters the implications of the convent's presence there.[17]

On 15 June 1989, Decourtay announced that a plot of land outside the camp had finally been purchased for the new center, but that building would not commence until 1990. Klein replied that even so, the nuns should leave the building as was agreed. When it became clear that they would not, Klein suspended official dialogue between Jews and Catholics, in order to measure the next step. In the meantime, according to Klein, Jewish and Catholic leaders continued to hold discreet negotiations, wary of the issue's combustibility in the event of an overly public airing. Their worst fears were realized in July 1989, when the American activist rabbi Avi Weiss and seven Jewish supporters scaled the walls of the convent and entered to chant prayers and read Torah. Polish workmen yelling anti-Semitic epithets dumped buckets of paint and water over their heads and beat them before dragging them out. The greater issues surrounding the convent thus ignited and were fueled further by inflammatory statements on both sides, culminating in Cardinal Jozef Glemp's poisonous insinuations that a "squad" of Jews had attempted to kill the nuns and that the Jewish-controlled media should call off its anti-Polish campaign.

After nearly two months of bitter recriminations, including a threatened libel suit by Weiss that prevented Glemp from making a planned trip to America and suspension by Macharski of the 1987 agreement, the Vatican finally stepped in. On 19 September 1989, the Catholic hierarchy affirmed the 1987 Geneva agreement and offered to fund the interfaith center. Though no mention was made of the nuns, their removal was implied in the Vatican's statement and acknowledged privately by Catholic spokesmen. What had begun with the Pope, it seems, would now end with the Pope.

The immediate crisis had been resolved, perhaps, but the issues it had crystallized remained as intractable as ever. For better or worse, the Carmelite convent at Auschwitz had brought the state of Polish-Jewish relations into painfully sharp relief: the cross here had served as a veritable lightning rod for the radically different memory each community was bringing to Auschwitz. Where the sign of the cross evoked mercy, compassion, and salvation in the Polish heart, it stirred resentment, dread, even panic for Jews. Where it reminded Polish Catholics of the meaning for all suffering, the reasons for life itself, European Jews recalled living under the shadow of the cross for two millennia, under unceasing pressure to convert, to relinquish their covenant, to disappear. Where the cross symbolized the redemption of millions of dead for Poles, it signified the very roots of the catastrophe for Jews. For them, Auschwitz could not be regarded as a figurative Calvary, so much as the ultimate—even logical—extension of Christian anti-Semitism. The convent was viewed in this case as a crowning achievement, a celebration of the massacre as a kind of Christian triumph.

Throughout Poland, Christians have consecrated their places of martyrdom, built shrines on the sites of executions and accidents, celebrated their martyrs and striven to keep the places of martyrdom holy. In a tradition in which the faithful are redeemed by martyrdom, these places play a crucial role in day-to-day religious consciousness. The Jewish respect for their martyrs calls for a fundamentally different approach: it demands that these defiled, profaned grounds of the death camp remain untouched, unconsecrated by institutional prayer. That such prayer might redeem these deaths in any way, but especially in a Christian scheme of redemption, strikes the Jewish mourner as unacceptable. Where Auschwitz has for Jews come to symbolize the uniqueness of the Holocaust, Christian tradition demands of the Carmelites that they offer penitential prayer in atonement for the evils visited on humankind by the Nazis.

The yawning chasm between the two sides grows wider with every attempt to bridge it. In agreeing to pray for the Jews as well, for example, the sisters seemed only to compound the offense. In the Jewish view, the nuns at Auschwitz inadvertently inflamed the anti-Semitic evil they claimed to expiate. All of which had international political repercussions: Glemp's ill-conceived remarks came precisely at a time when the new Polish prime minister, Tadeusz Mazowiecki, was appealing to the West for economic support. The great good will generated by the July elections a few months earlier, Solidarity's triumph, and open sympathy for Jewish interests was melting away fast with every new statement by Glemp—and later threatened by Lech Walesa's own initial reluctance to disavow unequivocally the cardinal's remarks.

But in trying to soothe the ruffled feathers of the American Jewish community, Walesa may also have given most succinct expression to the Polish position when he said that "the Jewish community is the nation that has paid the highest price in the history of the world. And we, the Polish nation, have paid the second highest price. Are we supposed to fight among ourselves? Auschwitz belongs to the world. It does not belong to any cardinals, it does not belong to Walesa, it does not belong to the Jews."[18]

Konstanty Gebert, writing under the pen name Dawid Warszawski, reminds us also that for most Poles, the interests of the Catholic church and of the Polish nation are identical: what is good for the church is good for Poland. Obversely, a perceived attack on the church is regarded as an attack on Polish national aspirations to independence. This dimension of the controversy is almost entirely lost on the rest of the world.[19] Forcing the Carmelites from Auschwitz seemed, in Polish eyes, not only to deny the martyrdom of Poles that took place here, but to threaten the very independence they seemed finally to be gaining.

The Poles hear still other political repercussions that are inaudible to the Western ear. Of great concern to Adam Michnik, the Jewish editor of Solidarity's newspaper *Gazeta*, is the accusation that Poles are somehow coresponsible for the annihilation of Jews in Poland, an accusation that, in his words, "has allowed public opinion in the West to approve the betrayal [of East Central European countries] by the West at Yalta. Do a people who would lend a hand at Treblinka deserve anything better than Soviet Communism?" In her elaboration of Michnik's point, Lillian Vallee insightfully concludes that "Western accusations against the posture of Poles in World War II which reduce world indifference to Polish anti-Semitism rankle because they are delivered from a position of luxury, of undeserved moral superiority; there is almost no evidence to indicate that people in the West were willing to cause themselves the least discomfort, let alone give up their lives, to change the fate of Jews during World War II."[20]

In addition, blanket denunciations of the Poles serve to obfuscate a number of other Polish memories of this time, as enunciated by Wladyslaw Bartoszewski: "The Poles feel as a nation they suffered terrible losses; that there was no political collaboration with the German occupier; that there was a large scale resistance movement within Poland; and in view of the Nazi terror there was no possiblity of saving Polish Jewry. The Second World War is considered by many Poles to be a Polish tragedy with six million Polish citizens—both Poles and Polish Jews—dead; the country destroyed and under alien communist rule; and the dream of an independent Polish state shattered. This is viewed to be an unjust and immoral end to a determined fight against the Nazis."[21]

Bartoszewski would remind us that it was not Polish police who rousted Jews out of their beds in Poland, as the French gendarmes did in Paris, or as the Ukrainian polizei did in Kiev; it was not Poles who conceived, designed, and operated the death camps, but Germans. In light of unfolding events in Eastern Europe, we might now begin to re-evaluate our own memories of this time, naturalized and reinforced over the years: after what happened in France and Germany, even in Holland and Belgium, we might ask to what extent our own sympathies and memories have been shaped by the alliances forged after the war. If Poles seem to have displaced the Germans as the first enemies of the Jews, it's time we asked why: not to diminish the specter of anti-Semitism in Poland, but to remember what our postwar alliances ask us to forget.

Coda: The Changing of the Memorial Guard

Amid the tumult of events during the fall of 1989, Prime Minister Mazowiecki quietly convened a commission to consider the future of the museum and monuments at Auschwitz-Birkenau. All too aware of his fragile tenure as head of state, perhaps, Mazowiecki dared to acknowledge openly what other leaders more often prefer to hide: the change in official memory that comes with a new government regime. And then, in a bold and conciliatory move, the prime minister called on a number of Jewish Holocaust scholars for guidance in the official remaking of public memory at Auschwitz.

Though now only a memory himself, Mazowiecki set in motion a complete restructuring of the memorial at Auschwitz. Under his direction, the Polish Ministry of Culture appointed the Auschwitz Council, composed of Jews from Poland, Israel, and other Western nations and of Polish Catholic intellectuals and government ministers. Charged with redesigning the museum and monuments at Auschwitz, reorganizing the ruins in ways that strip them of their previous Marxian undergirding, the council has met several times over the last two years. With little fanfare, it has already begun to redefine, literally to reshape, both memory of the Holocaust in Poland and its contested historical significance.

At the behest of the Ministry of Culture, Oxford University's Centre for Hebrew Studies invited a group of Jewish intellectuals from nine countries to meet in May 1990 at its Yarnton Manor to consider "the future of Auschwitz." After three days of polite, if occasionally vigorous disagreement, the twenty-seven academics, editors, religious leaders, and concentration-camp survivors formulated a list of six general principles and fourteen concrete proposals. The group hand-delivered this document—"The Yarnton Declaration of Jewish Intellectuals on the Future of Auschwitz"—to Poland's deputy minister of culture and art,

Polish youth
groups
commemorate
Christian and
Jewish victims
in the ash fields
of Birkenau
with crucified
stars of David.
Photo: Ira
Nowinski.

Krystyna Marszalek-Mlynczyk, who was accompanied by Stefan Wilkanowicz, the editor of the influential Catholic journal *ZNAK*. Both had attended all three days of talks, morning to midnight.

The Yarnton Declaration will never rival the Yalta Accords in significance, but it did seem like a treaty of sorts, a framework for settling the unseemly memorial wars conducted so long on the mass graves at Auschwitz. In its apparent consensus, this symposium might be regarded with suspicion. But in fact, unanimity was never its aim. Rather, the Yarnton meeting was simply the first time Jews had actually sat down to define the memory they wanted preserved at Auschwitz, their first opportunity to offer the Poles a public set of recommendations. What follows is a brief description of these proposals by one who was there, a glimpse into the process of this group's memory-work.

Specifically, the committee recommended that the museum and monuments at Auschwitz-Birkenau show clearly:

1. that 1.6 million men, women, and children were murdered there;
2. that over 90 percent of those murdered here were Jews, and that, aside from the tribes of Sinti and Rom, Jews were the only people condemned to death for the "crime" of having been born;
3. that huge numbers of non-Jews, especially Poles, died at Auschwitz, and that the camp played a key role in the Nazi campaign to destroy Polish nationhood;
4. that both Jews and non-Jews murdered there were drawn from all walks of life and all political persuasions, from dozens of cultural, religious, and national traditions;
5. that the atrocities committed at Auschwitz were perpetrated by the German National Socialist regime and its collaborators.

Finally, the group suggested that in reorganizing the museum and memorial, the commission established by the Polish government consult as widely as possible with survivors' organizations and other Holocaust research institutions.[22]

In addition to these general principles, the group agreed on a number of practical suggestions concerning the day-to-day operation of the memorial. These ranged from setting up a shuttle bus between Auschwitz-I and Birkenau to providing a historical orientation for visitors on entering and leaving the memorial; from reviewing existing inscriptions and signs to creating a "hall of names," where a continuous tape of the names of victims would be played. Members also proposed that the recruitment and training of guides be standardized, that cassette players and headphones be provided to those without a guide, and that the museum restaurant make kosher food permanently available.

At one point, after viewing slides of boisterous tourists, teenagers munching on ice cream and candy among the barracks at Auschwitz-I, one of the British participants demanded a dress and behavior code. "No way," shot back an incredulous American. "How are we going to force stuffy Western modes of dress on seven hundred thousand tourists a year, from all over the world? How are these tourists supposed to dress?" The American acknowledged that a dress code might pose no hardship on British visitors, or even on the Poles, who often travel in their Sunday best anyway. But by forbidding shorts and sandals, for example, the committee might automatically exclude half the Israelis who travel here. As a compromise, it was agreed that an ambiguous invitation to decorum might be posted instead, just to remind visitors that this memorial is, if not a holy site, also not just another tourist haven.

Another participant asked pointedly how one goes about preserving ruins, which by their nature grow more ruinous every day. Short of reconstructing the gas chambers, just how much renovation should be permitted? Someone responded that perhaps the camp should be sealed off altogether, called a "city of evil," and turned into a place apart, to be contemplated from afar. Or perhaps it should be treated as a cemetery, profaned ground, never to be trod upon by the priestly sect. Others wondered what to do with the vendors hawking concentration-camp trinkets and memorabilia. Coming from a culture of "Memorial Day Sales," some of us Americans wondered how we could ask the Poles to restrain their own entrepreneurial spirit.

Because the Carmelite convent was being moved from Auschwitz to a site five hundred meters distant, the group at Yarnton were relieved not to have to address it. All were shocked, however, by the broken-down movie sets left behind by the makers of *Triumph of the Spirit*. All were reassured by Jonathan Webber, one of the symposium's conveners, that the sets were being torn down. Nevertheless, the committee recommended that no material changes or innovations be introduced to the complex without authorization from museum administrators and consultants.

After Stanislaw Krajewski informed everyone that the old inscriptions at Birkenau describing four million murdered had been torn up, the issue of shared memorial space arose. For, as the historian Michael Marrus explained, between 1939 and 1942, the barracks at Auschwitz-I were used to intern Polish political prisoners and POWs. In its first two and a half years of operation, Auschwitz was primarily a concentration camp for Poles. Only in its last two years, from spring 1942 to the end of 1944, after Birkenau was built, was the complex devoted to killing Jews. How then to create a commemorative space large enough to accommodate the plural memories and symbols of disparate, occasionally competing groups? How are the correct proportions of space and significance allotted?

Is this, should this even be, the function of a memorial site? On one hand, it seemed intolerable that Jews should be buried beneath the crosses of the Carmelite order, a sign of Christian triumphalism in Jewish eyes. On the other hand, if Jews were to deny Christians their traditional forms of remembrance, they might also thwart their memory of Jewish victims. It was agreed that Auschwitz-Birkenau was the site of the greatest mass murder of Jews in history. But it was also in Poland, where some six million Poles (half of them Jews) died during the German occupation. Auschwitz would be, by geographic default, a Polish memorial to both Polish and Jewish victims, a shared shrine to both Jewish and Polish catastrophes.

With all these considerations in mind, the committee recognized that any such outline for memory would be, like memorials themselves, provisional. These proposals would be debated further and refined, augmented and perhaps elided altogether. The process reminded all that no memorial is ever-lasting: each is shaped and understood in the context of its time and place, its meanings contingent on evolving political realities. The wisest course, therefore, might be to build into the memorial at Auschwitz a capacity for change in new times and circumstances, to make explicit the meanings the site holds for us now, even as we make room for the new meanings it will surely engender in the next generation. For once it is made clear how many people died here, for what reasons, and at whose hands, it will be up to future rememberers to find their own significance in this past.

Chapter 6   The Biography of

a Memorial Icon:

Nathan Rapoport's

Warsaw Ghetto Monument

Up to now, the Jewish artist has not displayed
any specific inclination in the field of modern
plastic art, and now he will stride through
the arts of all nations and create a synthesis
through the prism of his specific material.
—Joseph Tchaikov, 1921

Could I have made a stone with a hole in it and
said, "Voilà! The heroism of the Jews"?
—Nathan Rapoport, 1986

Of the thousands of memorials created after the war to commemorate aspects
of the Holocaust, Nathan Rapoport's Warsaw Ghetto Monument emerges as possibly the most widely known, celebrated, and controversial. It was the first to
mark both the heroism of Jewish resistance to the Nazis and the complete annihilation of the Jews in Warsaw. But in its use of the broadest of cultural archetypes—
the lumbering mytho-proletarian figures of the Stalinist era and the typological
image of Jews in exile as they passed through the Arch of Titus on their way to
Samuel Hirszenberg's epic painting *Golus*[1]—the Ghetto Monument has found
little critical consensus.

Hailed by critics on its unveiling (19 April 1948, the fifth anniversary of the Warsaw Ghetto uprising), the monument has subsequently been scorned by museum
curators as kitsch figuration and by "cold warriors" as proletarian pap. Early
European reviewers insisted that the glories of the uprising demanded as literal

an articulation as possible; many guessed that, as the first rebellion in Nazi-occupied Europe, the Jewish revolt would come to stand for all others. Since then, however, other observers have found the figurative heroic art of the monument so far removed from contemporary aesthetic discourse as to be archaic and even irrelevant as art altogether.[2]

As I suggested earlier, in fusing public art and popular culture, historical memory and political consequences, monuments like this demand a critique that goes beyond questions of high and low art, tastefulness and vulgarity. For forty-five years, the Ghetto Monument has endured as a kind of screen across which the projected shadows of a world's preoccupations continue to flicker and dance. As its maker's hand initially animated cold, amnesiac clay, the monument has since been revitalized by the parade of public figures marching past it and by the ceremonies conducted at its base. With the state's blessings, it is now as much a gathering place for Polish war veterans as for Jews; to the former Communist government's consternation, the square in which it stands was also a gathering place for protests by Solidarity and other dissident groups.

The monument has been extravagantly visited by touring presidents, prime ministers, and even the Pope. Everyone memorializes something different here, of course; each creates different meaning in the monument. Elsewhere, its individual figures are echoed in dozens of other monuments to this era throughout Europe and Israel, its images exported as distinctly Jewish martyrological and heroic icons. The monument has been recast and nationalized in Israel; it is pictured on both Polish and Israeli postcards and stamps; and it has been animated to the tones of Schoenberg's *Survivor from Warsaw* in a short Polish film.[3] In this "biography" of Rapoport's memorial icon, I would like to reinvigorate the monument with memory of its ever-evolving life in the community and the reciprocal dynamic between it and ongoing historical events.

Life of the Monument Maker

On entering Nathan Rapoport's studio six months after his death in 1987, I was struck by the sheer vitality emanating from the scattered maquettes and sketches. The studio smelled not of death and decay, but of wet clay and soil. As the door opened, clustered figures and sketches around the room all seemed to pause in mid-movement; illumined by the skylight overhead, statues and maquettes seemed to turn on their pedestals ever so slightly as clouds passed over. It was almost as if the sculptor were still here, re-enacting the creation itself, breathing his life's spirit into these clay sketches, some of them still wet and shiny, as if freshly made. As the life of any one of these sculptures might be regarded as extension of the sculptor's own, the life of the Warsaw Ghetto Monument as it was conceived and constructed by its maker is no less an extension. To know the monument, we might turn first to the human being—living in inhuman times—who created it.

Rapoport was born in 1911 to working-class Jewish parents in Warsaw. It was by financial necessity, he has said, not artistic choice, that he trained in childhood as an architectural apprentice and renovator of the King's Palace in Wilanova, just outside the city.[4] At age fourteen he applied to a drawing class at the municipal school of art, hoping to study portraiture. Told there were places left in sculpture only, he adapted quickly to his new medium. Almost immediately, Nathan gravitated toward the monumental aspect of sculpture. Its size, drama, and social vision all moved him on a purely visceral level. In fact, he fairly prospered as a young student, being commissioned frequently by local families to do busts of their children, so that he could eventually afford to enter the Academy of Art in Warsaw. Within months of enrolling at the academy on scholarships, Rapoport was winning prizes for his architectural, metal, and sculptural work. He eventually received prestigious scholarships from the academy to study at the Fine Arts Academy in Paris and to travel in Italy.

In Rapoport's words, there was nothing particularly Jewish or contemporary in his sculptures during this period; he felt neither very ethnic nor fashionable. From the outset, in fact, both his Jewish and artistic identities were subsumed in a more capacious social and political vision. As a member of Hashomer Hatsa'ir (Young Guard of the Zionist Left Wing) and the grandson of Hasidim (one grandfather was a cantor, the other a *shohet*), he remained acutely aware of the Second Commandment's prohibition against making graven images—even as he resisted the taboo as a young, progressive thinker. When he turned to art and sculpture, therefore, he felt compelled to locate his work outside of Jewish tradition altogether, turning to the classics and to Rodin for his models.

In abstraction, Rapoport found a way to circumvent the Second Commandment altogether, since signs, symbols, and forms were all permitted. At the same time, he regarded his artistic mission in political terms: if, as a Jew, he was also a socialist, then as an artist he would be a realist. In spite of his time in France among cubist, expressionist, and other abstract artists, and partly because of his time in Italy among the figurative sculptures of Michelangelo, Rapoport's passion for the human form and portraiture intensified. Later he would insist somewhat ironically that his own figurative work was actually (if paradoxically) modern: after all, he would say, his figurative works were essentially cubist and formal— triangles, circles, and cylinders; he merely "invested [them] with human soul."[5]

During the 1930s, Rapoport regularly continued to enter and to win competitions, two of which held consequences he could not have foreseen at the time.

In 1936, his sculpture *The Tennis Player* was awarded a prize at the Warsaw Academy of Art for a "Sports in Art" contest. But when the Polish government tried to submit his work to an international exhibition in Berlin that year as part of the Summer Olympics, Rapoport refused to let it be shown in Nazi Germany. This cost the sculptor his prize money, but it won him the respect of antifascist artists and commentators throughout Europe. Two years later, Rapoport placed third (after Jacques Lipchitz, who placed second) in a competition for a monument to Paul Vaillant-Couturier, the socialist mayor of Villejuif and editor of *L'Humanité*.

Having run short of funds in Paris, Rapoport returned to Warsaw in June 1939, three months before the Germans invaded Poland. With Warsaw under siege on 7 September 1939, the twenty-eight-year-old sculptor fled north and east with thousands of other young Poles in search of the Polish army, which was supposed to be regrouping in the forests between Warsaw and Bialystok. After almost two weeks on foot, however, he found only more refugees, mostly Jewish. Though Russia was technically allied with Nazi Germany at this point, her borders with Poland were open to Jewish refugees, who could either pay for sanctuary or provide skills and labor deemed valuable by Stalin at the time. Identified as an artisan, Rapoport entered the Russian zone and continued to Bialystok, where he was invited to join a collective of 120 other Jewish artists who had fled the Nazis. Rapoport recalls that during his short stay on the collective, he felt he had been liberated by the Russians, who now fed, clothed, and housed him—all so that he could continue drawing and sculpting.

Later that year, members of the Communist party Arts Committee from Minsk came to Bialystok looking for artists and works for an upcoming exhibition entitled "Ten Years of Art from Byelorussia." Upon visiting the collective in Bialystok, the committee remarked Rapoport's work and so requested the artist's portfolio. They were as impressed, it seems, with the fiery political correspondence between the artist and the government concerning his *Tennis Player* and his prize in the Vaillant-Couturier competition as they were with his sketches and busts. The committee invited Rapoport to Minsk, where they installed him in a studio with another Jewish artist at work on a commissioned statue of Stalin. Rapoport relates that his new comrade-in-arts had been at work on the monument for three years, finishing everything but Stalin's head. The committee had rejected every head the sculptor submitted, fearing that if Stalin were displeased by his sculpted head, it might cost them their own. The sculpture was never finished.

This lesson in artistic discretion was not lost on Rapoport, nor could it have been far from mind throughout his ensuing career as state sculptor in Russia.

But in light of the Nazi assault on the Jews in Poland, he had come to regard himself as both survivor and beneficiary of the Soviet arts committee. In addition to submitting several pieces to the "Ten Years of Art in Byelorussia" exhibition, Rapoport commenced work on a model of liberated Polish and Jewish prisoners, which he hoped to turn into a monument one day. It was during this period that the second secretary of the Party, Kulagin, visited Rapoport's studio in Minsk, liked what he saw, and commissioned the first of several state projects.

This interlude could not last, however. When the Germans attacked Russia and overran Minsk in 1941, Rapoport and his wife were evacuated to Alma Ata, near Tashkent. While his wife was forced to stay behind, the sculptor was drafted into a labor battalion and shipped to Novosibersk. Priorities had changed, it seems, and the demand for state artists suddenly gave way to the the need for strong backs. After five months in the labor camp, Rapoport learned that his former patron, Kulagin, had also come to Novosibersk, now as the Party's first secretary. When Rapoport called his office, a woman answered in Yiddish-inflected Russian and promptly arranged a meeting between the Jewish artist and Kulagin. The first secretary was so horrified by the sculptor's deteriorating condition that he pulled Rapoport out of the labor camp and situated him once again in an expansive art-ist's studio in Novosibersk. Rapoport was supplied with great stores of food and vodka, the latter serving as currency in the wartime economy for clay, plaster, and tools. Liberated yet again, now from the liberators themselves, Rapoport re-paid his debt as recommissioned state sculptor. His new role in the war effort was straightforward: he would set in bronze and stone all the forms and faces designated worth remembering by the state. His numerous busts of Russian gen-erals, partisans, and workers—all heroes of the Patriotic War—are scattered to this day throughout the former Soviet Union. Although the official aim of these busts was to reproduce assorted partisans' and workers' likenesses, it was clear to all—especially to the artist—that their actual subject was heroism itself.

During his work as sculptor of People's Heroes, Rapoport continued to visualize and sketch various historical monuments: first to the liberation by the Russians of political and Jewish refugees, and then, amid further reports from Europe be-tween 1941 and 1943, to the deportation and massacre of Jews. His first model— long since lost—for a monument to the destruction of Polish and Russian Jewry consisted of a huddled family watching a young girl being led away by German soldiers. Still grasping his own condition as both political and Jewish émigré, Rapoport continued to mix his sets of archetypal figures; at this point in the sculptor's iconic lexicon, there seemed to be only the heroic and the victimized, one political, the other Jewish.

In the midst of these peregrinations and monumental sketches in late spring 1943, news of the Warsaw Ghetto insurrection reached Rapoport in Siberia. Nothing had ever moved him like this before: he lived only so that he might commemorate such an event, which he regarded as both a socialist and a Jewish revolution. Since all of his early sketches and maquettes remained in Siberia, we don't know what Rapoport's initial sculptural responses were. He described them as impossibly romantic and idealized, reflecting only a vague notion of events in Poland. Traveling to Moscow expressly to acquire more information, he met with the historian Ber Mark, who was receiving reports almost daily from the Jewish Antifascist Committee of the Soviet Union.

The Warsaw Ghetto Uprising

Since part of my aim is to reassert the Warsaw Ghetto Monument's relationship to events, I have relied on Mark for most of the following account of the uprising. In this way, we can keep in mind that what Rapoport knew of the uprising depended on how he knew it, and that, as his knowledge of events informed his memorial conception, it also contributed to our public memory of events as crystallized in the monument.[6]

Officially established on 2 October 1940 in a decree by Ludwig Fischer, SS governor of the Warsaw District, the Warsaw Ghetto was intended as both city-scaled concentration camp and transit center for Jews on their way to death at Treblinka. As was the strategic wont of the Germans, they informed the Jewish community of this edict ten days later, on Yom Kippur, to invest it with appropriate symbolic gravity. Within weeks, the Germans erected thirty miles of wall, ten feet high and topped with broken glass and barbed wire, around the Ghetto, located in what had been largely the Jewish slum section of Warsaw. In addition to its original 50,000 inhabitants, by April 1942 the Germans had crammed into the Ghetto another 500,000 Polish Jews, including 150,000 deportees from outlying provinces and *shtetlach*. Between slave labor and shootings, disease and starvation, 100,000 Jews died in the Warsaw Ghetto by June 1942. The first phase of the annihilation of Warsaw Jewry—starvation—as decreed and prosaically calculated by Fischer included both its means and its literal end: "The Jews will die from hunger and destitution, and a cemetery is all that will remain of the Jewish Question."[7] In this vision, the Ghetto would eventually be annexed by the adjoining Jewish cemetery.

After two years of concentration and starvation in the Ghetto came the Great Liquidation: in six weeks between 22 July 1942 and 12 September 1942, the Germans deported 310,322 Jews from the Ghetto to Treblinka, where they were gassed to the last child. Though a number of escapees returned in the first week to warn of the massacre that was under way, the Judenrat (Jewish council appointed by the Germans) dismissed these reports in favor of fabricated letters purportedly written by Jews resettled in eastern labor camps. When the enormity of this liquidation became clear by the end of August, the Ghetto's Antifascist Bloc— composed of Hashomer Hatsa'ir activists from the Zionist left wing, Po'alei Zion (Workers of Zion), Dror, He'halutz, and the Polish Workers party—transformed itself into the Jewish Fighting Organization (Zydowska Organizacja Bojowa) and replaced the discredited Judenrat as central authority in the Ghetto. This mostly young resistance coalition had hitherto deferred to the authority of their elders. But with the proportions of the catastrophe horribly clear, they moved at once to overturn the order: from now on, they declared, Jewish groups would no longer administer their own decimation, but would only rise in their defense.

The beginning of the Warsaw Ghetto revolt thus came not with the uprising itself the following year, but with the coalescing of all resistance groups during that bloody July into the Jewish Fighting Organization. Traditionally explosive rivalries between right- and left-wing Jewish political groups would give way to the active defense of all Jews—except those who either collaborated or refused to recognize the danger of traditional responses. Suffused in political manifestos and rhetoric from the left and right, all of these groups perceived at the outset that this could not be just an uprising of Jews against Nazis, but a revolt of new fighting Jews against the old passive order. In fact, the composition and aims of the Jewish Fighting Organization accurately reflected the intensely political atmosphere in which it was formed. Days before the Ghetto newspaper *Der Oifbroi* (The Ferment) had described Jewish resistance as an extension of a larger revolution in Europe,[8] the daily news organ of the Anti-Fascist Bloc, *Der Ruf* (The Call), was also exhorting "the Jewish masses" to rise: "Jewish people! Jewish workers! Jewish youth! Gather your forces and pool them for battle! Stand united shoulder to shoulder in a common front against fascism.Only destruction of the Nazi war machine by antifascist armies together with the masses of oppressed peoples will finally put an end to our enslavement and lead to full social and national redemption of the Jewish masses!"[9] The Antifascist Bloc would rise here not as Maccabees only, but also as workers, with whom they allied themselves in figure and in deed.[10]

Where the Antifascist Bloc had called repeatedly on "the Jewish masses" to rise up against the Nazis throughout 1941 and 1942 and to initiate a battle for both national and economic liberation, the right-wing Yiddisher Militerisher Farband (Jewish Military Alliance of Betar Revisionists) perceived itself primarily as a militant Jewish self-defense group. These two principal factions reflected the Ghetto fighters' dual inspiration as part of an international revolutionary movement and as a self-defense movement. The ultimate mixing of Jewish and proletarian figures in Rapoport's monument may thus have been as inevitable as the mixed identities of the fighters themselves. That the twenty-four-year-old commander of the Jewish Fighting Organization and leader of the revolt, Hashomer Hatsa'ir activist Mordechai Anielewicz, would come to emblematize all the fighters becomes all the more intriguing, given the explosive political rivalries at play. For just as he identified as a fighting Jew only insofar as he was also a Labor Zionist and socialist, using insurrection and revolution as his models, Anielewicz's ideological enemies on the right in the Farband fought alongside and under him as militant revisionists. The Farband was fighting primarily to save a remnant of the Jews for their homeland, not to bring about a new economic order. Anielewicz and the Fighting Organization saw each only as it facilitated the other. The fighters' senses of their Jewish, Zionist, and socialist identities were so intertwined as to make them inseparable in the sculptor's eyes.[11]

The first stages of rebellion came with the dismantling of the Judenrat, the emergence of a unified Jewish Fighting Organization, and the purging of traitors in the Ghetto. The armed struggle began on 18 January 1943, when a contingent of 800 Latvians and 200 SS entered the Ghetto without warning to begin rounding up the remaining 60,000 Jews. Although caught by surprise, the Jewish Fighting Organization forced the Nazis to withdraw from the Ghetto in a series of hit-and-run attacks that turned into full-blown street battles. Over the next three days, 1,000 Jews were killed fighting (nearly four-fifths of the Jewish Fighting Organization fighters) and 5,500 Jews were deported. But over 50,000 Jews remained, and both the Poles and Jews of Warsaw celebrated the success and significance of this resistance. "Beginning with January 18, the Jews of Warsaw have been in a state of permanent struggle against the Germans and their henchmen," Anielewicz wrote to the Polish Home Army headquarters. The Home Army immediately recognized the significance of this uprising for the one they were planning. On 25 February 1943, their information bulletin declared that "the echoes of the firings and explosions, which reverberated through the Warsaw ghetto in January, have been heard all over Poland."[12]

The actual date of the uprising's beginning, however, could never have carried the commemorative weight already assigned to the official date of the revolt's outbreak on 19 April 1943, the eve of Passover. Liberated from the strictures of an ancient paradigm, from waiting for God's intervention, the members of the Jewish Fighting Organization would now redeem themselves—as both Maccabees and socialists, Jews and workers. On the eve of Passover, when Jews celebrate God's deliverance of their forebears in the desert of exile, the Jewish Fighting Organization grasped fully that they were now their own deliverers. For the Germans' part, they had long recognized the strategic value in attacking on Jewish holy days: that Easter and Passover coincided in 1943 proved doubly fortuitous in that it inflamed the day's symbolic significance for both Jews on the inside and Poles outside the walls. Easter had always been a day of dread for Jews, a traditional day of blood libels and pogroms in Poland and Russia.

As Polish poet Adolph Rudnicki remembered it in his poem "Easter," the day of the uprising held special significance for the Poles gathering outside the Ghetto walls to watch and listen to the battles: "As soon as the words here heard, 'You may go, the mass is finished, halleluiah, halleluiah!' the congregations hurried from the overcrowded churches, their souls still aglow, all vernal, with freshly cut flowers in their hands, towards the walls to watch the spectacle. To watch Warsaw's Paschal spectacle."[13] This was to be a day of redemption all around: Christians redeemed by the sacrifice of their Jews in the Ghetto, Jews redeemed, if not by their God, then by themselves. For the Germans, there was the further inspiration of Hitler's birthday, 20 April, a day for delivering to their leader the present of a "Judenrein" (Jew-free) Warsaw.[14]

Full-pitched battles raged for six weeks after the opening skirmishes on 19 April. Six months after the last fighters had been buried in their bunkers or disappeared into the sewers, the ghetto rubble was a dangerous place for Nazi patrols. In all, SS Maj. Gen. Jürgen Stroop seemed able to account for over 50,000 Ghetto Jews captured or killed during the uprising. Almost all of the Jewish combatants died in fighting, while the remaining civilians captured were either shot on the spot or deported to their deaths in the camps. A handful of survivors escaped the Ghetto when the fighting was over and joined partisan groups and the Polish underground. "The Warsaw Ghetto is no more," Stroop declared. Depending on whether one relies on the Nazis' figures or those of the Polish Workers party, German losses during the uprising ranged from 16 dead and 85 wounded to 700 dead and 1,600 wounded. The precise number probably lies somewhere in between, close to the Polish Historical Association's estimate of 400 German dead and 1,000 wounded in the first ten days of fighting. As in all historical memory, the facts and their significance necessarily come to us intertwined, each represented in the figure of the other. Apart from Yugoslavia's national uprising, the Warsaw Ghetto revolt was the largest and longest armed resistance in Nazi-occupied Europe during World War II.[15]

The Monument

The first recorded call for a monument to the Warsaw Ghetto was issued not by the state, sculptor, or public—but by a poet. In his brilliant lament and manifesto "We, Polish Jews . . . ," the exiled Polish Jewish poet Julian Tuwim demanded such a monument exactly one year after the uprising—the interval in Jewish tradition between burial and tombstone dedication. Composed in New York in late 1943, immediately after news of the uprising reached Tuwim, the poem was circulated widely, reaching hundreds of thousands of Polish refugees in Russia by the following year, according to Ilya Ehrenburg.[16] Since the Polish text of the poem was published in Russia in 1944 by the Union of Polish Patriots, it seems certain that Rapoport knew of it: to what extent he may even have been inspired by it may never be known. Fittingly, Tuwim first read his poem publicly at the monument's dedication. His words were not engraved on the monument itself, but they might be said to be inscribed in the larger text of the memorial's performance:

> There also will be a Cross of the Ghetto—a deeply symbolic name. There will be the Order of the Yellow Patch, denoting more merit than many a present tinsel. And there shall be in Warsaw and in every other Polish city some fragment of the ghetto left standing and preserved in its present form in all its horror of ruin and destruction. We shall surround that monument to the ignominy of our foes and to the glory of our tortured heroes with chains wrought from captured Hitler's guns, and every day we shall twine fresh live flowers into its iron links, so that the memory of the massacred people shall remain forever fresh in the minds of the generations to come, and also as a sign of our undying sorrow for them.
>
> Thus a new monument will be added to the national shrine.
>
> There we will lead our children, and tell them of the most monstrous martyrdom of people known to the history of mankind. And in the center of this monument, its tragedy enhanced by the rebuilt magnificence of the surrounding city, there will burn an eternal fire. Passersby will uncover their heads before it.[17]

Whence, then, the original inspiration for the Ghetto Monument? In the poet's imagination, it had already come to exist. The history of the uprising and its perceived significance, the sculptor's own life and lost home, and the poet's lament all seem to have moved the stone that became the monument.

The specific form of Rapoport's early maquettes is not surprising, given his source of historical information (Ber Mark and the Jewish Antifascist Committee of Moscow), his vocation as state sculptor of Soviet heroes, his patron's place in the Party, the committees to which he submitted his work, his training in the heroic school of socialist realism, and his own Jewish identification as a member of Hashomer Hatsa'ir. As he asked later, "Where was a Jewish sculptor supposed to turn for his memorial icons?" On the one hand, Rapoport was unencumbered

by a Jewish artistic tradition in which icons were few and forbidden. On the other hand, in Stalin's Russia, he would not be able, in Joseph Tchaikov's postrevolutionary words, to "stride through the arts of all nations and create a synthesis through the prism of his specific material."[18] In fact, Rapoport was at work in a particular time (war) and place (Russia), with specific historic and public icons available to him. Like the fighters themselves, Rapoport visualized the uprising in both Jewish and proletarian figures, each embodied in the other. Since any proposal he made would have to be approved by the Arts Committee, it seems clear that in addition to his own political view of the uprising, he must have been haunted by the vision of Stalin's unfinished bust. It may not have been merely a matter of appeasing the authorities, but he must have anticipated both of his prospective audiences—government and public.

The art historical irony begins when Rapoport submitted his first model to the committee. Condemned by some postwar critics as being too Stalinist and not Jewish enough, Rapoport's monument was rejected by Stalin's own bureaucrats as "too narrow in conception, too nationalistic"—that is, too Jewish. Having never before had a project turned down by the authorities, Rapoport appealed for help to Ilya Ehrenburg, the Jewish-Soviet journalist and propagandist. Ehrenburg listened sympathetically but helplessly: *The Black Book of Soviet Jewry*, the literary memorial to the massacre of Russian Jewry which he coedited—originally

Original clay maquette of Nathan Rapoport's Warsaw Ghetto Monument, ca. 1947, frontal view. Photo: Courtesy of Estate of Nathan Rapoport.

Clay maquette of the bas relief, reverse side of monument, ca. 1947. Photo: Courtesy of Estate of Nathan Rapoport.

commissioned by Stalin to attract American Jewish sympathy and support—had also been denied production because it was too Jewish.[19] The authorities bought both the *Black Book*'s manuscript and Rapoport's maquette—possibly to ensure that they never be produced in Russia. The rejection so stung the young sculptor that he retreated empty-handed to Novosibersk in mid-1943 and vowed to continue the project.

Rapoport remained in Novosibersk until early 1945, completing projects for the state and continuing to modify his Warsaw Ghetto Monument. Since he could not know whether he would ever return to Poland, it is likely that official criticism and potential review committees continued to weigh upon the monument's evolving conception. At the end of the war, Rapoport and his family returned to Moscow, whence he was repatriated to Warsaw in early 1946. Upon arriving there, he asked the Warsaw Jewish Committee whether they might consider building a monument to the uprising and destruction of the Ghetto. They had not only considered such a monument, they replied, but had already received and rejected a submission from a local Polish artist. What did this proposal look like? Rapoport asked. "Two hasidim hoeing potatoes," came the reply, whereupon Rapoport unwrapped a small plaster cast of his own monument—smuggled out of the Soviet Union—which was accepted forthwith.

The Jewish Committee then asked whether the sculptor had a location in mind. Rapoport was adamant: the only possible site would be that of the uprising itself, where the first shots had been fired and Anielewicz had died in his bunker. In fact, the committee had already marked the site of the bunker in 1946 with a large red sandstone disc placed in a flower bed, inscribed to the Jewish Fighting Organization, and so they agreed to build the Ghetto Monument nearby.

Before taking the proposal to the Warsaw Arts Committee, however, Rapoport and the Jewish Committee needed almost a year to find funding for it. A former ghetto activist and survivor, Adolph Berman, made an initial bequest, which was supplemented by the Jewish Committee and the Joint Distribution Committee. When the city Arts Committee finally considered the monument and site, however, they demurred. Architects and planners did not know if Warsaw would be rebuilt on the site of its destruction; plans were afoot to relocate the Polish capital altogether, across the Vistula River near the intact Praga section of Warsaw.

City planners also wondered whether, with materials and resources so desperately short, they could afford politically to reconstruct the entire city around a Jewish monument. Sensitive to Stalin's hostility to the Jews, they feared for their own future at the hands of the newly established—and Russian-controlled—unicameral parliament. Among the committee members, Rapoport recognized one of his former professors of sculpture; other members included Party officials and former partisans who sympathized with what they regarded as the leftist roots of the uprising and its memorializer. After several days' deliberation, the Warsaw Arts Committee accepted the proposed memorial, but only under the condition that it be unveiled on the fifth anniversary of the uprising, 19 April 1948, now less than a year away. For, as they hinted darkly, given an unpredictable political climate and increasingly tight borders, they could not guarantee permission after that date.

With no studio space left standing in Warsaw—much less working materials or a foundry—Rapoport left for Paris to turn his plaster model into bronze statuary. Instead of setting immediately to work, however, he spent his first several weeks in Paris familiarizing himself with the nascent art of postwar Europe. As a figurative sculptor, Rapoport realized that his place in the contemporary art scene had always been marginal. But after his years as socialist realist bust maker in Russia, both his style and his aesthetic impulse seemed to belong to a completely different era. The more abstract and, in his view, nihilistic his peers' work had become, the more figurative and coherent his own mission as prospective witness seemed to him. Reluctantly, he visited his old mentors at the Academy of Fine Arts and showed them his project design. Even though they reassured him and even applauded his concept, Rapoport chose to insulate himself from further contemporary scrutiny and literally closed the door to his studio before going to work. "Could I have made a stone with a hole in it and said, 'Voilà! The heroism of the Jews'? No, I needed to show the heroism, to illustrate it literally in figures everyone, not just artists, would respond to. This was to be a public monument, after all. And what do human beings respond to? Faces, figures, the human form. I did not want to represent resistance in the abstract: it was not an abstract uprising. It was real."[20] So, using kibbutznikim as his models—that is, live heroes of the Yishuv in Palestine who were living in Paris after the war— Rapoport set out to make, in his words, "a clearly national monument for the Jews, not a Polish monument. I wanted to show the Polish people who we really were." Who "we really were" would depend, of course, on Rapoport's own identity as it was refracted through his mixed self-mythography as Jew, socialist, and sculptor of heroes.

As Rapoport began his work in Paris, a survivor and architect, Mark Leon Suzin, was commissioned to design and construct the base of the monument in Warsaw. Suzin planned at first to clear the mountain of rubble from the monument's site at the corner of Zamenhoff and Gesia streets, the latter already renamed M. Anielewicz Street, and to anchor the monument solidly in the ground. With no mechanical equipment at their disposal, however, architect and assistants undertook this clearing by hand, a broken stone at a time. After two weeks' work without discernible effect, Suzin abandoned this approach and decided to incorporate the ruins into the monument's base by pouring tons of concrete and reinforcement over them. As the ruins settled beneath the foundation, cracks later appeared in the monument's granite base, forcing the municipal authorities to reconstruct it in 1959.

At the end of 1947, while the foundry was casting the bronze part of the sculpture in Paris, Rapoport and Suzin traveled to Sweden in search of granite for the monument's retaining wall. The Jewish Agency in Stockholm directed them to the best quarry in the area, where they discovered a huge cache of perfectly cut labradorite granite blocks, ready to be shipped. "Where is this supposed to go?" they asked. They were informed that it had been ordered during the war by Arno Breker, the great German sculptor, for a monument in Berlin to commemorate Hitler's victory. Satisfied that the granite was in every way perfect for their own monument, sculptor and architect sent it directly to Warsaw.

One month before the official Warsaw unveiling, Rapoport's foundry in Paris wheeled out the bronze statuary for its critical debut the day before it was to be shipped: "This is a beautiful work . . . of intense pathos, lively, powerful, and

Sculptor Nathan Rapoport (middle) stands next to the labradorite granite blocks he found for his monument in a Swedish quarry, 1947. The granite had already been cut and stacked for Arno Breker, the German sculptor commissioned by Hitler to build a Nazi victory monument in Berlin. Photo: Courtesy of Sima Rapoport.

skillfully balanced," proclaimed Maurice Brillant, dean of Parisian art critics. He went on to suggest that its figures were painful, yet peaceful, evocative of Rodin and Emile Antoine Bourdelle, without being archaic. "It is pregnant with epic realism," Waldemar George wrote in the formerly clandestine resistance newspaper *Ce Matin*. "It goes to the heart of things and soars so high that it reaches symbolism." Other reviews followed suit: "A living symbol of ghetto resistance, treated with breathtaking lyricism and grandeur," according to Georges Pillement. "This is a grandiose creation alive with a mighty breath," in the words of Pierre Desquarque. "Nathan Rapoport shows himself exceptionally gifted, capable of recapturing the deeper meaning of heroic statuary."[21]

Aside from their unanimous praise, the most striking quality in these reviews was the critics' unwillingness to separate the work from the events being commemorated. In every case, they devoted as much space to descriptions of the Ghetto, the number of Jews killed, and the uprising as to the relief itself. Felt history and its public memory had not yet been riven by time but remained united in both artists' and critics' minds. Eyes that may have beheld actual events would now behold the memorial to them: memory of events was still almost visceral, so strong as to seem part of the monument itself. The link between events, memorial evocations, and viewers was critically palpable in 1948 in ways that are entirely lost to us now.

Only in Warsaw, however, would the same statuary be anchored literally in the destruction it commemorated. The journey between its debut in Paris and its unveiling in Warsaw transplanted the work from an aesthetic to a historical realm. Fearful that Soviet soldiers would stop the ninety pieces of statuary at the border if he shipped it overland, Rapoport sent it via waterway to Warsaw, where it arrived in the last week of March 1948, along with the cut stone from Sweden. This gave the Polish stonecutters in Warsaw, working from Rapoport's gypsum design brought from Paris, only weeks to carve the bas relief into the back of the monument before its unveiling on April 19. When Rapoport arrived in Warsaw, they had not finished, so together with five stone cutters, he carved the back side of the monument as the statuary in front was being installed.

On its unveiling, five years to the day after the first shots of the uprising were fired, Rabbi Dreistmann of Poland opened dedication ceremonies by reciting the mourner's Kaddish, joined by most of the twelve thousand survivors, visiting Jewish dignitaries, Polish politicians, and local spectators. According to witnesses and reporters, hundreds of flaming red banners of Socialist and Communist youth groups fluttered together overhead with blue-and-white star of David banners hoisted by Jewish and Zionist groups.[22] Wary of setting his makeshift altar and Holy Ark before such a monumental graven image, however, the rabbi kept the thirty-six-foot-high stone-and-bronze edifice covered discreetly with sheets during prayers. Only when speakers like Yitzhak Zuckerman, one of Anielewicz's surviving deputies then living in Palestine, ascended the platform was the monument itself unveiled. In his sensitivity to the spectacle of so many Jews praying before such an icon, the rabbi appears to have been prescient: for over the years, it has been the monument and its square (not the synagogue) that serves as a gathering place for both religious Jewish visitors from abroad and the largely unaffiliated young Jews in Warsaw. Ironically, it is as if the monument had retained the sense of sacred space created by the temporary Holy Ark and altar. For many young Polish Jews today, an annual visit to the monument to lay wreaths (not a traditionally Jewish ritual) on 19 April has become their only regular Jewish observance.[23]

Earliest sketches of the monument reflect both an insistence on Jewish themes and an emphasis on the figure of workers. Rather than trying to meld them into one set of figures, however, the sculptor joined them back to back, bound together by a free-standing wall of roughly hewn stone that would function both structurally and figuratively. As edifice, it literally supports the figures and meanings projected onto it; as metaphoric reference, it recalls the Ghetto wall that divided Warsaw's Jews from the rest of the city. And unlike other more abstract memorial forms such as the obelisk or pantheon, this free-standing wall resembles a great tombstone, with wreaths of flowers perpetually adorning its base. In Jewish custom, small pebbles and stones are piled into little heaps on its flat surfaces, only

to be swept off by groundskeepers. At night, the bronze figures come alive in the flickering light of *Jahrzeit* candles placed at their base, their shadows jumping and darting against the looming stone wall.

This wall's most significant resonance, however, has been almost entirely overlooked. For, as Rapoport explained, the wall was intended to recall not just the Ghetto walls, but the Western Wall (Kotel) in Jerusalem as well. Early photographs of his working maquette show that the granite stones were indeed conceived to be much more roughly hewn than in the final version, reminiscent of the giant blocks of the Kotel. These great stones would thus have literally supported and framed the memory of events in Warsaw in the iconographic figure of Judaism's holiest site, itself a monumental remnant of the Second Temple and, by extension, its destruction. We also see four *menorot*, not the final two, placed at each corner of the monument's base—another reference to the Temple Mount. Of all Jewish icons, the *menorah* in its visual resonance with the Maccabean *hanuki'ah* might be that most closely associated with classical Jewish resistance. As the Kotel has become the principal fragmentary icon of the Second Temple, the stones of this memorial would now suggest themselves as monumental remnants of the Warsaw Ghetto uprising.

Dynamited, torched, and then bulldozed by the Germans, the Ghetto had been

The figures of the Warsaw Ghetto Monument remained veiled during the rabbi's dedication speech. Moments later, it was uncovered to full military honors before some twenty thousand spectators, 19 April 1948. Photo: Courtesy Yad Vashem Photo Archives.

A few days after its unveiling in 1948, the Ghetto Monument remained the only standing structure in Warsaw's landscape of rubble. Photo: Courtesy of Estate of Nathan Rapoport.

demolished a block at a time. In 1948 all that remained was a moonscape of rubble, piled sixteen feet high, covering hundreds of acres. Anchored in this landscape of debris, the granite blocks in the monument appeared on its unveiling to rise out of the broken stones, emerging from them almost as congealed fragments of the destruction itself. As a singular tombstone rooted in this great burial mound, the monument seemed initially to draw its strength, massiveness, and authority from its solitariness. Its location reinforced the sense of its link to history as a metonymical fragment of the destruction it commemorates.

Today the monument still stands alone in a large, well-kept square, but it is now surrounded by block-style apartment buildings, which diminish its earlier monolithic impact. Instead of seeming to pull order together out of the mounds of rubble around it, even being vivified by these ruins, it appears from a distance as one rectangular block among many others. The trees, green lawns, and sunbathers during the summer combine to domesticate the memorial a little and to relieve some of the tension between its plastic, lifelike figures and massive granite base.

The seven figures on the monument's western wall facing the open square are classically, even mythologically drawn: fighting their way out of stone, out of the burning Ghetto, these heroically sculpted men and women are transformed from skeletal to legendary proportions. Together they would represent "all the people," at all stages of life. Except for one fallen youth at the lower right (a paean to the pathetic hero of World War I sculpture), the figures are rising to resist and protect

Frontal view of
the Warsaw
Ghetto
Monument's
fighters. Photo:
Courtesy of
Estate of
Nathan
Rapoport.

themselves. Each grasps a weapon of the sort found in the Ghetto: a muscular prophet figure on one knee picks up a rock; a young boy at the left clutches a dagger; a young woman at the right cradles a Kalashnikov rifle; the leader Aniele-wicz clenches a home-made grenade. Even the mother engulfed by flames raises her right arm defensively, as does the baby in her other arm. All are vulnerably exposed: none has armor or protective clothing of any sort, only a sheath of sculpted muscle. As others have noted, in her bared breast and pose, the woman clearly recalls Delacroix's Liberté and, by extension, the revolutionary insurrection she has come to symbolize in France.[24] In his bare chest, tattered clothes, and rolled-up sleeves, clutching his grenade almost like a hammer, Rapoport's Anielewicz is unmistakably proletarian, marching forth as both worker and partisan to lead his fighters.

The monument's dedication is inscribed in Hebrew, Yiddish, and Polish "To the Jewish People—Its Heroes and Its Martyrs," but to see the martyrs we must walk around to the stone bas relief on the shaded side of the monument. In numerical reference to the tribes of Israel, twelve stooped and huddled figures embody archaic, archetypal Jews in exile. Only three Nazi helmets and two bayonets barely visible in the background distinguish this expulsion from any other. Eyes to the ground, all trudge resignedly to their fate—except for a rabbi holding a Torah scroll in one arm, who looks up and reaches to heaven as if to beseech God. By his own admission, Rapoport clearly recalls Hirszenberg's *Golus*, which became, as David Roskies reminds us, "the first icon of Jewish suffering to gain a mass audience"—itself echoing the procession on the Arch of Titus.[25] As such, it was used by Rapoport as a recognizably public archetype for his newly deported Jews. And like the poet Avraham Sutzkever, who never portrays a German except as a type, Rapoport has chosen never to represent the faces of Nazis, instead referring to them only metonymically, by the tips of their bayonets, the distinctive slope of their helmets.

The result is a two-sided monument that represents two Jewish types, each to be viewed separately. But in addition to the narrative movement on each side of the wall (the martyrs marching laterally right to left, the heroes ascending vertically), I detect a movement between opposing sides within the core of the wall itself, from dark side to light. For as we see from a side view of the monument, the engraved martyrs recede into the granite and become invisible, as if absorbed into the stone. On the western side facing the open square, however, the heroes' profiles stand out in distinct relief. In this movement between sides, the ancient type seems to pass *into* the shaded wall only to emerge triumphantly out of the other side into the western light: one type is literally recessive, the other emergent.

The Monument's Life in Mind and Community

Memory is not merely passed down from generation to generation in the Warsaw Ghetto Monument, but is necessarily recast in the minds of each new generation at the memorial's base. Every official visitor, every tourist, every government ceremony and dissident counterceremony adds one more patina of meaning to the bronze and stone in this square—and, by extension, to the events commemorated here. This recasting of memory has not been uniform or continuous, however; until recently, the Ghetto Monument has led an altogether precarious life in the minds of local, non-Jewish Poles. To some extent, this reflects its dual life in two communities: one Jewish, the other Polish. Had a larger remnant of Polish Jewry survived in Warsaw, the monument might have retained a specifically Jewish voice. But in the center of a non-Jewish population regarding itself under still another foreign occupation, it has become a more universal focal point for its present community's memory.

In his early recollections of the Jewish uprising, Polish historian Jerzy Kirchmayer wrote that "the military importance of the Warsaw Ghetto Uprising is above all in its repercussions among the Polish people."[26] During the war and immediately afterward, Poles regarded the Jewish rebellion as inspiration for their

Bas relief on the reverse side of the Warsaw Ghetto Monument's martyrs. Photo: Monika Krajewska.

own uprising a year later. Over the years, however, they have found an increasingly mixed and contrary inspiration in the Ghetto Monument. For until its recent adoption as *place de résistance* by dissidents of all ranks and stripes, the monument was widely disdained by Poles as a place of resentment, not resistance. In the minds of many survivors of the 1944 Polish uprising, the Ghetto Monument recalled not the Jewish rebellion so much as the absence of a memorial to their own uprising.

Poles remember well the 1948 campaign in the Communist press to discredit the Home Army's role in the Warsaw uprising, the vilification of their national heroes as quasifascists. This led some to suspect that when authorities approved the Ghetto Monument, it was not only to substitute socialist heroes of the Jews for Polish heroes of the Home Army but, even worse, to expunge memory of the Red Army's passive role in the Nazis' brutal crushing of the rebellion. No monument remembers what all Poles will never forget: that while 180,000 Poles died in the 1944 uprising and the Germans razed the city a block at a time, the Red Army camped quietly across the Vistula River. A 1945 memorial statue of Russian soldiers dedicated to the Soviet liberators of Warsaw—*Brotherhood in Arms*—just over the river in the Praga section is thus dubbed by locals as "Monument to the Sleeping Soldiers." Though the Warsaw evening paper *Ekspres wieczorny* made the first proposal for a monument to the Polish uprising as early as 1946, and various memorial committees offered others in 1956, 1981, and 1984, political and aesthetic disagreements over every aspect of the monument—for example, its name and whether it should be devoted to the uprising itself or to the Home Army heroes—have paralyzed final production. Until August 1989, the only existing national memorial to the 1944 uprising—a Polish Nike, or Victory figure, ambiguously inscribed to "the heroes of Warsaw"—was held in ambivalent esteem as little more than a token gesture to remembrance, transcendent and confused in its classical reference to victory.[27]

Given his own political battles within the Jewish Fighting Organization, Mordechai Anielewicz might well have appreciated the bitter memorial wars waged at the foot of the Ghetto Monument every 19 April during the government's annual ceremonies. As it turns out, not even the most vigilant efforts by the state could save the monument from performing the memory of other, conflicting interests. Of course, any commemoration other than the official one undermines the authority of meaning—and its naturalness—imputed to events by the government. In response to the government's charge that competing commemorations at the Ghetto Monument aim only to exploit memory of the uprising for these groups' own causes, the sole surviving leader of the Ghetto uprising still in Poland, Marek Edelman, answered, "We came to the conclusion that it would be good to do something, not against the official commission, but parallel to it."[28] His group's remembrance of the Bundists shot by the Russians after the war was not supposed to displace the state's memory but, perhaps more dangerously still, to add to it. In this way, the overall effect would not be one clear memorial message, but a cacophony of competing voices.

Painfully aware of the need for a site to endow their own struggle with nationalist and collective identity, Solidarity trade union leaders have always been loudest in their demands for a monument to the 1944 uprising. Both the former Communist government and its opposition fully grasped the consequences of providing such a memorial site, a ready-made arena for the performance of contemporary resistance infused with the righteousness of past resistance. This became especially clear during the 1988 ceremonies marking the Ghetto uprising. "We commemorate this struggle today in a special way," then Solidarity leader Lech Walesa proclaimed, "because in this land, the land of so many uprisings, the uprising of the Jewish fighters was perhaps the most Polish of all uprisings."[29] In this conciliatory gesture, Walesa meant to enlarge the Poles' national sense of themselves to include memory of the Jews, to suggest that they were (and, by extension, still are) part of Polish heritage. By thus incorporating the Jewish rebellion into Polish national history, Walesa made the Ghetto uprising available to all Poles as a national figure of resistance, one with increasingly tangled consequences.[30]

Over the years, parallels between past, present, and prospective uprisings were encouraged in official Polish interpretations of the Ghetto Monument, even as they were carefully constrained. This was accomplished partly by the monument's central location in the city and partly by the government's canny incorporation of it into the national commemorative cycle. Challenged by Solidarity's gradual unionization of the Ghetto Monument since 1980, the government launched its own campaign to nationalize it after 1983. As the government seemed to recognize, the memorial space, if left vacant, would be filled by someone else's meaning and memory. The square surrounding the Ghetto Monument had thus become both a dangerous and a necessary memorial space for the state, whose best interest ironically was to preserve the memorial's literal reference to the Jewish uprising while assiduously avoiding its symbolic reference to current resistance. Every year the government seemed to fear that, left to its own devices, Solidarity might commemorate the Ghetto uprising not just by presenting speeches and wreath-laying ceremonies, but by actually re-enacting it. In fact, this is precisely what happened in 1988, when commemorations begun at the Ghetto Monument on 19 April ended in a strike at the Gdansk shipyards six weeks later.

This is why the government hopes that a recently dedicated memorial route

Dissidents from Poland's then-banned Solidarity union use the monument as a rallying point, 18 April 1983. Photo: AP/ Wide World.

DISSIDENTS RALLY AT WARSAW MEMORIAL: Supporters of the outlawed Solidarity union flash victory signs at an unofficial ceremony for victims of Nazi persecution. The police broke up the gathering. The monument honors those killed in the Warsaw Ghetto uprising 40 years ago. Page A3.

originating near the Ghetto Monument and running to the Umschlagplatz (site of the Jews' transfer to death-camp trains) will, in the words of the state press, "link the already existing monuments commemorating the martyrdom of the Jewish people, endow them with due rank, and include them in the symbolic landscape of Warsaw."[31] The monument is now joined deliberately to surrounding memorials by a path that leads from one memorial tablet to the next, a visitors' walking narrative that confers meaning on all parts of the route, each in light of the others. Memory begins here in front of a "Tree of Common Remembrance" dedicated both to Jews who perished and to Poles who died trying to rescue them; with Polish and Jewish memory seemingly unified, visitors turn to face the Ghetto Monument itself, the next station on this path. From here the trail continues with stops—nineteen in all—at syenite tablets commemorating specific heroes of the Ghetto, including Ringelblum and Korczak, and various fighters; after winding through several city blocks, the route ends at the new Umschlagplatz memorial, whence 350,000 Jews were deported to their deaths. As one node among others in a matrix of monuments devoted to remembering Polish history, the Warsaw Ghetto Monument would thus be incorporated into a national memorial landscape.

The tendency by Solidarity to figure its contemporary resistance in the memory of the Ghetto uprising was thus matched by the official move to represent memory of the Poles' averted genocide in the trope of the Jews' actual fate. The result is a reaffirmation both of the new Polish memory of Jews as fighters and of the Jews' destruction in Poland. In fact, with so few living and breathing Jews left in Poland, Jews have come to exist primarily in the twin memorial references embodied by the Ghetto Monument: as metonymies for destruction and heroism. "The uprising in the Warsaw Ghetto belongs to the history of both the Polish and the Jewish nations," the editors of Warsaw's *Trybuna ludu* write. "The present observances . . . occur at a time of wide upsurge of interest in Poland in the centuries-old Polish-Jewish history, in the role of Polish Jews in cultural, economic, and social life, *in our common fate. This also includes a growth of interest in the last stage of the common fate, prepared for the Jews and Poles by the Nazis.*"[32] As is already clear in Poland's many other memorials and museums to the time of Holocaust, the annihilation of Polish Jewry increasingly serves as the primary figure by which Poles have come to remember their own suffering during World War II.

Other national leaders and groups continue to adopt the monument as their fighting icon as well. The accompanying photographs recall a few of the heads of state who have visited the monument. To what and to whom is each of these people paying respects? How well do visitors remember the heroes of the War-

DER SPIEGEL

Cover of the German newsweekly *Der Spiegel*, showing Willy Brandt kneeling at the base of the Warsaw Ghetto Monument. It asks, "Should Brandt have kneeled?" Photo: Courtesy of *Der Spiegel*.

saw Ghetto uprising and to what extent are their own heroes now figured by the Ghetto fighters? Was Nehru remembering the Jewish fighters or his country's own independence a few years before? As clearly moved as Willy Brandt was on his historic and conciliatory visit to the monument on 7 December 1970, his German compatriots were more preoccupied by the propriety of such a gesture when they asked later, "Should Brandt have kneeled?"[33] In the midst of planning to bring Menachem Begin and Anwar Sadat together at Camp David, Jimmy Carter also visited the monument. Featured on the front page of the *New York Times* (31 December 1977), the president's pilgrimage of remembrance may have been intended as much to reassure worried Jewish leaders as to recall the uprising itself. When John Paul II returned to Poland as Pope, it was as a national hero that he visited the monument. Having remembered the Ghetto fighters, he was in turn remembered as a fighter in the Polish resistance.

In 1983, a delegate of the Palestine Liberation Organization laid a wreath at the monument and pronounced that "as the Jews were then justified to rise up against their Nazi murderers, so now are the Palestinians justified in their own struggle with the Zionists." Whether the PLO found actual or only rhetorical inspiration in the Ghetto uprising, during the Palestinians' intifada five years later in Gaza and the West Bank, another delegation of Palestinians laid a wreath dedicated in Polish "to those who perished in the Ghetto Uprising from those who perished

President Jimmy Carter bows his head in front of the Warsaw Ghetto Monument just before beginning his peace talks between Egypt and Israel, 31 December 1977. Photo: AP/Wide World.

Pope John Paul II visits the Warsaw Ghetto Monument in 1983. Photo: Courtesy of Estate of Nathan Rapoport.

in the Palestinian Uprising."[34] Ironically, the monument may finally allow this kind of appropriation, for even though the Ghetto uprising was conceived and carried out largely by Zionist groups within the Jewish Fighting Organization, no trace of the rebels' Zionist origins is evident in the monument itself. Were its figures more explicitly Zionist, the monument might hold significant new consequences for the kind of self-understanding it now generates in its Palestinian visitors.

In fact, the decision to recast the Ghetto Monument in Israel after 1967 came about partly amid fears that its Jewish life in Poland could not be guaranteed. During Poland's anti-Semitic purges following the Six-Day War, American Jews and Israelis worried that, as Polish Jews were being expelled from the Communist party and unions, Jewish meaning would be elided from the memorial landscape. It was not that anyone feared the actual dismantling of the monument; in being left to stand alone in an environment both hostile to and bereft of Jews, however, the monument's Jewish significance and character seemed threatened as never before. With this in mind, the American philanthropist and Warsaw survivor Leon Jolson commissioned a slightly modified reproduction of the monument to be installed at Yad Vashem in Jerusalem, where its Jewish national spirit would be preserved.

By the time the frontal relief had been installed in 1975, Rapoport's Anielewicz had already been adopted as an honorary Israeli archetype, reproduced on postage stamps, book jackets, tour pamphlets, and commemorative guides to Holocaust Remembrance Day programs.[35] Conceived by a nationalist sculptor, inspired by a Jewish uprising, this monument recalls simultaneously both the traditional weakness of Diaspora Jewry and the consequent need for organized defense, which was embodied first in the Warsaw rebellion and then again in the new Jewish state. In Israel, therefore, this cannot be a memorial to victims so much as to victory: it recalls the Jews' ultimate triumph over the Nazis in their survival and, in having risen at all, the Jews' victory over their own past responses to persecution. If, in being framed by the stones of the Kotel, Anielewicz and the Jewish Fighting Organization can be perceived as direct descendants of the Maccabees, then the Israel Defense Force can now see itself as directly descended from the Ghetto fighters. That a handful of these fighters lived to fight as well in Israel's War of Independence only reinforces the link between past and present heroism.

In effect, Rapoport has helped resolve the dilemma of Jewish monument makers working in a tradition with so few monumental icons. For he has in the end contributed to popular Jewish iconography its own icon of resistance and martyrdom. Located now in the matrix of Israeli memory at Yad Vashem on Har Hazikkaron

Members of Warsaw's local Jewish community gather in commemoration of the Ghetto uprising, 18 April 1986. Photo: Monika Krajewska.

(Remembrance Hill) in Jerusalem, the reproduction of the Ghetto Monument figures Holocaust memory in the images of heroes, even as it is in turn refigured by Israel's own wars. By uniting past and present heroism and resistance, the monument reciprocally invites Israelis to remember parts of their own war experiences in the image of the Ghetto uprising. In the monument's square at Yad Vashem, Israeli soldiers, new immigrants, and Baptist tourists alike linger before it. The tourists might be forgiven if they occasionally glance between bronze Ghetto fighters and young soldiers gathered nearby to fix them in analogue; after all, the soldiers themselves are bused to this square as part of their military education precisely to know themselves in light of past fighting Jews.

In fact, when the Ghetto Monument reproduction was unveiled, it memorialized only the heroes: the bas relief to the martyrs followed eighteen months later. Instead of emerging from actual blocks of Jerusalem limestone recalled by the monument's base in Warsaw, however, the Ghetto fighters are set against a red brick wall that recalls the Ghetto Wall, not the great stones of the Kotel. Moreover, unlike the back-to-back setting in Warsaw, the monument is opened up like a book to show both sides simultaneously, inviting the eye to follow the proces-

sion from archetypal martyrs from right to left to heroically rising fighters. Even
here the subtler movement within the stone of the Warsaw monument is recalled:
the martyrs' facade is recessed into the brick, while the adjacent fighters emerge
from it. Unlike the Warsaw version, however, Liberté's right breast is draped modestly in deference to Jerusalem's religious sensibilities, no longer quite as free as
she had been in Europe.

In several countries, one or two historical figures have come to embody memory
of the Holocaust period, each reflecting and affirming a nation's ethos and understanding of events. As Mordechai Anielewicz and Hannah Senesh—two who
rose to resist destruction—might exemplify national memory of the Sho'ah in
Israel, Elie Wiesel and Anne Frank figure popular American remembrance of the
Holocaust in images of victimization and hope. While *Sho'ah* and *gvurah* (Holocaust and heroism) are almost always twinned in Israel (as illustrated by Rapoport's monument, or the designation of Yad Vashem as "Martyrs' and Heroes'
Authority"), American memory of this period is most often figured by the Holocaust only. Even Yom Hasho'ah Vehagvurah (Day of Holocaust and heroism),
decreed by an act of the Israeli parliament in 1953 to fall on the twenty-seventh
of Nissan (the middle of the uprising period), is marked by the abbreviated Yom
Hasho'ah (Day of Holocaust) in America (see chapter 10). Aside from a much
modified version of the fighters at the Workmen's Circle Building in New York,
only the Ghetto Monument's bas relief of martyrs has been recast in America.
Bronze reliefs entitled *The Last March* taken from the original cast have been
reproduced at synagogues and seminaries in New York, Syracuse, and Dallas—
and are dedicated to the six million Jews who perished, without reference to the
monument's heroes.[36]

When Walter Benjamin observed that "even the most perfect reproduction of a
work of art is lacking in one element: its presence in time and space, its unique
existence at the place where it happens to be," he suggested two greater truths as
well: that part of the work of art is its particular time and place, and that even
though a work can be reproduced, once transported, its presence may not be re-
coverable.[37] Later in the same essay, Benjamin brings to our attention something
that we have considered at greater length: in new times and places, reproductions acquire new kinds of presence, new meanings and significance. The Warsaw
Ghetto Monument, in particular, has undergone as many personality changes as
it has reproductions in Israel and America. Depending on which part is reproduced, in what medium, and where, the monument remembers only heroes, only
martyrs, only Jews, or only Poles. The monument's image has become a kind of
memorial currency, an all-purpose iconographic tender, whose value fluctuates
in every new time and place.

Chapter 7   Broken Tablets

and Jewish Memory

in Poland

Sandstone is good
for honing scythes
so all that is left
is a rib of stone
here a foot of stone
a tibia
there a shinbone
a bone of sto
a shank of st

In an architectural impulse akin to the poet's broken epitaph, fragments of shattered Jewish tombstones have become the predominant iconographic figure by which public memory of the Shoah is constructed in Poland today.[1] Unlike the suspended sounds and broken lines in Jerzy Ficowski's poem, however, which we mend by completing the unfinished rhyme, memorial makers suggest that neither past worlds nor memory of them can be made whole again. For even as these remnants are gathered up and pieced together in Polish villages like Kazimierz, Przasnysz, and Wegrow, the fragments are not recuperated so much as reorganized around the theme of their own destruction. They represent a newly collected Jewish memory, retrieved piece by jagged piece in a form that emblematizes both the destruction and the impossibility of recovery. Rather than mending the words in a fissured epitaph, they preserve the break: in this way, broken tombstone monuments commemorate their own fragility, gather and exhibit the fragments *as* fragments, never as restored wholeness.

Broken tombstones and similar remnants of Jewish life in Poland have now become the loci around which contemporary memory assembles. In dark storerooms, or scattered over the countryside, such remnants remain inert and amnesiac. But gathered and consecrated, they project a specific public image of both the Jewish past in Poland and its destruction. The fragments may still be broken, but finally they are pieced together into some order, if only that which signifies disorder. I would like to explore here both the construction of Poland's "tombstone monuments" and how they embody Holocaust memory in a land nearly bereft of Jewish rememberers.

Emblems of brokenness have their own history in Jewish funerary tradition. The rent garment and broken artifacts of daily life have long served as communal signs of mourning, for example. Tombstone reliefs of broken candlesticks, or a splintered tree, or a bridge half torn away, are among several repeating images recalling life interrupted by death. In a gesture to this tradition, Polish architects not only incorporate stylized versions of the Jewish cemetery as a memorial motif, but often rend the monuments themselves.

In the expansive memorial at Treblinka, for example, perhaps the most magnificent of all Holocaust memorials, seventeen thousand granite shards are set in concrete to resemble a great, craggy graveyard. At the center of this landscape of fragments, an eight-meter-high obelisk of granite blocks stands cleaved from top to bottom. In fact, fifteen years after the end of the war, no memorial of any kind marked Treblinka, the deadliest of all death camps, where some 850,000 Jews were gassed and burned. In 1960, the road between Warsaw and Bialystok was still narrow and clogged with horse-drawn carts and herds of livestock; the trip from Warsaw could take five hours. The country was still rebuilding, and Treblinka was long regarded as almost too terrible a site even to visit. For even though the Germans had completely destroyed the camp in 1944, plowed it under and planted it over in pine trees and grain fields, sun-bleached bones and skulls still poked through the sandy earth as late as 1957.

Work on a mausoleum began and ended in 1958 at the former site of the gas chambers, and the land itself was cleared of loose remnants of the killing fields. Unsure of an adequate commemorative form, the Warsaw Regional Council called a national memorial competition for Treblinka. On 28 February 1960, the council accepted a preliminary design for Treblinka-I (a Polish labor camp) by Franciszek Strynkiewicz and another design for Treblinka-II (the killing center) by sculptor Franciszek Duszenko and architect Adam Haupt. In their early conceptual statements, the designers of the memorial declared that their aim would be to suggest iconographically the greatest of all genocidal cemeteries.[2]

Concrete
railroad ties
recall the tracks
that once fed
the death camp
at Treblinka,
Poland. Photo:
Donald
Woodman.

The memorial at Treblinka, designed by Adam Haupt and Franciszek Duszenko and dedicated in 1964, consists of seventeen thousand granite shards set in concrete around a twenty-six-foot obelisk. Photo: James E. Young.

Neighboring land would have to be bought from peasant farmers, and the construction costs were expected to be as much as fifteen million zlotys, most of which would come from the Warsaw Council, leaving nearly a million zlotys to be raised by public donations. But because the martyrdom of Poland's three million Jews was to be regarded as an integral part of the nation's martyrdom during the war, the Polish Ministry of Culture stepped in to sponsor the monument, along with an honorary committee headed by Prof. Jan Turski, a rector at Warsaw University. Between 1961 and 1964, hundreds of freight trains rolled slowly back into Treblinka, filled not with human cargo but with thousands of sharp granite stones. At the same time, a two-hundred-meter path of rounded cobblestones was laid parallel to a path of concrete railway ties symbolizing the tracks that once fed the death camp.

At the end of the line, the visitor steps into a huge expanse of open land, enclosed by trees. The broken obelisk stands in its center, surrounded by the immense graveyard of sharp-toothed stones set in slabs of concrete, several hundred of them bearing the names of Jewish communities in Poland destroyed during the Holocaust. In 1978, on the hundredth anniversary of Janusz Korczak's birth, a stone inscribed with his name was set amid the thousands of others, the only one dedicated to an individual. Every year, on the anniversary of his deportation to Treblinka, Korczak is remembered here with freshly cut flowers and colorful wreaths, some with bunting printed in Polish, some in Hebrew.

Like sentries to the memorial area, a separate row of granite stones two to three meters high stands before the clearing. On each one is inscribed the name of a country, the national homes of Jews who perished at Treblinka—Poland, France, the USSR, Germany, Yugoslavia. Thus the martyrdom of the Jews seems at first to be fragmented into that of so many nations.

But the Jewish identity of victims at Treblinka is not displaced altogether. After a direct narrative reference to Jewish victims at the entrance, the Jewish character of the memorial only grows more subtly iconographic: a menorah is carved into the cap of the obelisk on its reverse side; jumbled together and protruding in all directions, the densely packed stones bear striking resemblance to the ancient Jewish cemeteries in Eastern Europe. At the base of the obelisk, a stone plaque reads from top to bottom in Yiddish, Russian, English, French, German, and Polish: "Never again."[3]

Another striking example, on the former site of the Plaszow concentration camp near Krakow, displays a gargantuan stone sculpture of six sharply etched figures in mourning, cut front to back, edge to edge, by a great horizontal gash at about lapel level. As reflected in both figurative and abstract Holocaust monuments in Poland, as well as in the broken tombstone monuments themselves, this contemporary memorial motif appears to descend directly from ancient Jewish funerary images.

Immediately after the war, some 250,000 Polish Jews returned to find themselves aliens in communities that may have been 50 percent Jewish before the war. With the synagogues destroyed or gutted, survivors coming home to Sandomierz, Lukow, and Siedlce, among other small towns, walked out to their cemeteries to mourn their murdered families. But many returnees found only ruins: even the mourning places had been demolished. In wiping out a people, the Nazis not only destroyed those who would have preserved the memory of past generations; they also took pains to obliterate the spaces where the murdered might be remembered. Some of the oldest cemeteries, like that of Warsaw's Praga neighborhood, where tens of thousands lay buried, were literally scraped off the face of the earth. In other instances—recalling the treatment of Jews at the hands of Germans—the tombstones were machine-gunned, clubbed into pieces by sledgehammers, ground into dust. Or the *matzevoth* were put to work: uprooted, carted off, and used to pave roadways, sidewalks, and courtyards. Those left in place often bore scars inflicted by other vandals, their graves robbed by

The obelisk in the center of the memorial at Treblinka is riven by a great crack. The inscription reads, "Never again," in Polish, Yiddish, Russian, English, French, and German. Photo: James E. Young.

The memorial at Treblinka in the winter. Photo: Monika Krajewska.

Jumbled together and protruding in all directions, the stones at Treblinka recall to Polish eyes the sense of a Jewish cemetery. A menorah is carved into the cap of the obelisk. Photo: Monika Krajewska.

The only individual commemorated at Treblinka is a Polish-Jewish hero, Janusz Korczak, the head of a Jewish orphanage who chose to accompany his charges to Treblinka, where they were all murdered. Photo: Adam Kaczkowski.

The monument at Plaszow, near Krakow, designed by Ryszard Szczypczyski and Witold Ceckiewicz, 1964. Photo: Monika Krajewska.

A survivor returns to his hometown, Chmelnik, after the war to find a devastated Jewish cemetery. Photo: Courtesy of YIVO Institute for Jewish Research.

Vandalized
Jewish
cemetery in
Szydtowiec.
Photo: Monika
Krajewska.

local Poles searching for buried gold. Without a Jewish community to maintain them, the cemeteries crumbled, and many were eventually buried beneath the earth's own cover of trees and tall grass. Still others were paved over for highways and playgrounds.[4]

The returning survivors set about reconsecrating these sites, a memorial-work necessary before memory could begin. Occasionally this meant gathering up pieces of matzevoth and piling them into great, loose heaps, as in Siedlce and Lodz. Other survivors in Lukow, Sandomierz, and Myslenice built pyramids and pastiche obelisks out of the scattered tombstone fragments. In Lodz, they began but never finished such a monument. Near the center of this, the largest Jewish graveyard in Europe, hundreds of tombstones still lie stacked in immovable piles. They were gathered shortly after the war by survivors who hoped to build a

Returning survivors design and build a monument in the Jewish cemetery of Siedlce after the war, using fragments of broken tombstones. The monument was destroyed by local Poles some twenty years later. Photo: Courtesy of YIVO Institute for Jewish Research.

Tombstones in the Jewish cemetery of Lodz, gathered by survivors after the war and stacked in preparation for a tombstone monument that was never built. Photo: Monika Krajewska.

tombstone pyramid like those at Sandomierz and Lukow. Not being able to agree on a final conception, the Jews who eventually left Lodz once more had also to abandon their memorial project. When I came across these layered sheaves of matzevoth forty-five years later, I couldn't help but see them still as a memorial: not to the destruction itself, but to vacated memory. The unerected monument reminded me of one consequence of so vast a destruction: with no one left to preserve the memory of those who came before, memorial activity ceases altogether, except in the eyes of visitors.[5]

In many towns, not even one survivor returned to mourn: formerly Jewish districts were either taken over by Polish neighbors or left to crumble. In Ostrowitz, what had once been the Jewish neighborhood—the center of the village—was torn down a board at a time by the war-ravaged townspeople and then left untouched for forty years, a haunted no-man's land. Gradually, a thick forest began to cover the empty center of Ostrowitz; today the town itself seems built in a circle around this tangled wood. Without intending it, the town has created its own memorial wood, the town's very shape now commemorating its lost Jewish center.

For years, the Jewish cemetery in another small town also remained relatively untouched for years after the war. After marching Wegrow's Jews fifteen kilometers off to the Sokolow Podlaski train station for transport to Treblinka, the Nazis returned to liquidate the remaining thousand Jews who had hidden themselves along the way. All were shot and then buried at the Wegrow Jewish cemetery, whence their bodies were exhumed and taken to be burned just north of town, a place the locals nicknamed "Little Treblinka." During the 1960s, when Wegrow's authorities planned an expansion of the town, they decided to take over what was left of the Jewish cemetery—and at the same time to memorialize the their lost Jews, who had once made up over half of the town's fourteen thousand citizens.

Work crews gathered both human and tombstone remains into one site at a corner of the former cemetery, ravaged first by the Germans, then by time. Here a memorial designed by local architect Wieslaw Ratajski was unveiled in September 1982, the fortieth anniversary of the Wegrow Ghetto liquidation. Though still a small town, with more dirt than paved roads, Wegrow's citizens gladly, even proudly, show visitors the monument. A local truck driver led us several miles off his route to show us the memorial: two polished tablet-shaped stones inscribed in Polish and Hebrew, set atop a granite platform and surrounded by a semicircle of remnant tombstones from the cemetery, several rows deep. The stones' broken edges had been softened by a local stone mason, their Hebrew-inscribed texts weathered almost beyond legibility. Facing in toward the tablets,

an ark of sorts, the stones look like so many battered congregants, standing shoulder to shoulder. The two new tablets of the law now read, in Polish and Hebrew: "The world will remember the Jews killed at the hands of the Nazis in the years of Shoah, 1939–1944."

By turning to the only materials available—broken bits of matzevoth and mortar—survivors and community volunteers in Krakow and Warsaw did not restore the sites of remembrance so much as create new ones, formalizing the destruction. The collage retaining walls are made of wedges of black syenite cutting into shards of white marble. Epitaphs are preserved in pieces, with chunks of the aleph-bet splintered in all directions: Polish script breaks into Hebrew, sentences are cut off midword, midletter. When legible, the epitaphs read stammeringly, like this one from the wall in Krakow:

> Here lies our teach rab
> Benjamin Zeev Wolf the son of Ga
> of blessed mem

A broken-tombstone retaining wall in the Warsaw Jewish cemetery. Photo: James E. Young.

Mind pours itself into the gaps between fragments, like so much mortar, to bind the remnants together. We are reminded that memory is never seamless, but always a montage of collected fragments, recomposed by each person and generation.

Where the Germans could destroy synagogues, they always did: every last one of Poland's old and distinctive wooden synagogues was burned to the ground. Once in a while, they also exerted themselves in razing the sturdier masonry synagogues. The caretaker of the Jewish cemetery in Miedzyrzecz Podlaski relates that it took a German demolition unit more than one month to level the eighteenth-century synagogue there.[6] But in most cases, these stone structures were so well built—and useful to the Germans—that nearly all of Poland's masonry synagogues remain standing to this day. Without Jewish congregations to inhabit them, most have been converted to some other use: a hotel in Biecz, a bakery in Gorlice, a factory in Radymno, a garage in Ostroleka.[7]

The synagogue in Kazimierz on the Vistula, one of the oldest examples of masonry architecture in Poland, still stands just off the market square in the center of town: it is now the Vistula Cinema. Though not quite half of its five thousand inhabitants before the war were Jewish, this picturesque village is remembered by many Poles as essentially a Jewish town. Merchants today still speak a smattering of Yiddish learned from their Jewish neighbors. Scholem Asch once said that in Kazimierz even the Vistula River spoke to him in Yiddish. As is the case, however, for every former Jewish village in Poland, only a few cultural traces remain: some Yiddish idioms, a handful of buildings, the cemetery, and now a memorial to the town's murdered Jews.

On a Sunday afternoon during the summer of 1988, the market square in Kazimierz was alive with the colors of women's flowered skirts, farmers' fruits and vegetables, and dozens of children at play. My Polish friend asked a young girl selling ice cream where the synagogue was. She pointed directly across the open square and replied matter-of-factly, "The cinema is there." No, not the cinema, my friend repeated, the synagogue is what we're looking for. "Yes, I know," the young girl looked up, "but the synagogue is the cinema." We walked across the square to number 7 and passed through a narrow alley where we found an old stone building set just behind the marketplace, its facade covered by scaffolding. Next to the open wooden door, teenagers crowded around a small window box with a sign announcing movie times for the Vistula Cinema. Inside the lobby, at the door into the sanctuary, a ticket taker stood instead of a shammes, and moviegoers streamed in like congregants on the high holidays.

Entering, we found girls still sitting upstairs in the women's gallery, but now with their sweethearts. The windows were boarded up on the outside and plastered over on the inside to keep light from coming in. The walls were whitewashed and clean, and the original wooden floor was polished to a shine. No one seemed to mind when I pulled the screen slightly away from the wall to peek behind it: the frame for the holy ark was intact. The graceful arches, cool limestone walls, and masonry all combined to frame the film in progress. The ark might be covered by the movie screen and its images, but devoted viewers still faced in its direction. Later, we overheard teenagers asking each other about the film they had seen the night before at "the synagogue." What the villagers may have forgotten, their language still remembers, if only as a dead metaphor.

The friendly manager insisted that the decision to put a cinema in the synagogue was made with the Jews in mind. "After all," he said, "this could not be just a restaurant or work space, but a monument to culture. Only a museum or music hall would have been more appropriate." In fact, he continued, the initial aim of the city planners in 1953 had been to restore the synagogue to its prewar condition and turn it into a Jewish museum. But because there were no Jews left to visit the synagogue even as a museum, and no film house in Kazimierz, the planning committee decided to turn it into a cinema and all-purpose auditorium. Just recently, he told us proudly, UNESCO had held an international symposium there on the world's dwindling supply of drinking water. He couldn't recall whether the speakers knew of the auditorium's origin. A plaque on the back of the building, dedicated in 1985 to the Jews of Kazimierz murdered by the Germans, does not mention that this had been the community's house of prayer.

With nothing but this tablet to remind visitors of the town's Jewish past, the imposing tombstone-wall monument just outside town, on the road to Szreniawy, is all the more startling. On one of their photo expeditions, Monika and Stanislaw Krajewski, two members of the Citizens' Committee for the Preservation of Jewish Monuments in Poland, met with Kazimierz architect Tadeusz Augustynek, who had been commissioned by the town to build a monument at the Jewish cemetery. He showed them his design for a great pastiche wall, three meters high and twenty-five meters long, composed of salvageable tombstones from the cemetery, and torn vertically by a jagged crack. Anxious to see this conception realized, the Krajewskis spent most of the summer of 1983 sorting and cleaning tombstones and helping to construct the monument.[8]

According to Monika Krajewska, the first step involved a literal digging up of the past, a memorial archeology that reminded all involved of what was lost. It had been nearly forty years since tombstones in the Jewish cemetery were uprooted by the Germans and laid as paving stones in the town's Franciscan Monastery, converted into Gestapo headquarters. People in Kazimierz now recall with satisfaction that the Polish laborers had taken pains to lay the inscribed sides of the stones face-down in in a graded layer of soft dirt, which saved the epitaphs from being erased beneath the feet of pedestrians and wheels of carts. But one man remarked that with the blank side up, villagers were not reminded of the source of these paving stones every time they walked on them.

Dug out of the streets by a few of the same laborers who had laid them forty years earlier, the stones were first gathered into great leaning heaps in the town square. They were then transported back to the nearly empty Jewish graveyard. The Krajewskis spent most of that August marking tops and bottoms of gravestones and separating those of the men from those of the women. Since men and women had been buried separately here, the architect and his helpers chose to preserve this separation in the monument itself: not to affirm an archaic custom, they said, but to respect this particular community's tradition.

In Poland, a careful balance is constantly being struck between building new structures and preserving the remains of old ones. With the country chronically plagued by shortages of building materials, no one was surprised to learn that there would not be enough mortar to finish the monument that summer. The following winter, snow and rain washed off the marks distinguishing women's

from men's tombstones. It wasn't until a year later, in August 1984, that more materials were forthcoming. The Krajewskis returned to mark the stones again, and by that autumn the monument was complete.

Today, while the approaching visitor rounds a curve on the road out of town, a free-standing wall comes strikingly into view: the tombstones in it catch the western light well into the late afternoon, and glow almost incandescently against the lush forest behind. Perched atop a steep green knoll, the fragment-wall dominates the clearing, and a great crack dominates the monument. Drivers always slow down, and many leave their cars to study the monument and its Polish inscription to the murdered Jews of Kazimierz. Men's tombstones are on the right, women's on the left. Monika Krajewska says that the designer has placed all the rounded stones with candlesticks and candelabra at the top, as if to allow their flames to burn into the sky. A small cluster of unbroken tombstones is arranged in front of the wall—a visual echo of the newly restored headstones standing out of sight behind it. Unlike the polished marble surfaces of the fractured tombstone walls in Warsaw and Krakow, these limestone matzevoth

A broken-tombstone memorial wall in Kazimierz on the Vistula, designed by Tadeusz Augustynek, 1984. Photo: James E. Young.

A visitor to the
memorial wall
in Kazimierz
contemplates
the breach.
Photo:
James E. Young.

are porous and rough to the touch. Their faces are weathered and textured by time that wears down all inscriptions. The wall commemorates the painstaking piecing together of lost Jewish memory, but its jagged breach also suggests the devastation that remains.

These monuments lead a curious double-life in Poland: one in the consciousness of the local community, and another in that of Jewish visitors. On the one hand, they continue to serve as essential commemorative sites for the visitors. But in a country with only five thousand Jews left, it was inevitable that Jewish memory would also be collected and expressed in particularly Polish ways. It could not be otherwise. For once the state reassembles the fragments, it necessarily recalls even the most disparate events in ways that unify them nationally. The state's "recollection" of Polish Jewry has been accomplished—to some extent—in Warsaw's new "Memorial Route of Jewish Martyrdom and Struggle," dedicated in 1988 on the forty-fifth anniversary of the Warsaw Ghetto uprising.

Unveiled along with the new Umschlagplatz memorial, this tour is a walking narrative that unites several monuments in the area of the former Ghetto—now a great burial mound of rubble sixteen feet high, covered by trees, parks, and apartments. According to the Umschlagplatz Memorial Committee, the existing flagstone dedicated to the Jewish Fighting Organization headquarters on Mila Street, Nathan Rapoport's Ghetto Monument on Zamenhof Street, and a small plaque on nearby Stawki Street inscribed to the Umschlagplatz "were not linked together, did not form a legible whole." That is, they could not be "read" in such a way as to make them cohere in narrative sequence. The new route proposes to "link these monuments together, confer on them their rightful status and incorporate them into Warsaw's symbolic space." Thus, the state integrates Jewish memory into its own national constellation of meaning. Whether or not the Jewish fighters of the Ghetto uprising were regarded as Polish national heroes at the time, they are now recast as such whenever the state commemorates the uprising.

The result is a prescribed trail winding through several city blocks, its nineteen stations marked by black, matzevah-shaped syenite tablets, each inscribed in both Polish and Hebrew. To bind together Polish and Jewish memory from the outset, the route begins with a "Tree of Common Remembrance," suggesting that Jews' and Poles' experiences cleave to one another. The tablet at the first station is inscribed to "the common [*meshutaf*] memory of Polish Jews murdered at the hands of the Germans between the years 1939 and 1945 and to the Poles who died extending aid to the Jews." But as my friend and I—Pole and Jew—stood side by side before this tree, I wondered whether each of us actually shared the other's memory of events. Was ours a "common remembrance"? Or was it only the site of remembrance we shared, a common *place* of memory, where each was invited to remember in his own way?

From here, we followed the memorial trail with stops at the foundation of the Ghetto in 1940, Rapoport's monument, and the Jewish Fighting Organization's bunker. Having commenced our walk in common memory, we now continued along the trail of heroism. The path leads to tablets recalling the archivist Emmanuel Ringelblum, Polish Workers' party activist Jezef Lewartowski, and fighters Arie Wilner, Meir Majerowicz, and Frumka Plotnick. In addition, inspirational figures like Shmuel Zygelboim, Janusz Korczak, Rabbi Yitzhak Nyssenbaum, and poet Yitzhak Katzenelson are remembered just before the path ends at the Umschlagplatz—the last Warsaw stop for 350,000 Jews on their way to Treblinka.

For years both visitors and local survivors complained that the small plaque on a free-standing brick wall next to a petrol station was inadequate to mark the Umschlagplatz. But the new memorial, which replaces the old one at the corner of Stawki and Karmelicka streets, is clearly visible at this busy intersection. Now it is the Polish taxi driver who complains. "Forty-five years later," one driver confided to me, "the Jews have taken their revenge on us. Look, no more gas pumps." Warsaw's favorite filling station has indeed been closed down, its empty driveway now adorned by flower planters. The Umschlagplatz memorial, adjacent to it, is an outdoor enclosure, open overhead.

One morning, an old woman carrying groceries entered the marble space, apparently to rest on her way home. She was joined by two young men strolling by. All pauseed to examine the four white marble walls, about ten feet high, as was the Ghetto Wall. A horizontal band of black marble rings the outside walls about two-thirds of the way up, reminiscent of a *tallit* (Jewish prayer shawl). When I asked what they saw, the two young Poles replied that it looked like a black mourning band. They weren't so sure what to make of the black, round-topped slab balancing over the entrance off Stawki Street, which turns the entrance itself into a kind of absent matzevah. Inside, directly opposite the entry, a section of the wall extends upward into another tablet shape, broken by a narrow vertical portal just wide enough to permit one to view a tree growing outside the wall—a symbol of hope, according to the designers.

Standing in the center of this space, we were gently nudged off balance by the skewed angles of the walls: the corners are disjoined, leaving narrow gaps between walls, and the area itself is trapezoidal. Instead of being consoled through reassuring closure, square angles, and predictable forms, our senses were jarred by disquieting and oblique shapes. Architecture, normally a comfort in the strength of its regular forms, here uses broken geometry to recall disjunction and skewed realities.

The white marble walls were so bright when the sun shone that their inscriptions became difficult to read: "On this path of suffering and death in the years 1942–43, over 300,000 Jews from the Warsaw Ghetto were driven to the gas chambers of the Nazi extermination camps." According to committee members, debate during the design sessions centered not on the content of the inscriptions so much as on the languages to be used. Would this memorial be inscribed in the language of the community, its visitors, victims, or all of these? The committee recognized that the choice of languages could not be innocent but would imply the kinds of audience and, by extension, the kinds of remembrance. Some committee members argued for Polish and Yiddish only, since it was, after all, a Polish monument to Jewish victims. Others insisted that both languages of the victims—Yiddish and Hebrew—be included. One hardliner complained that Hebrew was also the language of the Zionists and shouldn't be used (as it was not used in the Jewish pavilion at Auschwitz, for example, where for many years inscriptions came in Polish and Yiddish only). But these are the living Jews now, rejoined another committee member, so we must incorporate both the Yiddish of the victims and the Hebrew of the survivors, many of whom live in Israel. Besides, he pointed out, the Jewish Fighting Organization in the Ghetto was composed almost entirely of Zionist fighters from both left- and right-wing parties. Other committee members insisted that since so many of the survivors are now in

The Umschlagplatz memorial in Warsaw, dedicated in 1988. Photo: James E. Young.

America—the main source of potential visitors—English must also be included as the tourist's lingua franca. It was finally agreed that victims, survivors, community, and tourists all be invited to remember here: the monument is dedicated in Yiddish, Hebrew, Polish, and English.

At first, the committee had also hoped to inscribe every one of the three hundred thousand names belonging to Jews who passed through the "transfer place" on their way to Treblinka. But this idea was quickly abandoned as the difficulties of tracking down every victim became apparent. Instead, the committee decided to list the different first names of as many of the victims as could be accounted for. Listed alphabetically without regard to gender, every Batia, Chaim, Dina, and Mordechai inscribed here would thus remember all so named. By referring to first names of the dead this way, the wall recalls the memorial function implicit in the European Jewish naming tradition, wherein every newborn is a *yad vashem*—a figurative monument and name, that is, memorial to a deceased family member.

The Polish government has several compelling reasons for preserving Jewish memorials to the Holocaust period and even building new ones like the Um-schlagplatz Monument and the Memorial Route. First, by reincorporating Polish Jewry—even in absentia—into the national heritage, the state creates the possibility for representing the Polish experience of World War II through the figure of its murdered Jewish part; the Jews' destruction in Poland comes increasingly to represent (and thereby magnify) the devastation of the entire country and points toward the averted genocide of the Polish nation as a whole. Next, by nationalizing the memory of the Holocaust, the former government prevented it from being marshaled against the state's interests by dissident groups. State commemorations at the Warsaw Ghetto Monument, for example, used to make it more difficult for the Solidarity trade union to adopt this space as its own place of resistance. The essential question is less whether Poles remember themselves or their former Jewish compatriots in these monuments, than what the consequences are for one people's understanding of its past when remembered in the figure of another people.

On a recent trip to the Jewish cemetery in Lodz, I was reminded of yet another impulse underlying the renaissance of Jewish memory in Poland today. So many years after survivors left Lodz, their memorial project abandoned, the cemetery is beginning to stir with new activity. Workers hired by the Nissenbaum Family Foundation have begun to restore the chapel and to cut new paths into the cemetery's forested grounds—great swaths that allow visitors to survey the massive scale of this graveyard. On the day I was there in July 1988, the workers were idle, though still happy to show me around. According to their foreman, they had not been paid since April and were worried that the restoration project—and hence their jobs—had been terminated. "The workers are resentful," the foreman told me, "because they were promised long-term jobs restoring the cemetery, constructing monuments out of the tombstones, and they are supposed to be paid well by Jews from the West." He then asked me why the Jews wouldn't take better care of their cemetery here in Lodz, why, with all their Western money, they wouldn't want to repair their former "home." In turn, I asked why the local community was so interested in such a project. "It is good work," the foreman replied, "and it will bring good tourists."

He was right. Hundreds of Jewish tourist groups from America, Western Europe, and Israel visit Poland every year on so-called Holocaust tours. Led by scholars and survivors, groups from the United Jewish Appeal, the American Jewish Congress, and even various survivor and ghetto fighters associations spend anywhere from three days to three weeks taking in the sights of the Polish memorial landscape: death camps, cemeteries, former synagogues, Jewish museums, and monuments. In fact, there is a burgeoning memorial industry in Poland today: first, a memorial is proposed to a lost Jewish community; next, funds are solicited from abroad to pay for materials and labor; then local craftsmen, architects, and builders are paid to build the memorial. When finished, these memorials become great tourist attractions, drawing hundreds of tourists to villages that have little else to offer but this memory of an absence. In lieu of waiting families and communities, monuments built for and often funded by Western visitors now invite survivors to return as tourists.

Though it is by no means clear that the Polish government is quite so calculating, new Jewish memorial projects find increasing sympathy at both state and local levels. With more Jewish memorials than any other country in Europe (nearly twenty-one hundred, by the state's count), Poland has plans for hundreds more. Before we pass judgment on such memorial intentions, however, we need to recognize similar impulses underlying any nation's landmarks: most are built simultaneously to remember and to attract rememberers. In America as in Poland, tourists are invited primarily for their contribution to local economies. The touristic consumption of monuments may not be as lofty, or as praiseworthy, as other aspects of the memorial process. But it is a dimension that cannot be ignored in coming to understand the combination of thought, work, and motives that sustain Holocaust memory in any land.

The final tragedy in Poland may be that images of death and rituals of mourning have all but displaced traditional tenets of life and learning as central figures of Jewish faith. In the aftermath of the Holocaust, much of Jewish life in Poland has become one long commemoration of the dead, transforming young Polish Jews and non-Jews alike into perennial caretakers and archivists. Instead of communities, we have community records; instead of a people, their gravestones. In a country without rabbis or a Hebrew press, young Jews are as likely to learn their

Hebrew from the inscriptions of tombstones as from Torah scrolls—a violation of the Talmudic warning not to study the texts of matzevoth. Instead of being versed in mishnah and gemara, a generation of Polish Jews that is painfully renewing itself will know the psalms, if at all, only from conventional citations on tombstone epitaphs. Theirs will be a Hebrew of lamentation only, whose narrative describes lost lives, whose sole prayer will be the Kaddish.

Stunted as it is, this conception of Jewish life does suggest a qualified return to another tenet of Judaism: the memory-work by which Jews have traditionally defined themselves in relationship to past events. In this sense, the memorial activity retains distinctly traditional proportions. The constant repair of Jewish graveyards, the gathering of fragments to save them from further deterioration, the maintenance of archives at Auschwitz and the Jewish Historical Institute in Warsaw: these also keep the ancient obligation to remember. Perhaps the only lasting memorials to the era of the Shoah will come not in finished monuments at all, but in the perpetual activity of memory: in the debate over which kinds of memory should be preserved, in whose interest, for which audience. Instead of allowing the past to rigidify in its monumental forms, we would vivify memory through the memory-work itself—whereby events, their recollection, and the role monuments play in our lives remain animate, never completed.

For neither time nor its markers ever really stand still. Even as I write, chunks of mortar holding these monuments together crumble and fall away, lichens cover their surfaces, and grass grows high around their bases. All the while, hundreds of miles away, a political regime is toppled, and a whole generation of monuments suddenly becomes obsolete, their past meanings now irrelevant to the new order. Of course, a monument's meanings were always changing, along with the changing face of the monument itself. But every regime, even the new, hopes that the meanings in its monuments will remain as eternal as it imagines itself to be.

Indeed, since writing these last words, the fall of old regimes and the rise of new throughout Eastern Europe have made the fragile and transient nature of monuments all the more apparent. The inscriptions marking four million victims at Birkenau, for example, have been removed while historians revise downward their politically inflated number. Likewise, the museum narratives at Auschwitz are being carefully rewritten to excise their formerly Marxist cast. As official understanding of the period changes to reflect that of the new non-Communist regime, alternative forms and sites are found to accommodate new memory. Any record of the memorials in Poland must therefore be as provisional as the memorials themselves. In fact, perhaps the "everlasting memorial" exists only in the mind of the visitor, who recalls a single journey to the memory-site, unmodified by later visits never made.

Part III

Israel:

Holocaust, Heroism,

and National

Redemption

The one suitable monument to the memory of European Jewry . . . is the State of Israel . . . where the hope of the Jewish people is expressed . . . and which serves as a free and faithful refuge to every Jew in the world who desires to live a free and independent life.
—*Davar* editorial, 1951

Introduction

Memory of historical events and the narratives delivering this memory have always been central to Jewish faith, tradition, and identity. For if the Jewish God is known only insofar as he reveals himself historically, as Yosef Hayim Yerushalmi and others suggest, then to remember history and to interpret its texts assumes religiously obligatory proportions.[1] Throughout Torah, the Jews are enjoined not only to remember their history but to observe the rituals of faith through remembrance: "Remember the days of old, consider the years of ages past"

(Deut. 32:7); "Remember what Amalek did to you" (Deut. 25:17); "Remember this day, on which you went free from Egypt, the house of bondage, how the Lord freed you from it with a mighty hand" (Ex. 13:3).

The memory of historical trauma, in particular, has long played a pivotal role in Jewish national consciousness. We are reminded, for example, that some ultra-orthodox communities continue to count the calendar years beginning with the Second Ḥurban (destruction of the Temple) of 70 C.E. and the dispersion; that is, Jewish time itself is measured in the distance between proto-catastrophe and present moment. In this way, both the impulse to remember the Holocaust and the meanings engendered in such remembrance are to some extent prescribed by the tradition itself. To this day, history continues to assert itself as a locus of Jewish identity, memory as a primary form of Jewish faith.

Like any state, Israel also remembers the past according to its national myths and ideals, its current political needs. Unlike that of other states, however, Israel's overarching national ideology and religion—perhaps its greatest "natural resource"—may be memory itself: memory preserved, restored, and codified. In cultivating a ritually unified remembrance of the past, the state creates a common relationship to it. The past remembered, recounted, and interpreted collectively becomes, if only vicariously, a shared experience. Having defined themselves as a people through commemorative recitations of their past, the Jews now depend on memory for their very existence as a nation.

Like the Holocaust memorials of other lands, those in Israel reflect both the past experiences and current lives of their communities, as well as the state's memory of itself. At times ambivalent, at times shrill, the official approach to Holocaust memory in Israel has long been torn between the simultaneous need to remember and to forget, between the early founders' enormous state-building task and the reasons why such a state was necessary, between the survivors' memory of victims and the fighters' memory of resistance. On the one hand, early statists like David Ben-Gurion regarded the Holocaust as the ultimate fruit of Jewish life in exile; as such, it represented a diaspora that deserved not only to be destroyed, but also forgotten. On the other hand, the state also recognized its perverse debt to the Holocaust: it had, after all, seemed to prove the Zionist dictum that without a state and the power to defend themselves, Jews in exile would always be vulnerable to just this kind of destruction.[2] As a result, the early leaders found little reason to recall the Holocaust beyond its direct link to the new state.

Ironically, however, by linking the state's raison d'être to the Holocaust, the early founders also located the Shoah at the center of national identity: Israel would be a nation condemned to defining itself in opposition to the very event that made it necessary. The question for the early state became: how to negate the Diaspora and put it behind the "new Jews" of Israel, while basing the need for new Jews in the memory of Shoah? How to remember the Holocaust without allowing it to constitute the center of one's Jewish identity? In part, the answer has been a forced distinction between the Israeli and the "galut," or exilic, Jew. Where the Jew in exile has known only defenselessness and destruction, the Israeli has known fighting and self-preservation. Where the Diaspora Jew continues to identify as a member of a religious faith and a minority population, the Israeli's major Jewish experience has been the building of a state, fighting its wars, and living day to day in Hebrew.[3]

To some extent, this essential dichotomy is resolved in Israel by the ubiquitous twinning of martyrs and heroes in Israel's memorial iconography. In this mixed figure, the victims are memorable primarily for the ways they demonstrate the need for fighters, who, in turn, are remembered for their part in the state's founding. When placed against the traditional paradigmatic backdrop of destruction and redemption, the memorial message in this dialectic comes into sharp relief: as destruction of the martyrs is redeemed by those who fought, the Shoah itself is redeemed by the founding of the state.

Immediately after the war, however, this and nearly all traditional paradigms that might have sustained memory of the Shoah were vigorously resisted by the early founders of the state. Even when survivors comprised half the state's population, the link between Jewish identity and Shoah was rejected as a self-fulfilling exilic phenomenon. The Jews' traditional self-image as victim would be explicitly supplanted by new, Zionist ideals of strength and self-determination. Only years later, after the public "coming out" of Holocaust survivors during the Eichmann trial, were survivors and martyrs accorded full Israeli identity—which is to say, assimilated to the ideals of the new state. After years of being linked on the official day of remembrance (Yom Hashoah Vehagvurah) and in the national shrine (Yad Vashem Heroes' and Martyrs' Memorial), Shoah no longer signified defeat in the eyes of many young Israelis, but actually emerged as an era of heroism, of triumph over past passivity.

In fact, this expanded definition of heroism is one of several remembrance themes recommended in the army's "Informational Guidelines to the Commander on Yom Hashoah":

The bravery of the Jewish people in the Holocaust cannot be examined only through the question: did they fight? The examination contains within it a prior question: what is bravery? This must be explored in the light of the conditions under which Jews lived in World War II. Despite these conditions we are witness to Jewish rebellion and revolt when it was possible. Together with this, bravery was revealed in unfurling the banner of communal institutions, mutual help, education of the children, maintenance of the customs of Israel and its holidays, and in fostering the values of culture. *By standing up under these conditions and refusing to surrender to despair the Jews made possible the continuation of the Jewish people even in the inferno of the Holocaust and thereby helped the creation of the State of Israel.* The stance of the Jews in the Holocaust reflects moral and spiritual power which provides the basis for our stance in the continued conflict.[4]

Memory of the Holocaust is brought into the present moment: that which sustained Jews during the Holocaust now sustains the current generation. Israel's defeat here would not be another Holocaust so much as an extension of the first one. In this way, Holocaust remembrance fosters a unity of identity between martyrs and a new generation of Israelis. The martyrs are not forgotten but are recollected heroically as the first to fall in defense of the state.

Due partly to the sheer enormity of events, partly to the great proportion of Holocaust survivors in Israel (nearly half the population in 1948), and partly to the central negative place of the Shoah in Zionist ideology, images and figures from this period have all but displaced their historical precedents in Jewish memory. Not only have remembered experiences from the Shoah been used to comprehend earlier disasters—lending them significance they would not otherwise have had—but they have also become a new standard in Jewish memory by which all kinds of post-Shoah catastrophes, Jewish or not, are now being measured.

On the one hand, the very existence of a museum in Tel Aviv—Beit Hatfutsot—dedicated to the Diaspora seems to epitomize the official Israeli view of dispersed Jewry as a dead and withered civilization. As museum object, life in the Diaspora is addressed in the past tense. At the same time, however, where memorials and museums in Europe, especially those located at the sites of destruction, focus relentlessly on the annihilation of Jews and almost totally neglect the millennium of Jewish life in Europe before the war, those in Israel locate events in a historical continuum that includes Jewish life before and after the destruction.

In Israeli museums at kibbutzim like Lohamei Hageta'ot, Tel Yitzhak, Givat Haim, and Yad Mordechai, Jewish life before, during and after the Holocaust is given first priority. At Yad

Vashem, Israel's national Holocaust memorial, the Holocaust marks not so much the end of Jewish life as the end of viable life in exile. In the narrative created by Holocaust Remembrance Day's placement on the national calendar, the end of the Shoah came not in the liberation of the camps, but in the survivors' return to and redemption in the land of Israel. In all cases, the Holocaust is integrated into a long view of Jewish history: it may be a turning point, a confirmation of Zionist ideology, but it is linked nevertheless to a millennium of Jewish life in Europe before the war and to Jewish national rebirth afterwards.

In every community, in every corner of Israel's landscape, one is reminded of the Shoah by a plaque, a building's dedication, an inscribed tablet. Streets are named after ghetto fighters like Mordechai Anielewicz, schools after martyrs like Janusz Korczak. A granite harp in a Kiryat Gat park is entitled "Shoah 1933–1945" and stands beside a stone etched with a list of victims. German-Jewish refugees who arrived to build a moshav at Shavei-Zion near Nahariya erected a memorial in their synagogue to 134 of their former townspeople who did not leave Germany in time. A wall sculpture on the front of Jerusalem's Great Synagogue is dedicated both to the six million martyrs and to Israel's war dead: all of whom "died so that we might live." Denmark Square, with its skeletal boat sculpture, recalls the Danish rescue of Jews to residents of Jerusalem's Beit Hakerem neighborhood. In Haifa, the actual hull of one of these rescue boats on the former site of a refugee center reminds us that the rescue voyage begun in Denmark did not end in Sweden at all, but in Israel's Sha'ar Ha'aliya reception camp in 1948.

Over time, these markers recede into consciousness, as parts of an inanimate cityscape, but continue to function as the coordinates of daily life in Israel, even when unrecognized. My aim in the following chapters will be to draw back into view the complex cast of memory in Israel, both as it is obliquely reflected in the countryside and as it officially legislated in the national memorial authority and day of remembrance. Although both the official and unofficial memorial sites in Israel share many of the same national assumptions, together they constitute a memorial landscape as broad and diverse as the population of Israel at large.

Chapter 8 Israel's

Memorial Landscape:

Forests, Monuments,

and Kibbutzim

The Martyrs' Forest and *Scroll of Fire*

In both its practical and ceremonial significance, tree planting in Israel has played an essential part in resettling the land. On the symbolic level, early pioneers regarded "the greening of Israel" as a metaphor for the people's return from exile. Uprooted and dispersed two thousand years before, the Jews had remained rootless, hence powerless, ever since. In cultivating the land of their origin and thereby rerooting their lives in its soil, according to Zionist thought, the Jews would derive new strength and security. The very language of this figure reinforced the seeming naturalness of the people's return, of the people's relationship to the land. Even the physical act of planting was suggestive in its mix of natural and symbolic imagery: digging one's hands into the soil, scooping out rocks and dirt and planting a seed seemed to be a spiritual mating of a people and its land, a becoming one with it again. To work the land was to become part of it and the natural cycle it represented.

On a more practical level, early afforestation projects by the Jewish National Fund paralleled the kibbutz movement's own reason for being: to make this rocky, inhospitable land habitable. Trees provided shade for the workers, secured the soil against erosion, and protected crops from searing desert winds. The forest encouraged life itself amid its branches and glens, gave refuge to birds and animals. Sowing and reaping demanded the kind of labor, in Zionist-socialist eyes, needed to make the new Jews strong, better prepared to withstand a hostile world. Finally, as planting a tree might signify the founding of a kibbutz, the kibbutz in turn pointed toward the birth of a state.

This link between the state's founding and tree planting is further reinforced on Israeli Independence Day, when new buildings and monuments are dedicated—and when ceremonial tree plantings are held around the country. Even the new year for trees, Tu B'shvat (fifteenth of Shvat), is transvalued by the state. Where traditional celebration of the sap rising in the trees of the Holy Land had included partaking of the fruits of the land—such as apples, almonds, figs, and pomegranates—and sitting up late reciting biblical passages on trees, it is now customary on this day to go out into the fields of Israel and plant saplings. Indeed, after the state's founding, it has become common to plant a tree in Israel to honor any and all of life's milestones: the birth of a child, bar- or bat-mitzvah, marriage, and death. As a memorial gesture, tree planting remains freighted with statist meaning.

In cooperation with the Jewish National fund in 1954, B'nai B'rith thus dedicated the Martyrs' Forest near Kesalon in the Judean Hills outside Jerusalem. Its first half-million trees were planted around a sanctuary hewn of rock, in B'nai B'rith's words, "as a living memorial to the six million Jews who perished in the Holocaust."[1] Since then, nearly two million trees have been planted in the forest, with another four million planned—one for each victim. This forest takes on double-edged significance: it remembers both the martyrs and a return to the land. Memory of the victims is cultivated in the founding of the state: in taking root in the land, memory of the martyrs binds rememberers to the state itself.

When combined with the Israeli's traditional reverence for *yedi'ath ha'aretz* (knowledge of the land), this notion of memorials as part of the natural landscape assumes still greater significance. Nature is defined by the Society for Protection of Nature in Israel as "not only plant and animal life, but also the landscapes and relics of the country's past."[2] Teacher-guides still lead tours around the country, teaching a people its relationship to the land, a bond that is both sustained and created in the teaching process. If, as part of the landscape, monuments become extensions of the land, then the teacher-guides in Israel teach not only the relationship between a people and its land, but also that between a people and its monuments. As a result, ancient biblical sites and Holocaust memorials alike become the landmarks by which Israelis continue to know their relationship to the land and, by extension, to their history.[3]

Several years after the Martyrs' Forest was founded, the essential bookishness of Israel's landscape found further expression in Nathan Rapoport's *Megilath-esh*— Scroll of Fire—a twenty-six-foot monument planted in 1971 atop the forest's highest hill at the end of an isolated road near Kesalon. The two great trunks of these scrolls seem almost to have sprung indigenously from the soil. On any

given day, we are as likely to find busloads of schoolchildren studying their bas relief pictographs as we are to find solitude at its base.

B'nai B'rith first invited Jacques Lipchitz to design a monumental shrine for the Martyrs' Forest, but the celebrated sculptor declined, citing an impossible backlog of unfinished projects, and recommended Rapoport for the job. When B'nai B'rith representatives visited Rapoport's New York studio in 1965, he led them immediately to a model for the *Scroll of Fire*. The guardians of America's public memory may not have been ready for the particularity of its immigrants' experiences in Europe, but Israel's national memory had always been defined by that of Jews everywhere, a continuum of generational memory transcending borders. By the time B'nai B'rith delivered a contract to Rapoport in June 1967, Israel had fought the Six-Day War. Rapoport asked, therefore, whether he could now devote one scroll to the heroism and martyrdom of the Shoah and one to Israel's national rebirth, leading to the reunification of Jerusalem. In stitching together the experiences of Jews in and out of Israel, he said, the *Scroll of Fire* would cast Jewish memory in a classically Jewish storytelling form. B'nai B'rith happily agreed, recognizing that in an unbroken narrative continuum, these two scrolls

Nathan Rapoport's *Scroll of Fire,* dedicated in 1971 near Kesalon, Israel. Photo: James E. Young.

would link Jewish martyrdom and resistance, the end of exile and redemption in Eretz Israel.

When first erected in 1971, the *Scroll of Fire* stood alone, visible from all directions. Now it is surrounded by a forest of pine trees, in a clearing created by its forty-by-forty-foot concrete base. From a distance, the monument seems as ancient as the land, two great Doric columns covered in hieroglyphs. On closer examination, we find that they are scrolls of bronze, not columns of stone. The bas-relief images are not strange, but recall familiar scenes from the sculptor's other memorials: the heroes and martyrs of Warsaw, a herald angel from Philadelphia, Korczak and his children from New York. The two leaning scrolls form an archway, open inside and at the top, so visitors can enter their space and listen to the wind whistling through.

The iconic narrative in the first scroll—devoted to the Holocaust era—begins with a familiar exilic motif: a family clings together, looking out in all directions while being herded off by the Nazis, whose helmets and bayonets are just visible over the heads of the Jews. In this gesture to "the last march" bas relief on his Warsaw Ghetto Monument, itself an echo of both Titus's march and Hirszenberg's *Golus* painting, the sculptor recalls every exile in the figure of original Jewish exile from the land of Israel. This procession moves left to right, through scenes of barbed wire, on to a jumble of bodies, folded over and into each other like rolls of clay. Directly above these deportations on the same scroll, fighters arise amid flame and ruin, their fists raised and weapons brandished—again, echoes of Rapoport's figures on the Ghetto Monument.

On this kind of scroll, one can begin anywhere and eventually be taken back to the beginning; that is, the present moment in such a circle always leads to remembrance of the past. In narrative sequence, martyrdom is followed by uprising, which leads then to liberation from the camps—followed by yet another march. The first marchers hold arms to their brows, as if to shield themselves from the surrounding terror. Above them, another family with bags now marches more hopefully, eyes fixed forward in resolve. This megillah of the Shoah ends with these survivors coming ashore by boat, reaching out and falling into the arms of Israelis distinguished by strong limbs, kibbutz work clothing, and temple hats—all recognizable to schoolchildren here, many of them dressed in exactly the same way.

The second, adjoining scroll begins with the battle at Kibbutz Negba during the War of Independence: kibbutznikim rising to fight, some falling, all still in procession. The rabbi carrying a Torah scroll from Rapoport's Ghetto Monument reappears again here: only now his direction is reversed. Instead of going into exile, he is returning from it. Above him, another sage looks up, his hand upraised: but instead of beseeching God, he helps to hold aloft a great menorah, carried by Israeli soldiers and workers. The procession on the Arch of Titus is reversed here, the menorah returned from exile. The end of the narrative on this scroll comes with soldiers praying at the Western Wall, in a reunified Jerusalem.

This is an unabashedly literary, even bookish memorial, in both theme and performance. As a scroll, it is meant to be read, its pictographs unfurling into a didactic historical narrative. In approaching this monument as a text to read and interpret, students and their teachers turn this memorial space into an open-air classroom. Students listen attentively while their teacher-guides, often with a pointer—a *yad*—lead classes from image to image, explaining and commenting on each. Occasionally, teachers correct the text itself. "Will someone please tell me what's wrong with this picture?" asks a tour leader, pointing to the scene of a soldier, wrapped in *tefillin*, praying at the Western Wall. A hand shoots up immediately. "Yes?" A young boy volunteers, "The tefillin is on the wrong arm— it should be the left arm, not the right." "Very good," nods the teacher. "But why did he do that," asks the puzzled student. "Because he was just an artist," replies the teacher, "and didn't think about details like that."

The meanings in images, even those arranged into narrative sequence, remain somewhat indirect and depend on both the teachers' commentaries and, as it turns out, the many poetic *aggadot* inscribed on markers around the site's perimeter. In this way, the images serve to illustrate not just the teachers' words but the monument's dedication, the sculptor's seeming epitaph, and the poets' verses: all become part of the memorial text. To the dedication, which reads "In memory of the martyred six million and in reverent celebration of Israel's rebirth," Rapoport has added what appears to be his own epitaph: "My words have been made of stone. They are silent, heavy, and everlasting."

The literary message of these scrolls is echoed more explicitly still inside their portal space, where we read in Hebrew and English from Ezekiel 37:

> Behold, O my People, I will open your graves
>
> And cause you to come up out of your graves
>
> And bring you into the land of Israel
>
> And shall put my soul in you
>
> And ye shall live and I shall place you
>
> In your own land.

On another marker near the perimeter of the monument's platform, Nelly Sachs has contributed her own "Epitaph for the Martyrs," as if in warning to the schoolchildren swarming near its base:

> Mutely the stone speaks
>
> Of the martyrdom of the six million

A teacher using
Rapoport's
Scroll of Fire as
history text.
Photo:
James E. Young.

Whose body drifted as smoke through the air

Silence—Silence—Silence

You who were born afterwards

Remember the men, women, and children in a time of violence

Lower your heads in humility.

To these lines, one of which was pulled directly from Sachs's poem "O the Chimneys," the Israeli poet Chaim Gouri added his voice at the cornerstone laying on 30 October 1967. His words merely affirmed the redemptory link between the martyrs and the rebirth of Israel already expressed in Ezekiel and Sachs's poetry:

From the fires of the ruins of the Ghettos

We picked a stone all charred and broken

That stone was made here into the cornerstone

and the foundation stone.

Their words about silence notwithstanding, these pillars are never completely mute, even in their solitary setting. Between the teachers' questions, students' answers, and the poets' verses, the landscape resounds with the words of visitors making memory articulate. For by themselves, these monuments in the landscape remain insensate stone and concrete, lost to meaning. But as part of a nation's memorial rituals, they are invested with national soul and significance. Together, these markers in the wilderness comprise a cartographical matrix by which Israelis navigate their new lives in the land. Memorials like the *Scroll of Fire* serve as landmarks in and around which histories are woven and a people's past is explained to itself.

Memorials and Museums on Kibbutzim

Under the cover of a moonless night in 1939, a group of recently arrived immigrant-refugees from Germany set up their tents on a lonely hillock in Israel's Jezreel Valley. Within days, they had sunk a well, dug a latrine, and begun to clear the area of rocks and prickly pear. At first, they called their kibbutz Even Yitzhak (Yitzhak Rock). Later they renamed it Gal-Ed (after Laban's witness pile of stones), a gesture by which the kibbutz likened itself to a monument. Like the founders of other kibbutzim at this time who had come to escape the Germans, the members of Gal-Ed regarded their kibbutz as a direct response to the gathering storm in Europe. Whether established by the youth wing of He'halutz before the war, or by refugees barely escaped during the war, or by survivors and ghetto fighters afterwards, kibbutzim like Gal-Ed frequently figured themselves as living memorials: to the end of life in exile, to survival in Israel. Eventually, a handful of these kibbutzim built Holocaust museums and memorials on the land itself. On the one hand, given the pioneers' socialist ideals and emphasis on the renewal of life, there might have been little time for commemorating the destruction of the Shoah at all. But in fact, some of the reasons for Holocaust memorials on the kibbutzim are tied inextricably to these same ideals.

After the Shoah, the contrast between living independently in the land of Israel and dying so horribly in Europe could not have been more stark. As life crumbled in exile, it blossomed in the Yishuv. Every daily act on the kibbutz seemed to affirm the continuation of life after Europe, the rejection of death in exile. Having borne out all of the Zionists' darkest prophecies, Europe now epitomized the Golah, or exile from the land. By contrast, in the tilling of soil and cultivation of crops, the kibbutz in Israel seemed to represent the very creation of life. To some extent, this contrast is evident in every memorial exhibit to the Holocaust in Israel, but especially so in the memorials and museums on kibbutzim. For, like other memorials, those located on kibbutzim reflect the image of their makers, their experiences and understanding of this time.

In the eyes of these pioneers, the Shoah was not the end of Jewish life as such, but only the end of Jewish life in exile. On the kibbutz, where life continued, remembrance would be gathered around the ideals and preoccupations of life in the Yishuv. For many already in Israel, in fact, this era was not merely a time of destruction at all, but of vibrant renewal and rebuilding. As a result, kibbutz museums and memorials at Lohamei Hageta'ot, Yad Mordechai, Tel Yitzhak, Givat Haim, Ma'ale Hahamisha, and Mishmar Ha'emek tend to recall primarily the resistance of kibbutz movement comrades in Europe, the musky death-stench of life in exile, and the newfound ability to create and defend Jewish life in Israel. As the kibbutz exudes life and strength, it tends also to refract memory through images of life and strength, resistance and renewal.

Kibbutz Mishmar Ha'emek

One of the earliest memorials in Israel to commemorate the Shoah was dedicated in 1947, a year before the state's independence, at Kibbutz Mishmar Ha'emek—"guardian of the valley"—near Megiddo. In its theme—*L'Yeldei Hagolah* (To the Children of the Exile)—and gently cubist form, this work by Israeli portrait sculptor Ze'ev Ben-Zvi blends the artist's vision of Shoah and his own aesthetic mission. Regarded by some as Israel's "first-born sculptor," Ben-Zvi struggled most of his life to carve an "Eretz Israel art" out of Jerusalem stone. On the one hand, he did not want to become, in his words, "a mere broker between European and Oriental traditions."[4] On the other hand, he fully recognized that "Eretz Israel artists" could not create without a sustaining tradition of some sort. The dilemma for Ben-Zvi was that, as an artist, he necessarily remained rooted in the Golah, even as he created in the land of Israel.

Instead of seeking to resolve this conundrum, Ben-Zvi chose to humanize the cubist edges in his work and to design what he called "Temples of the Idea." These temples would be isolated, even hidden, public spaces where people of the land could commune with pieces of art. In this way, European forms would derive new meaning from their new contexts. As sanctuaries of art, they would encourage a contemplative turning inward: meaning in "Eretz Israel art" would derive not from European or Oriental traditions, but from its place in the land, the sanctification of aesthetic space, and the private responses of Jews newly redeemed in the Jewish state.

Tucked away in a corner not far from the kibbutz kindergarten at Mishmar Ha'emek, Ben-Zvi's memorial *To the Children of Exile* is the only "temple" he ever built. It is composed of four reliefs installed in a stone wall surrounding a small open square, three by fifteen meters. Originally a grassy enclosure, it has been paved over in pebbles and concrete. On entering, our eyes are drawn first to a large, softly cubist figure of a mother and child, and then to three progressive reliefs on the left leading to this figure. I watch as a woman in kibbutz work clothes and her child enter the space, hand in hand. The mother begins to remark the redness of a blossom fallen to the ground when the little girl hushes her. "Don't talk here, mother," she says, "this is a place for quiet." Other children enter, and one by one each goes silently to a tiny figure at the far left. Nearly hidden behind a small shrub, it is a miniature relief of a child curled into fetal position. The children crouch before this little form and study it intently, before stepping right to the next relief.

Here four figures seem to rise in an arc from the ground, as if straightening from fetal to upright position. To their right, seven other figures march in a row, bunched together in profile, their hands stiffly at their sides—a stylized exilic procession. Our eyes follow them back to the mother and child. The mother's long arm holds the child close; the child reaches up, its mouth opened around the word "mama" or "ema," who half turns her head away. Her eyes are closed, her mouth open slightly but buried in her shoulder as if to stifle a cry. In sequence, the figures of these children seem to emerge from earth and stone, growing like the small plants nearby into a disciplined little row. Stretching its limbs to mother, the child reaches up like a flower to the sun.

"Let artistic signs and symbols be set up in every private and public place," Ben-Zvi once wrote, "to express this sense of pain in our souls." This corner at Mishmar Ha'emek is both a private and public place: once a year the kibbutz holds its Yom Hashoah ceremonies here, at what members now call *pinat hago-lah*—Diaspora corner. Shoah and Golah are twinned here in their rhyme as near equivalents in the mind of the kibbutz, wherein one is reciprocally known by—

Ze'ev Ben-Zvi's *To the Children of Exile*, dedicated at Kibbutz Mishmar Ha'emek in 1947, was Israel's first Holocaust memorial. Photo: James E. Young.

even substituted for—the other. In this space, one's thoughts are gathered inward, contained by the forms surrounding memory. It is a place of quiet contemplation: birds chirp, pine and eucalyptus trees rustle overhead, young voices emanate from the school just above—all in haunting counterpoint to the stone-muteness of the "children of the golah."

Kibbutz Ma'ale Hahamisha

Another rarely noticed memorial statue just outside Jerusalem on the road to Ma'ale Hahamisha molds memory of the Shoah in the figure of the kibbutz itself. This kibbutz was established as a memorial to five young members of the Polish Zionist movement Gordonia who were ambushed and killed by Arabs while working on an afforestation project near Kiryat Anavim for the Jewish National Fund in 1938. A year later, other young pioneers from Gordonia chose the site of this ambush to found a kibbutz in memory of their murdered comrades. They named it Ma'ale Hahamisha—Ascent of the Five—a dual reference to their deaths and to their immigration to Eretz Israel. The kibbutz later served as a base for Haganah (prestate army) forces during Israel's War of Independence and still hosts public ceremonies on Yom Hashoah.

Monument to Warsaw Ghetto fighters and Eliezer Geled and his comrades, designed by Andre Revesz at Kibbutz Ma'ale Hahamisha. Photo: James E. Young.

In 1961, this memorial kibbutz erected another kind of monument in its midst —a memorial within a memorial—to commemorate one of Gordonia's members who fought and died in the Warsaw Ghetto uprising. Constructed of Jerusalem stone, this statue by Andre Revesz stands at a fork in the road leading to the kibbutz and gleams white against the forest green of pine trees. Its muscular, life-size figures emerge from a rectangular, broken-topped pillar—a reference to the Ghetto's destruction. A Hebrew inscription reads "Monument to the Fighters of the Warsaw Ghetto—Eliezer Geled and his Comrades." "His comrades" in the statue include one man poised to throw a grenade, a woman cradling a child, and a muscular figure without shirt straining to support his fallen friend, who still clutches the barrel of an automatic weapon. The kibbutz archivist insists that there is no connection between the ascent of the original five and those who "rose up" in the Ghetto. But we cannot help noticing that this stone statuary comprises five figures.

By virtue of its location at a central crossroad at Kibbutz Ma'ale Hahamisha, in fact, this memorial recalls the ascent of the original five tree planters in the figure of the latter five fighters who rose up in Warsaw. To some extent, the fighters even displace the pioneers. Does the name of the kibbutz refer to the five pioneers who fell establishing the state, or to the five ghetto fighters in the monument, or simultaneously to both sets of heroes, each now known in the figure of the other? By creating this ambiguity, the monument commemorates both sets of heroes. That is, by recalling the memory of the young pioneers in the figure of the ghetto fighters, this memorial binds them into one image of national heroism: all remembered now as having fallen for the state.

230
Israel

Kibbutz Yad Mordechai

A similar, but much more striking, instance of this exchange between memorial images of the Shoah and the state's founding can be found at Kibbutz Yad Mordechai, near the town of Ashkelon in the Negev. Originally located in the north near Netanya and called Mitzpe Ha'yam (Sea Lookout), this kibbutz was composed largely of Polish immigrants from the Hashomer Hatsa'ir movement. In 1943, the kibbutz moved to its new site near Ashkelon, where word of the Warsaw Ghetto uprising and the fate of Mordechai Anielewicz reached his comrades in May. Inspired by the uprising led by one of their own, the kibbutz adopted Anielewicz's name to memorialize the courage of its leader, and thus became Yad Mordechai—literally, monument to Mordechai—arguably the first Holocaust memorial in Israel. In this case, however, it was not only a matter of the kibbutz shaping memory in its image. In light of subsequent events, it seems that the kibbutz redefined itself in Mordechai's heroic image, as well.

For five years later, one month after the dedication of the Warsaw Ghetto Monument, Kibbutz Yad Mordechai fell under Egyptian siege during Israel's War of Independence. To what extent the kibbutz wittingly enacted its heroic self-figuration may never be clear, but its desperate stand against several Egyptian battalions in May 1948 seemed to affirm a direct link between the courage of the Warsaw Ghetto and that of the kibbutz in the national mind of Israel. This memorial may have led to a particular kind of self-understanding: Israelis had acquitted themselves in the memory of their fallen comrade. The consequences of memorialization, never really benign, were palpable here. As the ghetto fighters had withstood the Germans for several weeks, a smaller number of kibbutznikim had held off the Egyptians just long enough to allow Israeli forces to regroup behind the battle lines: each resistance is now recalled in light of the other, the latter both an extension and a possible consequence of the former.

Today, Yad Mordechai is home to three major memorial spaces: a recreated battlefield on the site of Yad Mordechai's heroic stand; a large statue of Mordechai Anielewicz; and a museum whose narrative sequence links the Shoah and national independence. Kibbutz walking tours begin with the battlefield: from a strategic lookout point, we survey both the trenches of the kibbutz defenders and the cutout figures of Egyptian soldiers charging across the field below. Loudspeakers spaced over the trenches and machine-gun nests broadcast a recorded story of the battle of Yad Mordechai.[5]

In Hebrew, one arrives in Israel by going up *(aliya)* and exits the land by going down *(yerida)*. At Yad Mordechai's museum, we literally descend into the exilic past, down through a dark, narrow passageway into a vault where the Jewish past is dead and buried. In this economy of images, nearly two thousand years of Jewish life in the galut is represented by the shtetl and the tired remnants of a vanished shtetl life: a few weathered books, two tarnished candlesticks, faded photographs, a stack of crumbling Yiddish newspapers. Buried in this mausoleum, these artifacts are arranged almost as if to say that this life was hardly worth preserving anyway. The "way of life" in the Shtetl is captured in a handful of images: a belt maker, umbrella maker, and metal worker, all locked in a cramped and dingy past. Accompanying captions suggest that it is a struggle for life built on trade, faith, education, community, and redemption.

As narrated in the exhibition panels, it is also a hopeless struggle, which leads to the rise of the Nazis, the ghetto, deportations, and death. The dank shtetl is turned into a suffocating ghetto, crowding relieved only by deportations to the death camps. Having reascended to the second floor, we squint as the bright light of the kibbutz pours into the exhibit hall. Set in the wall side by side, dingy black-

Nathan
Rapoport's
monument to
Mordechai
Anielewicz at
Kibbutz Yad
Mordechai.
Photo:
James E. Young.

and-white images of Jews being led away are back-lighted by great picture windows filled with trees and sun-dappled lawns. On one side, we have light and life, teeming greenery, agriculture and construction; on the other side, darkness and death, starvation and destruction. On one side, freedom and the laws of a Jewish state; on the other side, Nuremberg laws and yellow stars, Nazis and a synagogue going up in flames. Life is here, in the orchards, in hard work, in freedom to be Jews. Death is there, in the musty shtetlach, ghettos, and concentration camps.

Then we move to a great "wall of the uprising," emblazoned floor to ceiling with the names of Jewish fighting groups from the ghettos, forests, camps, and allied armies. Where the martyrs are noted in their absence—abandoned and empty shtetlach, bags strewn in the streets, the very artifacts that greet visitors in the vault downstairs—the fighters are remembered in face, name, and deed. From here we move abruptly to the escape from Europe and rescue in the promised land. The exhibition then jumps to another era: a photographic record of water pipes laid to connect the early settlements of the Negev. A caption reminds us that this water was the lifeblood of the desert—and that the pipes themselves were reddened by the blood of those guarding them. By extension, the pioneers become an infusion of lifeblood into the desert, the kibbutz a remnant seed from Europe now replanted in the homeland. Next come the siege between 1947 and 1948, the destruction of many of these settlements, the story of Yad Mordechai, and the birth of the state. Three stories are told in this museum: that of a life in exile (as exemplified by the Shoah), that of resistance (as exemplified by both ghetto uprisings and the heroism of the kibbutz itself during the war of independence), and that of redemption in the promised land.

With only three years separating the liberation of the camps and the birth of the state of Israel, the link between the Holocaust and national independence was self-evident for most Israelis in 1948. In choosing a kibbutznik living in Paris as the model for his Ghetto Monument's Anielewicz, the sculptor Nathan Rapoport may have only affirmed the link he already felt between heroes of the ghetto and those of the Yishuv. For not long after the dedication of the Warsaw monument (nearly coincident with the founding of the Jewish state), Rapoport immigrated to Israel, where he was commissioned to build yet another memorial to Anielewicz at Yad Mordechai. He relates that when he arrived at the kibbutz to survey sites for the monument, he was shocked to find the kibbutz itself nearly destroyed. "After rebuilding your houses, then maybe you should think about statues," he advised the kibbutz.[6] But they wanted to begin with a monument: that is, they would now refound the kibbutz, itself a memorial, literally around a monument of its namesake. This was, after all, the locus of Yad Mordechai's identity. We might now ask, When the leaders of the kibbutz commissioned this monument, whom and what did they intend to commemorate—the courage of Mordechai Anielewicz or the courage of the kibbutz itself, as now represented by Anielewicz?

Rapoport responded by creating a patently Davidic figure, twelve feet high, armed with a single hand-grenade instead of a sling—the third memorial space at Yad Mordechai. Garbed as a kibbutznik, almost surly, this Anielewicz turns slowly to meet his attacker. Viewed from below, he stands against the backdrop of a water tower partially blown away by Egyptian shelling. The kibbutz wanted to remove the tower altogether, but Rapoport insisted that it remain. For in it, he saw a simultaneous reference to the ruins of both the Ghetto and life on the kibbutz. From the area of the monument itself, we look over Anielewicz's shoulder and survey the rest of the kibbutz and neighboring fields. This Anielewicz is recast as a kibbutznik to commemorate both destructions, both acts of heroic resistance, and in so doing links one to the other in national continuum.

Beit Terezin at Kibbutz Givat Haim-Ichud

Unlike other kibbutz museums and memorials, Kibbutz Givat Haim's Beit Terezin was not established in the image of state or kibbutz movement. Nor was it founded to remember to the world a general meaning or record of the Shoah. Instead, it seeks to remind Israelis both of the victims who perished in Terezin and of the unique essence of this "model ghetto," which was deception itself. For in the eyes of many survivors of Terezin now living in Israel, the Germans' meticulous deception not only succeeded in blinding victims and the world to Terezin's awful realities at the time. But the German-created illusions and lies surrounding Terezin had even begun to permeate other Israelis' and survivors' remembrance of the ghetto, as well.

The fortress-town of Terezin had been built one hundred kilometers north of Prague at the end of the eighteenth century by Austrian emperor Josef II, in memory of his mother, Maria Theresa. Surrounded by walls and moats, Terezin suggested itself to German occupiers as a convenient site for herding together the Jews of the Czech Protectorate and so was converted from an army citadel into a city concentration camp—Theresienstadt. The first transport of Jews from Prague came in November 1941; a few months later the remaining 5,000 townspeople were evacuated to make room for another 50,000 Jews. In "giving the Jews a city," Hitler turned the victims' culture and civilized incredulity to his own advantage. Elderly Jews were promised a convalescent spa here; artists, writers, and musicians were encouraged to continue their work within Terezin's walls—

all as a means of fostering the illusion of normalcy in their incomprehensible circumstances.

By 1943, when 90 percent of the protectorate's mostly assimilated Jews were housed here, many still believed this was an alternative to the camps in the East and so welcomed the chance to live in a wholly Jewish city. In reality, however, Terezin was little more than a transit camp—a way station—on the road to Auschwitz. Thus masked, the Final Solution was that much easier to accomplish: of the nearly 150,000 men, women, and children who passed through this "model ghetto," only 12,000 survived the war. Some 33,000 people died in Terezin between 1941 and 1945 of disease, starvation, beatings, and shootings. Another 90,000 were eventually murdered in Auschwitz.[7]

For many Terezin survivors now living in Israel, the Nazis' deception continues to haunt. One survivor recalls that when asked by other Israelis whether she was a survivor of the camps, she replies, "Yes, but forgive me—I was only in Terezin." Like her, many survivors feared that the German propaganda films and deluded Red Cross reports of Terezin would gradually displace both the reality of the ghetto and their own memory of it. It was mostly in response to this fear that members of He'halutz proposed a museum and archives devoted to Theresienstadt at Kibbutz Givat Haim-Ichud, which would teach about Terezin's special circumstances. Rather than erecting a passive, silent monument that might have acquiesced in visitors' misconceptions, even reifying certain myths, the Theresienstadt Martyrs' Remembrance Association opened the museum in 1975 as an educational center, a critical corrective for remembrance.

Beit Terezin comprises two sections: a study center with reading room, library, and archives; and a remembrance hall housing a small exhibition. The archives contain copies of the transport cards for 150,000 Jews transported to Terezin, documenting whence they came, when they arrived, when and where they were deported. Other materials include nearly every book and article published on Terezin, diaries and letters of inmates, photographs, and whole sets of the literary and political journals printed by the children of Terezin. Set amid lawns and trees not far from the kibbutz dining hall, the center hosts annual ceremonies and conferences on both Yom Hashoah and on 6 May, the date Terezin was liberated.

The twelve-cornered design of the adjacent memorial hall recalls the twelve corners of the fortress city and is constructed of red brick, a reference to the red brick of the ghetto walls. A permanent exhibition on the walls displays ghetto artifacts, transport lists, and photographs to tell Terezin's story. But on entering the remembrance hall, our eyes are drawn immediately to a colorful and intricate mosaic floor depicting an overhead view of the ghetto itself, surrounded by river and moats. The blocks are red, the town square and parks green. In a region

The museum gallery at Beit Terezin on Kibbutz Givat Haim-Ichud, with a mosaic floor depicting a map of the ghetto walls and blocks at Terezin. Photo: James E. Young.

where the only remnant of past civilizations is often the fragments of mosaic floor, the designer Albin Glaser sought to ensure some visual trace of both the ghetto and museum, were anything ever to happen to the building itself. "After all," the curator reminds me, "all we now know of the Byzantine period here are the mosaic floors left behind. The floor is always left." In this land of ruins and new buildings, the museum founders were ever mindful of the precariousness of both memory and the houses of memory. So, as an added precaution, they have also buried a scroll inscribed with Terezin's story beneath the mosaic floor, literally embedding further meaning in this memorial edifice.

Visitors are not the only human element comprising memory here. The archivist at Beit Terezin, Alisah Schiller, was actually born in Tel Aviv to Czech immigrants who came to Israel in the 1930s. But her parents' families so longed for their return that they finally persuaded them to come back to beautiful Prague— just before Hitler annexed the Sudetenland. Trapped, Alisah and her family were sent to Terezin in 1941, but only Alisah lived to see the liberation of the camp.

Within months of her repatriation, she returned to Israel at age fourteen.

The archivist's story is part of the memory being conveyed here, not because she tells it to every visitor (in fact, she guards her story to prevent it from dominating other parts of the museum), but because, as a survivor of Terezin now keeping memory's record in order, she represents a palpable link between the memorial house and its source in Czechoslovakia. Unlike the memorials located at the sites of destruction in Europe, those in Israel cannot invoke the ruins for their authority. At Beit Terezin and other museums at geographical remove from their sources, survivors often represent this lost link to events. As part of the experiences being commemorated, survivors simultaneously guard the communal memory and animate the memorial text with their presence.

Kibbutz Lohamei Hageta'ot

Nowhere in Israel does the survivors' spirit animate a museum more than at Kibbutz Lohamei Hageta'ot—literally, Fighters of the Ghettos Kibbutz. Not only do the fighters who live here embody the link between memorial sites and an actual past, but their experiences have left an unmistakable imprint on the very forms remembrance takes here. As the survivors of camps have organized remembrance of this time around their experiences as victims, the ghetto fighters and partisans recall this era in the images of their own resistance and fighting. In both cases, the survivors' and fighters' experiences have come to serve as paradigmatic figures for public remembrance.

Where other kibbutzim have recollected the period of Shoah around and in contrast to the ideals of the kibbutz movement, Lohamei Hageta'ot has defined itself explicitly in the memory of two fighting founders: Yitzhak "Antek" Zuckerman and Zivia Lubetkin. As young guards of the Zionist left wing, both fought in the Jewish Fighting Organization as deputies to Mordechai Anielewicz during the Warsaw Ghetto uprising. On Anielewicz's death, Zuckerman assumed command of the organization and fought until the ghetto was reduced to smoldering ruins, when he and a handful of other fighters escaped through the sewers to the Aryan side of Warsaw. Once outside, they joined Polish partisan units in the woods and, in August 1944, Zuckerman and Lubetkin led a Jewish brigade in the Polish Warsaw uprising. After surviving these battles and the obliteration of the rest of Warsaw, they returned to the forests to continue fighting as partisans until the end of the war.[8]

In 1946, Lubetkin arrived in Palestine to testify to the fighters' ordeal in the ghetto and woods. The next year, when Zuckerman finally reached the land of Israel, he and Lubetkin, together with another seventy former fighters, partisans, and survivors, founded this kibbutz in their name: Lohamei Hageta'ot. Finally, these pioneers of Shomer Hatsa'ir (Young Guard) would fulfill the movement's raison d'être: settling a collective farm in Eretz Israel. Until that moment, however, despite their youthful agricultural training before the war, the Zionism of these young guards had been realized only in organizing resistance and fighting. The continuity between their past lives in Europe and their new lives in Israel was forged precisely in their capacity to fight. For some, in fact, the "war" never really ended at all. After rising up in the Ghetto in 1943, joining the Poles in their 1944 uprising, and fighting as partisans until 1945, they arrived in Israel in 1947 just in time for the War of Independence. In their minds, there was a direct link between fighting in Warsaw—a struggle, in their words, for national and economic liberation—and the founding of the state: the war for Jewish nationhood begun in Warsaw ended in Israel. Little wonder that memory's mission would be so clear after Israel's independence, that they would regard their kibbutz—the flower of Zionism—as monument to the ghetto fighters.

In founding the museum here in 1949, Zuckerman and his comrades literalized the more figurative memorial of the kibbutz itself. Their intent was clear from the beginning: in the words of the curator, "We wanted to build a Yishuv as a monument to what we had seen in the ghettos and camps." Instead of standing for memory, the kibbutz would actively cultivate it. Over the years, the museum here—Beit Lohamei Hageta'ot—has grown from a small archive and library housed in a hut the size of a tool shed to a grand, classically designed stone-and-concrete building. This and a Roman-style amphitheater were constructed within sight of an actual Caesarian aqueduct: together, the aqueduct, amphitheater, and museum dominate the architectonic space of the kibbutz, lending it a timeless, ancient dimension.

With so few Jews left in Europe to recall Jewish life there before the war, little sign of it now exists in European memorials and museums. In Israel, by contrast, the survivors' recollections necessarily include their lives before the war, their suffering and struggle during the war, and their return to life in Israel afterwards. In the eyes of survivors who build these museums, their experiences link Jewish life in Europe and Israel. As part of this still unfolding historical continuum, their lives may be indelibly marked by the Shoah, but insofar as Jews continue to live and work in Israel, life itself continues. This longer view of Jewish history is explicitly reflected in the configuration of the museum at Lohamei Hageta'ot. Out of twelve exhibition halls, only two are devoted to the killing process; the rest relate what had come before and what now comes after in Israel. Built as it was by the hands of a kibbutz ploughman, Zuckerman, who, five years before

sowing these fields, had been commanding the Jewish rebellion in Warsaw, it could hardly have been otherwise.

The first three exhibition halls, therefore, depict what was lost in Europe: Jewish Vilna, the Shtetl Olkienicki, and the Zionist youth groups of He'halutz. Even here, however, there is a striking contrast between the images of a withered past in Vilna and Olkienicki and the youthful vitality of the Zionist youth groups. Where Vilna and Olkienicki reek of stale old books and tired life, the images of young, kerchiefed pioneers exude vitality, optimism, and athletic strength. In contrast to the past-obsessed *yeshiva bocher* (students) of Vilna, these teenagers look forward to new lives in Eretz Israel, where they seem already to be living. The seeds of both European destruction and Israeli rebirth have already been sown: of the Halutzim who stayed behind, most fought and died; those who came to Israel survived. Unlike the continued sentimentalization of Shtetl life in Diaspora literature and art, the models and photos of Shtetl life in the museum are tinged with death and decay, constructed with their end in mind.

In the next two rooms on the ground floor, killers and victims are recalled, each in succinctly suggestive images. In order to reach the killers, we descend half a

The outdoor amphitheater at Kibbutz Lohamei Hageta'ot is bordered on one side by a Caesarian aqueduct. Adjacent to the museum building, the amphitheater is filled to capacity during commemorations of the Holocaust and resistance. Photo: James E. Young.

flight of stairs: a descent to hell, descent to the gas chamber, descent to graves, descent to the Diaspora. The killers are represented by their effects: intricate models of the the Treblinka death camp and of the Vapniarka work camp, and an SS uniform. We exit this hall to enter that of the victims, here exemplified by the story of Janusz Korczak and his orphaned children. Together, Korczak and his children represent two sides of a victim ideal: the heroic director of the Jewish orphanage in Warsaw, who refused to abandon his innocent and defenseless charges. On this floor, we can also view a proposal for a memorial to all the children of the Holocaust—Yad Layeled. This "monument to the child" would represent not only the children of the Holocaust but, in its generic title, all children, both then and now.

On the next floor, photographs and text narrate the rise of Nazi Germany, its war conquests and initially invincible military machine. As conquerors of powerful nations, the exhibit suggests, the Nazis could not be stopped in their destruction of European Jewry. The ghettos and deportations are described in the room following, equal in space to the section on the Nazis' war: a victim's eye-view from the end of the rifle barrel. Our walking narrative continues past a model of the Anne Frank house in Amsterdam and the actual glass booth in which Adolf Eichmann sat during his Jerusalem trial. The bulletproof glass that once preserved Eichmann is now empty and preserves only the memory of his absence, of Israeli justice served.

Then come two long halls of Auschwitz sculptures, a map of Jewish resistance in Eastern Europe, paintings and drawings from Terezin—and the Warsaw Ghetto uprising. With resistance as its organizing theme, the museum highlights aspects of resistance in all events, turns all responses into acts of heroism. The map of Jewish resistance on the second floor transforms all within its perimeter into variations on the theme: the practical resistance of Eichmann's capture, partisan activity and the Ghetto uprising; the spiritual resistance of Anne Frank, Auschwitz sculptures, and art from Terezin. Even Janusz Korczak exemplifies the resistance implied in facing one's death with dignity. In this sequence, the Warsaw Ghetto uprising becomes the most stirring, but only one of several instances of heroism and resistance.

In the last room, on the top floor, we find more art: drawings by Marcel Janko and others, and a section on Yitzhak Katzenelson, the elegist of the Holocaust, to whom the museum is dedicated. This is not transcendent art, however, but poetry and painting anchored in events themselves. The exhibition that began with a reconstructed past—models, photographs, documents—ends in aesthetic responses to events and thereby encourages viewers' responses, as well.

To a great extent, the main operating principle of all museums is metonymic: we come to know the whole of an age, an event, or a people through the fragment presented to us. In the case of Holocaust museums in Israel, this era is delivered to us primarily through images of resistance and heroism, references to martyred children and the survivors' new lives in Eretz Israel. In each case, the representative part creates a larger meaning for the whole. By remembering all the victims of the Shoah in the figure of children, for example, an exhibition suggests the innocence and defenselessness of all the victims, the irredeemable barbarity of their killers. At the same time, such a presentation also casts doubt in viewers' minds on the traditional rationalizations for such tragedy: divine justice and punishment.

Conversely, when remembrance of the Holocaust is organized around the figure of heroic uprisings, some of this same helplessness is denied: this period becomes significant not in its unprecedented destruction, but in the unprecedented spectacle of armed revolt by the Jews—who rose up against both their enemies and their own traditional responses to persecution. Armed resistance was not only possible but, in the eyes of early museum makers here, obligatory. In the end, Zionist pioneers had also overturned the traditional image of Jew as victim. One of the tragic ironies, however, may be that if fighters remember in the shape of their resistance, and survivors remember in the shape of their experiences, who can remember the death of martyrs? In addition, we might note that of the survivors in Israel after the war (nearly half the population in 1948), only the fighters had a receptive state audience. The survivors who had simply endured, or had survived the camps by more luck than strength, remembered well their murdered families. But with rare exceptions, their remembrances were given little public voice until the 1960 Eichmann trial in Jerusalem.[9]

Given the five-year span in which one's people was murdered, oneself saved, and one's country founded, it might have been difficult to conceive of events any differently. We remind ourselves that in choosing resistance as their theme, the makers of kibbutz memorials have not deliberately tried to obfuscate or diminish the far greater number of martyrs; the icons of heroism here are not the mere whitewashing of slaughter or the calculated exaggeration of Jewish resistance in Europe. Rather, in remembering the Shoah, these groups inevitably remembered themselves, their parts in events, their comrades and movements who stayed in Europe. Since it was often these movements' members who made up the leadership of resistance organizations in Europe, when the kibbutz ploughman remembers these years, it will be in the image of himself, recalled in the figure of fighting comrades left behind.

Chapter 9   Yad Vashem:

Israel's Memorial

Authority

> Sometimes when Momik lies on his stomach
> in ambush, he sees the tall smokestack of the
> new building they just finished over on Mt.
> Herzl, which they call Yad Vashem, a funny
> sort of name, and he pretends it's a ship sailing
> by full of illegal immigrants from Over There
> that nobody wants to take in . . . and he's going
> to have to rescue that ship somehow . . . and
> when he asked his old people what the smoke-
> stack is for, they looked at each other, and
> finally Munin told him that there's a museum
> there, and Aaron Marcus, who hadn't been out
> of his house for a couple of years, asked, Is it
> an art museum? and Hannah Zeitrin smiled
> crookedly and said, Oh sure it is, a museum of
> human art, that's what kind of art.
> —David Grossmann, *See Under: Love*

Of all the memorial centers in Israel, only Yad Vashem Martyrs' and Heroes' Remembrance Authority bears the explicit imprimatur of the state. Conceived in
the throes of the state's birth and building, Yad Vashem would be regarded from
the outset as an integral part of Israel's civic infrastructure. It would both share
and buttress the state's ideals and self-definition. An eclectic amalgamation of

outdoor monuments, exhibition halls, and massive archives, Yad Vashem enacts the state's double-sided memory of the Holocaust in dozens of media.

Yad Vashem functions as a national shrine to both Israeli pride in heroism and shame in victimization, a place where Holocaust history is remembered as culminating in the very time and space now occupied by the memorial complex itself. As if trying to keep pace with the state's own growth, Yad Vashem has continued to expand its reservoir of images, sculptures, and exhibitions: as the state and its official memory of the Holocaust evolve, so too will the shape of memory at Yad Vashem. In its role as the national Memorial Authority, Yad Vashem is the final arbiter of both Holocaust memory in Israel and the very reasons for memory.

According to Shmuel Spector, the genesis for a Holocaust memorial institution in what was still Palestine came just as the first reports of the unfolding catastrophe reached the Yishuv.[1] At a board meeting of the Jewish National Fund in September 1942, Mordechai Shenhavi from Kibbutz Mishmar Ha'emek proposed to commemorate both what he called the "Shoah of the Diaspora" and the participation of Jewish fighters in the Allied armies. Shenhavi suggested that the

site be called "Yad Vashem" (literally, a monument and a name; figuratively, a monument and a memorial), after a quotation from Isaiah (56:5), in which God declares how he will remember those who keep his covenant: "I will give them, in my house and within my walls, a monument and a name, better than sons and daughters. I will give them an everlasting name that shall never be effaced."

With the Yishuv itself under Nazi threat, however, the proposal lay dormant until the very last days of the war. In May 1945, when the scope of destruction became clear, Shenhavi resubmitted his proposal, now named "Yad Vashem Foundation in Memory of Europe's Lost Jews: An Outline of a Plan for the Commemoration of the Diaspora." From the start he had conceived of a multidimensional site by which the Yishuv would remember both the Holocaust and former Jewish life in exile, each in the figure of the other. A month later, the Jewish National Council recommended the establishment of such an institution in Jerusalem, which would include an eternal flame for the victims; a list of their names; a memorial for the lost Jewish communities; a monument for the fighters of the ghettos; a memorial tower to honor Jewish fighters in Allied armies; a permanent exhibit on the concentration and extermination camps; and a tribute to the Gentile rescuers of Jews. Two years later, on 1 June 1947, Yad Vashem convened its first plenary session, putting on public display a plan entitled "Yad Vashem for the Diaspora."

Once again, however, implementation of the memorial was interrupted by events as dire as those that would be commemorated, in this case the 1948 War of Independence. Not until 1950 did Shenhavi resume his lobbying on behalf of a national memorial authority. He proposed an audacious and startling law. Shenhavi hoped not merely to register all the victims of the Shoah, which would be to fulfill the traditional Jewish mandate to remember the dead by naming them; now that the Jews had a state of their own, he proposed granting honorary, posthumous citizenship to all the martyrs, as well. For the next two years, the memorial project was put on hold while Israel's best legal minds wrestled with the concept of commemorative citizenship. Unable to extract a ruling one way or another, the government decided to move ahead nevertheless and defer the issue of citizenship until the memorial authority was established.

In 1952, the minister of education and eminent Israeli historian Benzion Dinur submitted to the parliament a bill for the establishment of Yad Vashem. As always in the Knesset, debate was long and tangled, though the bill itself enjoyed an almost unheard-of consensus among Israeli lawmakers.[2] On 18 May 1953, spurred on by the imminent unveiling of a "memorial to the unknown Jewish martyr in Paris," the Knesset unanimously passed what was officially called the "Law of Remembrance of Shoah and Heroism—Yad Vashem" (Hok hazikaron hashoah vehagvurah—yad vashem), after which the entire assembly rose for a minute's silence in memory of the victims. On 19 August, one day after the Paris memorial's unveiling, the law passed its final reading and became the first remembrance law of the land.

In its immediate temporal context, in fact, the link between the Holocaust and the establishment of the state was palpable for legislators in ways lost to and occasionally denied by subsequent generations. This was partly the result of the fact that national independence followed liberation of the camps by three years, as well as of a sense that Israel's War of Independence was fought as an extension of the Jews' struggle for survival in Europe. In the words of Nachum Goldman, former president of the World Jewish Congress, "If the State came into being, it was not only by virtue of the blood spilt by those who fell in the battles for its existence, which is the highest price, but also, indirectly, because of the millions murdered in the Holocaust."[3] In this view, the blood spilt for Israel's independence is seen to mingle with that spilt in Europe's slaughterhouses. If the state came about by virtue of the blood spilt in both places, it is little wonder that the murdered Jews of the Holocaust would be conferred posthumous Israeli citizenship, for in this scenario they, too, have given their lives for Israel. Conversely, once martyrs of the Holocaust are united with those who fought and died for the state, the War of Independence itself might be said to have begun not in 1947, but in 1939.

Even more significant to many of Israel's leaders at the time, however, was the overt political cause and effect between the Holocaust and the UN vote for

Israeli statehood. For even in the practical side of its birth, the state of Israel was tied closely to other nations' perceptions and recent memory of the Holocaust. In order to persuade the UN commission appointed to study the partition of Palestine into Jewish and Arab states, Goldman reported, Abba Eban and David Horowitz spent much of their time recalling to the delegates the story of the Holocaust. In their retellings, they were able to establish a persuasive link between Holocaust and statelessness, between rehabilitation and national rebirth. As a consequence, the commission visited displaced persons camps in Germany on fact-finding missions to determine the depth of Zionist commitment among survivors—and came away stunned by what they saw and heard. According to several accounts, every last one of the survivors they interviewed had insisted that after Treblinka, Bergen-Belsen, and Auschwitz, their future existed only in Palestine.[4] Even the Soviet delegate Vishinsky is reported to have risen at a meeting of his Eastern bloc comrades and declared flatly that the main factor in their deliberations was the Holocaust, for which they owed the Jews "this measure of rehabilitation."

All of which was fresh in the minds of legislators as they sought to embody the link between Holocaust and statehood in what would become Israel's preeminent national shrine. As defined by the Law of Remembrance of Shoah and Heroism, the memorial at Yad Vashem thus commemorates a reflexively Israeli understanding of the Holocaust, including "the six million members of the Jewish people who died a martyr's death at the hands of the Nazis and their collaborators"; "the communities, synagogues, movements . . . and cultural institutions destroyed"; "the fortitude of Jews who gave their lives for their people"; "the heroism of Jewish servicemen, and of underground fighters"; "the heroic stand of the besieged ghetto population and the fighters who rose and kindled the flame of revolt to save the honor of their people"; "the sublime, persistent struggle of the masses of the House of Israel, on the threshold of destruction, for their human dignity and Jewish culture"; "the unceasing efforts of the besieged to reach Eretz Israel in spite of all obstacles, and the devotion and heroism of their brothers who went forth to rescue and liberate the survivors"; and "the high-minded Gentiles who risked their lives to save Jews."[5]

Unlike memorials that attempt to remove their national origins and interests from view, Yad Vashem's mission as simultaneous custodian and creator of national memory was explicitly mandated in its law. Among the additional tasks of Yad Vashem, as defined in Article 2, are "to collect, examine, and publish testimony of the Holocaust and the heroism it called forth and to bring home its lesson to the people"; "to promote a custom of joint remembrance of the heroes and victims"; and "to confer upon the members of the Jewish people who perished in the days of the Holocaust and the resistance the commemorative citizenship of the state of Israel, as a token of their having been gathered to their people."[6] Shenhavi would have his wish. Among the early tasks of Yad Vashem was the "Memorial Page," launched on 19 April 1955 (Uprising Day), to record the names of every Jewish victim of the Germans. As defined in the *Yad Vashem Bulletin*, the purpose of the Daf-Ed (Memorial Page) project is "to perpetuate the memory of the millions of martyrs, whose graves are unknown and unmarked, by registering their names and other particulars in 'Memorial Pages' and awarding them 'memorial citizenship' of the State of Israel."[7] In bestowing posthumous citizenship on the victims, the state effectively created an invisible but ever-present shadow population of martyrs. As the state's newest citizens, these martyrs are understood in this context as having been murdered not only because they were Jews, but because they were Israelis as well.

The function of memory in this project is precisely what it has always been for the Jewish nation; in addition to bringing home the "national lessons" of the Holocaust, memory would work to bind present and past generations, to unify a world outlook, to create a vicariously shared national experience. These are the implied functions of every national memorial, of course, merely made visible in Israel's legislation of such memory.

The Chamber of the Holocaust at Mount Zion

As a creation of the state, Yad Vashem was necessarily conceived in political time, in response to specific political realities. Among these was a perceived threat by France to pre-empt Israel's national memory of the Holocaust with its own in its memorial to the "unknown Jewish martyr." But even more immediate was a memorial competitor from within Israel itself, a religious formulation of memory completely unacceptable to the secular Zionist founders of the state. Even though Yad Vashem was the first memorial complex proposed for Israel, it was not the first one built. This honor went to Rabbi S. Z. Kahana and his "Chamber of the Holocaust" on Mount Zion, just outside Jerusalem's old city walls.

As an official of the Ministry of Religious Affairs in 1950 (and later its director general), Kahana had hoped to reestablish a Jewish presence in this area, abandoned and ravaged during the 1948 War of Independence. He accomplished this by building a memorial to Europe's destroyed religious communities as close as possible to the heart of Jewish sacred space at the Kotel, forbidden to Jews when it was captured by Jordan in 1948 and held until 1967. At first, the Chamber of the Holocaust was supported by government funds allocated by the Mount Zion Association. After the Six-Day War in 1967, Kahana designated further land and buildings nearby to house the recently initiated Diaspora Yeshiva, which would then administer the Chamber of the Holocaust.

Since then, the chamber has served as a small museum and repository of relics: mock furnaces, the actual ashes of incinerated Jews, tallow made from the victims' remains, tattered uniforms, prayer shawls, and photographs. Nearly one hundred visitors a day, mostly tourists on their way to the Western Wall, enter to the echoes of yeshiva students chanting prayers and arguing disputations. After examining the exhibits of relics, visitors pass through a study room: a long wooden table and chairs, surrounded on two sides by walls lined floor to ceiling with memorial plaques inscribed to the destroyed religious communities of Europe. From here, we step into an outdoor courtyard, its walls similarly covered in tablet-shaped plaques, reminiscent of the broken tombstone walls of Jewish cemeteries in Poland. Each one is dedicated to an entire community or family, however, not to individuals: "to the martyrs of the community of Shavel"; "to our brothers and sisters, martyrs from Tsotsowitz." Adjoining the courtyard is one last room housing an exhibition entitled "Nazism Today," replete with newspaper clippings and headlines from "white power" newspapers and pamphlets.

According to one of the Yeshiva's instructors, Shabtai Herman, who teaches Talmud-Torah in the chamber itself, "This place gives you a sense of exactly what

Study room in Jerusalem's "Chamber of the Holocaust," replete with memorial books and barbed wire. Photo: Ira Nowinski.

the Germans destroyed: learning." Studying before a large photo of mass graves at Bergen-Belsen on the one side and a matzevoth-covered wall on the other, Yeshiva students regard their learning itself as a form of commemoration. As one student remarked, "Studying Torah here raises up the souls of the six million Jews to heaven."[8] As Torah studies are shaped to some extent by the surrounding images, memory and understanding of the Shoah are shaped by its Yeshiva context. Specifically, the Holocaust is studied here in the religious continuum of Jewish catastrophe beginning with the destruction of the First Temple. On each of the traditional fast days, special classes are held: the destruction and significance of the First and Second Temples are examined literally in the shadow of the Holocaust, which is commonly regarded here as the Third, and greatest, Hurban. In the words of Herman, expanding the Yeshiva on the grounds of the Holocaust chamber is not only likened to the rebuilding of the Temple in Jerusalem, but it will be, he suggests, an actual "stepping stone toward rebuilding the Temple."

Courtyard in the "Chamber of the Holocaust," lined with tombstone-shaped tablets commemorating religious families and communities destroyed. Photo: James E. Young.

Yad Vashem

Yad Vashem, on the other hand, was conceived by the state's founders as an explicit tearing away from the religious continuum and its meanings—another kind of countermemorial. This would be the beginning of a new, civic religion whose genesis would coincide with the creation of the state itself, whose new infrastructure would include Yad Vashem. Toward this end, a new historical space would be created, in which events of the Holocaust and the state's founding would quite literally be recalled side by side. The foundation stone for Yad Vashem was therefore laid into the hillside just west of the national military cemetery at Har Herzl on 29 July 1954, in a ceremony that turned this entire area into Har Hazikkaron (Memorial Hill).[9] In this way, Yad Vashem could be regarded as a topographical extension of the national cemetery, where Israel's ideological founder, Theodore Herzl, lay alongside Israel's fallen soldiers, including Hannah Senesh, Israel's martyred heroine ideal of the Holocaust.[10]

Immediately after the consecration of Memorial Hill, before construction even began, organizations of survivors and fighters gathered here for open-air conferences and talks. By 1957, the building housing the archives, library, and administrative offices was completed. The Hall of Remembrance (Ohel Yizkor) was dedicated four years later, on 13 April 1961, followed by the first tree plantings by government-recognized rescuers along the "Avenue of the Righteous" in May 1962. The synagogue, with its salvaged ark and Torah, was dedicated, appropriately enough, during Kristallnacht commemorations in 1965. The historical museum, located below the Hall of Remembrance and its plaza, opened in July 1973, and was followed by the Art Museum and its complex in 1981.

From the beginning, almost every year has witnessed another unveiling at Yad Vashem of a new memorial sculpture or gardens placed around the grounds, including a reproduction of Nandor Glid's haunting Dachau sculpture. A monument and plaza commemorating Jewish soldiers in the Allied forces was added in 1985, a children's memorial in 1988. A memorial sculpture commemorating four martyred women, heroines of the Auschwitz Sonderkommando uprising, was dedicated in 1991. A huge project, "The Valley to the Destroyed Communities," was to be completed in 1992. All told, the construction of memory at Yad Vashem has spanned the entire history of the state itself, paralleling the state's self-construction. For this reason, it seems clear that the building of memorials and new spaces will be never be officially completed, that as the state grows, so too will its memorial undergirding.

Today, the official route for visitors begins with the "Avenue of the Righteous Gentiles," a promenade lined with trees planted by non-Jews to honor their rescue of survivors during the war. The end of the walk is crowned with a very small, fragile-looking rowboat used by Danish fishermen to ferry some six hundred Jews out of occupied Nazi-occupied Denmark on the eve of their roundup. Just beyond the boat, the memory path leads up a short flight of steps, from Gentile to Jewish heroism, into the Warsaw Ghetto Square, bordered by a reproduction

of Rapoport's Ghetto Monument. As will be described at length in the next section, the state's official Holocaust Remembrance Day ceremonies are televised live from this square, filled to overflowing with dignitaries, survivors, soldiers, and government leaders—all framed by the fighters of the Ghetto Monument.

From the Warsaw Ghetto Square, we enter glass doors of the historical museum's open lobby, where we are confronted with a wall-sized monumental relief by Naftali Bezem, entitled *M'shoah l'tkumah* (From Shoah to Rebirth). Set in a black background, the first molten aluminum figure is, like the three that follow, a composite of symbolic forms: a factory emits round rings of smoke; two arms attached to two breasts hold two candlesticks upside down; a dead fish with broken wings floats at the side. In the second figure, the human form is fragmented: an arm, a boot, a head, all disconnected. One hand grasps a ladder, a symbol of uprising and *aliya* (ascension or immigration to the land of Israel), while the other clenches a spear: on the left is destruction, and on the right revolt. Destruction is but one element in this sequence, known only in the context of its consequences. For in the next panel depicting the ascent to Israel, a man brings the fire that has destroyed his family; the survivor in the third panel's boat is now a lion, with his paws on the ground. The overturned candlesticks of the first panel are set aright in the last section and burn brightly. Somewhere between figuration and abstrac-

Tourists at Jerusalem's Yad Vashem rest in the shade of trees planted along the "Avenue of the Righteous Gentiles" to remember non-Jews who saved Jews during the Holocaust. Photo: James E. Young.

tion, these surreal pictographs trace Israel's conceptual matrix of the Holocaust: Shoah, Revolt, Immigration, Rebirth.

Thus introduced, the History Museum itself is divided into three principal sections, their sequence echoing more literally the symbolic narrative of the bas relief. In the first section, the rise of anti-Jewish laws and actions between 1933 and 1939 is traced through a powerful mixture of photographs, leaflets, Nazi propaganda, and historical narrative. The harassment, deportations, and even the pogroms of Kristallnacht are all presented here as part of the prewar anti-Semitic tradition in Europe. From this room, one goes around the corner into a section entitled "The Struggle to Survive: 1939–41"—an extension of the first phase. Here we are brought face to face with the physical persecutions and attacks on Jews in Nazi-occupied Europe: a Jew has his beard cut off by a group of laughing Germans; a group of smugglers is lined up against a Ghetto wall in Warsaw; Jewish leaders dangle from the ends of ropes in Lodz. A group of young officer cadets required to visit the museum confess to being sickened by such photographs. But it is not the the images of death or the sense of terror that offends them, they say: it is the humiliation and degradation of Jews unable to defend themselves.

After leaving this section, we must move physically from one hall—one era— to another. We re-enter the museum lobby on our way to the next hall, devoted solely to the killing process itself between 1941 and 1945. As the layout already suggests, the proportions and methods of this killing were so unlike anything before that it cannot be located spatially within the context of traditional anti-Jewish persecutions. The first image provides a figure by which the rest of the victims will be known: a German soldier is shooting point-blank at a woman cradling her child away from the soldier's gun. The rest of the victims are now perceived no less helplessly: mounds of tangled corpses, medical experiments, and other images from the death camps epitomize the Final Solution. Joined physically to this room, another section labeled "The Gates of the World Were Sealed" offers a metaphysical conclusion. Images of the Evian conference (where the world decided against accepting Jewish refugees), the steamships *St. Louis* and *Struma* suggest a silent complicity on the rest of the world's part: there was no refuge then, as there is now in Israel.

In the logic of the museum's narrative, this leads inevitably to the next phase: Jewish armed resistance. With no other way out, we join Europe's desperate Jews in the sewers of the ghettos and in the forests, as partisans. A long, narrow passageway tells the story of the Warsaw Ghetto revolt, the partisan activities in the woods, all with photographic images familiar to the eyes of young Israelis: bands of partisans in the woods, posing together with carbines and hand grenades. Unlike European memorial expositions, the history of the Holocaust traced here does not end with the liberation of the camps. In adjoining exhibits, the ghetto revolts and partisans are linked spatially to the current historical moment, to the state of Israel itself. For as the photographs of survivors coming ashore at Haifa and Caesarea illustrate, the "end of the Holocaust" comes only with the survivors' return to and redemption in Eretz Israel.

In fact, as we exit the last room of the exhibition, the hall of names, we pass alongside the Baal Shem Tov's words, gilded in gold lettering, a distillation of this memorial's raison d'être in Israel: "Forgetting lengthens the period of exile! In remembrance lies the secret of deliverance." With these words in mind, we walk outside into the blindingly bright light of Jerusalem, the present moment. The memorial message is reinforced further still: "That has all come to this," the museum seems to be saying. "That was the galut, where Jews had no refuge, no defense only death and destruction; this is Israel, its people alive."

From here, visitors ascend steps back up to the Hall of Remembrance plaza, an open square overlooking the ghetto fighters' square below and the Jerusalem hills behind, now ringed with shiny white new neighborhoods. The cool darkness of the Ohel Yizkor (Memorial Tent), standing adjacent, invites us in. Designed by Israeli architect Arieh El-Hanani, the shrine functions on a number of practical and symbolic levels, beginning with its shape and materials. From a distance, its massive, flat concrete top appears as a slab of stone on the hillside, a matzevah. As we approach it, however, the great basalt boulders of its base come into view. These huge stones have been rounded and smoothed by water and wind, transported from a quarry in the Galilee. The piling of stones here recalls both the very first monument cited in Genesis, a gal-ed (witness heap of stones), and the Jewish custom of piling small stones on the flat surfaces of matzevoth. As Yosef Lishinsky reminds us, the rawness in such material also recalls the biblical commandment forbidding chiseled stone for the temple altar.[11] Like the names we assign these events, the materials here also work to bring into analogue the great destructions of the Temple and the Jews of Europe.

Whether or not the Temple analogue needs to be made more explicit, the subtler issue of the sacredness of this space comes to mind. For, as I enter, the shammes hands me a paper kipa, to cover my head in this sacred space, and asks women to cover their shoulders. The air is cool inside, a relief on hot summer days, and it takes a moment for our eyes to adjust to the darkness. The floor panels of the Ohel Yizkor—literally, Tent of Remembrance—bear the names of twenty-two of the largest concentration camps and are arranged in rough geographical order. In one corner, directly beneath an open skylight, an eternal flame flickers amid a sharp-pronged sheath of bronze, which seems to open up like petals of a black flower. It is bathed in a smoky beam of light from the opening above it and set

The Ohel
Yizkor
(Memorial Tent)
at Yad Vashem
embodies stone
heaviness on
the outside,
dark absence
inside. Photo:
James E. Young.

just behind a white, one-by-three-meter granite slab, which covers a pit holding ashes from the death camps. Since this stone entombs the remains of victims, it might be regarded more literally as a collective matzevah for unknown victims, a crypt. Often the slab is covered with wreaths of flowers, recently laid by visiting dignitaries or foreign delegations.

With its four-cornered ceiling rising to the small opening far above the eternal flame, and its walkway circling along the perimeter of names and tomb, the memorial tent objectifies emptiness and absence. The building and its form seem unyielding and permanent, stone-heavy and rock-hard to the touch. It is a space where one's eyes cannot readily fix on anything but the names on the floor, the flame and slab covering ashes. Our glance is first drawn downward by the flame, bringing us into the repose of prayer, and then it turns inward, as if to surround memory on the inside. Here we stand silently to meditate on the order of events, of memory, created for us here. Invited to remember and then to contemplate remembrance in this great dark space, we do so within an ever-vigilant context: exile, memory, and redemption.

From here, visitors can walk around to the synagogue and plaza adjacent to the Hall of Remembrance, whence they can walk either to the art museum and Jewish soldiers' monument behind, or traverse a path alongside the Pillar of Heroism to the children's memorial. If we take the first way, we come to Bernie Fink's monument *Soldiers, Ghetto Fighters, and Partisans*. In this installation, the artist has arranged six great oblong hexagonal granite blocks in two stacks of three, so that a window in the shape of a Jewish star is formed. The window is, in turn,

Bernie Fink's monument to Jewish soldiers, partisans, and ghetto fighters was installed at Yad Vashem in 1985. Photo: James E. Young.

bisected by the blade of a stainless steel sword. The six blocks are intended to recall the six million victims; the blade recalls the fighters; and the star represents the Jewish people. Constructed of granite, steel, and air, this monument explicitly remembers the 1.5 million Jewish soldiers who fought in Allied armies and partisan groups during the war. Though its parts might commemorate the victims, in its wholeness, it projects itself as a victory monument. At the monument's dedication in 1985, conducted with full military honors, the five thousand guests and dignitaries were reminded that Jewish fighters had been part of the forces that defeated the Nazis.

Behind us, in the very center of the complex, stands the tallest memorial at Yad Vashem. What Momik's imagination mistook for a great smokestack is actually the Pillar of Heroism, dedicated to the Jewish ghetto fighters. But the speaker in David Grossman's magical novel is not alone in imagining it as a chimney. Both Israelis and the millions of tourists who have been there continue to remark the great chimney monument they saw at Yad Vashem.

On 26 November 1962, a jury met to decide which of forty-one submissions would be realized as the "Monument of Heroism" at Yad Vashem. A hundred-foot-high tower of tangled and interlocking iron by Naomi Henryk, a student of Israeli sculptor Ze'ev Ben-Zvi, was awarded first prize—though it was never built. Instead, a much more highly polished stainless steel pillar by Buki Schwartz was erected some fifteen years later. In its three-sided configuration, it recalls Henryk's much more roughly cast tower, but it stands only twenty-one meters high, rather than the originally planned thirty meters. It is set in its own little valley, between two walls of black concrete, representing the abyss of destruction whence the tower of heroism rises. In the words of its Hebrew inscription, the pillar of heroism stands for all—immigrants, martyrs and fighters alike: "Now

לפקוד ולשמר הם
לנצח זכר רבבות אלפי
בית ישראל הנלחמים
במחנה ובגיטו ביערות
במחתרת ועם בנות הברית
אשר נלחמו ונפלו על קדוש השם

The *Pillar of Heroism,* designed by Buki Schwartz, soars above all else at Yad Vashem. Photo: James E. Young.

and forever in memory of those who rebelled in the camps and the ghettos, who fought in the woods, in the underground and with the Allied forces, of those who braved their way to Eretz Israel and those who died sanctifying the name of God."

Built not long after the Yom Kippur War, the tower seeks to unite past fighters of the ghetto with current Israeli soldiers, as Yitzhak Arad, the chief education officer of the army and former partisan, made clear in his dedication address. "The world wonders from where our soldiers draw their inspiration for their bravery, what are its sources?" Arad asked.

> The answer is that the source of our heroism in the present lies in the heritage of the heroism of the Jewish people, a heritage that is as old as the history of the Jewish people. . . . In this long chain we must see the special place of Jewish heroism in the Holocaust period: the heroism of the rebels in the ghettos and the death camps, of the Jewish partisans in the forests of Eastern Europe and in the Balkan mountains, of the Jewish underground fighters all over Europe. This chain of heroism also includes the heroism of the ordinary Jew who, under the conditions of the ghetto and the death camps, preserved his image as a human being, fought for his survival day after day, and thus heroically fought the battle of survival of the entire Jewish people.[12]

Not only are past fighters united with present in Arad's address, but all victims and survivors—even those who died sanctifying the name of God—are remembered now as heroes.

Together with Rapoport's Ghetto Monument and Fink's monument to Jewish soldiers, this, the largest, most visible monument at Yad Vashem, thus reminds us of the distinction between martyrs' and heroes' monuments. Where the memory of the heroes is concretized in presence, in thrusting vertical figures, an uprising of form, the martyrs are generally recalled in their absence: the Hall of Remembrance, the children's memorial.

In 1976, the well-known Israeli architect Moshe Safdie was invited to Yad Vashem and guided to a small hillock behind the administrative offices, where he was asked to design a small museum to the 1.5 million Jewish children killed in the Holocaust. A year later, he presented a model for his "museum," which was actually an architectural space, a room lined with mirrors and reflected candles, without an exhibition. It was not exactly what the executive committee had expected, they told the architect. But they would proceed nevertheless, as soon as they found the money to build it. For the next seven years, the model languished in the archives at Yad Vashem, unfunded, until it was shown to an American survivor and philanthropist, Abraham Spiegel. Remembering his own son, killed by the Germans, Spiegel is said to have written a check on the spot, and the monument was unveiled in June 1987.[13]

When first approached to design the monument, Safdie assumed that it would be a testimonial space, gesturing to the specific crime of the children's murder. On further reflection, Safdie decided on a more symbolic conception. "The more I entered the material," he has said, "the more I became convinced that what was needed was a *ner neshama,* a memorial candle, multiplied to infinity through its mirror image."[14] Such a conception would also allow the architect to remain answerable to the discourse of contemporary art and architecture, which demands self-conscious reference both to the art object's materiality and to the illusory nature of representation.

In its realization, the children's memorial works at several levels, some highly evocative, others overly so. To enter the completed memorial space, we pass a large, mounted square of clear glass, inscribed to the memory of the murdered children. The rest of the inscription tells us that this is a gift from Abraham and Edith Spiegel of Beverly Hills, California, in memory of their son, Uziel, who was murdered in Auschwitz. In the daylight, with a hillock of rocks and shrubs directly behind, these words are difficult to read. Then, in contrast to the thrusting tower of heroism nearby, the memorial forces us to descend between walls of Jerusalem stone into a bunkerlike tunnel. On the wall to our right there is plaque with an engraved picture of Uziel Spiegel, one murdered child whose memory will be reflected and refracted into the memory of 1.5 million children.

As we approach a door around the bend in our path, we become aware of the strains of synthesized, atonal music, which give way to the recorded recitation of children's names, their ages and places of origin, in Hebrew and English. We enter a pitch-black room through a door that closes behind us. Our eyes adjust to the dark as we shuffle carefully along a rail, behind which the faces of five boys and four girls from the Holocaust era shift, vanish, and reappear in a hall of mirrors, almost like ghosts. Beyond the music, which tends to overwhelm memory in a sea of sensations and sounds, the names of the children concentrate one's memory, contextualize it in the tradition of a Yizkor service.

From here, we continue into what seems at first to be a planetarium: the dancing light of five memorial candles is splintered into millions of sparks, like stars, reflected in the dark hall by five hundred angled mirrors on the walls and ceilings. It is disorienting, this all-encompassing, star-specked heaven. At first the strange music impairs meditation, the reflections of mind on these reflections of light. The slickness of the installation makes us feel a little self-conscious and reminds some of a theme park ride. Our own response of wonder and awe comes back to haunt us as almost unseemly somehow.

On the one hand, the architect seems to be reminding us that not only is memory illusory, but so are the monuments whose surfaces necessarily reflect our memory back to us: both memory and monument here are smoke and mirrors. But beyond its formal and material properties, this memorial space is organized around two very traditional memorial motifs: candles and the star-studded heavens. By transforming the light of five Jahrzeit candles lighted every morning into an infinite number of stars in heaven, Safdie combines the most traditional memorial gesture of all—the Jahrzeit candle—with the ancient Talmudic opinion that souls of unburied dead never find rest in their endless wanderings about the universe.

Increasingly, the children will be memorialized. For in their innocence, their unrealized potential, and as symbols of the next, never-to-be-born generation, children continue to represent the victim-ideal. In his address at the monument's dedication ceremonies, President Chaim Herzog thus reminded the audience that "these potential citizens of Israel were taken from us and it is our duty to turn their memory into a powerful demand, that the world pledge not to repeat such a crime."[15] It may exaggerate the matter slightly to suggest, as Avishai Margalit has, that these child-victims are being cynically used to emblematize all Israelis, thus turning every soldier and settler into a picture of total innocence.[16] But by turning these children into "potential citizens," the memorial may also suggest that the Holocaust was a crime against the state of Israel itself.

A frieze by
Boris Sakstier
depicting Janusz
Korczak and
children of the
Warsaw Ghetto
is dwarfed by
the nearby
*Pillar of
Heroism* (right).
Photo:
James E. Young.

A path descends from here to the kiosk, where books, postcards, and trinkets are sold. An open lawn between the kiosk and administrative buildings is often covered by youth groups, some seated quietly and meditatively, others boisterous after being pent up inside. They have come either from the museum or from the library and auditorium housed inside the office buildings, which also hold the world's most exhaustive archival and scholarly collections on the Holocaust. Ironically, it is almost as if compiling and examining the testimony and documents, Yad Vashem's initial memorial mandate, has been lost to the public. Images, gardens, and monuments now dominate the public's perception of Yad Vashem's memory-work.

Over the years, Yad Vashem has assumed an increasingly visible profile in Israel's civic and diplomatic landscape. It is the first site visited by foreign dignitaries on their way to meet with Israel's leaders. The obligatory wreath-laying at the Hall of Remembrance reminds all not just that six million Jews died but that other nations did so little to prevent the massacre. As a ceremonial preamble to state talks at any level, such a visit provides more than a little added negotiating leverage, since subsequent discussions are thus conducted with the Holocaust in mind.

If Yad Vashem is indeed second only to the Western Wall in its sacredness as a shrine of Israel's civil religion, as Liebman and Don-Yehiha have suggested, then it also becomes more than just a civic shrine. For, as Liebman and Don-Yehiya point out, the new civil religion in Israel invites a certain confusion between traditional and civil religion. After substituting civil religious values like heroism, bravery, and courage for traditional values like faith and patience, the ministers of the civil religion would have all forget that such substitutions were made.

As a result, not only are traditional Jewish paradigms and holy sites reinvested with civil religious meaning, but civic sites and their meanings acquire a certain religious fervor. Civil religion seeks to recapture—even remake—the spontaneous experience, the initial moment of redemption. It would like to remake it by imputing to contemporary experience the sacred sense of past religious experience. If the objective of civil religion is to sanctify the society in which it functions, as Liebman and Don-Yehiya believe, then we cannot ignore the simultaneous sanctification of particular images of the Holocaust produced in sacred spaces like Yad Vashem. For such sanctification not only integrates, legitimizes, and mobilizes society, it also makes some interpretations of events holier than other interpretations. While this may well be the traditional prerogative of the state, critical visitors must also retain the right to remark the ways divine authority tends to accrue to a state's institutions. In all these ways, Yad Vashem continues to function as Israel's ever-legitimizing national shrine par excellence.

Among Yad Vashem's many outdoor sculptures is Leah Michaelson's *Silent Cry*. Photo: James E. Young.

Chapter 10   When a Day Remembers:

A Performative History

of Yom Hashoah

As ordered by the Jewish calendar, time offers itself as an insuperable master plan by which Jewish lives are lived, past history remembered and understood. For only time, when patterned after the circular movements of earth around the sun, and moon around the earth, can be trusted to repeat its forms perpetually. Grasped and then represented in the image of passing seasons, in the figures of planting and harvest, cycles of time have traditionally suggested themselves as less the constructions of human mind than the palpable manifestations of a natural order. As a result, both our apprehension of time and the meanings created in its charting seem as natural as the setting sun, the rising moon. By extension, when events are commemoratively linked to a day on the calendar, a day whose figure inevitably recurs, both memory of events and the meanings engendered in memory seem ordained by nothing less than time itself.

Of all ways to commemorate the destruction of European Jewry, perhaps none—save narrative—is more endemic to Jewish tradition than the day of remembrance. Neither monuments nor paintings, neither fiction nor reportage is anchored as firmly in the tradition as commemorative fast days, which have been part of normative Judaism since the sixth century B.C.E. Beginning with the prophet Zecharia's reference (8:19) to fasts of the tenth month (Tenth of Teveth), fourth month (Seventeenth of Tammuz), fifth month (Ninth of Av), and seventh month (Third of Tishri), through the geonic period when up to thirty-six commemorative fast days were observed, the *ta'anit tzibbur* (public fast day) may be the most ancient of all traditional Jewish responses to national and communal catastrophe. That each of these fasts commemorates an event linked to the destruction of the First Temple suggests and affirms the centrality of this proto-catastrophe to the very measure of Jewish time itself (recall also the ultra-orthodox community's counting from the Second Hurban). Even the beginning of the Jewish festal year, Rosh Hashana (the first of Tishri), is described in Torah (Lev. 23:24) as *zikkaron teruah* (literally, remembrance of *teruah*, a shofar blast), traditionally called Day of Remembrance.

In Jewish tradition, time and memory, sacred texts and history are intricately interwoven, whereby we know the precise date by the weekly portion of Torah, our place in the text by the date. In this sense, the year is refigured as narrative, albeit a repetitive one. As written narrative imposes the order of language onto historical events, creating in Gerard Genette's terms "narrative time," both the Gregorian solar and Jewish lunar calendars impose yet another order onto historical time, a temporal pattern by which a day's memorial significance will be understood.[1] Like historical incidents related in narrative, the Jewish holidays, festivals, and fasts also acquire meaning according to their places on time's grid. As the placement of a monument in its city matrix generates meaning in it, the location of a commemorative day on the religious and national calendar will create meaning in remembrance, as well. When twinned with historical events, remembrance days assign specific significance to them, depending on where these days are located on the Jewish calendar. The same event might carry several different kinds of significance depending on both the time of year it happened and the time of year it is remembered, which do not always coincide. Conversely, entirely disparate events acquire parallel meaning when commemorated on the same day.

Though it is not a public fast day, Yom Hashoah Vehagvurah (Day of Holocaust and Heroism) owes its existence to the tradition, even as it was proposed in dialectical opposition to it. As such, Yom Hashoah inscribes memory of events into the Jewish calendar even as it finally nationalizes and secularizes such memory. In addition to being shaped by its place on the calendar, Holocaust Remembrance Day also lends its own cast to other, already existing holy days. Passover and Hanukka, for example, are transformed and revalued in Israel's remembrance of heroism during the Shoah. Their traditional significance as times when God

April 1, 1993	2	3	*Parashat Ẓav*
NISSAN 10		NISSAN 11	*Shabbat ha-Gadol* NISSAN 12

actively interceded on behalf of the Jews is now colored by new readings emphasizing the Jews' own actions. In all cases, the calendar figures prominently in the contemporary grasp of realities and responses to them: its narrative continues to bear the consequences of both meaning and action.

Beyond its place on the calendar, Holocaust remembrance is enacted by a variety of observances encompassed by the day, including commemorative ceremonies and speeches, moments of silence, and mass-media programming. Even this cultural history of Yom Hashoah—itself a narrative "telling of time"—might be regarded as an extension of the remembrance day. In this performative history of Holocaust Remembrance Day, I would like to bring into view a few of the ways in which memory and its meanings are generated on this day, how Yom Hashoah turns time itself into memorial space. For, like most commemorative spaces, whether topographical or calendrical, this day has come to remember nearly everything but its own ambivalent genesis and evolution. Part of my aim, therefore, will be to reinvest this day of remembrance with the memory of its own history.

The Calendar Renewed

In Israel today, where the religious calendar is overlaid by the civil calendar, symbolic time serves both national and religious ends. But even though Israel's resulting "civil religion" is rooted in the Jews' traditional symbols and figures, it is by no means synonymous with these figures, as Charles Liebman and Eliezer Don-Yehiya have shown so well.[2] Occasionally, a traditional religious date will unobtrusively serve a civil need: for example, the Seventh of Adar, which marks Moses' birth and death, is now designated as the day of mourning for Israeli soldiers whose final resting place is, like Moses', unknown. But in other cases, a vibrant tension is created between the two calendars, whereby ancient forms and symbols are used to legitimate civil ceremonies, and the state's remembrance days infuse traditional holy days with national significance.

In fact, perhaps nobody better recognized the potential consequences in a calendar's narrative than Israel's early state makers. The New Jews were simply going to need a New Calendar, a new time-map by which to navigate the future. For the

4	5	6
	Erev Pesaḥ	*First Day of Pesaḥ*
	Fast of the	*Sefirat ha-Omer*
Palm Sunday NISSAN 13	*Firstborn* NISSAN 14	*begins* NISSAN 15

traditional calendar was as discredited in the Zionists' eyes as the self-destructive delusions it had seemed to foster in Jewish minds over the ages. It was a matter not only of rejecting two thousand years of decayed Jewish life in the Diaspora, but also of discarding the calendar that had perpetually recirculated the myths sustaining the misery of life in exile. Time would no longer be measured in the distance between the Temple's destruction and the present moment. Instead, the redrawn calendar would find its genesis, its anchor, in the birth of the state itself. All else, including memorial days, would now be regarded as either culminating in Independence Day or in issuing from it.[3]

Thus declared in 1949, Israel's first and most joyous public holiday marked the Fifth of Iyar as Yom Hatzma'ut, anniversary of the day in 5708 (14 May 1948) when independence was proclaimed and the state established. One year later, the government dedicated the day preceding Independence Day to the memory of those who had fallen in the 1948 war. The choice of this date for Yom Hazikkaron initially rankled many of the bereaved families, who found such a solemn day violated by the unabashed revelry immediately following it. But the government was steadfast, its reasons for linking the state's war-dead with national independence clear. On the level of pure statist ideology, no better model would be found than dying for the state: as the sole reason for living, the state would now be the only reason for dying. By yoking the deaths of its soldiers together with the birth of the state, the government in effect nationalized the oldest of all Jewish paradigms: destruction and redemption. A memorial day turning at sunset into Independence Day would make explicit that the destruction of these men was redeemed in the birth of the state: mourning was to be relieved literally by the celebration of Independence.

The aim, however, was never merely to find a new world view for the New Jew, but to select which governing views to advance and which to abandon. For Ben-Gurion's statists, one of the least palatable aspects of the old calendar lay in the way its fast days had explained past disasters. Traditionally, the four minor fast days had been associated with different events from the siege and fall of ancient Jerusalem, each purportedly marking the actual anniversary of a disaster during the destruction of the Temple in 586 B.C.E. In fact, none of them probably

7	8	9
Second Day of Pesaḥ NISSAN 16	*Ḥol ha-Mo'ed* NISSAN 17	*Ḥol ha-Mo'ed Good Friday* NISSAN 18

had any actual historical connection to the events being commemorated.[4] Nor did that matter. More important was the way that four historically independent fast days had come to be associated with the destruction of the Temple—the ur-catastrophe—and that over time, these days accumulated the commemorative weight of later catastrophes as well.

For traditional dates seem to have attracted commemoration of other events and then organized them around a teleological locus, creating a single meaning in all events. Remembrance days of multiple disasters sprang not from the coincidental occurrence of events on the same day, but from the assuredly noncoincidental single meaning assigned by the tradition to all disasters, no matter how disparate. As a result, not only were entirely unrelated disasters reported to have occurred on exactly the same day, centuries apart (the destructions of the First and Second Temples, for example),[5] but all disasters were assigned the same meaning— *Mipnei Hataeinu* (because of our sins). According to the Rambam, the aim of the four fasts is to "stir the hearts, to open roads to repentance, and to remind us of our own evil deeds, and of our fathers' deeds which were like ours, as a consequence of which these tragic afflictions came upon them and upon us."[6]

For the founders of modern Israel, such meaning created in the Shoah by the traditional calendar was repulsively unacceptable. The first movement toward a national Holocaust remembrance day, therefore, came in the movement away from traditional commemorative dates marking former disasters. This is also where the needs of the state and those of the rabbinate came into direct conflict. On the one side, there was a pressing need among the religious community in and out of Israel for a rabbinical ruling to set a day on which Jahrzeit candles could be lighted and Kaddish recited for those whose actual dates of death during the Shoah were unknown. For the rabbinate, which date to choose was relatively simple: after all, they were already in possession of at least four ready-made days of mourning. So, in 1948, they adopted the Tenth of Teveth as Yom Kaddish Klali (Day of Communal Kaddish), for little better reason, according to some, than to reinvigorate an otherwise dormant fast day.[7]

On the other hand, the obvious problem for the state and predominantly non-religious population was that, according to the tradition, this day would not

10	11	12
	Ḥol ha-Mo'ed	*Seventh Day*
Ḥol ha-Mo'ed NISSAN 19	*Easter* NISSAN 20	*of Pesaḥ* NISSAN 21

merely link the Shoah to the fall of Jerusalem; it would suggest as well the theological reasons for this fall—Mipnei Hataeinu—all as a justification for current exile. None of which could be tolerated by a state dedicated to the rebuilding of Jerusalem and the Jews' mass return from exile. If there was a "meaning" for the Holocaust in the national view, it was the necessity for a Jewish state to protect Jews from just this sort of destruction—not a divine punishment for supposed sins committed. Even here, the archaic religious paradigm is occasionally, if reflexively, reinvoked also as a Zionist explanation of events. As Liebman and Don-Yehiya have noted, the lead story in the newspaper *Davar* on Yom Hashoah in 1960 concluded that the "function of Holocaust Day is to remind the Jewish people of its own sin in not unequivocally having chosen Zion."[8]

In fact, once recast in the image of the statists themselves, this day would not commemorate mere destruction at all. In keeping with their vision of a new, fighting Jew and their rejection of the old, passive Jew as victim, the founders would prevent this day from entering the commemorative cycle of destruction altogether. Six years after the liberation of the concentration camps, three years after the state of Israel was founded, the Israeli Knesset thus moved to adopt a national Holocaust and Ghetto Uprising Day. As proposed by Member of Knesset Mordechai Nurock on 12 April 1951, "The first Knesset declares and determines that the 27th day of the month of Nissan every year shall be Holocaust and Ghetto Uprising Day [Yom Hashoah Umered Hageta'ot]—an eternal day of remembrance for the House of Israel." It remains significant that Nurock, an orthodox Jew, would agree to sponsor this bill. In an impassioned floor speech bristling with allusions to the Book of Lamentations, he was able to validate the bill at both the political and religious levels. Not Nebuchadnezzar, nor Titus, nor the crusades, nor the pogroms could compare, he proclaimed. This was a third Hurban, greater than all the rest, and so demanded its own day.[9]

"We need to choose a date," he continued, "that coincides with most of the slaughter of European Jewry and with the ghetto uprisings that took place in the month of Nissan." In the next sentence, Nurock added that the Knesset commission had chosen this day because "it was during the Sfirah, when the crusaders, ancestors [avot avotehem] of the Nazis, destroyed so many 'holy' [that is, Jewish]

13	14	15
Eighth Day of Pesaḥ NISSAN 22	NISSAN 23	NISSAN 24

communities." Since the Sfirah period (counting the omer) was already a traditional time of semi-mourning, during which marriages, haircuts, and music were forbidden to the religious, Nurock deemed it all the more appropriate. In addition, the only other secular date put forth until then, that of the Warsaw Ghetto uprising (19 April 1943, the Fifteenth of Nissan), would not have been allowed by the rabbinate because it overlapped with Passover. In fact, the ultra-orthodox delegation to the Knesset requested that the entire month of Nissan be protected from the violation of an official day of mourning—a demand vociferously rejected by former ghetto fighters, who wanted to place the day as close as possible to the anniversary of their uprising. In effect, this left only a few choice days during a period bordered on the one side by the Fifteenth of Nissan (the first day of Pesach and Uprising) and on the other by the Fifth of Iyar, Israel's Independence Day. Forbidden to set a day of mourning during Hol Hamo'ed (the week of Passover) and not wanting to crowd Yom Hazikkaron and Yom Hatzma'ut, the committee was left with only twelve days in which to place Yom Hashoah Umered Hageta'ot.

In the end, by choosing the Twenty-seventh of Nissan (five days after the end of Hol Hamo'ed, seven days before Yom Hazikkaron), the committee dramatically emplotted the entire story of Israel's national rebirth, drawing on a potent combination of religious and national mythologies. Pulled from both the middle of the six-week Ghetto uprising and the seven-week Sfirah, this day retained links to both heroism and mourning. Coming only five days after the end of Passover, Yom Hashoah Umered Hageta'ot extended the festival of freedom and then bridged it with the national Day of Independence. Beginning on Passover (also the day of the Warsaw Ghetto uprising), continuing through Yom Hashoah, and ending in Yom Hatzma'ut, this period could be seen as commencing with God's deliverance of the Jews and concluding with the Jews' deliverance of themselves in Israel. In this sequence, biblical and modern returns to the land of Israel are recalled; God's deliverance of the Jews from the desert of exile is doubled by the Jews' attempted deliverance of themselves in Warsaw; the heroes and martyrs of the Shoah are remembered side by side (and implicitly equated) with the fighters who fell in Israel's modern war of liberation; and all lead inexorably to the birth of the state.[10]

16	17	*Parashat Shemini*	18	
	Shabbat			
NISSAN 25	*Mevarekhim*	NISSAN 26	*Yom ha-Sho'ah*	NISSAN 27

Unfortunately, this resolution was passed at the height of statist influence in Israel and so, effusive parliamentary sentiments notwithstanding, was widely ignored. It could be argued that memory of the Shoah was not neglected so much as merely subsumed in the greater task of state building during the early 1950s. But this was also a time in Israel when bare mention of the Shoah, or the fact that one had survived it, might have been met with surly contempt. It was a time when survivors were still being shamed into silence by those claiming the foresight to have left Europe before the onslaught. In the early statists' view, the Shoah was redeemable—hence, memorable—by little more than instances of heroism and the Jewish courage it evoked in some of its victims, the hopelessness of Jewish life in exile, and the proven need for a state to defend Jews everywhere.[11]

Though this resolution was passed by the Knesset in 1951, it generated little public notice until 1953, when, as part of its mandate, Yad Vashem Memorial Authority was assigned control over how the day was to be observed. Even then, and for the next several years, it seemed that the day of remembrance had been forgotten by all but survivors and partisans. In response, Nurock and others decided in 1959 that only a law, not just another parliamentary resolution, could guarantee public observance. Some of the questions arising during the Knesset floor debate on the law's wording might now be reintroduced to the day of remembrance. First, the name: one member of Knesset found the notion of Ghetto uprising too specific. After all, she asked, wasn't there also heroism in Kiddush Hashem, that is, in martyrdom itself? She proposed that since the main principle at hand was what the uprising stood for—heroism—this principle be included in the name as well: Yom Hashoah, Hagvurah, Uhamered. Others wondered whether we ought to remember only the killing, or only the uprising, or only heroism. Why a day to remember all these? And what about the killers? How do we remember them? Or maybe this day should mark the inquisition as well. Or Chmielnicky. Or the Ukrainian pogroms.

Still others argued unsuccessfully for the day to be incorporated into Tesha B'av (the Ninth of Av), the most widely observed fast day recalling the destruction of the Temple. As Saul Friedländer and others have noted, years later Menachem

270
Israel

19	20	21
NISSAN 28	NISSAN 29	*Rosh Ḥodesh* NISSAN 30

Begin asked that Yom Hashoah Vehagvurah be divided between two already existing days. Yom Hashoah (Holocaust Day) would be observed on Tesha B'av, and Yom Hagvurah (Heroism Day) on Memorial Day for Israel's fallen soldiers.[12] Begin's proposal was primarily a reflection of Rabbi Joseph B. Soloveitchik's proposition that the religious community would give up the Tenth of Teveth if the state gave up the Twenty-seventh of Nissan—and all would commemorate the Shoah on Tesha B'av. But such a compromise would have been no compromise at all, of course, since the meaning engendered on this fast day would have been basically the same as that created on the Tenth of Teveth.[13]

So the Twenty-seventh of Nissan prevailed and was eventually generalized slightly in name and assigned concrete observances. As finally passed by the Knesset on 7 April 1959, the law for this Day of Remembrance of Holocaust and Heroism reads:

1. The 27th of Nissan is the Day of Remembrance of the Holocaust and Heroism, dedicated every year to remembrance of the catastrophe of the Jewish people caused by Nazis and their aides, and of the acts of Jewish heroism and resistance in that period. Should the 27th of Nissan fall on a Friday, the Day of Remembrance shall be marked on the 26th of Nissan of that year.

2. On the Day of Remembrance there shall be observed Two Minutes Silence throughout the State of Israel, during which all traffic on the roads shall cease. Memorial services and meetings shall be held in Army camps and in educational institutions; flags on public buildings shall be flown at half mast; radio programmes shall express the special character of the day, and the programmes in places of amusement shall be in keeping with the spirit of the day.

3. The Minister authorized by the government shall draft, in consultation with the Yad Vashem Remembrance Authority, the necessary instructions for the observance of the Day of Remembrance as set forth in this Law.[14]

In 1961, an amendment required that all places of entertainment be closed on the eve of Yom Hashoah VeHagvurah. Yad Vashem also suggested that the siren for Yom Hazikkaron be sounded to enforce the two minutes of silence on Yom

22	23	24	Parashat Tazri'a / Meẓora
Rosh Ḥodesh IYAR 1	IYAR 2		IYAR 3

Hashoah, yet another move linking the martyrs of the Shoah to the heroes who fell for the State.

The Memorial Performance of a Day

How then is the remembrance day publicly performed? What do people remember in its ceremonies and moments of silence? To what extent do the forms of observance shape remembrance itself? Rather than cutting across all locations and communities, answers to these questions depend very much on the specific site. Outside of Israel, Yom Hashoah increasingly assumes the trappings of a "holy day" and so is often observed in and around the synagogue. When conducted at civic centers or at public memorial sites, "services" are as likely as not to be led by a rabbi or member of the religious community. In America, where the main organizing ideology is pluralism, ecumenical ceremonies bring together clergymen from diverse faiths and ethnic groups, Jewish survivors and Christian liberators. Each commemoration reflects the ethos and tradition, the piety or politics of a given community. In fact, the first national Days of Holocaust Remembrance in America, proposed by Sen. John Danforth (28–29 April 1979), were to commemorate the thirty-fourth anniversary of Dachau's liberation by American troops—an explicit reflection of America's Holocaust experience. Only later were these days moved to coincide more closely with the Twenty-seventh of Nissan. In New York, the Warsaw Ghetto Resistance Organization gathers thousands of people into the Felt Forum to light candles to heroism and martyrdom. In Brooklyn, a *minyan* at a small *shul* (synagogue) holds an all-night vigil—Leyl Shmurim—to study all that was lost. In Tennessee, a Catholic priest has set aside parallel days on the Christian liturgical calendar, during which he leads his congregation in a "Feast of Atonement." Scholars, writers, and religious leaders across the religious spectrum continue to fashion new commemorative liturgies for this day.[15]

While all of these ceremonies and liturgies comprise a total text of this day, for the purposes of this inquiry, I shall concentrate on the performance of this day in Israel. Like all Jewish commemorative and holy days, Yom Hashoah begins at sundown the night before. In the years immediately following the law's passage,

25		26		27	
Yom Hazikkaron	IYAR 4	*Yom ha-Aẓma'ut*	IYAR 5		IYAR 6

there was little perceptible change in the streets on this evening: it was not so different from other nights. At first, Yad Vashem asked the prime minister's office to enforce the clause in the Remembrance Law closing places of entertainment and amusement. When the office replied that it could not without an impossibly strict reading of the law, Yad Vashem resorted to sending notices to movie houses and theaters requesting that they show only films or plays appropriate to Holocaust remembrance. Over the years, this has achieved a partial compliance, with many cinemas continuing to show their regularly scheduled films.

The state-controlled mass media are another story. For days before and after Yom Hashoah, Israel television airs along with its regular programming a variety of documentary and fiction films on the Shoah, specially produced shows on resistance and destruction, histories of anti-Semitism, interviews with survivors and partisans, and panel discussions featuring scholars of the Holocaust. On the day itself, all programs are devoted to the Holocaust, beginning with a live broadcast of the state memorial ceremonies at Yad Vashem. Between 1986 and 1989, the first evening's programs also included—incredibly—a Holocaust quiz show, *The International Quiz on Jewish Heroism during World War II.* Taped in front of a live audience, panels of students would take questions from the state's president on names, dates, places, and events of the Shoah period highlighting instances of resistance and heroism. Correct answers would elicit respectful applause from the audience, wrong answers finding only silence.

In the days leading to Yom Hashoah on the four state-run radio stations, music composed in the ghettos and camps is interspersed with interviews, roundtable discussions, readings of diaries and poetry from the era, and dramatic presentations. On the Twenty-seventh of Nissan, somber music mixes with liturgical melodies drawn from the days of awe—except on Abby Nathan's independent radio station, "The Voice of Peace," which broadcasts a full schedule of popular antiwar and protest songs from the sixties and seventies.

In the state's early years, hundreds of members of ghetto fighters' organizations would march through Tel Aviv on the eve of remembrance. Setting out from Malkei Yisrael Square, carrying placards and banners identifying themselves as

28	29	30
IYAR 7	IYAR 8	IYAR 9

partisans, ghetto fighters, and anti-Nazi war veterans, these men and women would wend their way from Rehov Frishman and Rehov Dizengoff through Dizengoff Square and then arrive at the Mann Auditorium to hold their own annual memorial meeting. Similar gatherings convened at Lohamei Hageta'ot, Yad Mordechai, Ma'ale Hahamisha, and the Martyrs' Forest outside Jerusalem. The content of these meetings still varies from year to year, group to group. But generally they include addresses by survivors and former partisans, the singing of partisan songs, a recitation of Kaddish, and end with the national anthem.

There is only one official Opening Ceremony of Holocaust Martyrs' and Heroes' Remembrance Day that evening, however, and it takes place at Yad Vashem on Har Hazikkaron (Remembrance Hill) in Jerusalem. In front of thousands of guests, all monitored carefully by security forces, the president and prime minister of Israel lead the national remembrance service. An Israel Defense Forces Honor Guard opens the ceremony with a presentation of arms, followed by a lowering of the flag to half-mast. Then the president lights a flame of remembrance, and addresses are delivered by the chairmen of the Yad Vashem Directorate and Council, as well as by the chairman of the Council of Organizations of Former Partisans, Fighters, and Nazi Prisoners. After "Eli, Eli" is sung by the chief cantor of the Israel Defense Forces, the prime minister reads his keynote speech. This is followed by the *Partisans' Hymn* and the lighting of six memorial torches, each by a new immigrant from a different land—formerly Jews of the Diaspora remembering those who died in exile. The ceremony ends with a powerful reading of Psalm 79 by the chief rabbi of the Army, a recitation of Kaddish, "Ani Ma'amin," and *Hatikva*, the national anthem.

The entire ceremony is conducted at the foot of the Wall of Remembrance at Yad Vashem, a reproduction of Nathan Rapoport's Warsaw Ghetto Monument. As a figurative backdrop, this site frames the proceedings in especially significant ways: the Ghetto fighters tower heroically overhead the dais and speakers; the martyrs are on their last march, barely visible behind a row of Honor Guards. Illuminated from below by colored floodlights, the hulking figures of the fighters glow spectacularly before the seated audience, though somewhat grotesquely when viewed on television. The adjacent bas relief depicting the last march is seemingly guarded by Germans from behind (their helmets and bayonets just visible) and by Israeli soldiers from the front. The wall itself is draped not in black memorial bunting, but in the national colors, blue and white.

On this evening, Yad Vashem's exhibition hall remains open to the public until midnight to accommodate thousands of extra visitors. Early the next morning, an honor guard composed of former partisans and current soldiers takes its position inside the great Memorial Hall. They stand at attention amid the names of death camps inscribed on the floor, while the eternal flame flickers silently nearby. Even as these soldiers symbolically guard memory of the martyrs, they more literally embody—and thereby remind us of—the heroic fighters. In fact, after being twinned with heroism for so many years, the Shoah itself no longer signifies defeat in many of the young soldiers' eyes, but actually emerges as an era of heroism, of triumph over past passivity. Through its explicit coupling of Shoah and gvurah (heroism) this day encourages rememberers to find heroism wherever it may be: from active resistance to the spiritual resistance of artists and writers; from the self-sacrifice of parents for their children to the quiet dignity of Jews bravely facing certain death.

In fact, how Yom Hashoah will remember the Holocaust to these young soldiers is made explicit in the bulletin especially prepared for army commanders on Yom Hashoah, "Informational Guidelines to the Commander":

> 1. The Zionist solution establishing the State of Israel was intended to provide an answer to the problem of the existence of the Jewish people, in view of the fact that all other solutions had failed. *The Holocaust proved, in all its horror, that in the twentieth century, the survival of Jews is not assured as long as they are not masters of their fate and as long as they do not have the power to defend their survival.*
>
> 2. A strong State of Israel means a state possessed of military, diplomatic, social, and economic strength, and moral character which can respond properly to every threat from outside and provide assistance to every persecuted Jew wherever he is. The consciousness of the Holocaust is one of the central forces which stand behind our constant striving to reach this strength and behind the solidarity and deep tie with Diaspora Jewry.[16]

This conception was elaborated in Chief of Staff Mordechai Gur's address at the base of Yad Vashem's Wall of Remembrance in 1976, in which he made clear the current generation's debt to the Holocaust: "If you wish to know the source from which the Israeli army draws its power and strength, go to the holy martyrs of the Holocaust and the heroes of the revolt. . . . The Holocaust [] is the root and legitimation of our enterprise."[17] The vocabulary of both the guidelines and the chief of staff is aimed at young soldiers, whose identity with the victims depends almost entirely on the martyrs being presented now as heroes. The martyrs are not forgotten at Yad Vashem, but are recollected heroically as the first to fall in defense of the state.[18]

In addition to its codification in the "informational guidelines," this unity created in the memory of the Holocaust is reiterated every year in the speeches on this day—all of which constitute part of the remembrance day's text. "Today, the 27th of Nissan, the people of Israel unites with the memory of its sons and daughters, the fighters of the heroism and the victims of the Holocaust," declared Joseph Burg in 1989. "In their heroic deaths, they commanded us to live." A few minutes later, Prime Minister Yitzhak Shamir echoed this refrain: "Every year, the House of Israel unites with the memory of our people who were destroyed during the Holocaust years by the Nazi beast . . . . And those who were swept away commanded us to live. . . . The people of Israel unites in the strength of memory commanded us in the Torah, 'Remember what Amalek did unto you, do not forget it.'"[19] As we will see, however, there is a difference between uniting in "the memory of our people" and uniting in the meaning of this memory.

The next morning, at the base of the Western Wall—the ultimate iconographic symbol of destruction in Judaism—survivors take turns reciting the names of victims from a list of three hundred thousand provided by Yad Vashem. Ultra-religious Jews in black come and go, oblivious to the recitation of names. Their remembrance is not the state's remembrance, after all, but still Yom Kaddish, the Tenth of Teveth: they virtually ignore this and other ceremonies on the Twenty-seventh of Nissan. As the names drone on, tourists gather nearby for a group photograph; two soldiers in combat gear pause and listen intently, as if for specific names, before moving on. Then a woman interrupts the readers with a list of her own, which she is permitted to read in quavering voice. On this day, even the holiest of religious spaces takes on statist meaning. One side of the Western Wall commemorates the destruction of Jerusalem and the resulting dispersion; the other recalls ancient Jewish statehood and the rebellion against the Romans. Meanwhile, Prime Minister Shamir begins a parallel recitation in front of the Knesset by reading the names of his family killed by the Nazis.

Since only a small part of Israel's population actually attends any of the official ceremonies, many Israelis find this day's most powerful moment in the two-minute siren that sounds across Israel at 8 a.m. on Yom Hashoah. For most Israelis, this siren is their only direct experience of the remembrance day. Commemoration, which might otherwise be avoided, is inescapable during this moment. Instead of the clarion call of the Shofar relayed from hill to hill, as in ancient times, an unwavering air-raid siren—a terrible *tekiah gedolah*—now transfixes an entire country. Its wartime shades of danger and warning meld with the Shofar's traditional echoes denoting God's memory of all events, past and future, and the call to penitence: secular and religious Jews alike pause before its memorial significance.[20] Because this moment of silence is the one ritual text shared by all in Israel, we might consider what literally occurs over these two minutes—both on the street and in the minds of those, like the author, who "observe" this moment.

Just before the hour, some people in the street begin to hesitate and wait. Then the siren begins, low and deep and rises until it reaches scream pitch, an open-mouthed wail. Depending on where one stands, the siren can be unbearably loud or is muffled by buildings and trees. All in the street stop in their tracks: taxis, buses, trucks, pedestrians. Drivers get out of their cars, some look up at the sky, then at their watches, and then down at the ground. Most stand with heads bowed, shoulders hunched. At the corner of King George and Ben Yehuda streets in Jerusalem, where I stand, an old man shakes uncontrollably. A young mother clenches the hand of her child, who looks up wondrously at the suddenly still streets. A soldier shifts impatiently from foot to foot, seemingly embarrassed. An elderly couple sets down their shopping bags, full of groceries. An Arab construction worker laying paving stones stands up and looks straight ahead into space, at no one. Tourists caught unaware pause uncertainly, some fingering their cameras but too ashamed by the awful solemnity to snap photos. Then a professional photographer, laden with equipment, begins to scuttle from corner to corner, shooting everything in sight. How will he convey this moment? He risks turning into still life what is already and significantly still. How will he capture the sense of Israel's frenetic motion stopped so suddenly by a sound?[21]

Then I wonder: What do the Sephardic immigrants remember? Their own former misery in Islamic countries? The stereotype images of Ashkenazim going like sheep? What do Arab-Israelis make of this day, of these two minutes? What do they remember of Jewish experience? Their Jewish neighbors' past lives, or the intifada of their West Bank cousins? What do I remember? I remember watching a tired-looking woman in a kibbutz kitchen, years ago, as she turned off the water, squeezed out a rag, wiped her hands on a smudged apron, and leaned against the counter. I remember her telling me that every year, she recalls the same image during this siren: leaving her parents' Hamburg home in 1938, a nine-year-old girl on her way to Palestine, her last moments in Germany. Born in America after the Shoah, I remember only what I have heard from others on past remembrance days.

For two minutes, the siren turns all moving things and people into standing monuments. For two minutes the siren encircles us with sound, gathering all into one great space of time, turning the very ground we share into public memorial space. The moment stretches on, the wail growing tighter and thinner, like a

In a photograph
of the Tel Aviv–
Jerusalem
highway during
the morning's
siren on Yom
Hashoah, the
sense of stilled
movement is
captured
against a
background of
implied
movement.
Photo: Frederic
Brenner.

taut thread, binding all together, until it unwinds. A half-hour later, I look into strangers' eyes and wonder where they were, and if they remember the moment we shared. But what is it that we are sharing in this ritual instant? The survivor remembers her experiences in Auschwitz, her lost family and friends, her lost past life. At the same time, she remembers why she is in Israel, why her sons are in the army. Am I to remember her life as well, as she has told it to me? And if so, do we indeed share memory, her memory, even if I know it only vicariously? Or must I concentrate on my own experience of this period, which amounts to nothing more than its effects on me, my felt rage and desolation?

As reflected in Yad Vashem's explicit mandate "to foster a unified form of commemoration of the heroes and martyrs of the Jewish people,"[22] many feared from the outset that without standard forms of observance, national meaning in the Holocaust might also be lost. As the meaning of former catastrophes had been unified in ritual texts, national meaning of the Shoah would require a unified memorial text. "We have not devised as yet adequate rites so as to install the 27th of Nissan among our days of mourning," Arye Kubovy wrote in 1957. "The Lamentations which should be read from year to year and in which our people will bewail its dead has not yet been written."[23] Ten years later, this call was repeated by Benjamin West, who proposed a scroll of the Holocaust: "We need an 'Aicha' [Lamentations] of the Holocaust, something short and strong that will have an effect on believers and non-believers alike."[24] Since then, many other—mostly religious—leaders have bemoaned the plurality of observance, what they perceive as a splintering of memory and its meanings. David Golinkin has not only argued passionately for a more unified public commemoration of the Shoah, based on the elements of Jewish religious tradition, but has also proposed a detailed plan for commemorating Yom Hashoah in our homes.[25]

At this point, however, we might distinguish between unified forms of commemoration and the unification of memory itself, between unified meanings and unified responses to memory. For despite unified forms of commemoration, memory in these shared moments is not necessarily shared, but in fact varies distinctly from person to person. This is not a day of shared memory, but rather a shared time of disparate remembrance. Taken together, these discrete memories constitute the *collected*, not collective, memory evoked on Yom Hashoah. In this light, we might see Yom Hashoah not as a day of national memory so much as a nationalization of many competing memories.

In its conception, Yom Hashoah was intended as neither a fast nor a holy day. It was pulled out of the religious continuum precisely to be observed as a national day of remembrance. As such, this day would mirror one of the nation's own functions: to bind into one polity a diverse people. Nations traditionally accomplish this unification in a number of ways, including the propagation of common laws, ideals, and language. As it turns out, generating a national memory is yet another way to unify a nation. For the very act of commemoration provides a common experience for a population otherwise divided by innumerably disparate lives. This is not a unity of Holocaust experience, however, or even the unification of memory itself. It is only the unity of shared ceremony, which creates the sense of a shared past.

This is the painful necessity and impossibility of a public remembrance day, its blessing and its curse. On the one hand, the creation of common memorial experience can indeed unify plural segments of a population, even if it is only during a brief "memorial moment." This is both the right of the state and, many would argue, its obligation. On the other hand, in heeding the traditional call to "remember events *as if* they happened to us," we risk confusing the shared moment for a shared memory. We are invited to mistake our common memorial experience for a common Holocaust experience—thereby literalizing the metaphorical command to remember *as if* it happened to us. In this sense, the nation always asks for more than common commemoration: remembering one's national history is not merely to learn about the experiences of others, but to make these experiences one's own. It is to adopt a nation's past as if it were one's own past, and then to respond to the current world in light of this vicariously gained legacy. By creating the myth of a common past, a national remembrance day like Yom Hashoah creates the conditions for recognizing a common future, as well.

While recognizing this tendency in remembrance days to unify both memory and responses to it, however, we must also guard against it. We need to distinguish between the beauty in a day that unites a people in common moments of remembrance and the danger in a day that creates a single meaning in such memory. In this way, we might encourage Yom Hashoah to encompass a multiplicity of memories, without allowing the day to subjugate memory to univocal meaning. For the life of memory and its commemorative day depend on their capacity to adapt to new times, on the evolution of their meanings in new historical contexts. Unlike monuments in the landscape, in whose rigid forms memory is too often ossified, the remembrance day can reinvigorate itself and the forms it takes every year. By virtue of its place on the calendar, certain meanings will also be renewed. But if we encourage the day to encompass multiple memories and meanings on this day, we ensure that Yom Hashoah remains more the perennial guardian of memory, less its constant tyrant.

Part IV

America:

Memory and the

Politics of Identity

Memory is important, letting that memory be sufficiently ambiguous and open-ended so that others can inhabit the space, can imbue the forms with their own memory.
—James Ingo Freed

Introduction

As the shape Holocaust memory takes in Europe and Israel is constrained by political, aesthetic, and religious coordinates, that in America is no less guided by both American ideals and experiences of this time. Unlike European memorials, however, often anchored in the very sites of destruction, those in America are necessarily removed from the "topography of terror." Where European memorials located in situ often suggest themselves rhetorically as the extension of events they would commemorate, those in America must gesture abstractly to a past removed in both time and space. If memorials in Germany and Poland composed of camp ruins invite visitors to mistake themselves for the events they represent, those in America inevitably call attention to the great distance between themselves and the destruction. The meaning in American memorials is not always as "self-evident" as that suggested at the camps, places of deportation, or destroyed synagogues. In this sense, American memorials seem not to be anchored in history so much as in the ideals that generated them in the first place.

In America, the motives for memory of the Holocaust are as mixed as the population at large, the reasons variously lofty and cynical, practical and aesthetic. Some communities build memorials to remember lost brethren, others to remember themselves. Some build memorials as community centers, others as tourist attractions. Some survivors remember strictly according to religious tradition, while others recall the political roots of their resistance. Landsmanschaften organizations continue to erect hundreds of inscribed markers to lost teachers, communities, and families in the Jewish cemeteries in and around New York City.[1] Veterans' organizations sponsor memorials to recall their role as camp liberators. Congressmen support local monuments to secure votes among their Jewish constituency. Even the national memorial to the Holocaust now under way in Washington, D.C., was proposed by then-President Jimmy Carter to placate Jewish supporters angered by his sale of F-15 fighter planes to Saudi Arabia. All such memorial decisions are made in political time, contingent on political realities.[2]

The reasons for memory change with every new generation, as well. While the survivors remember themselves and loved ones lost, their children build memorials to remember a world they never knew, an act of recovery whereby they locate themselves in a continuous past. In the words of Alex Krieger, a child of survivors and professor of architecture active in Boston's proposed memorial, "It's not for my parents that I pursue this endeavor. . . . This memorial will be for me. Because I was not there, and did not suffer, I cannot remember. Therefore, I very much need to be reminded. This memorial will be for my six-month-old daughter, who will need to be reminded even more. It will be for her children who will need to be reminded still more. We must build such a memorial for all of the generations to come who, by distance from the actual events and people, will depend on it to activate [memory]."[3] That is, the memorial will become for post-Holocaust generations a surrogate experience, something other than the survivors' recollections to inspire their own memory.

In the pages that follow, I trace the generational change in American public memorialization of the Holocaust, from its early place along the margins of historical consciousness to its more recent overshadowing of nearly all other Jewish past and present. Like the preceding sections, this one on American memorials does not attempt a comprehensive survey of American memorials and museums, of which there are now hundreds. For want of space, this means that many celebrated memorials in Miami, Atlanta, Baltimore, Toledo, Philadelphia, Long Island, and New Haven, among dozens of other communities, have not been addressed here. The memorials I do examine were chosen as illustrations of the critical themes I have pursued until now: their embodiment of national ideals, difficult aesthetic debates, and political contingencies. I hope that this inquiry will inspire others to critical tellings of the dozens of memorials that have been undeservedly passed over here.

Chapter 11

The Plural Faces

of Holocaust Memory

in America

American public memory of the Shoah began with the first newspaper reports of mass murder early in 1943. Though often buried beneath accounts of military battles, these stories haunted both the Jewish refugees who had arrived in the mid-1930s and second-generation Jewish Americans with family still in Europe. To this vicarious memory of events, newly liberated survivors arriving after the war added their personal experiences. At first, Jews in America enacted such memory in traditional, ritual forms: remembering the dead in Yizkor services during the high holidays, lamenting the catastrophe on the Ninth of Av, or even leaving place-settings empty at home festivals in honor of those recently lost. Relatives who knew the exact dates of their loved ones' deaths lighted Jahrzeit candles, while those who did not know where or when their family was killed waited for the rabbinical ruling that deemed the Tenth of Teveth such a day of mourning and remembrance.

The first public Holocaust commemoration in America took place at the very height of the killing, on 2 December 1942. On this day, according to the Jewish Telegraphic Agency, some five hundred thousand Jews in New York City stopped work for ten minutes, both to mourn those already killed and to call attention to the ongoing massacre. In a gesture of sympathy, several radio stations observed a two-minute silence before broadcasting memorial services at 4:30 that after-noon.[1] Similar commemorations followed the next spring, culminating in several mass public memorial ceremonies, including a pageant held at Madison Square Garden in March 1943, called "We Will Never Die" and dedicated to the two million Jews who perished at the hands of the Germans that year.[2] Other public memorials included mass rallies called by the Jewish Labor Committee to mourn the destruction of the Warsaw Ghetto. The largest single Holocaust memorial event during the war took place on 19 April 1944, the first anniversary of the Warsaw Ghetto uprising. On the steps of New York City Hall, over thirty thousand Jews gathered to hear Mayor Fiorello La Guardia and prominent Jewish leaders honor the memory of fighters and martyrs who had died in the uprising.

Much of the horrifying information that moved these groups to memorialize Europe's dying Jews had been distributed by the man at the Polish News Agency who later proposed the nation's first Holocaust monument. After fleeing to France from Vienna in 1938 during the Anschluss, A. R. Lerner came to New York, where he edited bulletins for the Polish News Agency describing the plight of Polish Jews under Nazi occupation. His parents had died in France after following him there, and the rest of his family—Polish Jews—had perished in the death camps. In 1944, using photographs and documents supplied by the Polish underground, Lerner published a pictorial history of the Nazis' annihilation of European Jewry. Later, he organized an exhibition of these same materials at the Vanderbilt Gallery on Fifty-seventh Street in New York, sponsored by the Jewish Labor Committee. In January 1946, as vice president of the National Organization of Polish Jews (NOPJ), he proposed that the group establish an eternal flame in tribute to the "Heroes of the Warsaw Ghetto and the Six Million Jews Slain by the Nazis," to be situated somewhere in New York City.[3]

Within days, according to Lerner, the NOPJ had petitioned the new mayor of New York, William O'Dwyer, for a place to build their "Eternal Light." The mayor endorsed the project, as did Robert Moses, commissioner of the Parks Department, who enlisted the aid of Stuart Constable, the department's chief designer. Moses wrote to the NOPJ that he preferred a monument to an eternal flame and would proceed when they found a suitable site in the city. At Lerner's suggestion, Constable and Jo Davidson, a well-known sculptor and friend of Constable, drove to Riverside Drive to look for an appropriate site. Constable reported back to Lerner that on approaching Riverside Drive between Eighty-third and Eighty-fourth streets, he and Davidson watched as an old, bearded Jew stood quietly in the park as if in deep contemplation. Apparently struck by the apparition, they stopped the car and decided that the spot on which the Jew stood, monumentlike, would be the future site of the memorial.

The date for the dedication was chosen less arbitrarily. "My decision to hold the dedication ceremony in September or October," Lerner said, "was chiefly influenced by the acute situation in Palestine where a bitter fight raged between the Jews and the English which caused the United Nations to put the Palestine question on the agenda before the Assembly in October, 1947."[4] Between May and

A mass rally on the steps of New York City Hall commemorates the first anniversary of the Warsaw Ghetto uprising, 19 April 1944. Mayor Fiorello La Guardia listens as Sen. Isaac Rubinstein, former chief rabbi of Vilna, reads. Among those standing in the second row are writer Sholom Asch, poet Julian Tuwim, and, on the far right, miniaturist Arthur Szyk. Photo: Courtesy of YIVO Institute for Jewish Research.

October, Lerner mounted a furious public relations and fundraising campaign. Before long, letters from all the European ambassadors began to pour in, each requesting some role in the ceremonies. Hundreds of civic and religious leaders from all sectors pledged their support, as well, also expecting to take part in a public way. Arrangements were made for television, newsreels, and the Voice of America to cover the dedication ceremonies. Hundreds of thousands of admission tickets were sent to civic organizations for distribution and mailed to all delegates at the United Nations.

At 12:30 on a rainy Sunday afternoon, 19 October 1947, tens of thousands of people jammed the Riverside Park mall from Eighty-third to Ninety-fifth streets. With people crowded onto rooftops above and blocking the streets below, Mayor O'Dwyer dedicated the site of the future monument and marked it with a cornerstone slab inscribed with the words: "This is the site for the American memorial to the Heroes of the Warsaw Ghetto Battle, April–May 1943 and to the six million Jews of Europe martyred in the cause of human liberty." Descriptions of the ceremony and excerpts from speeches filled the next day's newspapers. In its editorial two days later, the *New York Times* declared, "It is fitting that that a memorial to six million victims of the most tragic mass crime in history, the Nazi genocide of Jews, should rise in this land of liberty." The stone slab remains to this day, but the memorial itself was never built.

THIS IS THE SITE FOR THE AMERICAN MEMO- RIAL TO THE HEROES OF THE WARSAW GHETTO BATTLE APRIL- MAY 1943 AND TO THE SIX MIL- LION JEWS OF EUROPE MARTYRED IN THE CAUSE OF HUMAN LIBERTY

The First American Monument: Forever Unbuilt

As is often the case, the subsequent story surrounding the unbuilt memorial can be more instructive than a finished memorial could ever have been. The first proposed monument, designed by Davidson and architect Ely Jacques Kahn in 1948, consisted of a series of steplike blocks forming a pedestal, atop which stood a muscular, heroic figure. With his arms swept back, his chest thrust forth defiantly, and sleeves rolled up, the bare-handed fighter towered over a rabbinical figure below, hands up as if beseeching the Almighty; another figure aided a fallen comrade, and yet another slumped dead against the front of the pedestal. Within months, however, and without much commentary, the New York City Arts Commission rejected the model and began a search for another.

A year later, another model was submitted by the Memorial Committee for the Six Million Jews of Europe. Designed by a Columbia University architecture professor, Percival Goodman, it had a 25-foot-high wall stretching 120 feet long, crowned by a 45-foot pedestal and menorah. It was rejected on two counts, according to Arthur Hodgkiss, executive secretary of the Parks Department. Not only would the memorial take up an inordinate amount of space, but in its sheer visibility, it could well cause automobile accidents by startling motorists on the Henry Hudson Parkway.[5]

Two years later, ground was actually broken for an 80-foot-high black granite pylon of two tablets, on which the Ten Commandments were to be inscribed. In this design by architect Erich Mendelsohn and sculptor Ivan Mestrovic, the tablets would rise at one end of a long plaza, bordered on one side by a 100-foot-long wall of bas-relief figures depicting the struggle of humankind to fulfill the Commandments—all urged on by a giant carving of Moses. Though the design was accepted by the Arts Commission, Mendelsohn's death in 1953 discouraged

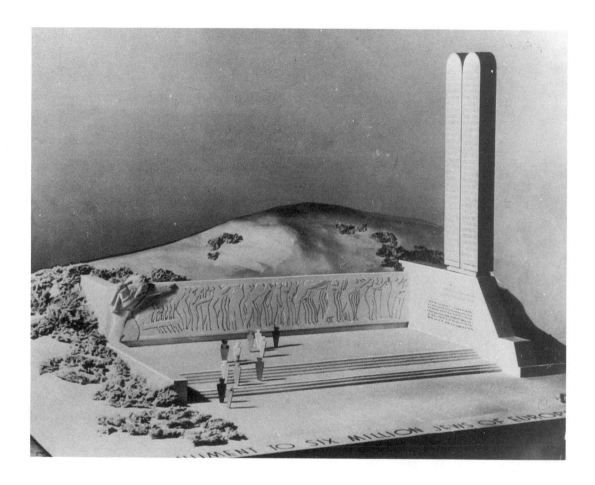

potential donors, and fundraising efforts eventually broke down altogether.

Nearly twelve years passed before two memorials by Nathan Rapoport were submitted for consideration in 1964. One, the *Scroll of Fire*, was proposed by the Warsaw Ghetto Resistance Organization (WAGRO). The other, submitted by the Artur Zygelboim Memorial Committee, was a sculpture of the committee's namesake, engulfed by flames, about to pitch forward—a reference to Zygelboim's 1943 suicide in London to protest the world's indifference to the plight of Jews in Poland. After rejecting the Zygelboim sculpture on behalf of the commission as too tragic for recreational park land, too distressing for children, Eleanor Platt, a sculptor and Arts Commission member turned to the *Scroll of Fire*. "This proposed work seems to be excessively and unnecessarily large," she wrote. "Even if it were to be smaller and in better taste, artistically, I believe that by approving it or the Zygelboim sculpture, we would set a highly regrettable precedent."[6]

In the eyes of Rapoport and his sponsors, however, the crux of Platt's response came in her concluding remarks, which incensed the Jewish community. "How would we answer other special groups who want to be similarly represented on

Model of memorial designed for Riverside Park site in New York City, designed by Erich Mendelsohn and Ivan Mestrovic but never built. Photo: Courtesy of YIVO Institute for Jewish Research.

public land?" she asked. Stunned by her reference to "special groups," the sponsors were further bewildered by Parks Commissioner Newbold Morris's opinion that "monuments in the parks should be limited to events of American history." They saw numerous examples of other immigrant groups' national heroes immortalized in stone and bronze, from Central Park to Washington Square. Eventually, Rapoport's *Scroll of Fire* was erected in Israel, where national memory had always been defined by that of Jews everywhere, a continuum of generational memory transcending borders.

But these American survivors of the Warsaw Ghetto may have continued to wonder what the difference was between "events of American history" and those of "Americans' history." For, like many American immigrants, they included both old and new worlds in their historical memory. In a culture composed of immigrants, they assumed that their "foreign" experiences would come to be regarded also as American, that as part of their European past, the Holocaust would become part of America's past. As a land of immigrants, the survivors had hoped, America would also be a land of immigrant memories, of pasts that were "foreign" only insofar as they transpired in other lands, but American in that they explained why immigrants had come to America in the first place. If the survivors' history was not a part of the public memory, could they still regard themselves as part of the public?

The New York Holocaust memorial was never built at its assigned place in Riverside Park. The square stone remains, however, protected by a short cast-iron fence, largely unknown to most New Yorkers. Once a year, around 19 April, wreaths of flowers appear inside the enclosure. Undeterred, WAGRO continued its search for funds and an acceptable design. In the mid-1960s, with the city's blessing, a new site on the lower tip of Manhattan across from Ellis Island and the Statue of Liberty was chosen as more suitable for a truly civic monument. An umbrella committee calling itself Memorial to the Six Million Jewish Martyrs, Inc. and comprising some twenty major Jewish organizations commissioned a model from the celebrated architect Louis Kahn. In October 1968, Kahn's model of six great glass blocks was exhibited to wide acclaim at the Museum of Modern Art. A season of fundraising dinners was kicked off to raise the 1.5 million dollars necessary to install the monument. Five years later, the committee had raised $17,000, barely enough to pay the architect for his model. Kahn died in March 1974, and the following May, the executive committee announced that fundraising efforts had been stymied by a worsening economic recession, Israel's recent wars, and the crisis of Soviet Jewry. Fearful that a drive to fund memory of the past could be at the expense of endangered Jews in the present, the memorial committee suspended further work on the New York monument.[7]

Louis Kahn's
model for a
Holocaust
memorial in
New York City,
designed in
1967 for Battery
Park but never
built. Photo:
Courtesy of
Vladka Meed.

Which is not to say that New York was left without its share of Holocaust monuments and memorial centers. Most synagogues in New York continue to reserve some space for a small memorial: a bas relief of Janusz Korczak and his children frames the doorway of the Park Avenue Synagogue; a miniature memorial garden invites quiet meditation at the Brotherhood Synagogue on Gramercy Park. In other places, Rapoport's Warsaw Ghetto Monument has been divided thematically and reproduced: the exilic bas relief has a home at the Jewish Theological Seminary, while a version of the fighters occupies the lobby of the Workmen's Circle Building.

Other memorial motifs depend similarly on their sites and sponsoring institutions. Sculptor Harriet Feigenbaum's marble bas relief is set vertically along the corner edge of the Appellate Division Courthouse of the State Supreme Court on Madison Avenue and Twenty-fifth Street. Carved swirls of flame and smoke climb gracefully from an etched plan of Auschwitz, up along the corner, cut off bluntly at the top. This memorial "to Victims of the Injustice of the Holocaust" is inscribed with words that echo its placement as a kind of cornerstone for the courthouse, the reason for its commission: "Indifference to Injustice Is the Gate to Hell."

The American Memorial Terrain: Denver

With little national coordination, other memorials did begin to appear across the country, quietly as plaques on synagogue walls, or as small memorial gardens in the courtyards of suburban synagogues. Occasionally, the rabbi would read from a pulpit salvaged from a destroyed synagogue in Germany, Poland, or Czechoslovakia. Eventually, as a community's confidence grew, small memorials were dedicated publicly in civic spaces usually reserved for state and national monuments. Open competitions were occasionally held, though more often it was the donor him- or herself who conceived of the monument's form and commissioned it. Typically, a Holocaust memorial committee would invite a local artist to submit proposals until they could agree on one they liked. Even as community projects, these memorials rarely achieved popular consensus: if they were too figurative, religious leaders balked at their not being Jewish enough. If they were too abstract, survivors protested that their all-too-literal experiences were betrayed.

Today, nearly every major American city is home to at least one, and often several, memorials commemorating aspects of the Holocaust. What each remembers depends on who commissioned the monument, under what financial conditions, and in what context. For example, not long after Yevgeny Yevtushenko's poem "Babi Yar" came to the attention of Americans, the city council in Denver passed a motion "to recall the past tragedy of Babi Yar, as well as the necessity to speak out against anti-Semitism in the Soviet Union today."[8] As the plight of Soviet Jewry had paralyzed one memorial in New York, it would now inspire a new one in Denver. Accordingly, the city council designated a twenty-seven-acre parcel of undeveloped city land for a Babi Yar Memorial, chosen for its apparent topographical resemblance to the site of the infamous massacre at Babi Yar: a ten-meter-deep drainage culvert recalled to their minds the ravine at Babi Yar. After several years of fundraising, a dedication ceremony addressed by Elie Wiesel, and a Congressional motion commending the committee for its work, plans for the memorial were nearly completed.

But when the model and inscriptions were publicly announced, representatives from the local Ukrainian community rose in protest. There was no mention of the massacre of Ukrainians that took place at Babi Yar in 1942, they argued, which included the martyrdom of the nationalist poet Olena Teliha, among others. After several rounds of negotiations between the Babi Yar Foundation and a newly formed committee of Ukrainian Americans, the foundation agreed to change the monument's inscriptions to reflect the Ukrainian dimension of the killings at Babi Yar between 1941 and 1943. In return, the Ukrainian group would contribute $25,000 to finish the memorial. Two massive, polished chunks of charcoal granite at the entrance to the Babi Yar Memorial in Denver now commemorate the "Two Hundred Thousand Victims Who Died [at] Babi Yar, Kieve, Ukraine, U.S.S.R.,

September 29, 1941–November 6, 1943. The Majority Jews with Ukrainians and Others."

Beyond the portal stones, a number of other, mixed symbolic markers dot the great expanse of green, rolling park land. One hundred crabapple trees were planted to represent Jews killed at Babi Yar. A narrow, high-sided wooden bridge spans the culvert, an oblique reference to boxcars that once carried Jews to their deaths (though not at Babi Yar). Across the park, a round granite slab in the shape of a tree trunk sheared near the ground signifies a people cut off, mid-growth. Near the entrance, a large round marble stone is inscribed with the names of the park's founders, its chief donors, and the politicians who participated in its establishment.

Today, Denver's Babi Yar Memorial Park lies quietly unvisited by much of the community. The city's park service continues to maintain the grounds, and neighborhood children on bicycles still careen down the park's grassy slopes. But the voice box that once narrated Babi Yar's history to visitors has long been broken, its tape lost. Holocaust Remembrance Day ceremonies have been moved to

other sites throughout the city. For, as was the case in many American communities, the building process itself was occasionally so bruising and contentious, that much of Denver's Jewish community grew alienated from the very site that was meant to unify them. In time, wounds may heal and the community may yet return to their Babi Yar Park, but as of this writing, the memorial seems all but forgotten by its community.

Dallas

As terrain and fundraising combined in Denver to shape the Babi Yar Memorial's message, the artists' and primary sponsors' visions dominate in other American memorials. Though survivor Michael Jacobs says he had wanted an outdoor site for the memorial he had long planned for his Dallas community, he gratefully accepted the downstairs space donated to him by the local Jewish Community Center in 1980. This would be the future home of the Dallas Memorial Center for Holocaust Studies, a professionally run museum and study center for Holocaust education and research. As the chief donor and fundraiser, Jacobs wanted the center to bear some mark of his personal experiences during the Holocaust, some trace of the survivor's vision.

This vision was defined for him when he was led downstairs to see the space for the first time. As he descended, Jacobs has said, the stairs appeared to be so many railroad ties, the handrails seeming to lead him into the boxcar he'd been forced into as a young Jewish child in Poland.[9] Committed to presenting a rhetorically authentic reconstruction of events, the survivor-sponsor traveled to Europe in

1983 expressly to find one of the boxcars that once transported Jews to the East. He first tried the Dutch national railway, but they had disposed of all the now ancient boxcars. He then called the Belgian railway, who believed they had one car left, which they were about to destroy. Assured by authorities that its murderous credentials were beyond reproach, Jacobs arranged to have the car shipped intact to Galveston, whence it would be trucked overland to Dallas. At first, the railway tried to sell the boxcar to the survivor; but when told of its purpose and Jacobs's own past, they agreed to donate it, as shippers did their services over the entire length of the boxcar's journey to America.

On its arrival in Dallas, the boxcar was shortened by one third of its length to fit into the building. It was then placed at the bottom of the center's stairs as an entry hall to the museum, a kind of antechamber, just to give visitors the sense

Boxcar entryway to the Holocaust memorial museum and study center in Dallas. Photo: Courtesy of the Dallas Memorial Center for Holocaust Studies.

297

The Plural Faces of Memory

of "having been there." As the survivor's memory had been dominated by his experiences in boxcars, so too would the visitor's museum experience be framed. But here a minor memorial crisis ensued. During the museum's dedication, a few of those who really "had been there"—the survivors—refused to enter the boxcar at all: once had been enough. When they complained that they were, in effect, barred from visiting a museum devoted to their experiences, a solution followed immediately. The boxcar remained, but survivors were given their own, hidden entrance, a secret door for survivors only. To this day, the boxcar entryway is the only one of its kind.

Tucson

In Tucson, local topography and landforms combined with the Jewish Community Center's design to influence the shape of Holocaust memory in still other ways. Unveiled on 22 April 1990, the coincidental convergence of Earth Day and Holocaust Remembrance Day, the Holocaust memorial at the center seemed to embody the simultaneous gesture every monument makes to both landscape and memory. As the "Grand Canyon State," Arizona had long linked its identity to its monumental natural setting. Artist Ami Shamir thus conceived and built Tucson's Holocaust memorial in direct proportion to the wide-open landscape it would inhabit. With its 43-foot-high, broken-topped column, a reflecting pool, and 150-foot-long bas-relief wall, it would be the largest Holocaust monument in America.

For its size would correspond to that of Tucson's landscape, not to that of its small but vibrant Jewish community of some twenty thousand. In this sense, Tucson confirmed the general wisdom that the smaller the community, the more manageable and streamlined the memorial building process will be. In a community of relatively uniform aesthetic tastes and historical concerns, the Holocaust memorial committee found little disagreement in evaluating some eighty submissions and proposals from artists around the world. When the local Jewish federation decided to build an expansive new recreational and educational community center, one open to the entire non-Jewish Tucson community, they voted to commission the memorial as part of the complex, thus avoiding the usually fractious fundraising chores. Costs of the memorial would be built into the center's ten-million-dollar budget.

Though the building's architect had not designed a specific space for the monument, he had planned for a long, free-standing wall to extend outward from the main structure by some 150 feet to define and enclose the surrounding open desert. Instead of sitting isolated and exposed, the center would seem linked both to nearby roads and to the landscape; such a structural arm would also create a large, inviting plaza and parking lot in front, breaking the landscape into manageable parts. As it turned out, the wall and the plaza it created also provided an ideal space for the monument; indeed, by building the monument into the freestanding wall, Shamir has made it seem part of the center's original structure. As a result, the monument now functions as the architectural entryway visitors pass through on their way into a stunning complex of auditoriums, cavernous gymnasiums, weight rooms, swimming pools, and tennis courts. Built as it is into the wall and plaza, the memorial houses and thus lends a certain cast to all the activities that take place in the center.

From a distance, only the three-sided concrete column and long white wall are visible. The open country around it is dotted with postcard-perfect, three-armed saguaro cactus trees, sandy dry gulches, and low-slung Santa Fe–style homes— all dwarfed by the craggy Santa Catalina mountain range looming eight thousand feet high a couple of miles to the west. As we approach, we see that the column and walls are poured in white concrete sections. Like many of the monument's other elements, the broken top of the column resonates in several ways at once: some iconographic, some symbolic. By itself, the column suggests an architectural remnant from a shattered civilization, or, in the tradition of Jewish funerary motifs, a broken tree, or a broken candlestick recalling a life interrupted by death. Survivors, as well as those who have only visited the camps since the war, say they see in the lone column a crematorium chimney.

Both tower and wall seem to take on the color and cast of the natural earth forms nearby. The tower's broken top, for example, recalls the craggy peaks of the nearby mountains. At sunset, the entire wall complex radiates the warm pink glow of evening. The pastel hues of the desert—reds, yellows, and browns—are picked up, seemingly cast into the raw white concrete of the wall and monument, while the sky's sunset gold is reflected in the pool of water at its base.

Other elements simultaneously reinforce and undercut the tranquility of the setting, which takes on the taut stillness of ruins. A section of the wall appears to have toppled forward into the reflecting pool, leaving a wide gap in the wall's length. With its round-topped edges, the section leaning into the pool recalls the tablets of the law, broken and reinscribed with the names of some 147 concentration, death, and labor camps. According to the project's director, Fred Steiniger, the artist made sure every local survivor's former camp was listed here, a place where individual stories might be recalled together. A piece of stone from Dachau was also embedded in the slab of concrete bearing the camp's name, linking the removed memorial sign to its place on earth.

Rivulets of water run down from cracks in the column to feed the pool, on which seems to float a stylized Hebrew quotation from Jeremiah 31: 15–17:

The Holocaust memorial at the Jewish Community Center in Tucson, Arizona, designed by Ami Shamir, 1990. Photo: Courtesy of the Jewish Community Center of Tucson.

"There is hope for thy future." The aim, according to the artist, was "to conjure up the essences of complementary archetypes such as destruction and rejuvenation, hopelessness and hopefulness . . . death and life with the emphasis on the power and vitality of life forces to overcome unspeakable difficulties."[10] Together, images and words suggest that from brokenness, life still flows. Shamir, an Israeli living in New York, seems to combine Israel's sense of continuing Jewish life after the Holocaust with America's ever-sanguine view of the future.

In addition to resonating the nearby "lay of the land," Shamir's design seems to have incorporated some of its local lore as well. For as stark and raw as the wall looks from a distance, on closer inspection we find that its entire length is covered with a bas relief of what appear to be etched hieroglyphs: geometric lines and squiggles, randomly drawn arrows and a star of David, Hebrew lettering (Zachor, or remember), and round intermeshing gears. According to the artist, these abstract signs gesture to the identity of the memorial maker, on the one hand, and to the railroad tracks and machinery of death, on the other. Further down the wall to the right, a stylized menorah cut out of the top of the wall serves as both part of the monument and the only icon marking the site as specifically Jewish.

Whether intentionally or not, Shamir's wall signs also recall yet another kind of local iconography, known primarily to the inhabitants of Tucson familiar with the history of their environs. For wherever someone digs in Tucson—for a new sidewalk, swimming pool, or even a monument—handfuls of red-clay pottery shards are churned up, remnants of a now extinct tribe of Native Americans, retrospectively named "Hohokam"—loosely translated as "the Disappeared Ones." The Hohokam tribe left more than broken vessels: they also left what has been called a "legacy on stone," thousands of petroglyphs carved into nearby stone faces, caves, and cliff sides. Variously abstract and anthropomorphic in design, the petroglyphs now function in the popular imagination as indecipherable epitaphs for an extinct people. The visual resonance between Shamir's wall etchings and the petroglyphs of the Hohokam tribe may be apparent only to those who have seen both, yet it still links the memory of one genocide to another and in so doing ties the monument that much more closely to its surroundings.[11] The result is a Holocaust monument whose elements speak directly to its habitat, even as it commemorates events so distant in time and space that they may seem more mythical than real to much of Tucson's non-Jewish community.

It also becomes clear that in its many elements, the monument draws on much more than local landscape and lore. For, like any artist, the monument maker has drawn from his own particular repertoire of memorial figures and materials, forms and motifs. With several memorial commissions to Shamir's credit, it is not difficult to trace the recirculation of elements from memorial to memorial, each recalling some aspect of its predecessors. In fact, it seems likely that the Tucson memorial, with its seemingly unlimited space, invited just such a compilation of previous Holocaust memorials designed and built by the artist in New Jersey and Los Angeles. The forms of a memorial Shamir built in 1983 for Temple B'nai Abraham in Livingston, New Jersey, for example, are repeated here: a broken-topped column, cut-out menorah, and leaning tablets are slightly rearranged and enlarged in scale to the monumental surroundings of their new home in Tucson. To them, Shamir has added the long wall that will be part of his new design for the Simon Wiesenthal Center in Los Angeles. Even the broken column in Livingston appeared in Shamir's earlier commission for the Wiesenthal Center's first memorial courtyard, built in 1977. By rearranging a number of repeating elements from his previous work, the artist might even be said to have created a kind of modular monument, eminently adaptable to its new surroundings.

Los Angeles: Three Memorials

In general, the larger a particular Jewish American community and the greater its diversity, the more difficult it will be to reach agreement on a unified memory of the Holocaust, much less a single memorial space. Conversely, the more compact and homogeneous the community, the easier and more single-minded the memorial-building process usually is. This is why Tuscon has a memorial and New York does not, why San Francisco finally agreed to build its controversial monument while Boston is still raising funds for its memorial. This may also be why Los Angeles has ended up with two major Holocaust museums, plus a large public monument.

In Los Angeles, with a Jewish population second only to New York's in size, public memory of the Holocaust has been riven into three unequal shares: the Jewish Federation's Martyrs' Memorial and Holocaust Museum, the Simon Wiesenthal Center's Beit Hashoah—Museum of Tolerance, and a striking monument of black granite columns set in Pan Pacific Park. In a Jewish community of six hundred thousand, including some thirty thousand Holocaust survivors and refugees, rival memories and competing interests were inevitable. Practically the only common trait uniting an otherwise diverse weave of pious and secular, left- and right-wing, European and Mediterranean Jews has been the desire to remember. But questions of how, what, whom, and where to remember have divided the community no less than in other cities. While the Jews of Los Angeles have not decided on the single best way to commemorate the Holocaust, all agree that there is, for better or worse, more than enough memory to go around.

Indeed, even the desire to remember was born in conflicting needs. "At first, we wanted to forget," local survivor Otto Schirn has said. "But when we realized that our forgetting might lead to others never knowing about the Holocaust, we began to work on remembering—both for ourselves and so that others would know what happened. That's when the idea of a monument was born."[12] Each side of this twin memorial impulse would eventually demand its own corresponding space: one would be a substitute gravesite where survivors could mourn their lost families, the other a public exposition of Holocaust history. From its inception in the 1960s, the Los Angeles memorial was thus to plod painstakingly along two parallel tracks—one monumental, one museological—until it was joined—some say challenged—later by an energetic newcomer, Rabbi Marvin Hier.

By 1973, Schirn and his committee of fellow survivors had found what they believed to be a friendly neighborhood park for their projected memorial, the Pan Pacific Park in the traditionally Jewish Fairfax district of Los Angeles. That the neighborhood was not quite as Jewish as it had been in the past, but had become a more representative mix of African Americans and new immigrants from Mexico and Asia, made the space even more appealing in the "new Americans'" eyes. An open competition for a memorial design was called in 1977, and ten artists submitted drawings. Within weeks, a jury of survivors, local academic art historians, and Jewish community leaders had chosen Joseph Young's proposal for six triangular columns of black granite, each twenty four feet high, equipped with gas flames to be kindled on commemorative days.

But when the survivors' group turned to the county for use of the public park, the Board of Supervisors balked. According to the Los Angeles County Parks code, a public park was a civic, and therefore nonsectarian, space. This was, after all, *Pan* Pacific Park and so could not display the religious symbols or forms of any single group. The Holocaust, in the board's view, would have to be broadly defined to include all of its victims, Jews and non-Jews. The monument would have to invite the entire community into its space, without the implicit boundaries suggested by stars of David, crosses, or moons and crescents. As good "new Americans," the survivors agreed to omit all religious iconography. While the original design had included a hexagonal arrangement of columns inside a larger star of David, the final version would be the granite columns only—arranged in the outline of the now missing star.

Likewise, other specific references to Jewish victims would come only in oblique symbolism, according to the artist, forms that allowed the memorial projections of both Jews and non-Jews. The six columns, for example, would be open to many interpretations: their number would suggest in Jewish eyes the approximate number of Jewish dead, six million; others might count each as signifying one of the six death camps in Poland. Some would see the black columns as commemorative candles or torches, others as crematoria chimneys belching flames. In their vertical reach, they could be regarded as soaring emblems of heroism, while their triangular shape could recall the patches worn by all concentration camp inmates. Young has also suggested that the space between columns could recall the absence of victims, the missing generation of children.

In fact, rather than conveying a sense of comfort or reassurance, the artist has attempted to suggest some of the pain that comes with mourning and remembrance. "I did not want to make something beautiful," he said, "but something to evoke the experience itself, which was not pretty."[13] The 75-by-100-foot space includes both the black granite columns set in a floor of black and red granite and a wall of broken-topped, unfinished granite chunks. A low black granite bench is meant to evoke the uncomfortably short bench traditionally used when Jewish mourners sit Shiva. And rather than inspirational memorial inscriptions, two sides of each of the three-sided columns will be incised with a historical text, each one of twelve panels describing a year of the Nazi rule. On the third side of each column, a bronze bas relief will illustrate images from the period, with a special text set at child's eye level.

Though conceived in 1973, the monument at Pan Pacific Park was dedicated eighteen years later, in the fall of 1991. Meanwhile, the other half of the city's memorial project, its expository part, was also under way. What had begun as a small, traveling exhibition of photographs in 1976, organized by a group of survivors, finally found a home on the twelfth floor of the Jewish Federation office building on Wilshire Boulevard in 1978. In both conception and style, the exhibition reflected its modest origins—a meeting over coffee between an American-born businessman, Morton Silverman, and survivors from the area. We did not want a "pigeon-roost" in a park, said Silverman, but "something to teach, to document."[14] With this in mind, Silverman and his group gathered photographic documents, labeled them, and solicited space from local universities and community centers. The exhibition's designers forswore a slick, high-tech appearance for a more understated, books-on-walls approach, one that would fit in flexibly with whatever space it occupied. Eventually, the local Jewish Federation found space to mount the exhibition permanently at its offices.

For a while, this room was the first and only Holocaust museum in America, a small sister to Yad Vashem in Jerusalem, which had sent consultants to advise the Jewish Federation. Working closely with Los Angeles County schools, the federation's small staff of survivors brought thousands of students from neighborhoods throughout the city to tour the museum. In fact, as instructive and powerful as the photographic panels were, students and teachers agreed that the exhibition's principal resource was the survivors who led them through the museum. In their presence, the photo montages came alive. The survivor-docents' living commentary seemed to invigorate the "book on walls," filling in the gap between a grainy black-and-white past and the present moment. The director, Michael Nutkiewicz, recalls that after visiting the museum in 1982, Elie Wiesel told him, "You have a little jewel up here."

Over the years, the center amassed a huge archive of photographs and artifacts—everything from uniforms to badges, letters to train schedules. For twelve years, visitors found their way up to the little jewel on the twelfth floor, but when the Bank Hapoalim vacated the space next door, the federation mounted a million-dollar campaign to endow a much larger, more accessible museum on the ground floor. In 1991, the new Martyrs' Memorial and Museum of the Holocaust took its place on Wilshire Boulevard's museum row, just down from the Los Angeles County Museum of Art, the Page Museum, and the Craft and Folk Museum.

Survivors still lead tours, but rather than focusing only on a long road to death, the redesigned exhibition begins with descriptions of Jewish culture and life in

Survivor Marc Salberg leads students on a tour of the Martyrs' Memorial and Museum of the Holocaust in Los Angeles. Photo: Courtesy of the Martyrs' Memorial and Museum.

nineteenth-century Europe—showing what was lost. And instead of emphasizing the end of Eastern European Jewry only, the new space will include elaborate displays of French and Greek Jewish communities whose destruction is often overlooked. According to Nutkiewicz, the exhibition story line does not end in 1945 with the liberation of the camps, but also covers the ensuing three years to suggest the continuation of Jewish life in Israel and America. "The content committee doesn't want to give the impression of Jews as [just] victims," Nutkiewicz has said, "but [also] to demonstrate that they had a rich life before 1933."[15]

About the time in 1977 when the Jewish Federation decided to open the Holocaust museum, a young orthodox rabbi was on his way to Los Angeles to found the city's first orthodox Yeshiva. New York–born and –trained, Rabbi Marvin Hier had taken a sabbatical from his congregation in Vancouver to spend the year before in Israel. He had been much impressed by two institutions there: a small yeshiva called Or Sameach for young Ba'alei Tshuva (secular Jews who "return" to the orthodox fold) and the Yad Vashem memorial and museum. On his return

to Vancouver, Hier decided to found his own yeshiva in Los Angeles, after Or
Sameach's example. With encouragement and financial backing from philanthropist Samuel Belzberg, whose children Rabbi Hier had shepherded back into the
Jewish flock, the young rabbi moved to Los Angeles in 1977 to open a West Coast
branch of Or Sameach. Within months, not only had Hier opened a Yeshiva (later
affiliated with Yeshiva University) but, to the consternation and amazement of
his newly adopted community, he had appended to it a Holocaust memorial and
museum, the Simon Wiesenthal Center.

To this day, the motivation and timing underlying Hier's yoking of the yeshiva
and Holocaust remain a festering sore point in the Jewish community. In the
eyes of his well-to-do supporters, Hier's timing and vision were propitious: his
Wiesenthal Center was to be the advanced edge of the Holocaust museums boom.
But to his many detractors, including much of the academic and religious community, the rabbi was an interloper and opportunist, a self-promoting media
hound who beat Angelenos at their own game. Many believe that while his original plans to open a Yeshiva were sincere, once he tapped the immense potential
in the Holocaust as a fundraising theme, he allowed the means to become synonymous with the ends: Holocaust and Jewish education would become one.
Critics charged that in this city of illusions, Hier had cleverly mixed Holocaust
fundraising with Holocaust consciousness raising; even worse, in their minds,
the public—especially the wealthiest sector—had bought it.[16] Furthermore, Hier
was accused of dividing the area's financial resources, having jumped into the
pool of potential donors precisely at the point when the Jewish Federation began
raising funds for its long-planned museum.[17]

With its 380,000 contributing members, the Simon Wiesenthal Center is now
the largest Jewish organization in the world and home to a sparkling new, five-
story, fifty-million-dollar Holocaust museum and memorial complex. For better
or worse, it has in fact borne out the words of the center's principal financial
backer, Samuel Belzberg, who once told a reporter, "It's a sad fact that Israel and
Jewish education and all the other familiar buzzwords no longer seem to rally
Jews behind the community. The Holocaust, though, works every time."[18]

Ever mindful of both the differences between civic and Jewish constituencies
and how they overlap, the Wiesenthal Center has constantly refined its mission
to reflect the contingencies of audience and funding. As the recipient of state
funds, the center was forced, in a lawsuit brought by local Jewish groups anxious to preserve the separation of church and state, to divorce itself completely
from the yeshiva it once supported. Both the mission of the new museum and
its name have been refined accordingly: it will now be a nonsectarian, public
museum whose stated aim will be to confront bigotry and racism. Its new name,

Beit Hashoah—Museum of Tolerance, suggests that tolerance can be propagated precisely through the study of its greatest antithesis, the Holocaust, and other examples of racial and religious persecution.

In keeping with its new civic mandate to be answerable to Los Angeles' large black, Hispanic, and Asian communities, Beit Hashoah—Museum of Tolerance plans to examine the history of all social and ethnic prejudice and its consequences in America. In the words of a promotional brochure, "The museum's main exhibit area is organized in two sections: the history of racism and prejudice within the American experience . . . and then the story of the most quintessential example of man's inhumanity to man—the Holocaust." The exhibition hall on the ground level will include multimedia presentations of the civil rights movement in America, with a biographical section on Martin Luther King, Jr. After examining American forms of racism and bigotry, visitors will meet the Holocaust—now part of a distinctly American continuum. In this way, European and Christian anti-Semitism will be thematically subsumed to a more universal propensity in humankind toward prejudice and race hatred.

Model of Beit Hashoah–Museum of Tolerance, Los Angeles. Photo: Courtesy of the Simon Wiesenthal Center.

According to the exhibition model, the second main exhibition hall is devoted to "the Shoah—the Destruction of European Jewry." As at the U.S. Holocaust Memorial Museum in Washington, D.C., visitors entering the Holocaust section of the Museum of Tolerance will receive a passport bearing the photo of a child "enmeshed by events of the Holocaust." At every station, visitors insert their cards into machines to learn further details of their adopted child's life. In anticipation perhaps of a near future without survivors to lead us through such exhibits, technology makes former victims themselves our new guides. The first tableau in a succession of installations—"Berlin 1932: A Streetscape in Pre-Nazi Germany"—features a Jewish woman and child dining amicably at Café Kranzler with a German businessman, doctor, and military officer. On a screen above, according to the plan, visitors "see these same people ten years later as they are transformed into the victims and perpetrators of the Holocaust." From here, we will be led through a series of dioramas and multimedia presentations presenting the subsequent twelve years—Kristallnacht, the invasion of Poland, the Wannsee Conference, ghetto uprisings, and finally the entry gates to Auschwitz. Only at

the last station will visitors learn the fate of their child-guides.

At the end, visitors return to the present day in the form of a "situation room," complete with wire-service monitors relaying minute-by-minute instances of anti-Semitism and other human rights violations. Whether this will bring the past forward or make the present moment seem already historical and archaic in its museum setting remains to be seen.

Holocaust memorials not only reflect the aesthetic tastes of their communities, the topographies of their landscapes; in both process and execution, they tend also to embody the community's broader ethos. What happens when, in the words of Judith Miller, Hollywood meets the Holocaust? The results may have been all too predictable. Early conjecture surrounding the initial design of the Wiesenthal Center was not always without basis: in the land of Disney and entertainment theme parks, a Holocaust chamber of horrors, replete with piped-in smoke and screams, did indeed make its way onto the drawing board—only to be rejected by the project's organizers.

The ultimate design of the center showed both taste and Hollywood flash, even if the slickness of the promotional campaigns left many in the community uneasy. In media-saturated Los Angeles, where the strength of an idea or depth of talent is often measured in decibels and talk-show visibility, even the public institutions have had to rely on show-business techniques to draw some of the region's great wealth into its cultural and performing arts centers, its museums, and universities. Given the ethos of a region dominated by the "entertainment industry," the Beverly Hills Holocaust banquets featuring everyone from George

Bush to Arnold Schwarzenegger should not be surprising, no matter how surreal they seem at first blush. Because Los Angeles is a big city, where all kinds of people give all kinds of money for all kinds of causes, all kinds of memory are going to exist side by side: both the glitzy, entertaining productions of the Wiesenthal Center and the more measured, lower-key exhibitions at the Martyrs' Museum.

None of which is to ignore the serious consequences for Holocaust memory and understanding that also take root in this media wonderland. In the Wiesenthal Center's case, it becomes clear that those who live by the media sword may also be wounded by it. On the one hand, the center has succeeded masterfully in converting media attention into museum-building capital. At the same time, because discord and controversy elicit more media attention than anything else, the power plays, media coups, and bitter rivalries between Holocaust organizations in Los Angeles have generated far more publicity than any actual memorial-work yet accomplished. To a great extent, in fact, "public memory" of the Holocaust has been defined in Los Angeles explicitly by that which plays on the media waves.

As a result, publicity of the internecine wars between competing museums in Los Angeles, between national and state museums in Washington and New York, has become a kind of mutant variation of "public memory." Precisely because of the prurient attention these controversies attract, and because no community likes washing its dirty laundry in public, the entire process—necessarily a public one—grows ever more distasteful and painful. For those survivors whose dignity was already shattered by the Nazis, the unseemly charges and countercharges, the indignities of fundraising and political maneuvering, become almost too much to bear. For many survivors and others who always wanted their community's resources directed toward education and social services, such memorial scenarios grow ever more egregious and unpalatable. Few could have predicted that so much disunity would arise in the name of memory, the only activity that has traditionally unified the Jewish people over time.

San Francisco: George Segal's Holocaust

San Francisco has long prided itself on the often spectacular blend of its architectural and natural landscapes. So when Mayor Dianne Feinstein's Holocaust memorial committee conceived of its project in 1981, members set their sights high: theirs would be both a memorial and a work of public art great enough to stand on its own. The aim would not be to acquire merely a flame or a stone, "but a major work of art for the city."[19] In the words of Henry Hopkins, then representing the San Francisco Museum of Modern Art and a committee member, "the memorial should serve a dual audience: those who would go to see it because of the subject, i.e., a memorial, and those who would go to see it because it would be a great work of art and thus would learn about the Holocaust and its implications for mankind."[20] The committee could not have foreseen how a monument might succeed valiantly in its constituent parts—as memorial and as art—and yet divide the community and generate nearly as much controversy as memory.

With its lofty goals in mind, the committee acquired a prime site from the city Parks Commission at Lincoln Park's Palace of the Legion of Honor—a shoulder of land set amid pine and cypress trees overlooking the Pacific Ocean just west of the Golden Gate. An equally promising list of prospective artists was compiled, including some of the most distinguished sculptors of the century: Henry Moore, Joan Miró, Isamu Noguchi, Louise Nevelson, Max Lieberman, Menashe Kadishman, Robert Graham, Ya'akov Agam, and George Segal. Of those invited to participate, however, only Agam, Kadishman, Graham (together with Lawrence Halperin), and Segal submitted designs. The rest either declined (some respectfully, others dismissively) or ignored the invitations altogether.

Deliberations began with Agam's proposal, which was rejected out of hand for being, in the words of one committee member, "too Agam-ish, too kitschy and light-weight." And while the committee admired Kadishman's forty-foot memorial column, they balked at its cost and were sure that the Parks Commission would never allow such a tower to dominate the Legion of Honor. The short list came down to a conceptually innovative memorial tunnel proposed by Graham and the landscape architect Lawrence Halperin, and an installation by George Segal, who had turned reflexively to his hallmark white plaster figures. Though at first intrigued by Halperin's and Graham's negative-space concept, committee members feared that in its secluded location, the "black hole" could prove dangerous, inviting both crime and physical accidents.

Segal's design had almost never been conceived. The artist had long mulled over possible aesthetic responses to the Holocaust, but the loss of nearly all his parents' European family during the war and the prospect of immersing himself in such memory led him to resist the committee's repeated overtures. Nevertheless, on his way home from mounting an exhibition in Tokyo, Segal agreed to stop over in San Francisco to tour the proposed memorial site. It was early June 1982, and Israel had just invaded Lebanon. Shaken and anxious to hear more details, the politically dovish artist recoiled at the tone and language that American newscasters used in describing the war. "I was horrified for the first time in my life to hear anti-Semitic words coming out of American mouths," he related afterward. "In that instant, I decided to do the [Holocaust] piece. . . . It seemed precisely

George Segal's
Holocaust at
the Legion of
Honor in San
Francisco, with
a view toward
the Pacific
Ocean. Photo:
Ira Nowinski.

the wrong moment for me to abandon my support for the state of Israel and my fellow Jews, despite my objections to Begin and Sharon."[21]

Barely three months later, the committee received photographs of Segal's memorial: a tableau of eleven cast-white figures behind a barbed wire fence. One tattered, plaster-white figure (modeled on an Israeli survivor) stands looking out from behind the fence, his left hand resting on the wire. Behind him, ten bodies lie splayed in a pile, rife with both biblical and formal allusions: a woman with her head against a man's rib, a partly eaten apple in her hand; a father fallen near his son, both sacrificed; a man with outstretched arms, seemingly crucified. Radiating outward, the pile of corpses forms a rough star from one angle, a cross from another. On visiting the artist's New Jersey studio, committee members found that the work seemed to fit in with their original conception: it would be both high, cutting-edge art and an explicitly defined space for Holocaust memory. The committee agreed unanimously that it had found its design and returned to San Francisco to raise funds for its installation.

By this time in Segal's career, his plaster forms had long been celebrated as pop-cultural heirs to Duchamps' ready-mades, Warhol's soup cans, and Hopper's mundane slices of life. Widely acclaimed and exhibited in New York and European galleries, they were collected and shown in dozens of major museum installations. Before long, Segal's human-sized forms also began to find homes in public outdoor spaces, commissioned as commemorative bronze statuary to honor bus riders at New York's Port Authority, steelworkers in Youngstown, Ohio. For an artist who had turned away from the two-dimensional flatness of canvas to sculpture precisely for its material volume and three-dimensional space, this seemed to be the most natural memorial medium.

As a young painter during the 1950s, Segal had wrestled with the legacies of German expressionism and fauvism in the context of contemporary abstract expressionism. Still influenced by the broad brushstrokes and primary colors of these schools, he was also indebted to contemporaries like Jan Muller, Wolf Kahn, and Felix Pasilis. Segal thus worked hard to reconcile abstraction with his powerful desire to depict the human figure. This led him to explore the materiality of both his medium and his subject, the human form. Allan Kaprow's seemingly three-dimensional canvases and tar-babies moved Segal toward his own experiments with human volume and space. But, dissatisfied with his paintings, he turned to space itself (not its illusion on the two-dimensional canvas) for the third dimension: the material volume of human forms would follow the canvas's illusion of volume. In the late fifties, Segal began placing free-standing, roughly hewn human forms, made of chicken wire and burlap dipped in plaster, in front of large canvases painted with brightly colored, life-sized figures.

In the sixties, Segal won renown by casting first himself, seated at a table, and then others in plaster-dipped, cotton-gauze strips. Initially, both critics and, according to Phyllis Tuchman, the artist himself were unsure about these casts: they were disturbing, even morbid somehow in their echoes of the figures caught in the lava and ashes of Mount Vesuvius's eruption.[22] But it was precisely this capacity to formalize the pedestrian moment, captured in media res, that set Segal's medium apart. His figures clustered at street corners, arrested in midstep, or sat at tables; they stood in front of pinball machines or lay in bed. In its sudden stillness, its shocking whiteness, the human form was both affirmed in his plaster casts and abstracted as a formal object of study.

Long regarded merely as the step between a sculptor's clay maquette and the final bronze piece, the plaster model was preserved in its own right by Segal. Even after casting his plaster figures in bronze—his concession to the monumental—Segal began to return them to their penultimate stage of creation by covering the bronze in a permanent, plaster-white patina. As a result, both his sculpture and monuments suggest themselves as works still in process, provisional and unfinished.

By the time of his San Francisco commission, two other public memorial experiences had left Segal wary of, if inured to, the political and emotional agendas underlying all such public commissions: one at Kent State University in honor of the students killed there by the National Guard in 1971, and another in Tel Aviv in honor of the state of Israel. In both cases, he had submitted variations on Abraham's binding of Isaac, neither of which suited his sponsors. While Kent State had hoped for something like a soldier's gun being brushed aside by a young nude woman, his sponsors in Tel Aviv had inferred an unfavorable political comparison between the aborted biblical sacrifice and that made by young Israeli soldiers for the policies of the older generation.

Like that of most Americans, Segal's "Holocaust experience" was necessarily vicarious, limited to the photographs and newsreel footage taken at liberation. When asked to remember the Holocaust, therefore, it was the piles of corpses and barbed wire, the shock and revulsion that came back to him. To refresh his memory before starting work on the San Francisco memorial, Segal returned to the site of his memory: archival photographs of liberation. One in particular, by Margaret Bourke-White, stuck with him and became the image he decided to replicate in his tableau of plaster casts. Segal adds another reason for using the corpses as his motif: strewn as they were, the bodies seemed to exemplify the violation and degradation prisoners underwent at the hands of the Nazis. "I determined that I would have to make a heap of bodies that was expressive of this arrogance and disorder."[23]

Once his theme was decided, Segal told a reporter, he "had two options in dealing with that heap of corpses." One would have been to use bodies borrowed from a morgue, a prospect he rejected. The other was to ask his friends "to play dead," so that, in his words, he "could bury images of sensuality and myth in their gestures."[24] In fact, when several critics remarked not only the apparent robustness of the bodies but their teeming sensuality, Segal responded, "That was also put there purposefully, so there would be overtones of the life force amid all the tragic and carnage."[25] He had become, he said later, as interested in Eve's sensuality as anything else, adding, "It has to do with survival."[26] For Segal, questions of historical veracity were less important than the sense of recently passed life still emanating from his forms.

Back at his New Jersey studio, Segal gathered a number of his friends, young and old, and briefed them on their duties as models. They undressed, and then he asked his friends "to fall down, to collapse and imagine they were dead," after which the artist began the arduous process of wrapping bodies in plaster-soaked cotton-gauze strips. In the next hours, there was plenty of time for the models to meditate on their roles as victims. In fact, Segal had hoped from the outset to capture some expression of his models' responses to their task, some trace of their own memory. In the forms their bodies took, Segal hoped that their thoughts, too, would somehow become part of the cast: reflected in a frozen grimace, a contorted limb. In Segal's words, this piece would thus be "a summation of gestures and movements, of piling and heaving. It becomes a collection of each individual's ideas about death. Some were relaxed, some were rigid, some were drooped. It's a collection of a series of movements that are all ruminations on death."[27] In fact, the figures in the memorial seem only temporarily stilled, ready to rise and brush themselves off after a brief rest. By reminding us that the dead were once whole, living humans, the artist hoped to rehumanize all the victims, to undo some of the degradation that moved his conception in the first place.

Once the design became known, civic response was swift and predictably fractious. As new committees formed to raise funds, others were called to stop the monument's installation. Whereas survivors had hoped for a place to mourn lost loved ones, a substitute gravesite, other groups bewailed the want of similar monuments to mark their losses. Some art historians scorned what Peter Selz called the monument's "wax-work representation," while others, like Selz's colleague Brian Wall, applauded both the artist and his aesthetic conception.[28] Because part of the brilliance in Segal's earlier cast-white sculpture had been its formalization of the banal moments in life, other critics felt that his medium was at direct cross-purposes with his Holocaust theme, the least banal of subjects. Did it trivialize memory, they wondered, or expand the sculptor's medium? For

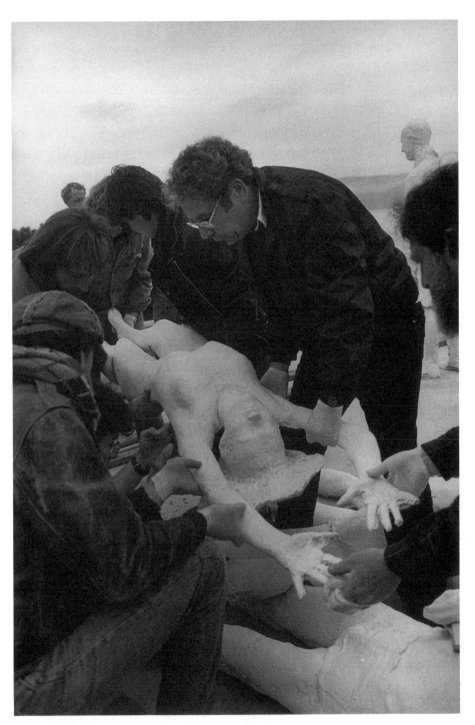

George Segal
installs one of
his plaster-
white figures
for San
Francisco's
Holocaust
memorial,
dedicated in
1983. Photo: Ira
Nowinski.

dissenting critics, the particularization of Segal's life-sized figures reduced both the scale of meaning and possibilities for memory in ways that abstraction would not have done.[29]

On arrival today at the turnaround at the Legion of Honor, the visitor is struck by a seeming dissonance between the Holocaust theme and its beautiful setting. But within a few minutes, this incongruity becomes less problematic. We see, for example, that Segal's white forms echo the tormented figures in Rodin's *Gates of Hell*, long installed nearby at the Legion of Honor, itself a memorial to the fallen of World War I. As we look around, we may be reminded, as well, that the concentration camps were often placed in stunningly beautiful, secluded countryside in Germany and Poland—an ironic perversion of pastoral oft noted by survivors.[30] During the dedication of the original plaster model at the Jewish Museum in New York, more than a year before the memorial was installed in San Francisco, Segal addressed this question directly. "That contrast may in itself speak volumes— about the beauty of the world and the dark underside of human nature," he said, adding later that "I intend this work in part as a memorial to all people who have been victims of that dark underside of human nature."[31] The issue may be less one of "agony in paradise" than the particular effect of the setting on the piece itself, which turns out to be considerable.

In fact, Segal has made two memorials, one an indoor sculpture, the other an outdoor monument. The plaster model of *The Holocaust* was unveiled to the public on 10 April 1983 at the Jewish Museum, as a part of its Yom Hashoah commemorations. The museum has since acquired the original plaster models for its permanent display. In their interior setting at the museum, the white plaster casts invite us to contemplate their forms as objets d'art, part of the artist's larger corpus. The survivor stands alone, estranged from the heap of corpses lying behind him and separated from us by the fence. Stooped slightly forward, he stares straight ahead at no one, at nothing. Enclosed by a ceiling overhead and spotlighted, he remains still and mute, encumbered by an interior memory too recent, too painful to articulate. At the memorial's Jewish Museum dedication in 1986, Segal reiterated this point. "It is fitting," he said, "that silent art represent the muted voices that were forever stilled in the Holocaust."[32]

The deathly stillness is now made palpable, affirmed and highlighted, in the indoor installation. On the other hand, it concentrates our attention on the forms themselves, made ghostly and strange by the white plaster. Without color, only line and shadow, these forms in their whiteness become emblematic and mythical. Surrounded by nothing but its dark borders, the installation remains all-absorbing: memory is defined as an interior, symbolic process.

But in the glory of the sculpture's California environment, with sunshine and spectacular view, memory is externalized, swallowed up by the vastness of its setting. The human forms in particular are miniaturized in such landscape, reduced and made less striking. Indeed, it could be said that we often seek out such beautiful surroundings precisely to lose ourselves in them, places where our thoughts and preoccupations are made to look small and inconsequential by comparison.

In such a context, these figures seem to refer neither to their material, nor to themselves, nor to the ghastly moment of liberation; instead, they are drawn outside themselves by the landscape, become less about themselves than part of their surroundings. While in the museum, they inspire quietude, stillness, and contemplation, at the Legion of Honor, they merge with the great outdoors—the song of birds, rustle of trees, thwack of golfers, roar of cars make them too much a part of the present moment. The white plaster forms lose the context of their material and the artist's corpus and acquire new, California-esque significance. Visitors remark that, at a glance, the sprawling bodies appear to become sunbathers, the barbed wire fence a volleyball net. From their elevated perspective in front of the monument's inscription, visitors look down at the scene, as from a cliff over a beach. Rather than lingering on the installation, the eyes of visitors are apt to join the survivor's own gaze over a spectacular landscape of sloping green grass, a golf course, the ocean, and sailboats—framed by trees on one side and the Golden Gate on the other. Whereas, indoors, the survivor seemed to be looking inward and asking us to do likewise, by his position in the park, he looks out—and invites us to join him, yet another tourist transfixed by the view.

On the memorial's unveiling on 8 November 1984, the eve of Kristallnacht, a steady rain dampened spirits and seemed to lend the setting an enclosed, interior feel; in the summer fog, visitors are also contained by the space, less apt to lose themselves in a landscape shrouded from view. Dazzling sunlight, on the other hand, can be almost blinding when reflected off the white bodies: our gaze over the space is quite literally repelled and seeks refuge in the green shade of golf course and trees, the cool blue of the ocean. In this respect, the fine black-and-white photographs by Ira Nowinski can assist memory here. For in his control of light and tone, his depiction of low-hanging, smoke-colored clouds, the photographer is able to cultivate a brooding, ominous setting. His cool, dark frames recenter the white forms in our consciousness, fence us back into the memorial space.

Despite, perhaps even because of, its transformation from museum sculpture to public monument, Segal's memorial continues to lead a vibrant life in San Francisco's civic mind. Ceremonies for Yom Hashoah are conducted here, as well as Kristallnacht commemorations. When former President Ronald Reagan went to

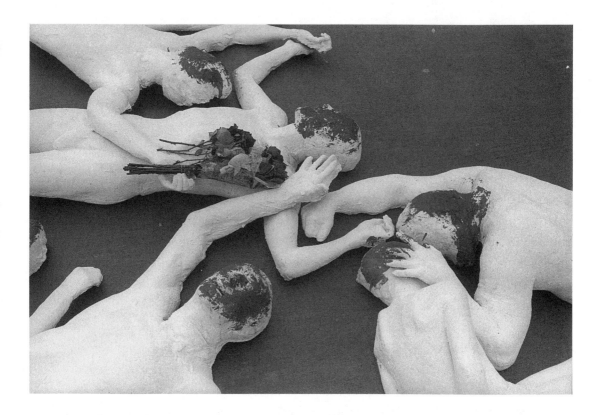

Bitburg, the memorial served as gathering space for a spontaneous countervigil. Four days after its installation and dedication, vandals spray-painted the faces of the figures black and added their own counterinscription to the wall behind it: "Is this necessary?" The monument has since been sprayed with Nazi swastikas and cleaned a number of times. When detractors suggested that its whiteness may well have invited its desecration, supporters responded that this sounded a lot like blaming the victim: were the Jews, by extension, responsible for their own murder? In a show of support, an anonymous donor has sent flowers to be laid weekly at the site ever since. Survivors still come daily to tend the memorial, as if it were a surrogate gravesite for lost loved ones.

In San Francisco, with its large population of Japanese Americans, aspects of the monument necessarily evoke other memories, as well. In fact, the project's landscape designer, Asa Hanamoto, could not help but recall his own experience in an American internment camp for Japanese Americans during World War II. "It's been a long time," he said, "but I still remember those barbed-wire fences and those guard towers with machine guns in them. It stays with you."[33] The designer reflects as much his experience as the artist's, making it a joint memorial, embodying plural kinds of memory. Knowing this, the busloads of Japanese tourists at the Legion of Honor may not recall the Jewish Holocaust so much as their own experiences, or perhaps those of their American cousins during the war. Like all memorials, this one depends on those who visit it, those who resist it, those who embrace it for its life in the mind, its many lives in many minds.

And like many communities before and after it, San Francisco has found that its effort to build a site for shared memory could not help but expose the many conflicting and contested assumptions underlying "public memory." Few communities are prepared for this kind of controversy, and most are embarrassed by it, ashamed that such a seemingly unifying cause like public memory should betray so much real disunity. In the heat of argument, bruised friendships and fractured political alliances, most communities are ill-prepared to acknowledge the value of the process itself. Largely unfazed by the argument, possibly even invigorated by it, Segal was able to take the long view of this process when he inspected the site a year before the monument's dedication. "What's at stake," he commented, "is the quality of the response, in the area of public education. Sculpture functions as a community memory. It's a civilized root to educate young people, to reinforce freedom and tolerance and respect for individuals. I don't mind all the discussion."[34] As Segal seemed to recognize early on, debate is also a form of memory.

Liberty State Park, New Jersey

Though his medium is not typical of other Holocaust memorials in America, the liberation motif in Segal's monument is. This is the one experience shared by both survivors and American soldiers during the war: one that conforms conveniently to America's most powerful self-idealization. For the young American GIs who liberated Dachau and Buchenwald, memory of the Holocaust necessarily excludes the conditions in Europe before the war, the wrenching break-up of families, deportations to ghettos and camps—even the killing process itself. American soldiers were not witnesses to the process of destruction, only to its effects.

Even the first national days of Holocaust remembrance in America were called for explicitly in light of the American liberators' experiences, independently of either the U.S. Holocaust Memorial Commission or Yom Hashoah. In 1979, Sen. John Danforth proposed that 28–29 April of that year, the days corresponding to the thirty-fourth anniversary of Dachau's liberation by American troops, be designated as national days of remembrance. The senator was unaware of Yom Hashoah and its proximity to these days, which have since been moved to coincide more closely with the Twenty-seventh of Nissan. Though they now seem to coincide with the Jewish calendar's day of remembrance, America's national

Nathan
Rapoport's
Liberation,
erected within
sight of of
America's
greatest
ideological
icon, the Statue
of Liberty
(right), and Ellis
Island (out of
photo on left).
Photo:
James E. Young.

days of remembrance necessarily recall both America's experience as liberator and the Jewish catastrophe—each in the figure of the other.

Because the "American experience" of the Holocaust in 1945 was limited to the grisly moments of liberation, it may not be surprising that one of the most widely visited monuments to this era in America, entitled *Liberation*, is located in Liberty State Park, New Jersey, within sight of America's greatest ideological icon, the Statue of Liberty—all part of a topographical triad including Ellis Island. In this work by Nathan Rapoport (sculptor of the Warsaw Ghetto Monument), a young, solemn-looking GI walks forward, his eyes on the ground, cradling— almost pietà-like—a concentration camp victim. With skeletal chest showing through shredded prison garb, his arms spread, and his eyes staring vacantly into the sky, the victim exemplifies helplessness.

Commissioned by the State of New Jersey and sponsored by a coalition of American Legion and other veterans' organizations, the monument is consonant with both the specific experiences of Americans in the war and with traditional self-perceptions of the nation's role as rescuer in war and as sanctuary for the world's "huddled masses." Indeed, the official state resolution dedicating the monument on 30 May 1985 defined explicitly its place in American history:

> Whereas the Liberty Park Monument Committee was formed by Governor Thomas H. Kean to raise funds for, and commission the construction of, a monument to honor American Servicemen of World War II as liberators of oppressed people, and
>
> Whereas the theme of the monument was to recognize that our servicemen fought, not to conquer nor to be aggressors, but rather to rescue and restore freedom to those persecuted and oppressed by the fascist powers . . . .[35]

According to the program notes from the dedication, though other monuments have honored American victory in World War II, this is the first one to show us the purpose of the fight. In *Liberation*, America's reasons for fighting World War II would thus reiterate America's memory of its origins.

The governor's remarks at the dedication emphasize the monument's American pedigree even more strongly. "To me," he said, "this monument is an affirmation of my American heritage. It causes me to feel deep pride in my American values . . . . This monument says that we, as a collective people, stand for freedom. We, as Americans, are not oppressors, and we, as Americans, do not engage in military conflict for the purpose of conquest. Our role in the world is to preserve and promote that precious, precious thing that we consider to be a free democracy. . . . Today, we will remember those who gave their lives for freedom."[36] As such,

Liberation has become an obligatory photographic stop on the campaign trail for national candidates, including George Bush, Dan Quayle, and Jesse Jackson in 1988.

Liberty and pluralism thus comprise the central memorial motifs in both current and proposed museums to the Holocaust in America. The museum at the Simon Wiesenthal Center in Los Angeles is being reconceptualized, moved next door into an expansive new complex, and renamed Beit Hashoah—Museum of Tolerance, both to reflect its pedagogical mission (tolerance) and to attract as wide an audience as possible. In New York, the new Museum of Jewish Heritage—A Living Memorial to the Holocaust is being planned for Battery Park City in lower Manhattan, within sight of Ellis Island and the Statue of Liberty, thus situating the Holocaust somewhere between American shrines to immigration and liberty. The twin names of these two museums illustrate both the dilemma each faces in professing civic values in a sectarian space and the attempt to overcome this dilemma by balancing Jewish and American memory in one line.

Chapter 12

Memory and the

Politics of Identity:

Boston and

Washington, D.C.

> All those who walk this Freedom Trail pause
> here to contemplate the consequences of an
> absence of freedom.
> —Alex Krieger

Boston: An American Process

Not long after the unveiling of *Liberation*, a Boston survivor decided to initiate
a similar memorial in his city to thank the American soldiers who had liberated him at Buchenwald. The survivor organized a small memorial committee
and approached sculptor Nathan Rapoport, who agreed to design a version of
Liberation for Boston. But when the committee turned to other survivors for
support, they found unexpected resistance instead. "Maybe some were liberated
by Americans," a fellow survivor complained, "but my family and I were never
liberated at all. They were killed at Auschwitz while American bombers flew
overhead, and I barely survived the death marches to Germany." While other
survivors sympathized with their friend's motive, they also feared that in *Liberation*, a millennium of Jewish civilization in Europe and all the lives lost would
be reduced to the one degrading moment they shared with American liberators.
Bitter arguments ensued, community support withered, and the project was put
on hold.

Yet Boston will soon have its Holocaust memorial. Moreover, the chain of
events that followed even suggests itself as an object lesson in American memorial building. For what began as one survivor's thwarted memorial mission eventually grew into a sophisticated and self-reflexive public art project. Still in

process, the Boston memorial provides a uniquely instructive glimpse of the inner workings—the tempestuous social, political, and aesthetic forces—normally hidden by a finished monument's polished, taciturn exterior. In this section on what has come to be called the New England Holocaust Memorial, I examine the working parts of a memorial in process, the ways in which a memorial's shape is determined as much by its own coming into being as by the ideals that first inspired it.

For a short time after "liberation" was rejected as its motif, the Boston project seemed doomed. But once relieved of its singular theme, the proposal for a Holocaust memorial was revived—and soon took on a second life. The committee hired a professional executive director, who in turn assembled an influential committee of local Jewish leaders, philanthropists, and academics. Kitty Dukakis, the Jewish wife of then-Governor Michael Dukakis, was recruited as honorary chairperson. And after being invited to serve as one of the founding chairpersons, Mayor Raymond Flynn helped arrange for the city to cede a prime piece of downtown real estate to the project, the Union Street Park.

Located between Faneuil Hall and City Hall, this long strip of land was both problematic and promising. For years, it had served as a no-man's land, a traffic island created accidentally by the city's urban renewal project of the 1960s. With cars whizzing by on both sides, some feared a memorial set there would get lost in the traffic's noise and tumult, hardly the setting for quiet meditation. On the other hand, it was centrally located and right alongside the Freedom Trail, visited by some sixteen million tourists a year. In effect, it would become one more stop on the trail: two stops after the Boston Massacre site, one after Faneuil Hall, and one before the Paul Revere House on a route wending from the Boston Common to the Bunker Hill Monument. No matter what shape the memorial here finally takes, it will be located both spatially and metaphysically in the continuum of American Revolutionary history. Almost thirty years after New York City forbade the survivors their place in American history, Boston will integrate the Holocaust into the very myth of American origins.[1]

Acutely aware that contested memory would be an inevitable part of this, or any, public memorial commission, the New England Holocaust Memorial Committee decided not to suppress argument and dissent but to turn debate itself into one of the project's reasons for being. Theirs would be a memorial whose memory-work began with the committee's own discussions, community education, even public challenges to the memorial. The process of the memorial's self-definition, finding its role in the community, would become the memorial's first function: it would either be built on the basis of its self-justification or, in failing to persuade the community of its mission, remain unbuilt. In either case, according to the committee, the project will have served both memory and education, and provided a public forum for the Jewish community's own self-definition amid American civic culture.[2]

To this end, the Memorial Committee sponsored a number of public debates on the merits and liabilities of the memorial, attended by survivors and their children, local politicians and urban planners, artists and architects. Over the course of several months, public symposia were called to view images of other Holocaust memorials, to hear art historians discuss the function of memorials. Survivors lectured on their experiences, took questions from a curious audience, and argued over the forms memory should take. At a public symposium held at Harvard's School of Design, Maya Lin reflected on the process of building the Vietnam Veterans' Memorial and its implications for the Boston memorial. By consulting the community every step of the way, making them part of a process they may even disagree with, the committee also made them accountable. In Boston's academically charged environment, debate began to assume the dignified, nearly sacred proportions of philosophical discourse. Where other communities had fretted over the unseemly appearance of squabbling and dissent, the committee in Boston encouraged it, and in so doing allowed debate to drive the process forward. Even the press, previously skeptical and reluctant to cover the memorial much beyond its controversy, had begun to show an interest in the critical issues in editorials and feature columns.[3]

At about the time the committee decided to hold an international competition, a few of its members admitted that they had hoped their own memorial visions might somehow be realized. "Let me tell you what I see there," said one of the most prominent backers, "a statue with water perpetually running over its sides, as if it were crying." After an awkward silence, another supporter piped up, "Maybe we should just invite someone we already know to do it. Why can't we ask Maya Lin to make us a monument? Then at least we know we've gotten the best." To which Alex Krieger, a Harvard professor of architecture, rejoined: "That is precisely why we must have an international competition. The only way to find the inspiration of a Maya Lin is to invite everyone to participate. Without the open competition in Washington, there would have been no Maya Lin memorial." Krieger's argument eventually carried the day. But the cost, moaned another committee member, what will such a competition cost? A lot, came Krieger's reply.

For as healthy and invigorating as the debate seemed in the community's eyes, it also had its practical costs. As the executive director soon discovered, an enlightened and creative memorial process is not always compatible with fundraising. The very debate and lively discussion that had attracted the public's attention scared off potential donors, who tend to shy away from controversial projects. Executive Director Stephen Dickerman was constantly amazed by the hesitation on the part of the city's most generous philanthropists—who all supported the project in name, but continued to gauge the support of others before giving large sums themselves.

And then there was the matter of a jury. Most of the committee recognized that the choice of jury members constituted the first step in their community's choice of the monument. So, in appointing a jury, the committee's overriding aim was to gather as formidable a group as possible, an authoritative body whose integrity and credentials could withstand any storm their final decision might provoke. There was also the matter of balance: at least two of the jurors needed to be of international stature, so that no single authority would dominate the proceedings. Each of the major relevant disciplines would have to be represented: urban and landscape architects, local art critics, curators and artists, a historian and survivor. In the end, the jury was composed of Marshall Berman, a cultural historian; Rosemarie Bletter, an architectural critic and historian; Henry Friedlander, a modern German historian and survivor; Frank Gehry, world-renowned architect; Katy Kline, an art historian, critic, and curator; Michael Van Valkenburgh, a renowned landscape architect; and Elyn Zimmerman, a sculptor and environmental artist. All would be held accountable by their respective constituencies.

In the fall of 1990, announcements in several trade journals proclaimed the opening of an international competition for the New England Holocaust Memorial. More than 1,000 potential designers registered for the competition, of whom 520 finally submitted designs. Entrants hailed from seven countries and included architects, artists, sculptors, and landscape designers. The thick registration packets they received included a detailed statement of purpose, site description and photographs, discussion of the site's architectural and historic context, a summary of other public art works in downtown Boston, survivors' testimonies, and a resource bibliography. The registration packet was meant not only to provide topographical and social context, but also to invite artists to enter into their own dialectic with memory.

The principles of the memorial and competition were defined thus:

> This will be a memorial to the Shoah—the Holocaust—in which the Nazi Third Reich systematically murdered six million Jewish men, women, and children. . . . The memorial will be for the six million—a place to grieve for the victims and to mark the loss of their culture to history.
>
> The Nazis and their collaborators victimized many other groups, murdering countless other people, each of equal worth

and importance. Still others, including survivors, those who aided them, and those who liberated them, were caught up in this great tragedy and carry the burden of that memory throughout their lives. In seeking a universal understanding of the Shoah, we acknowledge the place of each experience in the horror of that collective history.

To remember this suffering is to recognize the danger and evil that are present whenever one group persecutes another. The Holocaust was the ultimate act of prejudice—in this case, anti-Semitism. Wherever prejudice, discrimination and victimization are tolerated, evil like the Shoah can happen again.[4]

In its carefully written statement of purpose, the Boston Memorial Committee remained acutely conscious of its place in America, its mission in a plural society. Beyond this definition, it left the forms open to potential designers, hoping to inspire as much memory as it would eventually codify.

The range of responses was extraordinary: one entrant, a professor of art and design from North Carolina, had made this a semester-long class project, where students examined every aspect of the event, public art, and memorial design before submitting a meticulously researched team design. Others included teams of artists and architects from New York City, the principals from prestigious architecture firms, young, old, trained, and amateur. In several other cases, the entrants underwent profound personal and spiritual changes. Many wrote to say that the experience itself had brought a new depth to their work, a greater appreciation of their medium's limitations. Were the monument itself never built, the committee might still console itself for having generated this kind of massive memory-work on the part of 520 souls: hundreds of hours multiplied by hundreds of teams and individuals.

Originally, the jury had planned to select three finalists and to make a small number of merit awards. But after three days of deliberations, without a trace of consensus, a variation on the initial plan emerged. "You will notice," Krieger observed wryly in announcing the results, "that there are seven jurors and seven finalists when there were originally supposed to be three."[5]

Even at this stage, the community was invited to respond to the models and thereby to sustain debate, if only hypothetically, since their votes would not bind the jury. The process, if not the monument, would be interactive; it would remind the community as often as possible how much memory depended on them, and not on the space. To this end, the models of the seven finalists were unveiled and exhibited publicly before the final decision was made. Visitors to the exhibition were asked by both the design committee and the local Jewish newspaper, the *Advocate*, to voice their likes and dislikes. Among specific questions posed to visitors were: What do these memorial designs help us to remember about the Holocaust? How do these designs and the Freedom Trail location help us see the relevance of the Holocaust in today's world? What sort of experience can a Holocaust memorial provide to the individual and to the community?

As was expected, responses reflected a wide cross-section of public opinion. A few had difficulty accepting the Holocaust's place on the Freedom Trail, wondering what it had to do with the American Revolution. Others felt it would heighten the significance of all Americans' former oppression and liberation. Many wanted to broaden the general scope of memory to include non-Jews as well as Jews, so that it would invite as much of the general population as possible into its space. Still others had specific suggestions for alternatives, recalling other memorials in other places. And of course, a few denied that the Holocaust had ever happened. Like the "countermonument" in Hamburg, this memorial had begun to serve as a great fingerprint for society.

Though the *Advocate* tallied responses to particular models, ranking them in order of popular opinion, its poll was not to be binding on the jury. That the jury chose the popular favorite does leave some room, however, for speculation as to whether the poll had some bearing, after all. For in fact, while the first stage was a blind-jury selection, the second-stage model submissions included the names of the designers, names whose significance could not have have escaped the jury members. The winner, Stanley Saitowitz, was well known to the influential architects on the jury, Gehry and Van Valkenburgh. It may not have been a matter of calculated political deliberation, but at the final stage, the jurors also understood (even if unconsciously) that the better known the winner, the easier it would be to garner public and political support for the monument's construction.

The thousands and thousands of hours spent by the 520 teams on their memory-work bore an incredibly rich response, as exemplified in a few of the finalists' own statements. Nancy J. Locke and Jan Langwell, for example, proposed "an endless meadow" of two-foot-high yellow grass, sunk beneath a three-foot-high granite walk, both extending the length of Union Park. Definitions and meanings of the Holocaust would remain multiplaned, as fluid as the meadow, broken only by the concrete path over it. "The great emptiness of the fields hides the real horror of the event that cannot be expressed through words or sights," the designers wrote. "Explanations are replaced by a void—a beautiful, empty, boundless place. . . . The space above the meadow is as well a void, cut out in a mass of trees set on a grid."[6] Like a number of public respondents, the judges may have felt this recalled too much the Germans' planting over of the death sites with splendid grain fields, that it consoled visitors more than it provoked them.

Glass Star, South view

Two other designs were less reassuring, more haunted by events. Architects Chung Nguyen and Chuong Nguyen proposed cutting a great scar into the park space, 240 feet long, 40 feet wide, and 6 feet deep. "This path is seen as a wound that slits open the ground, unleashing the silent cries [of the murdered]," they wrote. At the same time, the path would be bridged in several places, self-conscious attempts to suture the wound, to repair the breach, through a memory-structure. In a similar vein, Troy West, Anker West, and Ginidir Marshall conceived of a series of monumental glass panels, fourteen by fourteen feet tall, connected by steel cables and configured in a great star of David. It would be bisected by a concrete path and railroad rails. In both cases, the artists evoked the sense of brokenness and simultaneous attempt at mending recalled in the broken tombstone memorials in Poland.

Three other designs drew inventively upon concept as much as form, inviting visitors to interact with the memorial and then to reflect critically on their presence there. In a proposed work by sculptors Cissy Schmidt and Matthew Pickner, twenty-four thresholds with doors ten feet high would be spaced in a grid on a granite floor amid the green grass and trees of the park. Wide-open doors on the outer thresholds would invite passersby in to contemplate words like Tolerance, Liberty, Justice, and Equality, cut out of their metal panels to reveal the sky and light behind. As visitors proceeded further, they would find the interior thresholds and doors half-closed, more difficult to enter; negative-value words like Prejudice, Tyranny, and Injustice would be printed in raised black letters

New England Holocaust Memorial Competition finalists Troy West, Anker West, and Ginidir Marshall proposed a broken glass star for the Boston competition. Photo: Courtesy of New England Holocaust Memorial Committee.

allowing no light to pass through these doors. One interior threshold and door would be closed entirely, a dead-end, inscribed on one side with the Memorial Committee's statement of purpose, and on the other with the words: "As they marched to their deaths, they recited for each the Kaddish, the Jewish prayer of mourning. They knew there was no one to say it for them."

In a similarly inspired vein, architects Robert J. Stein and Jerry Wedge suggested a labyrinth as spatial metaphor for the Jews' impossible journey during the Holocaust. Pedestrians would enter one end of a maze of polished, black marble benches, each inscribed with the names of concentration camps. Locust trees growing in the midst of the maze would be guarded by iron fences, so that visitors would be kept from touching them. The labyrinth would be a three-hundred-foot-long piece of environmental art, according to its designers, a part of the modern living city which would continuously invite new passersby into its recesses of memory.

Of the conceptual monuments not chosen, perhaps the most original was New York architect Hali Jane Weiss's "echo chamber." Based on the premise that some subjects simply elude the systems of knowledge and logic practiced by writers and architects, "this memorial design," wrote Weiss, "recedes from form so that the ineffable can enter in its own way. Conceptually, it juxtaposes fact and mystery, loss and regeneration, technology and nature, the ordinary and the sacred." In fact, the execution would have been as profoundly subtle as its concept was ambitious: a blend of sound and sense, visitor presence and victim absence. This design would have left the park's trees and lawns largely untouched, only the ground plane changed.

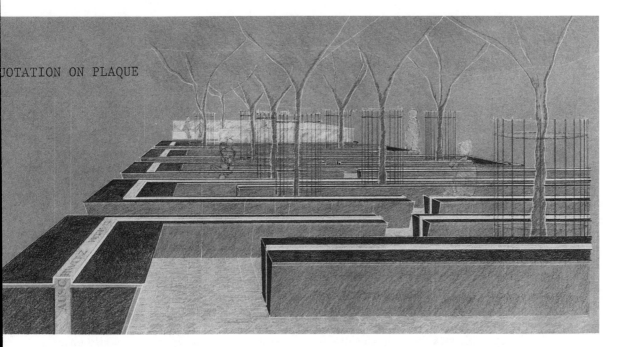

QUOTATION ON PLAQUE

Finalists Robert J. Stein and Jerry Wedge suggested a three-hundred-foot labyrinth of benches, marked with names of concentration camps. Photo: Courtesy of New England Holocaust Memorial Committee.

Finalist Hali Jane Weiss designed a memorial echo chamber for the space in Boston. Photo: Courtesy of New England Holocaust Memorial Committee.

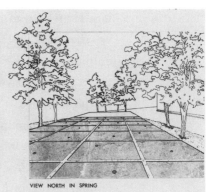

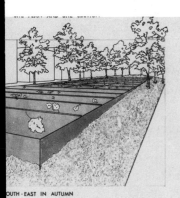

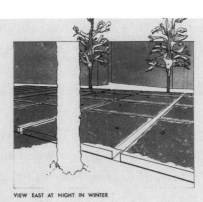

SOUTH-EAST IN AUTUMN

VIEW EAST AT NIGHT IN WINTER

VIEW NORTH IN SPRING

Using about one-third of the park space, a large, hollow rectangle of steel would be set flush in the earth, embedded with thirty-six small flames encased in thick clear glass, randomly spaced throughout the square. Our footfalls would reverberate loudly with every step, punctuating our movement over the surface of the memorial. Like an enormous drum, the surface would, in Weiss's words, "echo from the wound of people walking across it. The low-tuned reverberations in the sound chamber resonate in the non-verbal chamber of our being. The steel confronts our internal voids and the slate, grass and light begin to fill them." In this way, we would become experientially aware of the hollowness of this ground, now a symbolic grave, self-conscious of our very actions this space. With every step, we would attract undue attention to ourselves, each step a slow drumbeat to accompany our funereal procession.

Though its conceptual ingenuity made it a favorite with several of the more academic art and architectural historians, the echo chamber was not chosen partly because of its very subtlety. It would have remained invisible from the street and sidewalk, quiet in the absence of visitors. From above, the site would have

been partly screened by the trees left in place, even covered over by leaves in the autumn. At night or in fog, only the thirty-six flames would be visible, flickering like Jahrzeit candles in the darkness. Though they admired its conception, the jury felt that it would have been a difficult memorial to "sell" to a public conditioned to "the monumental."

In the end, the jury selected the most audacious memorial design, by the most prominent architect of the final seven. The design, by San Franciscan Stanley Saitowitz, along with Ulysses Kim, Tom Gardner, and John Bass, calls for six 65-foot-high armor-strength glass towers, set in a row, each illuminated from below by a black granite pit filled with electrically heated volcanic rocks. Visitors will be able to walk on a path leading through the bases of these towers, over the iron grates covering gleaming pits of light, beneath the hollow chambers of glass pillars. From a distance at night, the towers will cast a bright glow, illuminating the sky above and the faces of buildings nearby. Their glow can be expected to attract curious passersby in other parts of the city the way old-fashioned spotlights once did. It will be unavoidable, filling the empty park with light and life, pits of fire and pillars of ice.

From the beginning, Saitowitz and his colleagues envisioned the memorial as a process which included an almost ritualistic preparation of the site. Construction would, in the original plan, begin on Holocaust Remembrance Day with the "brutal cutting of all the trees on half the site." The remaining stumps would recall both the lives of Jews interrupted by death (as did the iconography of broken trees in Polish Jewish tombstones) and the destruction of life that usually pre-

cedes its memorialization—a truism for all memorial markers. We are reminded that destruction is part of memory-construction. Once again, while engaging in concept, this proposal will probably encounter stiff resistance from several quarters, including the Parks Commission and environmental groups. Were the debate lively enough, the memorial function might even be fulfilled without cutting the trees at all. Only after further debate will the great glass towers be erected atop the glowing pits, covered over with iron grating, each named after one of the six death camps: Chelmno, Treblinka, Majdanek, Auschwitz, Sobibor, and Belzec.

Jurors were struck by both the experiential and symbolic potential in this design. "By day, the play of natural light on the forms and the light filled shadows cast by the glass towers will be an ever changing phenomenon," they wrote, "constantly renewing the memorial experience." By night, the glow will create a new presence in that part of the city, lending life to forms hitherto unseen after dusk. The jurors felt that both the scale of the towers and their material would serve to mediate between soaring steel and glass skyscrapers on one side and the

Stanley Saitowitz's winning entry for the New England Holocaust Memorial competition comprised six glass towers, illuminated at night. Photo: Courtesy of New England Holocaust Memorial Committee.

older, colonial brick architecture of Faneuil Hall on the other, between new Boston on the west and old Boston on the east. The pits would glow hot, emitting warm air upward through the glass pillars, perhaps attracting homeless people in the winter for warmth. Jurors also recognized that the glass would attract vandals, as well, its seeming fragility an invitation to rock throwers, hammers, and chisels. But even this did not bother one of the jurors, cultural historian Marshall Berman, who remarked, "If all the skinheads in New England come and throw rocks at [the memorial], it will only become more eloquent. It will then be like a representation of the Kristallnacht of the 30s."[7]

The jurors were also moved by the memorial's abstractly symbolic references to Jewish culture, the ways its universal forms and light would include, rather than exclude, other groups. Like the six granite pillars in Los Angeles, these would suggest a number of possible references and so would not insist on any single meaning. In the architects' words,

> Once completed, many meanings attach to the memorial: Some think of it as six candles, others call it a menorah. Some a colonnade walling the civic plaza, others six towers of the spirit. Some six columns for six million Jews, others six exhausts of life. Some call it a city of ice, others remember a ruin of some civilization. Some speak of six pillars of breath, others six chambers of gas. Some sit on the benches, are cooled by the water and warmed by the fire. Some think it is a fragment of Boston City Hall, others call the buried chambers Hell. Some think the pits of fire are six death camps, others feel the warm air rising up from the ground like human breath as it passes through the glass chimneys to heaven.By remaining open in significance, the space's forms would sustain their liveliness in both present and later generations' minds.

As I write, the memorial-building project in Boston proceeds apace. It may be years before funding is completed, years more before the Boston Redevelopment Authority approves a final version. Debate will persist, some of it angry, some restrained: Do we etch numbers in the glass or not? And what about the trees? Do we cut them? How do we guard the monument from vandals? There will be further fundraising glitches and dinners, lectures and controversies. Some of its supporters will abandon the project, while its former detractors join in building. By the time it's built, the glass towers may well be half their proposed height, may not even be lighted except on commemorative days. Many of the controversies will be charted in its evolving forms, others forgotten or ignored by it. Each of its changes will function to chart the process itself, the ebb and flow of public sentiment and will. These, too, will become part of the memorial's performance. To the extent it continues to evolve and show the twists and turns of public needs and concerns, it will remain memory forever in process, never completed.

The U. S. Holocaust Memorial in Washington, D.C.:
Memory and the Politics of Identity

Of all Holocaust memorials in America, none can begin to match in scope or am- bition the national memorial and museum complex nearing completion in the heart of the nation's capital. Situated adjacent to the Mall and within view of the Washington Monument to the right and the Jefferson Memorial across the Tidal Basin to the left, the U.S. Holocaust Memorial and Museum will be a neighbor to the National Museum of American History and the Smithsonian Institute. At the time of this writing, nearly six thousand people have donated 105 of the projected 147 million dollars needed for its opening in 1993. It will contain ten thousand artifacts collected from around the world, including an authentic Treblinka box- car, a Danish fishing boat used in the rescue of that country's Jews, an actual barrack from Birkenau, and two thousand pairs of children's shoes from Ausch- witz, among thousands of other imported remnants. Its archives and library of a hundred thousand volumes will make it the largest Holocaust repository and study center in America.

Established in 1980 by an act of Congress, the U.S. Holocaust Memorial Council was charged with fostering Holocaust remembrance in America in three funda- mental ways. The council shall, in the words of the resolution,

1. provide for appropriate ways for the Nation to commemorate the Days of Re- membrance, as an annual, national, civic commemoration of the holocaust, and shall encourage and sponsor appropriate observances of such Days of Remem- brance throughout the United States;

2. plan, construct, and oversee the operation of a permanent living memorial museum to the victims of the holocaust, in cooperation with the Secretary of the Interior and other Federal agencies as provided in section 1406 of this title; and

3. develop a plan for carrying out the recommendations of the President's Com- mission on the Holocaust in its report to the President of September 27, 1979, to the extent such recommendations are not otherwise provided for in this chapter.[8]

Sticking both to protocol and to America's pluralist tenets, the statement re- flects the lowercase holocaust defined by Jimmy Carter when he appointed the President's Commission in 1978: eleven million innocent victims exterminated, six million of them Jews.[9] Beyond Carter's pluralist definition of the Holocaust, however, is the way this memorial would integrate the Holocaust into the heart of America's civic culture.

"What is the role of [this] museum in a country, such as the United States, far from the site of the Holocaust?" Charles Maier has asked. "Is it to rally the people who suffered or to instruct non-Jews? Is is supposed to serve as a reminder that 'it can happen here?' Or is it a statement that some special consideration is deserved? Under what circumstances can a private sorrow serve simultaneously as a public grief?"[10] Before such a museum could be built on the Mall in Washington, explicitly American reasons would have to be found for it.

The official American justification for a national memorial in the nation's capital was also provided by President Carter in his address at the first Days of Remembrance ceremonies at the Capitol Rotunda, 24 April 1979:

> Although the Holocaust took place in Europe, the event is of fundamental significance to Americans for three reasons. First, it was American troops who liberated many of the death camps, and who helped to expose the horrible truth of what had been done there. Also, the United States became a homeland for many of those who were able to survive. Secondly, however, we must share the responsibility for not being willing to acknowledge forty years ago that this horrible event was occurring. Finally, because we are humane people, concerned with the human rights of all peoples, we feel compelled to study the systematic destruction of the Jews so that we may seek to learn how to prevent such enormities from occurring in the future."[11]

Not only would this museum depict the lives of "new Americans," but it would reinforce America's self-idealization as haven for the world's oppressed. It would serve as a universal warning against the bigotry and antidemocratic forces underpinning such a catastrophe and call attention to the potential for such slaughter in all other totalitarian systems.

For, as a national landmark, the national Holocaust museum would necessarily represent the Holocaust according to the nation's own ideals, its pluralist tenets. In the words of a memorial brochure, therefore, the Holocaust began "before a shot was fired, with persecution of Jews, dissenters, blacks, Gypsies, and the handicapped. The Holocaust gathered force as the Nazis excluded groups of people from the human family, denying them freedom to work, to study, to travel, to practice a religion, claim a theory, or teach a value. This Museum will illustrate that the loss of life itself was but the last stage in the loss of all rights."[12] In being defined as the ultimate violation of America's Bill of Rights and as the persecution of plural groups, the Holocaust encompasses all the reasons immigrants—past, present, and future—ever had for seeking refuge in America.

When cultural critics protested that such a museum, though necessary, would be a blight on the Mall, the Memorial Council countered, "This Museum belongs at the center of American life because as a democratic civilization America is the enemy of racism and its ultimate expression, genocide. An event of universal significance, the Holocaust has special importance for Americans: in act and word the Nazis denied the deepest tenets of the American people." That is, the U.S. Holocaust Memorial defines what it means to be American by graphically illustrating what it means not to be American. As a reminder of "the furies beyond our shores," in one columnist's words, the museum would define American existence in the great distance between "here" and "there."[13] In effect, in being placed on the Mall, the museum will enshrine not just the history of the Holocaust, but American ideals as they counterpoint the Holocaust. By remembering the crimes of another people in another land, Americans will recall their nation's own idealized reason for being.

This will be the beginning of what the museum's project director, Michael Berenbaum, has termed the "Americanization of the Holocaust." In Berenbaum's words, the museum's story of the Holocaust will have to be "told in such a way that it would resonate not only with the survivor in New York and his children in Houston or San Francisco, but with a black leader from Atlanta, a midwestern farmer, or a northeastern industrialist. Millions of Americans make pilgrimages to Washington; the Holocaust Museum must take them back in time, transport them to another continent, and inform their current reality. The Americanization of the Holocaust is an honorable task provided that the story told is faithful to the historical event."[14] Of course, as Berenbaum also makes clear, the story itself depends entirely on who is telling it—and to whom.

Layers of Meaning: Topography, Architecture, Exhibition

The story also depends on several other layers of meaning: in the memorial's location in Washington, in the heart of America's monumental civic culture; in the architectonic form of the edifice itself, its place in relation to nearby buildings, to architectural trends and fashion; and in the exhibition narrative housed by the museum. Each conveys a different meaning that bears some relation to the other dimensions of the memorial's total text.

From the beginning, many people, like the architectural critic for the *Washington Post*, were unsettled by "the symbolic implications of the memorial's placement [adjacent to the Mall]—that the Nazi extermination of 6 million Jews [could be] an integral part of the American story."[15] Even local survivors came forth with their reservations, testifying against the memorial for its not being relevant to the American national experience and for enlarging the idea of the

Holocaust to include non-Jewish victims of the Nazis. Still others feared that such a memorial contradicted the very essence of the national Mall, that by recalling such horrible events, the memorial would cast a dark shadow across a monumental landscape dedicated to all that was high and virtuous in America's origins.

To all of which the memorial committee's chairperson, Harvey Meyerhoff, responded that precisely because the Mall celebrates human history and creativity, the Holocaust museum belongs on it, a reminder of dark side humankind's civilized works. "If the Smithsonian represents the accomplishments of civilization, the Holocaust raises fundamental questions about the capacity of individuals and of society, of technology and human genius for evil," Meyerhoff wrote.[16] This too, he seems to say, is part of Western civilization; this too can become part of a past on which we now build a "more perfect union."

Meyerhoff goes on to acknowledge that "because the Holocaust Memorial is located in the heart of our nation's capital and because it is a national memorial, the uniquely American dimension of the Holocaust will be consistently represented in the museum." The American dimension will include not only the American soldiers' part in defeating Nazi Germany and liberating the camps, but also less "memorable" aspects of the country's history: the restrictions on immigration, the rejection of refugees during the war, and the refusal to bomb the death camps. Ironically, of course, the memorial will thereby Americanize the Holocaust, making it a pluralistic, egalitarian event.

Finally, putting the memorial on the Mall will also set a national standard for suffering. It will formally monumentalize the Holocaust, hold it up as an ideal of catastrophe against which all other destructions will be measured. After the Vietnam Veterans' Monument nearby, the Holocaust memorial will become the second antimemorial on the mall: a national memorial institution that is also self-critical, that suggests a self-correcting national policy and actions.

The next layer of meaning was negotiated in the building's design. Chosen from a large field of competitors, James Ingo Freed, a principal in I. M. Pei's New York architectural firm, began by articulating the fundamental problems facing him on all fronts. He would have to begin, he said, by bridging the two landmark buildings on either side of the memorial's 1.7-acre lot: the grey limestone and neoclassical lines of the hulking Bureau of Engraving to the south, and the ornate red-brick Victorian Auditors Building to the north. From here, his aim would be to "take the conditional [that is, situational] circumstances of [the museum's] location and weave them together with its content."[17] This is, in some ways, the double-edged dilemma facing any architect and monument builder: How will design and material, which are used for the way they speak to the environment, speak to content? Specifically, in the case of a Holocaust memorial, how will the brick and limestone chosen for its neighborhood architectural resonance make meaning as a Holocaust edifice?

At the same time, Freed wanted to use this space to challenge—or at least to critique—Washington's monumental facade. How to challenge the Mall's monumentality from a monumental structure on the Mall? How to do this while remaining answerable to the capital's Fine Arts Commission, whose first principle is to regulate and keep a relatively uniform appearance on the Mall? How to make a building that would disturb consciousness on the one hand, while having to conform to a highly regulated and uniform architectural set of guidelines on the other?

For the self-conscious architect, every structure is also a metaphor, created for one physical purpose but also to stand figuratively for an idea, a time, an event, a people. In Freed's eyes, for example, "the metaphor of the guard tower was the watching, the overview, the distancing of the persecutors from the prisoners." How then would his building figure the memory it was designed to house? The essential problem of design for a plural nation was resolved by Freed in a relatively simple, yet profound formulation. It is important, in Freed's words, that "memory be sufficiently ambiguous and open ended *so that others can inhabit the space, can imbue the forms with their own memory.*"

Like other memorial designers before and after him, Freed insists on keeping forms open-ended, abstract enough to accommodate all rememberers, especially those who come after, who will after all comprise the great bulk of visitors. By not forcing what he called "one reading" on the visitors, Freed hoped to leave the symbols inclusive and inviting to all. "We wanted an evocation of the incomplete," he wrote. "Irresolution, imbalances are built in. For instance, the screen in the front portal is not there to force a reading, but to make evident the need for interpretation." The objective, Freed continued, was to "make it cohere without being explicit, without being one thing."[18]

"It is my view," Freed writes, "that the Holocaust defines a radical, but hopefully not a final, break with the optimistic conception of continuous social and political improvement underlying the material culture of the West."[19] The question, then, is how to preserve this sense of break in a setting whose very raison d'être is to unify memory and understanding of the nation's past. Would Freed suggest Holocaust memory as a part of, or separate from the Mall and all of its national ideals? Would it call attention to itself as an exception to, even a violation of, these ideals—thereby seeming to destroy the architectural harmony of the capital? Freed recognized early on what was only confirmed for him by the Fine Arts Commission in their first evaluations of his proposal. Differences, challenges, and resistance to surrounding motifs would literally have to be sanded away if the building were to be erected at all.

The commission rejected Freed's first design in 1986 on several grounds, mostly having to do with its sheer size and assertiveness. "The character of the building," according to Charles H. Atherton, the commission's executive secretary, "itself had an almost unintended link to fascist architecture. It was almost brutal. You could not escape identifying it with the architecture favored by Hitler. It seemed to be more a memorial to the perpetrators of the crime, not the victims."[20] Atherton went on to suggest that one of his commission's primary roles was to protect the integrity of the Mall, to keep any single project from upstaging the rest of the Mall's monuments.

One year later, the memorial's design was resubmitted, this time much more successfully. The entire project had been scaled back, though one part of it still stuck out a little too much: the Hall of Remembrance, a large, limestone-clad hexagonal building attached to the museum extended some forty feet beyond the line of its two neighbors. Back and forth they went, the Fine Arts Commission trying to scale back the museum's obtrusiveness and to bring it into line with the rest of the Mall's monuments, Freed trying to preserve his challenge to monumentality, a sense of disturbance on the Mall. Finally, Freed and the Memorial Committee members agreed to move the building back into line, reducing some of the space of the rest of the museum, but not taking any space away from the exhibits. This design was approved by the Fine Arts Commission in an 8–2 vote on 30 July 1987.[21]

The result is an exterior that will indeed join the Capital "urbanistically" and an interior that metaphorically removes visitors from the Capital. If, on the outside, this building had to conform with its surroundings, the architect could ensure that, once entered, it removed visitors from Washington as quickly as possible. "When you walked out of Washington, I wanted to separate you from the city formally and spatially; but before you stepped into the Hall of Witness, I also felt that you had to go through an acoustical change, a disturbance like a drumbeat. Something to tell you that you are coming to this place, to make you pay attention."[22] Since it is Freed's conception, I allow his words to become part of his architectual text. This is not to resolve questions with the architect's authoritative answers, but to show that in some places, the architect does not have answers—nor does he believe he should have answers. He relates going through his project-workers' drawings and pulling out any neat resolutions precisely to leave the space problematized, its difficulties intact.

When visitors enter, therefore, they will find themselves in a great "raw steel structure, without cover or enclosing planes, except that the walls have panels

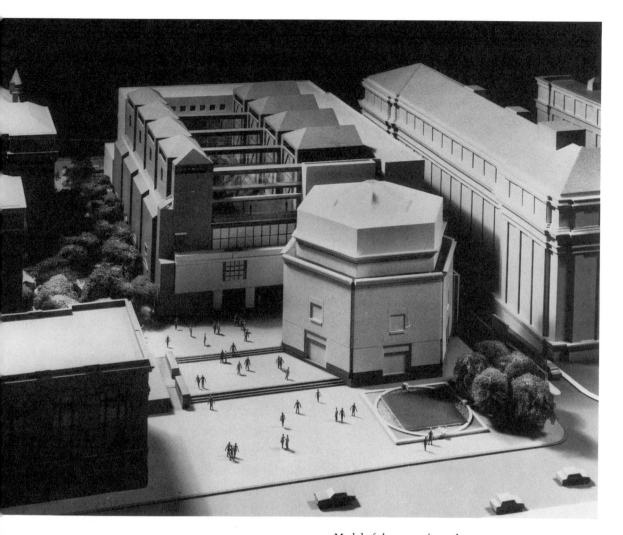

Model of the United States Holocaust Memorial Museum, designed by James Ingo Freed of I.M. Pei Associates, located four hundred yards from the Washington Monument, just off the Mall in Washington, D.C. Photo: Courtesy of the United States Holocaust Memorial Museum.

of glass. These panels are the Walls of Nations, where every nation that suffered deaths is identified by a panel of glass." Visitors will then proceed diagonally through the Hall of Witness, the path lighted by a diagonally cut skylight high above. Elevators at the end of this path will take visitors to the fourth floor, where the historical exhibit will begin. But to enter the exhibit, visitors must cross a bridge made of glass blocks, what Freed describes as "a dangerous path."[23]

The visitors' last stop at the detached Hall of Witness, like their first, will also resonate brokenness, an irresolution of form and meaning. In this great, open, sky-lit gallery, absence will reign, architectural emptiness to recall the void left behind by a people's mass murder. All structures and materials reflect brokenness, irreparability: from the floor of verde antica marble, naturally cracked and disintegrating, to a gigantic crack in the granite wall symbolizing a breach in civilization, to the roof and its skylight, skewed and fragmented with metal trusses. Lines inside are deliberately skewed and twisted, without reassuring angle or form.

The discontinuity and fragmentation preserved in the museum's interior architectural space could not, however, be similarly conveyed in the exhibition narrative itself. For, like all narrative, that created in the exhibition will necessarily depend on the continuity and coherence of its telling of history. Because the exhibits are not installed at the time of this writing, and will be in a state of relative flux until the museum's actual opening, I reflect here only on the written narrative of the project director's "walk-through."

According to Berenbaum, visitors will begin their exhibition walk-through with an immediate, personal leap of identity.[24] On entering the museum, all visitors will be asked to type their age, gender, and profession into a computer, after which they will be issued an identity card of someone like themselves who was caught up in the Holocaust. At three stages of the exhibit, visitors will have their cards updated, so that with every passing year in exhibit-time, the personal history of what might be called our phantom-guide will be revealed further. At the end of the permanent exhibition, visitors will insert their cards into a television monitor and meet the companion face-to-face through oral history—or, if the phantom-companion died, the memory of the deceased will be conveyed by surviving family and friends.

On the one hand, such a device allows individuals a chance to personalize history, to know it "as if it happened to us," in the Passover refrain. For a moment, at least, the victims are rehumanized, invigorated with the very life force of the visitors themselves. But at another level, the device perpetrates a small but significant deception. For by inviting visitors to remember their museum experience as if it were a victim's Holocaust experience, the personal identity card asks

Model of the
Hall of Witness
in the U.S.
Holocaust
Memorial
Museum, which
will serve as a
central
gathering space.
Note the open
rafters, skewed
angles, and
cracks on the
wall—all to
suggest a breach
in architectural
norms after the
Holocaust.
Photo:
Courtesy of the
U.S. Holocaust
Memorial
Museum.

The United States
Holocaust Memorial Museum

9341

Name: *Manya Petranker*
Date of Birth: *October 21, 1922*
Place of Birth: *Munich, German*
Place of Residence: *Stanislawow, Po*

We have a close-knit, happy family life within
this cosmopolitan city. My parents are always
going to Jewish community events. On Sunday
and other Christian holidays, people throw stones
at us as they go to church. We know we aren't
Jewish, and we know we aren't Sink...

Name: *Haskel Kernweis*
Date of Birth: *1920*
Place of Birth: *Kupno, Poland*
Place of Residence: *Kolbuchova, Poland*

Haskel comes from a small village in Galicia. His
family is very religious. His mother raises geese,
chickens, and vegetables for the family to eat.
Haskel walks 5 miles to public school in the
morning, and goes to religious school in the
afternoon.

1933-1939: Haskel now calls himself "Charley,"
for his passion is no longer religion but English.
He spends much of his time learning English from
a torn, old grammar book. He writes to Eleanor
Roosevelt telling her that he loves English and
wants to speak it in America one day. She responds
enthusiastically. The German police order Charley
to work for them.

1940-1944: Charley is told by the Germans to
dismantle the photos in Kolbuchova, then hears that
he is to be killed upon completion of the job. He
escapes into the woods with a group of Jewish
men. One day, Charley went into a town to buy
bread. Waiting for him were a group a Polish
peasants. His friends found him—dead, a
pitchfork stuck into his chest.

1945: Charley's entire family was gassed at
Belzec. Only one of the Jewish fighters who went
to the woods with him survived the war.

The United States
Holocaust Memorial Museum

5736

A personal identification card similar to this will issued to visitors to the U.S. Holocaust Memorial Museum. Each card will contain personal data entered into a computer by visitors, turning all into victims for the day. Photo: Courtesy of the U.S. Holocaust Memorial Museum.

us to confuse one for the other. While the "experiential mode" has come into increasing favor by museums, it also encourages a certain critical blindness on the part of visitors. Imagining oneself as a past victim is not the same as imagining oneself—or another person—as a potential victim, the kind of leap necessary to prevent other "holocausts." All of which obscures the contemporary reality of the Holocaust, which is not the event itself, but *memory* of the event, the great distance between then and now, between there and here. For this, not the Holocaust itself, is our pre-eminent reality now, no less than the Holocaust was the victims' pre-eminent reality then.

In addition, a further twist has been detected by Jonathan Rosen: "The irony is that many Jews during the Holocaust scrambled to acquire false papers in order to survive the war—the papers of non-Jews. There is a reverse principle at work here, as if everyone were expected to enter the museum an American and leave, in some fashion, a Jew."[25] If this is true, then precisely the opposite effect of a unifying experience has been achieved: Americans enter whole, only to exit in their constituent parts.

This is a victim-imagined museum: the visitor—now victim—returns to see it all through the victim's eyes. The Holocaust was, after all, a Holocaust only for the victims, something else for the perpetrators. By this logic, a perpetrator-made

Holocaust museum would turn visitors into potential murderers: the professor who collaborated, the schoolchild who taunted her Jewish classmates, the Hitler Youth who ended up in the SS, a concentration camp guard. How people became killers might be almost as interesting as how people became victims, though not nearly as inviting a motif as the latter, nor much of a basis for a national museum meant to affirm national ideals and values.

Despite their identity cards, the visitors' experience will begin appropriately with America's first direct Holocaust experience—through the eyes of the American GIs who liberated Buchenwald and Dachau. In this opening section, we will view footage of the camps at their liberation filmed by the Army, images that will convey both the shock of the Americans and the gratitude and relief of survivors on being liberated, many of them about to become new Americans. With a little chronological slippage, in fact, it could be said that as potential Americans, many of the victims in these films were already somehow American. Indeed, many became American solely on the strength of their experiences as Holocaust victims: for them, the Holocaust was the beginning of their becoming American, making the Holocaust an essentially American experience.

And then, unlike European Holocaust museums that begin and end with the destruction of its Jews, and unlike museums in Israel that often show the prewar European Diaspora as already half-dead, the U.S. Holocaust Museum will reflect an essential exilic bias, showing the great vibrancy and richness of Jewish life lost in the Holocaust. The tragedy in this context is not just how European Jewry was destroyed, or the gruesome remains at the end, but the richly complex life lost—the thousand years of civilization extirpated, unregenerated, unrepaired. The Holocaust is defined here not as mere killing, but as an immeasurable loss. (Even Israeli museums that include life before and after the Holocaust are not so generous in their appraisal of pre-Holocaust Jewish life in Europe—so decayed and decrepit in the Zionist view, so defenseless and weak, that it almost deserved to perish. For to do otherwise, to represent Diaspora Jewry in overly generous terms would be to undercut Israel's very reason for existence).

Because the American experience of Nazi Germany in the thirties was necessarily mediated by newsreels, papers, and radio broadcasts, the media experience itself is recreated in the next section. Visitors will enter a typical American living room in 1939, complete with a radio broadcasting news reports, newspapers and magazines discussing contemporary events. This was the American experience, in all of its limited and necessarily mediated ways.

After this, the visitors will reinsert their personal identity cards and so be transformed again from Americans to victims. To reach a section on the ghetto, visitors will traverse a narrow bridge like the ones that linked the outside world to the ghettos then. Then they will walk on authentic cobblestones from the Warsaw Ghetto and view other artifacts, such as a sewing machine, a baby carriage, a policeman's bicycle, and other items showing the range of life in the Ghetto: each artifact a metonymic reminder of the actual life once animating it. Though director Jeshayahu Weinberg believes such artifacts make the factuality of the Holocaust self-evident, an immunization against the negationist lies that deny the Holocaust, they also suggest something the Holocaust was not: a collection of ownerless items, junked. Of course, this is true for other museums as well, but any time an entire people is represented by the artifacts of their lives, something of life itself is lost. Because this museum will be showing entire cases of victims' shoes, their hair, and other remnants brought from the Auschwitz museum, the earlier critique I made of that museum would apply here as well.

After the ghetto experience, the narrative will turn to mass murder, beginning with the Einsatzgruppen, the mobile killing units of the SS responsible for murdering some 1.5 million Jews in the Soviet Union. According to Berenbaum, however, this part will also be X-rated: a four-foot-high tin wall will keep young children from looking into the abyss, visible only to their elder siblings and parents. From here visitors will enter a section on the Warsaw Ghetto uprising, whence they will be herded over a bridge narrowing from sixteen to five feet wide, crowded together while they view films of the deportations. For those survivors who, in Berenbaum's words, "don't need to see or feel what they can never forget," or who grow claustrophobic, or who just cannot bear the horrible images, there will be a detour, an escape ramp away from the crowds and horror.

A section on concentration camps will follow, replete with an actual barrack imported from Birkenau. Again, according to Berenbaum, this and other artifacts will be used to refute the lies of Holocaust negationists. Once inside the barracks, visitors will view a scale model of the gas chambers designed after a similar model on view at Auschwitz. Canisters of Zyklon-B, long deactivated, will attend this section, along with contracts of the construction companies who built the gas chamber and crematorium complexes, guaranteeing a longevity of twenty-five years. "Issues of corporate behavior—with all their ethical ramifications—must be confronted squarely in this tower," Berenbaum writes.

After the death exhibits, visitors will find both respite and some sense of vindication in sections on resistance and "the courage to care." Here the stories of ghetto fighters and partisans will be told alongside those of other heroes, such as Raoul Wallenberg (who saved a hundred thousand Jews in Budapest) and the French village of Chambon, where Jewish children were hidden and protected.

Finally, like the museum narratives in Israel, where lives were rebuilt after the

Holocaust, this exhibit will end with the "return to life." For this is the story of an ideal shared by America and Israel: both see themselves as lands of refuge and freedom. What will follow is a story of immigration, the long journey from "Old World" displaced persons camps, ravaged towns, and anti-Semitism to the "New Worlds" of Jewish statehood and American egalitarianism. It is the story of America's absorption of both immigrants and their memories, the gradual integration of Holocaust memory into American civic culture. At the end, the museum will suggest itself as the ultimate triumph of America's absorption of immigrants, the integration of immigrant memory into the topographical heart of American memory. All of which visitors will meditate upon in the Hall of Remembrance, a hexagonal hall adjacent the permanent exhibition gallery.

In his introduction to the museum walk-through, Berenbaum addresses the reciprocal exchange between a monument and its surroundings. It is not only a matter of a monument's meaning being shaped by its context—the Holocaust Americanized, in this case—but also of the surroundings being re-viewed in light of the Holocaust memorial. "When people leave the U.S. Holocaust Memorial Museum," Berenbaum writes, "the monuments to democracy that surround it—to Lincoln and Jefferson and Washington—will take on a new meaning." Such American icons of democracy will either be affirmed for the ways their ideals prevented similar events in America or, in the eyes of Native Americans, African Americans, and Japanese Americans, reviewed skeptically for the ways such ideals might have prevented, but did not, the persecution of these groups on American soil. Every visitor will bring a different experience to the museum, as well as a different kind of memory out of it.

In America, the traditional impulse to anchor memory in historical crisis is further complicated—and exacerbated—by a number of additional factors unique to the contemporary Jewish American experience. For in America's culture of assimilation, where explicitly religious differences are tolerated and de-emphasized, it is almost always the memory of extreme experience that serves to distinguish the identity of minority groups from the majority population. Indeed, one of the central topoi of American New World identity, beginning with the progenitors of America's "majority population"—the pilgrims—is the memory of Old World oppression.

During the rise of civil rights activism in the 1960s, in particular, new-found ethnic pride among African Americans, Jewish Americans, and Native Americans depended in great measure on the power of a remembered past to bind otherwise alienated groups. The myth of the American melting-pot rapidly gave way to a sense of America as patchwork quilt of ethnic, religious, and national constituencies. Jews, no less than other American ethnic groups, began to reassert their national identity, turning no less than other groups to their memory of mass suffering. As African Americans recalled their enslavement and Native Americans their genocide, Jewish Americans recalled the Holocaust as the crux of their common heritage.

In fact, without the traditional pillars of Torah, faith, and language to unify them, the majority of Jews in America have turned increasingly to the Holocaust as their vicariously shared memory. This preoccupation with the Holocaust may have led, in turn, to the massive outpouring of support for Israel in May 1967—when the Jewish state seemed threatened with destruction. For many Jewish Americans, the point of common identification with the Jews of Israel seemed to lie in their potential destruction. In a perverse way, love of Israel and Holocaust memory now seemed to be two sides of the same coin: the more acute Holocaust memory, the greater the fear that Israel stood on the brink of another Holocaust—and the greater the relief and pride when Israel emerged victorious.

Ironically, if true to the Israeli notion of a "Galut mentality," when Israel came to be perceived as less a potential victim, it also became less a source of identity and pride among American Jews. And as identification with Israel waned during the late 1970s, reaching its nadir during the Lebanon war, the other half of secular American Jewish identity—Holocaust memory—assumed a greater proportion of Jewish time and resources. Accordingly, as Israel absorbs more and more formerly victimized Soviet Jews, and is perceived to have been victimized itself during the Persian Gulf War in 1990, its stature as source of identity in American Jewish eyes will surely rebound. In this way, the fates of Holocaust memory and sympathy for Israel may always be intertwined.

Over time, the only "common" experience uniting an otherwise diverse, often fractious, community of Jewish Americans has been the vicarious memory of the Holocaust. Left-wing and right-wing Jewish groups, religious and secular, Zionist and non-Zionist may all draw different conclusions from the Holocaust. But all agree that it must be remembered, if to entirely disparate ideological ends. As a result, while Jewish day schools, research institutes, and community centers run deficits, millions of dollars continue to pour into Holocaust memorial projects and museums. As unattractive as this reality may be, its significance has not been lost on savvy fundraisers across the spectrum of Jewish organizations. For example, full-page advertisements in the *New York Times* appealing for donations to support the exodus of Soviet Jews in 1990 described this rescue in the image of another Holocaust prevented. "It starts with hate mail, name calling, and grave desecrations," the caption reads over a photo of Yad Vashem's memorial hall. "We all know how it ends. And now it looks like it's starting all over again in the Soviet Union."[26] On a more local level, nearly all community centers and Jewish Federation offices also include some reference to the Holocaust, a suggestion that every stone to build a new Jewish community be regarded as an implicit sign of Hitler's defeat.

By extension, Holocaust museums are increasingly becoming the centers for historical education, activism, and fundraising. Consequently, instead of learning about the Holocaust through the study of Jewish history, many Jews and non-Jews in America learn the whole of Jewish history through the lens of the Holocaust. Without other kinds of museums to a Jewish past, even to current life in the Diaspora to offset them, Holocaust memorials and museums tend to organize Jewish culture and identity around this one era alone. As a result, not only will the Holocaust continue to be suggest itself as a center of American Jewish consciousness, but it will become all that non-Jewish Americans know about a thousand years of European Jewish civilization.

In the end, the American Jewish community may not be able to have it both ways: it will be difficult to sustain the exclusively Jewish character of the Holocaust and continue to make it a public event. A Jewish memorial to the Shoah is one thing, a civic memorial to the Holocaust another. Each answers to a different constituency; each reflects different kinds of meaning in memory. Public Holocaust memorials in America will increasingly be asked to invite many different, occasionally competing groups of Americans into their spaces. African Americans and Korean Americans, Native Americans and Jews will necessarily come to share common spaces of memory, if not common memory itself. In this, the most ideal of American visions, every group in America may eventually come to recall its past in light of another group's historical memory, each coming to know more about their compatriots' experiences in light of their own remembered past.

Notes

Introduction

Epigraphs: Jean Baudrillard, *The Evil Demon of Images* (Sidney, 1988), 23; Jean Amery, *At the Mind's Limits: Contemplations by a Survivor on Auschwitz and Its Realities*, trans. Sidney Rosenfeld and Stella P. Rosenfeld (Bloomington, 1980), 84; André Schwarz-Bart, *The Last of the Just*, trans. Stephen Becker (London, 1961), 409.

1. Arthur Danto, "The Vietnam Veterans Memorial," *The Nation*, 31 Aug. 1986: 152. This particular definition is repeated in an otherwise excellent analysis of the memorial by Marita Sturken, "The Wall, the Screen, and the Image: The Vietnam Veterans Memorial," *Representations* 35 (Summer 1991): 118–42.

2. Friedrich Nietzsche, *The Use and Abuse of History*, trans. Adrian Collins (New York, 1985), 14–17.

3. Lewis Mumford, *The Culture of Cities* (New York, 1938), 438.

4. For the full, much more complex, context of Broszat's remarks, see his series of letters to Saul Friedländer and Friedländer's excellent replies printed first in *Vierteljahreshefte für Zeitgeschichte* 36, no. 2 (April 1988): 339–72, subsequently translated and reprinted as "Martin Broszat/Saul Friedländer: A Controversy about the Historicization of National Socialism," in *Yad Vashem Studies* 19 (Fall 1988): 1–47; also reprinted in *New German Critique* 44 (Spring–Summer 1988): 85–126. The exchange between Broszat and Friedländer was initially sparked by Friedländer's response to Broszat's "Plädoyer für eine Historisierung des Nationalsozialismus" [Plea for a historicization of National Socialism], *Merkur* 39 (1985): 373–85.

Broszat's specific reference to monuments comes in his comments on "mythical memory," which he distinguishes from "scientific insight" (*New German Critique* 44 [Spring–Summer 1988]: 90–91).

5. Rosalind Krauss, *The Originality of the Avant-Garde and Other Modernist Myths* (Cambridge, Mass., and London, 1988), 280.

6. Pierre Nora, "Between Memory and History: *Les Lieux de Mé-moire*," trans. Marc Roudebush, *Representations* 26 (1989): 13. Reprinted from Pierre Nora, "Entre mémoire et histoire," *Les Lieux de mémoire*, vol. 1: *La République* (Paris, 1984), xxvi.

7. John Hallmark Neff, "Introduction [to Public Art]: Daring to Dream," *Critical Inquiry* 16 (Summer 1990): 857.

8. See Maurice Halbwachs, *Les Cadres sociaux de la mémoire* (Paris, 1952); also see his *La Mémoire collective* (Paris, 1950).

9. From "Forwort," in *Sefer Yizkor le-kedoshei ir (Przedecz) Pshaytask Khurbanot ha'shoah*, p. 130, as quoted in Jack Kugelmass and Jonathan Boyarin, eds., *From a Ruined Garden: The Memorial Books of Polish Jewry* (New York, 1983), 11.

10. On the missing grave syndrome, see Joost Merloo, "Delayed Mourning in Victims of Extermination Camps," in Henry Krystal, ed., *Massive Psychic Trauma* (New York, 1968), 74.

11. See the catalogue for this exhibition, edited by Werner Fenz, *Bezugspunkte 38/88* (Graz, 1988). I discuss this installation at greater length in chapter 4.

12. For insights into this project by both the artist and curator, see Hans Haacke, "Und ihr habt doch gesiegt, 1988," and Werner Fenz, "The Monument Is Invisible, the Sign Visible," in *October* 48 (Spring 1989): 75–87.

13. See Albert Elsen, "What We Have Learned about Modern Public Sculpture: Ten Propositions," *Art Journal* 48, no. 4 (Winter 1989): 291. Also see Albert Elsen, *Rodin's "Thinker" and the Dilemmas of Modern Public Sculpture* (New Haven, 1985).

Without being too facetious in this context, we might speculate on what a monument to the Holocaust by video artist Nam June Paik might look like. Would it be a single video loop, replaying over and over images set in a concentration camp or deportation site? Or would he make an all-purpose monument, a chunk of marble, inset with a video monitor that played any memorial loop we wanted to insert? Depending on the day and location, this stone and video might commemorate Auschwitz, Hiroshima, or World War I—not to mention any number of future catastrophes.

14. For examples, see Albert E. Elsen, *Modern European Sculpture, 1918–1945: Unknown Beings and Other Realities* (New York, 1979), 122–25.

15. See Janet Blatter, "Art from the Whirlwind," in Janet Blatter and Sybil Milton, eds., *Art of the Holocaust* (London, 1982), 22–35.

16. For a much more comprehensive discussion of the difficulties in bearing literary witness, see James E. Young, "Interpreting Literary Testimony: A Preface to Rereading Holocaust Diaries and Memoirs," *New Literary History* 18 (Winter 1986–87): 403–23.

17. As might have been expected, even the most popular of abstract monuments, the Vietnam Veterans Memorial, was eventually forced to make concessions to the figurative demands of its public. Apparently dissatisfied with only seeing themselves reflected on its black marble surface, some of the veterans demanded a more figurative representation of "actual soldiers" nearby. As a result, a figurative statue of three representative soldiers was added to the setting—to be joined eventually by a figurative statue of nurses, also veterans, who served in Vietnam.

For discussion of the controversy surrounding the decision to add to Lin's original concept, see Elizabeth Hess, "A Tale of Two Memorials," *Art in America*, April 1983: 120–27; and Charles L. Griswold, "The Vietnam Veterans Memorial and the Washington Mall: Philosophical Thoughts on Political Iconography," *Critical Inquiry* 12 (Summer 1986): 688–719. Also see Jan C. Scruggs and Joel Swerdlow, *To Heal a Nation: The Vietnam Veterans Memorial* (New York, 1985).

18. See Peter Bürger, *The Theory of the Avant Garde*, trans. Michael Shaw (Minneapolis, 1984), 87. Bürger defines the "functional analysis of art" as an examination the artwork's "social effect (function), which is the result of the coming together of stimuli emanating from within the work itself and a sociologically definable public."

19. Marianne Doezema, "The Public Monument in Tradition and Transition," in *The Public Monument and Its Audience* (Cleveland, 1977), 9.

20. Robert Musil, "Monuments," in *Posthumous Papers of a Living Author*, trans. Peter Wortsman (Hygiene, Colo., 1987), 61.

21. I suggested a similar critique of monuments in much rougher form in "Memory and Monument," in Geoffrey H. Hartman, ed., *Bitburg in Moral and Political Perspective* (Bloomington, 1986), 112; reprinted in expanded form in James E. Young, *Writing and Rewriting the Holocaust: Narrative and the Consequences of Interpretation* (Bloomington, 1988).

For an excellent, much more fully adumbrated discussion of "the struggle between iconoclasm and idolatry," see W. J. T. Mitchell, *Iconology: Image, Text, Ideology* (Chicago and London, 1986), 160–208.

Introduction to Part 1

1. In the rare event when a state does commemorate its crimes, it is nearly always at the behest of formerly victimized citizens. The memorial unveiled on 30 Oct. 1990 in Moscow, for example, to "the millions of victims of a totalitarian regime" was instigated by a group calling itself "Memorial," composed of scholars, cultural figures, dissidents, and former victims of Stalin's terror.

Likewise, a new monument by Maya Lin to the civil rights movement in Montgomery, Alabama—inscribed with the names of those who died for the cause—was commissioned and constructed by the Southern Poverty Law Center there, which had chronicled and prosecuted civil rights cases. In neither the Soviet nor American case did the state initiate the monument, but in both instances representatives of the state later endorsed these memorials—a move by which both current governments sought to create an official distance between themselves and past, guilty regimes.

2. Cited in Elizabeth Domansky, "How to Remember What to Remember: Jenninger's Speech," paper given at a conference at Northwestern University entitled "Lessons and Legacies of the Holocaust," November 1989, p. 2.

3. In fact, what both sides of the *Historikerstreit* (Historians' Debate) in Germany seem to have in common is the resistance to remembering the Third Reich solely in the image of Auschwitz. The vociferous response inside Germany and out to Ernst Nolte's infamous charge that "certain interests," especially those of the persecuted (i.e., the Jews), kept Auschwitz in view only to sustain their privileged status among the nations, led to his revised explanation of the killings: that the Nazis committed "Asiatic deeds" only in fear of the deeds to be perpetrated upon the Germans by the Asiatics

themselves. In "Vergangenheit die nicht vergehen will," his essay in the *Frankfurter Allgemeine Zeitung* (6 June 1986) that ignited the Historians' Debate in Germany, Nolte wrote: "Did not the National Socialists, did not Hitler perhaps commit an 'Asiatic' deed only because they regarded themselves and those like them as potential or real victims of an 'Asiatic deed'? Was not the Gulag Archipelago more original than Auschwitz? Was not the 'class murder' of the Bolsheviks the logical and factual prius of the 'racial murder' of the National Socialists?" See also Nolte, "Between Myth and Revisionism? The Third Reich in the Perspective of the 1980s," in H. W. Koch, ed., *Aspects of the Third Reich* (New York and London, 1985), 17–38.

Though Martin Broszat was one of many who argued forcefully and eloquently against this revisionist critique, he also suggested that it would behoove all historians not to view the Third Reich solely through the lens of Auschwitz, that a historical normalization is necessary if we are ever to grasp the entire significance of Hitler's time. In his view, the hegemony of Holocaust memory had begun to bury the rest of Hitler's social and political crimes, losing them to further inquiry and understanding. See Broszat, "Plädoyer für eine Historisierung des Nationalsozialismus," *Merkur* 39 (May 1986): 373–85.

Chapter 1. The Countermonument

Epigraph: Friedrich Nietzsche, *The Use and Abuse of History*, trans. Adrian Collins (New York: Macmillan, 1985), 13.

1. For elaboration of this theme, see Matthias Winzen, "The Need for Public Representation and the Burden of the German Past," *Art Journal* 48 (Winter 1989): 309–14.

2. From Claude Gintz, " 'L'Anti-Monument' de Jochen et Esther Gerz," *Galeries Magazine* 19 (June–July 1987): 87.

3. See Michael North, "The Public as Sculpture: From Heavenly City to Mass Ornament," *Critical Inquiry* 16 (Summer 1990): 861. As North shows, such an impulse has a long history in its own right.For further discussion of these dimensions to contemporary sculpture, see Henry M. Sayre, *The Object of Performance: The American Avant-Garde since 1970* (Chicago, 1989); Lucy R. Lippard, *Changing: Essays in Art Criticism* (New York, 1971), 261–64; Douglas Crimp, "Serra's Public Sculpture: Redefining Site Specificity," in Rosalind Krauss, ed. *Richard Serra/Sculpture* (New York, 1986).

4. From Doris Von Drateln, "Jochen Gerz's Visual Poetry," *Contemporanea* (September 1989): 47.

5. Gintz, " 'Anti-Monument,' " p. 80.

6. From a public presentation by the Gerzes on the *Gegen-Denkmal* at a conference on art and the Holocaust, Evangelischen Akademie Loccum, West Germany, 20 May 1989.

Berlin-born and speaking in German to a German audience, Jochen Gerz was making an obvious, if ironic, allusion to the Nazis' own notoriously literal-minded reference to being "stabbed in the back" by enemies internal, external, and imagined. Appropriating the Nazis' language in this way was clearly intended both as a provocation and as an ironic self-identification by the Gerzes as "enemies of the Reich." See *Kunst und Holocaust: Bildiche Zeugen von Ende der Westlichen Kultur*, ed. Detlef Hoffmann and Karl Ermert (Rehburg-Loccum, Germany, 1990).

7. Quoted in Michael Gibson, "Hamburg: Sinking Feelings," *ARTnews* 86 (Summer 1987): 106–07.

8. Ibid., p. 106.

9. Ibid., p. 107.

10. See "Das Verhängnis," in *Kritischer Kalender Querschnitt I: 160 Lithographien von A. Paul Weber*, ed. Arnold Koster (Munich, 1981), 37.

11. For further insight into these images and the debate surrounding them, see Gabriele Werner, "Welche Realität meint das Reale? Zu Alfred Hrdlickas Gegendenkmal in Hamburg," *Kritische Berichte* 3 (1988): 57–65.

12. Norbert Radermacher, quoted in *Gedenkstätte KZ-Aussenlager Sonnenallee Berlin-Neukölln: Bericht der Vorprüfung* (Berlin, 1989), 20; my translation. I am indebted to Jochen Spielmann, the coordinator of this competition, for so generously providing me with all of its documentation.

13. See Norbert Radermacher, *Stücke für Stadt*, catalogue from the Kunstlerhaus Bethanien, Berlin, 1985.

14. From Horst Hoheisel, "Rathaus-Platz-Wunde," in *Aschrott-Brunnen: Öffene Wunde der Stadtgeschichte* (Kassel, 1989), unpaginated; my translation.

15. For this imaginative insight, I thank Gary Smith in Berlin, who suggested it to me in conversation.

16. From Aristotle's *Physics* 221b, 2, as cited in Edward Casey, *Remembering: A Phenomenological Study* (Bloomington and Indianapolis, 1987), 181.

17. Pierre Nora, "Between Memory and History: *Les Lieux de mémoire*," trans. Marc Roudebush, *Representations* 26 (1989): 19.

Chapter 2. The Sites of Destruction

1. For an insightful discussion of Germany's earliest postwar memorials, including the rallies, see Jochen Spielmann, "Gedenken und Denkmal," in Jochen Spielmann, Helmut Geisert, and Peter Ostendorff, eds., *Gedenken und Denkmal: Entwurfe zur Erinnerung an die Deportation und Vernichtung der jüdischen Bevölkerung Berlins* (Berlin, 1988), 7–46; also see Jochen Spielmann, "Steine des Anstosses— Denkmale in der Bundesrepublik Deutschland," *Kritische Berichte* 3 (1988): 5–16.

2. From "Plotzensee Memorial, Berlin," Informationszentrum Berlin (Gedenkstätte Deutscher Widerstand, 1985), 2.

3. For detailed accounts and analyses of the "Stauffenberg plot," see Harold C. Deutsch, *The Conspiracy against Hitler in the Twilight War* (London, 1968); James Forman, *Codename Valkyrie: Count Stauffenberg and the Plot to Kill Hitler* (New York, 1973); Peter Hoffmann, *The History of the German Resistance, 1933–1945* (Cambridge, Mass., 1977); and Hans Mommsen, *The German Resistance to Hitler* (London, 1970).

4. "Plotzensee Memorial, Berlin," 11.

5. Klemens von Klemperer, "The Legacy of the Plot to Kill Hitler," *New York Times* Op-Ed page, 21 July 1990.

6. For complete accounts of this incident and surrounding controversies, see Günther Schwarberg, *Angriffsziel Cap Arcona* (Hamburg: Stern-Buch im Verlag Gruner, 1983) and Rudi Goguel, *Cap Arcona: Report über der Untergang der Häftlingsflotte in der Lübecker Bucht am 3. Mai 1945* (Frankfurt am Main: Roderberg, 1982).

7. For descriptions of other memorials to the *SS Cap-Arcona* catastrophe, see Ulrike Puvogel, ed., *Gedenkstätten für die Opfer des Nationalsozialismus: Eine Dokumentation* (Bonn, 1987), 736–40, 750, 751. This excellent volume provides an exhaustive survey and documentation for all memorials to the victims of the Nazis in Germany.

8. See "Remarks of President Reagan to Regional Editors, White House, April 18, 1985," in Geoffrey H. Hartman, ed., *Bitburg in Moral and Political Perspective* (Bloomington, 1986), 240, 217. Other essays in this volume comprehensively document and comment on the entire course of events surrounding Reagan's trip to Bitburg.

9. See Helmut Sonnenfeldt in Judith Miller, *One by One by One: Facing the Holocaust* (New York, 1990), 48.

10. Theodor W. Adorno, "Valery Proust Museum," in *Prisms*, trans. Samuel and Shierry Weber (Cambridge, Mass., 1981), 175.

11. Terrence Prittie, "Dachau Revisited," *Manchester Guardian Weekly*, 16 Dec. 1954: 25.

12. Gaston Coblentz, "Dachau Crematorium Is Kept as Memorial," *New York Herald Tribune*, 3 March 1954: 1.

13. Of the 2,771 clergymen interred at Dachau, 2,580 were Catholic priests; of these, nearly 2,000 were Polish and 445 German. Seven hundred of the Catholic priests died in Dachau, and another 300 died in the trains leading to Dachau from Poland (Paul Berben, *Dachau, 1933–45: The Official History* [Munich, 1975], 276).

14. Johann Neuhaeusler, *What Was It Like in the Concentration Camp at Dachau?* (Munich, 1974), 70.

15. *New York Times*, 12 Nov. 1962.

16. Barbara Bright, "Tortured Prisoners Once Lived in GI Jail," *Overseas Weekly*, 15 May 1966: 15.

17. Philip Shabekoff, "Jews Gather in Prayer at Dachau to Dedicate a Memorial for Dead," *New York Times*, 8 May 1967.

18. "Grosse Kreisstadt Dachau," an unpaginated tourist pamphlet published by the County Town of Dachau.

19. Detlef Hoffmann, "Erinnerungsarbeit der 'zweiten und dritten' Generation und 'Spürensuche' in der zeitgenössischen Kunst," *Kritische Berichte* 2 (1988): 34.

20. See "Wiedergutmachen," in *DDR-Handbuch* (Cologne, 1985), 1484; also *Die Retliche Stellung der ankannten Verfolgten des Naziregimes in der DDR* (Berlin, 1950), as cited in Eve Rosenhaft, "The Uses of Remembrance: Some Preliminary Thoughts on the Legacy of the Communist Resistance in the GDR after 1945," in Leonides Hill, Francis R. Nicosia, and Lawrence D. Stokes, eds., *Opposition and Resistance to National Socialism in Germany, 1925–1945* (Berg, 1990). I am grateful to Eve Rosenhaft for sharing her manuscript and its many profound insights with me.

21. *Gesetzblatt der Deutschen Demokratischen Republik* 1 (1959): 212ff.; also see F. Bartel, *Auszeichnungen der DDR von den Anfangen bis zur Gegenwart* (Berlin, 1979), 157ff.

22. Rosenhaft, "Uses of Remembrance," 25, 26.

23. Bodo Ritscher, "Buchenwald: Guide to the National Memorial," published by the Dietz Verlag for the Buchenwald State Museum.

24. See Peter Hayes, *Industry and Ideology: I. G. Farben in the Nazi Era* (New York and Cambridge, 1987).

25. Ulrike Puvogel, ed., *Gedenkstätten für die Opfer des Nationalsozialismus: Eine Dokumentation* (Bonn, 1987), 795, 798.

26. See H. Koch, "Nationale Mahn- und Gedenkstätte Buchenwald: Geschichte ihrer Entstehung," *Buchenwaldheft* 31 (Weimar-Buchenwald, 1988); and V. Frank, *Antifaschistische Mahnmale in der DDR: Ihre kunstlerische und architektonische Gestaltung* (Leipzig, 1970).

Chapter 3. The Gestapo-Gelände

1. See the photograph in *Topographie des Terrors: Gestapo, S.S. und Reichssicherheitshauptamt auf dem "Prinz-Albrecht-Gelände," Eine Dokumentation,* ed. Reinhard Rurup (Berlin, 1987), 186. For many of the historical details in this section, I am indebted to this excellent documentation of the history of the Gestapo-Gelände and its subsequent memorial excavation. Also see *Zum Umgang mit dem Gestapo-Gelände* (Berlin, 1988).

2. Ibid., 198.

3. Ibid., 205.

4. Ibid.

5. Ibid., 202.

6. Ibid., 206.

7. From a tape-recorded discussion in the Town Hall of Kreuzberg, 13 July 1984, as cited by Rainer Kolmer in "A Holocaust Memorial in Berlin?" *Remembering for the Future* (Oxford, 1988), 1763.

8. See Aktives Museum Faschismus und Widerstand in Berlin, *Zum Umgang mit einem Erbe* (Berlin, 1985); and *Zum Umgang mit dem Gestapo-Gelände* (Berlin, 1989).

9. Rurup, *Topographie,* 202.

Chapter 4. Austria's Ambivalent Memory

1. John Bunzel, "Austrian Identity and Anti-Semitism," *Patterns of Prejudice* 21 (Spring 1987): 4.

2. It is estimated that even with one-tenth the population of Germany, Austria supplied one-half of the SS guards at concentration camps. Nearly all of Austria's 60,000 Jews were murdered, and footage of the annexation of Austria makes it clear that the masses regarded Hitler's arrival as something close to the prodigal son's return.

3. Werner Fenz, "Protocols of the Exhibition," in the exhibition catalogue for *Bezugspunkte 38/88* (Graz, 1988), 172. Fenz's fascinating essay is reprinted in *October* 48 (Spring 1989): 71–74.

4. Hans Haacke, "Und ihr habt doch gesiegt, 1988," *October* 48 (Spring 1989): 83–84.

5. Werner Fenz, "The Monument Is Invisible, the Sign Visible," *October* 48 (Spring 1989): 77.

6. See Andreas Razumovsky, "Wo die Toten nicht ruhen: Der Wiener Streit um Hrdlickas Mahnmal," *Frankfurter Allgemeine Zeitung,* 7 Jan. 1989.

7. Quoted in Horst Christoph, "Antifa mit Hrdlicka," *Profil* 48 (28 Nov. 1988): 94.

8. For these and other details, see Christoph, "Antifa," 91–95, and Judith Miller, *One by One by One: Facing the Holocaust* (New York, 1990), 74–77.

9. From Robert Singer's interview with Hrdlicka, "Ein Massenmord bedarf einer Masse von Mördern [A mass murder needs a mass of murderers]," *Judische Rundshau* 47 (24 Nov. 1987): 2.

10. Quoted in Razumovsky, "Wo die Toten nicht ruhen."

11. Singer, "Ein Massenmord," 2.

12. John Czaplicka, "The Unmasterable Past, Public Discourse, and National Identity: Alfred Hrdlicka's Monuments against War and Fascism," paper delivered at the College Art Association meeting, New York, February 1990, p. 13.

13. See Walter Podlesak's letter to the editor, "Der eigentliche Skandal liegt unter der Erde," *Die Presse,* 3 Dec. 1988.

14. Christoph, "Antifa," 95.

15. Quoted in Razumovsky, "Wo die Toten nicht ruhen."

Introduction to Part 2

Epigraph: Kazimierz Brandys, *A Question of Reality,* trans. Isabel Barzun (London, 1981), 62–63.

1. See Jan Tomasz Gross, *Polish Society under German Occupation: The General Government, 1939–1944* (Princeton, 1979), 185–86.

2. I am indebted here to Iwona Irwin-Zarecka's fine discussion of Poland's martyrological tradition in *Neutralizing Memory: The Jew in Contemporary Poland* (New Brunswick, N.J., 1989), 27.

3. Pierre Nora, "Between Memory and History: *Les Lieux de Mémoire,*" trans. Marc Roudebush, *Representations* 26 (Spring 1989): 9.

Chapter 5. The Rhetoric of Ruins

1. Nora, "Between Memory and History," 19.

2. Jozef Marszalek and Anna Wisniewska, eds., *Majdanek* (Lublin, 1983), 3.

3. Ibid., 4–5.

4. Wiktor Tolkin, "Die Denkmäler in Stutthof und Majdanek," *Zeichen* (March 1988): 21.

5. In an effort to replicate this rhetoric of the ruins, many memorial projects removed from the camps import ashes or bits of soil from the sites of destruction and bury them as the symbolic foundation of memory. Once the seed of authentic artifact is planted in either the memorial grounds or the visitors' minds, memory seems linked to something more than the mere forms of the memorial.

In this context, I should also make clear that this critique of museums at Majdanek and Auschwitz can be made of our own memorial institutions, as well. My aim is not merely to discredit any given presentation of memory, but to examine how all these memorials, both those in situ and those removed, create historical understanding in their memorial representations of the Holocaust.

6. For his invaluable discussion of artifacts in the museum, I am indebted to Eugenio Donato's "The Museum's Furnace: Notes toward a Contextual Reading of Bourvard and Pecuchet," in *Textual Strategies: Perspectives in Post-Structuralist Criticism* (Ithaca, 1979). One passage in particular is worth recalling in its entirety:

"The set of objects the *Museum* displays is sustained only by the fiction that they somehow constitute a coherent representational universe. The fiction is that a repeated metonymic displacement of fragment for totality, object to label, series of objects to series of labels, can still produce a representation which is somehow adequate to a nonlinguistic universe. Such a fiction is the result of an uncritical belief in the notion that ordering and classifying, that is to say, the spatial juxtaposition of fragments, can produce a representational understanding of the world. Should the fiction disappear, there is nothing left of the *Museum* but "bric-à-brac," a heap of meaningless and valueless fragments of objects which are incapable of substituting themselves either metonymically for the original objects or metaphorically for their representations" (p. 223).

7. For the beginnings of an architectural history of Auschwitz-Birkenau, see Robert Jan van Pelt and William Carroll, *Architectural Principles in the Age of Historicism* (New Haven and London, 1991), 345–69. At the time of this writing, van Pelt has a full study of the architecture of Auschwitz in process.

8. From Kazimierz Smolen, ed., *KL Auschwitz* (Warsaw, 1980), 16.

9. Janusz Wieczorek, chairman of the Council for the Perservation of Monuments to Struggle and Martyrdom, "Address delivered at the opening ceremony of the Jewish Pavilion at the former concentration camp of Oswiecim-Brzezinka, April 17, 1978," published by the State Museum at Oswiecim, unpaginated.

10. The rest of the jury included Giuseppe Perugini from Rome and Jakob Bakema from Amsterdam, representing the International Union of Architects; August Zamoyski from Toulouse, of the International Union of Art; Pierre Courthion from Paris, for the International Association of Art Critics; and Odette Elina from Paris and Romuault Gutt from Warsaw, on behalf of the International Committee of Auschwitz.

11. Henry Moore, *The Auschwitz Competition*, booklet published by the State Museum of Auschwitz, 1964, unpaginated.

12. Ibid.

13. See Jan Zachwatowicz, "The International Memorial at Auschwitz," *Poland* 1 (January 1965): 11.

14. See Georges Wellers, "Essai de détermination du nombre de morts au camp d'Auschwitz," *Monde Juif*, Fall 1983: 127–59; and Yehuda Bauer, "Fighting the Distortions," *Jerusalem Post* (International Edition), 9 Sept. 1989: 6.

15. Quoted in Sergio I. Minerbi, "The Kidnapping of the Holocaust," *Jerusalem Post*, 25 Aug. 1989: 6.

16. John Tagliabue, "A Place Where the Past Overwhelms the Present," *New York Times*, 13 Sept. 1989.

17. See "The Drama behind the Convent Deal," *Jerusalem Post*, 22 Sept. 1989: 9. For comprehensive discussions of the controversy surrounding the convent, see Wladyslaw T. Bartoszewski, *The Convent at Auschwitz* (New York, 1991) and Carol Rittner and John K. Roth, eds., *Memory Offended: The Auschwitz Convent Controversy* (New York, Westport, and London, 1991)

18. *New York Times*, 18 Nov. 1989.

19. Dawid Warszawski, "The Convent and Solidarity," *Tikkun*, November–December 1989: 29.

20. Adam Michnik, "The Irresistible Attraction of Truth [Regarding Philo-Semitism]," *Krytyka* 25 (1987): 37, as quoted in Lillian Vallee, "This Empty Place Hurts: The Jewish Question in Recent Polish Publications," *Studium Papers*, April 1989: 60–61.

21. Vallee, "This Empty Place Hurts," 62.

22. This is a summary of "The Yarnton Declaration of Jewish Intellectuals on the Future of Auschwitz," signed by its principal convener, Jonathan Webber of the Oxford Centre for Hebrew Studies.

Chapter 6. The Biography of a Memorial Icon

Epigraphs: Joseph Tchaikov, *Sculpture* (Kiev, 1921), as quoted in Avram Kampf, *Jewish Experience in the Art of the Twentieth Century* (South Hadley, Mass., 1984), 35. Rapoport quote from an interview with the author, 22 Feb. 1986.

1. David Roskies has discussed both this resonance and the exile motif in much greater detail in *Against the Apocalypse: Responses to Catastrophe in Modern Jewish Culture* (Cambridge, Mass., and London, 1984), 276–80.

2. Though Rapoport's monument continues to be celebrated in the popular press and Jewish journals, it has been almost completely ignored by the art historical and curatorial establishment. Selected essays about it include Eliezer Ben Hadash, "Nathan Rapoport: Sculptor of Jewish Resurgence," *Israel Today*, 12 Jan. 1960: 8–9; Leon E. Brown, "Monumental Works from Warsaw to Philadelphia," *Jewish Times*, 16 Feb. 1984: 1, 3; Helen Collins, "The Magical Works of Nathan Rapoport," *Jewish Horizon*, 25 March 1982: 1, 3; Anne Glass, " 'Never to Forget . . . ,' " *Jewish Standard*, 15 May 1972: 2–3; Bernard Gotfryd, "Casting the Holocaust in Bronze," *Jewish Monthly*, April 1985: 18–9; Freema Gottlieb, "Monument to Survival: A Talk with Nathan Rapoport," *Haddassah Magazine*, December 1981: 24–25, 37; Marc Kornblatt, "Nathan Rapoport Remembers the Uprising," *Congress Monthly*, April–May 1983: 13–14; Ernie Meyer, "Monument to Revolt Set up at Yad Vashem," *Jerusalem Post*, 15 Jan. 1975: 2; Nathan Rapoport, "Chronicler of the Holocaust," *Jewish Standard*, 15 June–1 July 1972: 3, 18; Bea Stadtler, "Remembering the 6,000,000," *National Jewish Monthly*, April 1968: 12, 16; Richard Yaffe, *Nathan Rapoport: Sculptures and Monuments* (New York, 1980).

3. In this seven-minute film by Jan Kulma, the monument is broken into cubist pastiche and filmed in its parts. The film is set to Arnold Schoenberg's *Survivor from Warsaw*, with a voice-over narration entitled "This I Cannot Forget." It was produced for Warsaw television, though never shown.

4. Much of the following material and all of Rapoport's words are culled from three days of interviews with him taped by the author on 15 and 22 Feb. and 1 March 1986. I have relied on Rapoport's recollections, not to privilege their accuracy so much as to make the sculptor's own memory and understanding of events part of the memorial work.

5. For examples from his work, Rapoport pointed to the triangle in his monument to Mordechai Anielewicz at Yad Mordechai in Israel; the circle in *Jacob Struggling with the Angel*, located in Toronto; the two cylinders in *Megilat-esh* (Scroll of Fire) at Kesalon in Israel; and the great rectangular block of the Warsaw Ghetto Monument itself.

6. A methodological dilemma emerges here: in focusing solely on the monument, I would risk turning events themselves into a mere footnote to their memorialization. As readers will recognize, this is, in fact, one of the critical liabilities in any study of a text's signifying activity: inquiries into how texts work seem often to exclude the historical events that spawned the texts in the first place. With this in mind, I reiterate that the issue of a text's relationship to events is at the heart of this particular inquiry: it is in only this context that I present any version of the uprising at all.

7. Quoted in Reuben Ainsztein, *The Warsaw Ghetto Revolt* (New York, 1979), 3. The precise source of this quotation is unclear, since Ainsztein's attribution of it to *The Black Book* (New York, 1946), 178, is mistaken.

8. Even before the Great Liquidation, on 7 June 1942, *Der Oifbroi* would proclaim that "the Jewish masses have not yet rid themselves of their distrust of their own fighting capabilities and given up the hope of salvation coming from outside. . . . Within the limited possibilities of the ghettos we must prepare the ground for a revolutionary Jewish deed. From Jewish pain and sufferings there must grow up the strength that together with all the revolutionary forces in Europe and the backing of the Red Army will rise to fight against Nazi slavery" (Ainsztein, *Warsaw Ghetto Revolt*, 29).

9. *Der Ruf*, 15 May 1942, as quoted in Ber Mark, *Uprising in the Warsaw Ghetto* (New York, 1975), 99.

10. A year after the Uprising, the Jewish Workers Alliance cabled this anniversary message from Warsaw (19 April 1944) to the Jewish Antifascist Committee in Moscow, requesting that it be printed in the Russian press: "In connection with the anniversary of the heroic struggle in the Warsaw Ghetto, we send battle greetings to the victorious Soviet Army, to General Berling's Polish Army, and to Jewish workers throughout the world, battling for economic and national liberation" (Mark, *Uprising*, 192). This appeared in Moscow at about the time Rapoport was submitting his sculpture to the authorities.

11. On a more personal level, it is also possible that Rapoport simply identified with Anielewicz. Both had been members of Hashomer Hatsa'ir before the war, and both had fled to Russian-occupied territory when Germany attacked Poland. While Rapoport stayed in Russia, however, Anielewicz returned to organize the Jewish resistance. During the Great Liquidation, Anielewicz had gone to Bedzin and Sosnowiec on an Antifascist Bloc assignment; when he returned, he found that his mother and sister had been deported and killed in Treblinka. Rapoport's own mother and sister were deported and killed in the same action. According to the sculptor, in one of his mother's last letters from the Ghetto to him in Russia, she complained that "all you left me were brushes and paints, when it should have been guns and bullets."

12. Ainsztein, *Uprising*, 79, 81.

13. Ibid., 108.

14. For more on this kind of apocalyptic coordination between Nazi "actions" and the Jewish calendar, see Roskies, *Against the Apocalypse*, 191, 202.

15. Among first-person and historical accounts of the uprising, these works in English offer full, occasionally competing, versions: Ainsztein, *Warsaw Ghetto Revolt*; Meyer Barkai, *The Fighting Ghettos* (Philadelphia, 1962); Wladyslaw Bartoszewski, *The Warsaw Ghetto: A Christian's Testimony*, trans. Stephen G. Cappellari (Boston, 1987); Marek Edelman, *The Ghetto Fighters* (New York, 1946); Philip Friedman, ed., *Martyrs and Fighters: The Epic of the Warsaw Ghetto* (New York, 1954);

Bernard Goldstein, *The Stars Bear Witness* (New York, 1949); Yisrael Gutman, *The Jews of Warsaw: Ghetto, Underground, Revolt* (Bloomington, Ind., 1982); Yisrael Gutman and Shmuel Krakowski, *Unequal Victims: Poles and Jews during World War II* (New York, 1986); Zivia Lubetkin, *In the Days of Destruction and Revolt* (Israel, 1981); Mark, *Uprising*; Vladka Meed, *On Both Sides of the Wall* (Israel, 1973); Sybil Milton, ed. and trans., *The Stroop Report* (New York, 1979); Yuri Suhl, *They Fought Back* (New York, 1965); David Wdowinski, *And We Are Not Saved* (New York, 1985).

16. See Julian Tuwim, *My, Zydzi Polscy . . .* ; *We, Polish Jews*, ed. and trans. Chone Shmeruk (Jerusalem, 1984), 7.

17. Ibid., 20. The next line of the poem reads, "And the Christians will cross themselves," which distinguishes somewhat ironically between Christians and Jews, who would traditionally cover their heads in such a holy place, not uncover them.

18. Joseph Tchaikov, *Sculpture* (Kiev, 1921), as quoted in Kampf, *Jewish Experience*, 35.

19. Ilya Ehrenburg and Vasily Grossman, eds., *The Black Book: The Ruthless Murder of Jews by German-Fascist Invaders throughout the Temporarily-Occupied Regions of the Soviet Union and in the Death Camps of Poland during the War of 1941–1945*, trans. John Glad and James S. Levine (New York, 1981). Though the original plates for this book were destroyed in Russia, most of the manuscript was eventually brought to Israel, where it was published in Russian in 1980 by Yad Vashem and the Israel Research Institute of Contemporary Society.

It may also be worth noting one of the goals set forth by the editors of this volume: "*The Black Book* should become a memorial placed over the innumerable graves of Soviet people viciously murdered by the German Fascists" (p. xii), another memorial denied by the authorities.

20. Interview with the author, 22 Feb. 1986.

21. Maurice Brillant, "Le Monument aux combatants du ghetto de Varsovie," *L'Epoque*, 14 March 1948. Waldemar George, "Le Monument aux défenseurs du ghetto de Varsovie . . . ," *Ce Matin*, 16 March 1948. Georges Pillement, "Monuments—expositions," *Les Lettres françaises*, 25 March 1948. Pierre Desquarque, "Paris a salué avant Varso[v]ie le monument aux héros du ghetto," *Arts*, 19 March 1948. All translations mine.

22. See "Warsaw Unveils Ghetto Memorial," *New York Times*, 20 April 1948: 1.

23. I am indebted to Stanislaw Krajewski for sharing these observations with me in his "To Be a Jew in Poland Today," a lecture and unpublished manuscript.

24. See Roskies, *Against the Apocalypse*, 297.

25. Ibid., 276.

26. Cited by Ainsztein in *Warsaw Ghetto Revolt*, 171.

27. Thomas S. Gladsky has already noted that, unlike other countries in the former Soviet bloc, Poland's memorial landscape remains relatively free of monuments to international socialism. Instead of monumental busts and statues of Lenin, Marx, and Mao, political memorials in Poland concentrate on Polish socialists and heroes. In this way, Social Democratic heroes like Felix Dzierzynski and Julian Marchlewski remain anchored in a Polish national continuum, even as they come to represent the larger revolutionary movement through its Polish part. See Thomas S. Gladsky, "Polish Post-war Historical Monuments: Heroic Art and Cultural Preservation," *The Polish Review* 31, nos. 2–3 (1986): 153–54.

By referring to the specific heroes of the Warsaw Ghetto uprising—all Polish Jews, most socialists—Rapoport's monument unwittingly or not adheres to this unwritten rule of Polish postwar memorial sensibilities. It thus seems to lend the uprising and its leaders an unmistakably Polish cast, especially when viewed through Polish eyes.

28. "Ad Hoc Events on Ghetto Revolt Irk Warsaw," *New York Times*, 14 April 1988: A17.

29. Ibid.

30. In a fascinating elaboration of the political nuances at stake here, Mark Erlich quotes the young leader of Warsaw Solidarity, Zbigniew Bujak, who declared in his address at the commemoration of Bundists Henryk Erlich and Victor Alter: "We need to find our connection to history. And Erlich and Alter are my past." See "Honoring the Past to Change the Future: Solidarity and the Warsaw Ghetto," *Tikkun*, September–October 1988: 25.

31. From the daily press review of the Polska Agencja Prasowa, 19 April 1988, p. 4.

32. Ibid., p. a (emphasis added).

33. See the cover of the German newsweekly *Der Spiegel*, 14 Dec. 1970.

34. My thanks to Barbara Kirschenblatt-Gimblett for providing photographs of this wreath, laid on 19 April 1988.

35. In choosing a kibbutznik living in Paris as the model for Mordechai Anielewicz, Rapoport may have only affirmed the link he already felt between heroes of the Ghetto and those of the Yishuv. (For more on this theme, see chapter 8.)

36. This is not to say that the Warsaw Ghetto uprising itself is forgotten in America. The Warsaw Ghetto Resistance Organization (WAGRO) sponsors an elaborate memorial ceremony every 19 April in New York, attended by thousands of survivors, children of survivors, former partisans, and dignitaries. In addition, every few years WAGRO publishes a commemoration journal collecting dozens of remembrances, official tributes, and newly surfaced details surrounding the uprising.

37. Walter Benjamin, "The Work of Art in the Age of Mechanical Reproduction," in Hannah Arendt, ed., and Harry Zohn, trans., *Illuminations* (New York, 1969), 220.

Chapter 7. Broken Tablets and Jewish Memory in Poland

1. The above lines open Jerzy Ficowski's "Script of a Dead Cemetery," in *A Reading of Ashes*, trans. Keith Bosley with Krystyna Wandycz (London, 1981), 21.

2. See M. Chmielewski, "Mauzoleum Mycienstwa w Treblince," *Trybuna ludu* 332 (1960): 1.

3. What would be "never again," however, depended on how the memorial itself would be remembered. This most terribly magnificent of all Holocaust memorials was nearly betrayed by its own unveiling on 10 May 1964. The blaring headline of *Prawo i Zyacie*—"We Must Remember—We will Remember"—may have caught the eyes of all readers, but the first sentence of the newspaper's account tells more: "The area of the former concentration camp at Treblinka, where over 800,000 citizens of European nations lost their lives at the hands of the Nazi oppressors, was the site of a great anti-

war gathering on 10 May, linked to the unveiling of the new monument there." (From the front page article, "Musimy pamietac—bedziemy pamietac!", *Prawo i zycie*, no. 11 (1964): 1.

4. According to the Office for Religious Denominations in Warsaw, of 434 major Jewish cemeteries in Poland, 22 were regarded as still in good condition in 1979. Of the remaining 412 cemeteries, 68 were half-destroyed during the German occupation; 78 more were 90 percent devastated; and 136 revealed only traces of burial grounds. The other 129 cemeteries were obliterated without a trace. Cited in *Everlasting Memory: Struggle and Extermination of Polish Jews* (Warsaw, 1988), 22–23.

5. For a complete history of the Lodz Jewish cemetery, see Bronislaw Podgarbi, *Cmentarz Zydowski w Lodzi: The Jewish Cemetery in Lodz* (Warsaw, 1990), 31–57.

6. See Malgorzata Niezabitowska, *Remnants: The Last Jews of Poland*, trans. William Brand and Hanna Dobosiewicz (New York, 1986), 67.

7. See Carol Herselle Krinsky, *Synagogues of Europe: Architecture, History, Meaning* (Cambridge, Mass., and London, 1985), 431, for a more complete list of extant Polish synagogues.

8. I am very grateful to Monika Krajewska for sharing with me her essay "Na Cmentarzu Cmentarza—Kazimierzu nad Visla" (Cemetery of a cemetery—Kazimierz on the Vistula), which appeared in *Nowiny-Kurier*, 3 May 1985, and to Tamara Slusarska for her fine English translation of the essay.

Introduction to Part 3

Epigraph: From an editorial in *Davar*, one of Israel's daily newspapers, on 22 April 1951, the first Holocaust Remembrance Day established by act of parliament.

1. Yosef Hayim Yerushalmi, *Zakhor: Jewish History and Jewish Memory* (Seattle and London, 1982), 9.

2. In a bulletin prepared for army commanders on Holocaust Remembrance Day in Israel, the meaning of Holocaust memory is made explicit: "The Zionist solution establishing the State of Israel was intended to provide an answer to the problem of the existence of the Jewish people, in view of the fact that all other solutions had failed. The Holocaust proved, in all its horror, that in the twentieth century, the survival of the Jews is not assured as long as they are not masters of their fate and as long as they do not have the power to defend their survival." See "Informational Guidelines to the Commander," as quoted in Charles S. Liebman and Eliezer Don-Yehiya, *Civil Religion in Israel: Traditional Judaism and Political Culture in the Jewish State* (Berkeley and Los Angeles, 1983), 184.

3. For further discussion of the complicated relations between Holocaust memory and Israeli identity, see Liebman and Don-Yehiya, *Civil Religion*, 100–107, 151–58; Saul Friedländer, "Die Shoah als Element in der Konstruktion israelischer Erinnerung," *Babylon* 2 (1987); and Sidra Ezrahi, "Revisioning the Past: The Changing Legacy of the Holocaust in Hebrew Literature," *Salmagundi* (Fall 1985–Winter 1986): 245–70.

4. From "Informational Guidelines to the Commander," as quoted in Liebman and Don-Yehiya, *Civil Religion*, 178 (emphasis added).

Chapter 8. Israel's Memorial Landscape

1. *B'nai B'rith in Israel: A Traveler's Guide* (Washington, D.C., n.d.), 14.

2. See Shaul Katz, "The Israeli Teacher-Guide: The Emergence and Perpetuation of a Role," *Annals of Tourism Research*, 12, no. 1 (1985): 66.

3. Born in the nineteenth-century Jewish pioneers' need to familiarize themselves with the terrain, a series of Sabbath tours promoting yedi'ath ha'aretz eventually gained respectability as an academic course of study. This was partly a result of the early Zionist-socialists' agricultural devotion to the soil, and partly to the mytho-geography of the land. In both cases, the land had become the Jews' newest unexplored text. Place-names never referred merely to geographic location, but to entire biblical stories, each rife with historical meaning. In an ironic way, a journey through the land of the Book likened itself to a journey through the Book itself. These tours have since been institutionalized in the extremely popular Society for the Protection of Nature in Israel, which has become the leading organizer for nature walks in Israel.

4. From Haim Gamzu, "Ben-Zvi 1904–1952," in *Ben-Zvi: A Portrait Album* (New York, 1962), unpaginated.

5. See Margaret Larkin, *The Six Days of Yad Mordechai* (Israel, 1965).

6. See Richard Yaffe, *Nathan Rapoport: Sculptures and Monuments* (New York, 1980), unpaginated.

7. See Yehuda Bauer, *A History of the Holocaust* (New York and London, 1982), 189–91.

8. See Zivia Lubetkin, *In the Days of Destruction and Revolt* (Israel, 1981).

9. As an engrossing spectacle, this trial might even be said to have transcended its juridical function to serve as a mass commemoration of the victims. Many regard it as having been as much a memorial as a legal process. See, for example, Annette Wieviorka, *Le Procès Eichmann* (Brussels, 1989).

Chapter 9. Yad Vashem

Epigraph: From David Grossman's novel *See Under: Love*, trans. Betsy Rosenberg (New York, 1989), 55.

1. See Shmuel Spector, "Yad Vashem," *Encyclopedia of the Holocaust* (New York, 1990), 4: 1681–86.

2. For the Hebrew transcript of part of the debate, see *Divrei Ha'knesset* (Minutes of the Parliament) 1953: 131–54.

3. From Nachum Goldman, "The Influence of the Holocaust on the Change in the Attitude of World Jewry to Zionism and the State of Israel," in *Holocaust and Rebirth: A Symposium* (Jerusalem, 1974), 103.

4. Ibid., 149.

5. From "Martyrs' and Heroes' Remembrance (Yad Vashem) Law, 5713—1953," reprinted fully in *Yad Vashem: The Holocaust Martyrs' and Heroes' Remembrance Authority, Jerusalem* (Jerusalem, 1986), 4. This law is also translated and reprinted in *State of Israel Yearbook* (Jerusalem, 1954), 250–51.

6. Ibid., 5.

7. See "Department for the Registration of the Martyred," *Yad [V]ashem Bulletin*, April 1957: 40.

8. See Ben Lynfield, "Raising 6 Million Souls," *Jerusalem Post* magazine section, 13 Jan. 1989: 4.

9. In the words of former Prime Minister Levi Eshkol, "The very struggle against the adversary [during the Holocaust] and the victory which followed [Israel's War of Independence] laid the foundations for the revival of our national independence. Seen in this light the Jewish fight against the Nazis and the War of Independence were, in fact, a single protracted battle. The geographical proximity between Yad Vashem and Mount Herzl thus expresses far more than mere physical closeness" (*Yad Vashem Bulletin* 16 [1965]: 62). Eshkol's words are also cited in an excellent discussion of Yad Vashem's proximity to Mount Herzl by Don Handelman, *Models and Mirrors: Towards an Anthropology of Public Events* (Cambridge and New York, 1990), 201.

10. Hannah Senesh occupies the same place in Israel's Holocaust hagiography that Anne Frank occupies outside Israel. Born in Hungary, she immigrated to the Yishuv in Palestine as a teenager just before the war. Here she was transformed from a weak "galutnik" (exilic Jew) into a strong Israeli, returning to the Galut during the war as a paratrooper fighting the Nazis. Captured and tortured to death by the Gestapo, Senesh was reburied at Mount Herzl as an Israeli war heroine. Hers is not a Holocaust monument per se, but she is remembered for having been killed by the Nazis as both a Jew and as an Israeli. For further details, see *Hannah Senesh: Her Life and Diary*, introduced by Abba Eban (New York, 1973).

11. Yosef Lishinsky, "Yad Vashem as Art," *Ariel: A Review of Arts and Letters in Israel* 55 (1983): 17.

12. See "Dedication of the Pillar of Heroism on Har Hazikaron," *Yad Vashem News* 5 (1974): 19.

13. See Moshe Safdie, "Holocaust Memorial," in *Jerusalem: The Future of the Past* (Boston, 1989), 195–98.

14. See Ernie Meyer, "Children's Memorial," *Jerusalem Post* International Edition, week ending 11 July 1987: 14.

15. Ibid., 14.

16. See Avishai Margalit, "The Kitsch of Israel," *New York Review of Books*, 24 Nov. 1988: 23. For an angry reply to Margalit's critique of the Children's Memorial, see Menachem Fogel's letter to the editor of the *Jerusalem Post*, 30 March 1989.

Chapter 10. When a Day Remembers

1. For elaboration of this distinction, see Gerard Genette, *Narrative Discourse: An Essay in Method* (Ithaca, 1980), 33–35.

2. For the best existing discussion and definition of Israel's civil religion, see Charles S. Liebman and Eliezer Don-Yehiya, *Civil Religion in Israel: Traditional Judaism and Political Culture in the Jewish State* (Berkeley and Los Angeles, 1983).

3. For keen insight into Israel's "counter-tradition," see Yael Zerubavel, "Invented Tradition and Counter-tradition: The Social Construction of the Past in Israeli Culture," a paper presented at the Association for Jewish Studies annual meeting, December 1990. Also see Zerubavel's "New Beginning, Old Past: The Collective Memory of Pioneering in Israeli Culture," in Laurence J. Silberstein, ed., *New Perspectives on Israeli History: The Early Years of the State* (New York, 1990), 193–215, and "The Holiday Cycle and the Commemoration of the Past: History, Folklore and Education," in *The Proceedings of the Ninth World Congress of Jewish Studies* 2 (1986): 111–18.

4. The Tenth of Teveth commemorates the beginning of the siege; the Seventeenth of Tammuz marks the first breach in the walls of the city; the Ninth of Av recalls the destruction of the Temple; and the Third of Tishri remembers the assassination of Gedaliah, the governor of Judah appointed by Nebuchadnezzar. For details surrounding the historical origins of these dates, see Theodor H. Gaster, *Festivals of the Jewish Year: A Modern Interpretation and Guide* (New York, 1978), 194–96.

5. In a further example, it is possible that the Chmielnicky massacres commenced on precisely the same day as the Blois blood libel murder of thirty-two Jews 477 years earlier, as is traditionally believed. But it is more likely that when the anniversary of the Blois massacre in 1171 became a day of fasting for Jewish communities in England, France, and the Rhineland, it also became the anniversary for subsequent massacres occurring in the same general period on the calendar.

6. From Yad, Hilchot Ta'aniyot 5:1.

7. See Irving Greenberg, *The Jewish Way* (New York, 1988), 330. Contrary to Greenberg's suggestion that this date never caught on with religious Jews, the Tenth of Teveth is, in fact, widely observed by much of the ultra-orthodox community in Israel, where Jahrzeit candles are kindled and ceremonies are conducted at the Mount of Olives cemetery.

8. Liebman and Don-Yehiya, *Civil Religion*, 107.

9. *Divrei Haknesset* 1951: 1657, 1656.

10. For a much more detailed, anthropological analysis of the calendar's narrative, see Don Handelman, *Models and Mirrors: Towards an Anthropology of Public Events* (Cambridge and New York, 1990), 194–200. In his rich study, Handelman also reminds us that in falling seven days before Yom Hazikkaron, Yom Hashoah recapitulates the Jewish mourning period (*shiva*) of seven days.

11. For a much more extended discussion of the statists' attitude toward the Holocaust, see Liebman and Don-Yehiya, *Civil Religion*, 100–118.

12. See Saul Friedländer, "Die Shoah als Element in der Konstruktion Israelischer Erinnerung," *Babylon* 2 (1987): 10–22; "The Shoah Between Memory and History," *Jerusalem Quarterly* 53 (Winter 1990); and "Roundtable Discussion," in Berel Lang, ed., *Writing and the Holocaust* (New York and London, 1988), 288.

13. Irving Greenberg also recalls that in 1984, Rabbi Pinchas Teitz proposed yet another alternative date for Yom Hashoah: the anniversary of Hitler's death—the Seventeenth of Iyar, the day before Lag B'omer, the festival celebrating the end of the Sfirah period (*Jewish Way*, 332–33).

14. Quoted from "Day of Memorial for Victims of the European Jewish Disaster and Heroism—27 Nissan, 5719," *Yad Vashem Bulletin*, October 1959: 27.

15. For some innovative examples, see David Roskies, *Night Words: A Midrash on the Holocaust* (Washington, D.C., 1971); David Roskies and Irving Greenberg, eds., *Holocaust Commemoration for Days of Remembrance* (Washington, D.C., 1981); Abba Kovner, *Megillot Ha'eduth* (Israel, 1989); Marcia Sachs Littell, ed., *Liturgies on the Holocaust* (Philadelphia, 1986); Albert Friedländer and Elie Wiesel, *The Six Days of Destruction: Meditations toward Hope* (Ramsey, N.J., 1988).

16. Quoted in Liebman and Don-Yehiya, *Civil Religion*, 178 (emphasis added).

17. Ibid., 184.

18. We might recall in this context the Yad Vashem World Council's first convention was held in 1957 on 19 April (anniversary of the Warsaw Ghetto uprising), which fell that year on the Eighth of Iyar and not on the Twenty-seventh of Nissan, at Har Hazikkaron. After reading a number of letters, the chairman, Benzion Dinur, asked all to rise for a moment's silence. According to one report, "The council rose in a minute's silence *in memory of the victims of the European holocaust and of those who fell in the defense of the homeland.*" In this equation, martyrs and fighters are united here by the memory of those who were both. See "Yad Washem World Council Convenes on Memorial Hill in Jerusalem," *Yad Vashem Bulletin,* April 1957: 31 (emphasis added).

19. From the Opening Ceremony of "Holocaust Martyrs' and Heroes' Remembrance Day, Nissan 26, 5747–May 1, 1989," courtesy of Yad Vashem Memorial Authority.

20. In Israel's more recent past, the long, steady siren acquired further memory still; it was the all-clear signal sounded in the wake of Iraqi missile attacks in January 1991.

21. Only one photograph I know, taken from the Tel Aviv–Jerusalem highway, conveys this sense of stopped motion. The stillness of the drivers standing at attention beside their cars outside is captured precisely by the figure of the roadway itself, which functions as a backdrop of assumed movement. See the photograph by Frederic Brenner in A. B. Yehoshua and Frederic Brenner, *Israel* (London, 1988), 2–3.

22. Benzion Dinur, "Problems of Research," *Yad [V]ashem Studies* 1 (1957): 9–10.

23. Arye L. Kubovy, "Nissan 27—A Day of Examen of Conscience," *Yad Vashem Bulletin,* June 1960: 2.

24. *Yad Vashem News* 2 (1970): 7.

25. David Golinkin, "Yom Hashoah: A Program of Observance," *Conservative Judaism* 37 (Summer 1984): 52–64; and "How Should We Commemorate the Shoah in Our Homes?" *Moment* 14 (June 1989): 30–35.

Introduction to Part 4

Epigraph: James Ingo Freed, "The United States Holocaust Memorial Museum," *Assemblage* 9 (1989): 61.

1. For a comprehensive survey and discussion of the Landsmanschaften memorials in New York City cemeteries, see Rabbi Alvin M. Poplack's doctoral dissertation, "Various Ways Jews Commemorated the Holocaust for Eternity by Permanent Memorials on Cemeteries in the Metropolitan New York Area" (Jewish Teachers Seminary, December 1981).

2. For more on the political dimension of memorials, see Michael Berenbaum, "On the Politics of Public Commemoration of the Holocaust," *Shoah,* Fall–Winter 1981–82: 9. Also see Berenbaum's collection of essays *After Tragedy and Triumph: Modern Jewish Thought and the American Experience* (Cambridge and New York, 1991), 3–16. For further details on the controversy surrounding the establishment of the U.S. Holocaust Memorial Commission, see Judith Miller, *One by One by One: Facing the Holocaust* (New York and London, 1990), 255–66.

3. From Alex Krieger's speech at the Founders' Dinner of the New England Holocaust Memorial Committee, 29 Nov. 1989, Boston.

Chapter 11. The Plural Faces of Holocaust Memory in America

1. From the Jewish Telegraphic Agency press bulletin, 2 Dec. 1942. I am grateful to Lucia Ruedenberg for bringing these announcements to my attention in her "Analysis of Civil Commemoration of the Holocaust in New York City" (January 1990), an unpublished essay from her doctoral dissertation in performance studies at New York University.

2. Citing a 1989 doctoral dissertation by Atay Citron, Lucia Ruedenberg reports that among the hundreds who performed in this pageant, twenty orthodox rabbis who had escaped from Nazi-occupied Europe held up torn Torah scrolls and recited the Kaddish. See Citron, "Pageantry and Theatre in the Service of Jewish Nationalism in the United States: 1933–1946," cited in Ruedenberg, "Analysis," 4.

3. The details surrounding this first memorial are culled from an unpublished manuscript, "The Case of the Memorial," by A. R. Lerner, part of the Schneiderman Archives at YIVO Institute of Jewish Research in New York.

4. Ibid., 4.

5. *New York Times*, 18 Jan. 1950.

6. "City Rejects Park Memorials to Slain Jews," *New York Times*, 11 Feb. 1965: 1; and "2 Jewish Monuments Barred from Park," *New York World Telegram and Sun*, 10 Feb. 1965: 1.

7. From a letter dated May 1974 to friends and colleagues, signed by the executive committee of the Memorial to the Six Million Jewish Martyrs, Inc. At the time of this writing, a state-sponsored, privately funded "living memorial to the Holocaust"—the Museum of Jewish Heritage—is planned for a site on the Battery in New York, near the site proposed for Kahn's monument. To date, it has received substantial financial support but remains mired in a slow economy, burdened further by its ambitious scale. Like its predecessors, the Museum of Jewish Heritage seems cursed by the very breadth and depth of the community in New York that has so long demanded a memorial equal to its size and importance.

8. From "A Presentation on Behalf of the Babi Yar Park Foundation" (Denver, n.d.), unpaginated. For this and other materials on the Babi Yar Park, I am indebted to Helen J. Ginsburg, one of the memorial's founders, who very generously supplied me with a complete record of the park's conception and construction. In providing me with further details of the local discussion, Michael Allen, the director of Denver's Holocaust Awareness Institute, was also extremely helpful and generous with his time and insights.

9. These and other details are culled from a personal interview with Michael Jacobs at the Memorial Center for Holocaust Studies in Dallas on 23 Aug. 1990.

10. From a press release dated 22 April 1990, quoted in Peter Ember, "Images of Light," *Bronx Herald Statesman*, 10 June 1990.

11. For information on the Hohokam tribe and their petroglyphs, I am indebted to Fred Steiniger, one of the Tucson memorial's founders and builders, who provided me with a study of Native American petroglyphs by Sally J. Cole, *Legacy on Stone: Rock Art of the Colorado Plateau and Four Corners Region* (Boulder, 1990).

12. From a telephone interview with Otto Schirn, 19 June 1991.

13. From a telephone conversation with Joseph Young, 19 June 1991.

14. See Naomi Pfefferman, "Martyrs' Memorial: Creating the Dream," *Jewish Journal*, 28 April–4 May, 1990: 22.

15. Leo Noonan, "The New Holocaust Museum Has a New Idea," *The Jewish Journal*, 4–10 Nov. 1989: 30.

16. For several discussions of Marvin Hier's and the Wiesenthal Center's controversial style and fundraising tactics, see Gary Rosenblatt, "The Simon Wiesenthal Center: State-of-the-art Activism or Hollywood Hype?" *Baltimore Jewish Times*, 14 Sept. 1984: 62–74; Sheldon Teitelbaum and Tom Waldman, "The Unorthodox Rabbi," *Los Angeles Times Magaine*, 15 July 1990: 6–11, 35–39; and Miller, *One by One by One*, 236–51. Though the Wiesenthal Center subsequently corrected a handful of specific inaccuracies in Miller's book, the author has stood by her interpretive conclusions regarding the center's propriety and tastefulness. For further discussion of the Los Angeles memorials, see Terry Pristin, "3 Perspectives on the Holocaust," *Los Angeles Times*, 12 June 1991: B-1, B-4.

17. There are several versions of the Wiesenthal Center's genesis, none confirmed by Rabbi Hier. In one version, Hier was sitting with friends around the dinner table in August 1977, "having [his] Shabos chulent . . . and telling a friend at the dinner table what a shame it is that there is no equivalent of a Yad Vashem in the United States." He realized then and there, according to this report, that "it will never happen unless we do it ourselves" (Rosenblatt, "Wiesenthal Center," 65). Within days, he was off on a plane with his wife and financial backers to meet with Simon Wiesenthal in Vienna and propose a Holocaust center that would be named after the famed Nazi hunter.

In another, less flattering version, Hier was sitting with others in the courtyard of Hier's newly acquired building on Pico Boulevard to plan the first fundraising banquet for his new Yeshiva. When they realized that the date of the banquet, Nov. 12, fell near Kristallnacht, Mara Kochba reported that Hier "chortled with glee—and declared, 'We're in business'" (Teitelbaum and Waldman, "Unorthodox Rabbi," 35). Hier angrily disputes the language and insinuations of both accounts.

18. Teitelbaum and Waldman, "Unorthodox Rabbi," 10.

19. Thomas Albright, "The Holocaust Memorial: A Critical View of the Concept for S. F. Sculpture," *San Francisco Chronicle*, 16 April 1983: 36.

20. "Statement of Purpose," Mayor Dianne Feinstein's Committee for a Memorial to the Six Million Victims of the Holocaust, p. 2.

21. Michael Brenson, "Why Segal Is Doing Holocaust Memorial," *New York Times*, 8 April 1983: C16; and Matthew Baigell, "Segal's Holocaust Memorial," *Art in America*, Summer 1983: 136.

22. Phyllis Tuchman, *George Segal* (New York, 1983), 19.

23. Baigell, "Segal's Holocaust Memorial," 136.

24. Douglas C. McGill, "Making of 'Holocaust,'" *New York Times*, 10 Jan. 1986: C-20.

25. William Wilson, "Segal: Private Visions in the Public Arena," *Los Angeles Times*, 19 Aug. 1984: 91.

26. Brenson, "Why Segal Is Doing Holocaust Memorial," C-16.

27. "A Sense of Stillness," *Art News*, Summer 1983: 12.

28. See "Editor's Mailbox," *San Francisco Examiner*, 11 Aug. 1983.

29. See Thomas Albright, "The Holocaust Memorial: A Critical View of the Concept for S.F. Sculpture," *San Francisco Chronicle*, 16 April 1983; and Allan Temko, "The Virtues and Flaws of the Segal Sculpture," *San Francisco Chronicle*, 8 Nov. 1984.

30. A survivor and president of the Holocaust Center of Northern California, Michael Thaler, told the author at one point, "I like the site because when the killing happened, the birds sang, the sun shone and still we were killed." From an interview with the author in San Francisco, 24 April 1990.

31. William Wilson, " 'The Holocaust' Unveiled in San Francisco," *Los Angeles Times,* 9 Nov. 1984: 13.

32. Douglas C. McGill, "A Muted Dedication for 'Holocaust,' " *New York Times,* 4 Jan. 1986.

33. Beth Coffelt, " 'The Holocaust' and the Art of War," *San Francisco Sunday Examiner and Chronicle Magazine,* 23 Oct. 1983: 15.

34. Ibid., 12.

35. From "Resolution," reproduced as part of the monument's dedication proceedings brochure, 30 May 1985.

36. From "Draft: Remarks of Governor Kean, Liberty Park Monument Dedication," 30 May 1985, courtesy of the estate of Nathan Rapoport.

Chapter 12. Memory and the Politics of Identity

Epigraph: Alex Krieger proposed these words as an inscription to be placed at the entrance to the new Holocaust memorial in Boston, which will be located on the Freedom Trail. As quoted in "Speaking to the Unspeakable," *Design Times,* March–April 1991.

1. Recall Alex Krieger's words, cited above.

2. For inviting me to sit in on these discussions and providing me with the minutes of committee meetings afterward, I am grateful to New England Holocaust Memorial Committee President Ruth B. Fein, its executive director, Stephen Dickerman, and its program coordinator, Katherine D. Kane.

3. See, for example, Jim Hight, "Divided in Memory," *Boston Sunday Herald Magazine,* 22 April 1990: 14–20.

4. "The New England Holocaust Memorial Competition Program," p. 1.

5. Otile McManus, "A Concrete Reminder of the Holocaust," *Boston Globe,* 12 April 1991: 86.

6. These and the other designers' statements have been supplied by the New England Holocaust Memorial Committee.

7. Robert Campbell, "Rich Images Enhance Holocaust Memorial," *Boston Globe,* 25 June 1991: 56.

8. From the U.S. Code Annotated, Title 36 (Patriotic Societies and Observances), Chap. 46 (United States Holocaust Memorial Council), Sect. 1401.

9. From Appendix C, "Address by President Jimmy Carter," printed in "President's Commission on the Holocaust: Report to the President," 27 Sept. 1979, 26. For more on the political context surrounding Carter's decision to establish a Holocaust memorial in Washington, D.C., see the introduction to this section on American memorials, as well as much more comprehensive discussions of the memorial's political origins by Michael Berenbaum and Judith Miller, cited earlier.

10. Charles Maier, *The Unmasterable Past: History, Holocaust, and German National Identity* (Cambridge, Mass., and London, 1988), 165.

11. From an undated press release of the U.S. Holocaust Memorial Council.

12. *The Campaign for the United States Holocaust Memorial Museum*, published by the U.S. Holocaust Memorial Museum, n.d., p. 4.

13. George Will, "Holocaust Museum: Antidote for Innocence," *Washington Post*, 10 March 1983.

14. Michael Berenbaum, *After Tragedy and Triumph: Essays in Modern Jewish Thought and the American Experience* (Cambridge and New York), 20.

15. See Benjamin Forgey, "In Search of a Delicate Balance," *Washington Post* 23 May 1987: B1–B2.

16. Harvey M. Meyerhoff, "Yes, the Holocaust Museum Belongs on the Mall," *Washington Post*, 18 July 1987.

17. James Ingo Freed, "The United States Holocaust Memorial Museum," *Assemblage* 9 (1989): 61.

18. Ibid., 64, 65.

19. From James Ingo Freed, "The United States Holocaust Museum: What Can It Be?" printed by the United States Holocaust Memorial.

20. From Irvin Molotsky, "Arbiters of Monumental Taste," *New York Times*, 8 July 1987.

21. For further discussions of the U.S. Holocaust Memorial's design, see Herbert Muschamp, "How Buildings Remember," *New Republic*, 28 Aug. 1989: 27–33; Robert Greenberger, "The Genesis of the Holocaust Museum," *Jewish Journal*, 12 May 1989; Paul Goldberger, "A Memorial Evokes Unspeakable Events with Dignity," *New York Times*, 30 April 1989.

22. Freed, "United States Holocaust Memorial Museum," 65.

23. Ibid., 70.

24. For details from the exhibition walk-through, I am indebted to Michael Berenbaum, who generously provided me with a copy of his plan, "A Visit to The Permanent Exhibition: The United States Holocaust Memorial Museum."

25. See Jonathan Rosen, "America's Holocaust," *Forward*, 12 April 1991.

26. *New York Times*, 10 Sept. 1990: B12.

Bibliography

This bibliography comprises all of the works consulted or cited in this study. Rather than listing them en masse, I have broken them into three sections, intended to assist further research in this area: I. Critical Literature: Holocaust-Related Memorials; II. Critical Literature: Theory of Public Art, Memory, and Memorials; and III. Historical, Cultural, and Other Resources.

I. Critical Literature: Holocaust-Related Memorials

Albright, Thomas. "The Holocaust Memorial: A Critical View of the Concept for S.F. Sculpture." *San Francisco Chronicle*, 16 April 1983: 36.

American Jewish Congress. *In Everlasting Remembrance: Guide to Memorials and Monuments.* New York: American Jewish Congress, 1969.

Amishai Maisels, Ziva. "The Complexities of Witnessing." *Holocaust and Genocide Studies* 2 (1987): 123–47.

Armanski, Gerhard. *"Und wenn wir sterben müssen": Die politische Ästhetik von Kriegerdenkmälern.* Hamburg: VSA, 1988.

Azaryahu, Maoz. "Renaming the Past: Changes in 'City Text' in Germany and Austria, 1945–1947." *History and Memory* 2 (Winter 1990): 32–53.

Baigell, Matthew. "Segal's Holocaust Memorial." *Art in America*, Summer 1983: 134–36.

Bartoszewski, Wladislaw T. *The Convent at Auschwitz.* New York: Braziller, 1991.

Benz, Wolfgang, and Barbara Distel, eds. "Erinnern oder Verweigern." Special issue of *Dachauer Hefte: Studien und Dokumente zur Geschichte der nationalsozialistischen Konzentrationslager* 6 (November 1990).

Berben, Paul. *Dachau, 1933–45: The Official History.* Munich: Lipp, 1975.

Blatter, Janet. "Art from the Whirlwind." In Janet Blatter and Sybil Milton, eds. *Art of the Holocaust.* London: Pan, 1982. Pp. 22–35.

Brebeck, Wulf E., et al. *Zur Arbeit in Gedenkstätten für die Opfer des Nationalsozialismus: Ein internationaler Überblick.* Berlin: Aktion Sühnezeichen Friedensdienste, 1988.

Brenson, Michael. "Why Segal Is Doing Holocaust Memorial." *New York Times,* 8 April 1983: C16.

Bright, Barbara. "Tortured Prisoners Once Lived in GI Jail." *Overseas Weekly,* 15 May 1966.

Brillant, Maurice. "Le Monument aux combattants du ghetto de Varsovie." *L'Epoque,* 14 March 1948.

Bringmann, Fritz, and Hartmut Roder. *Neuengamme—Verdrängt, vergessen, bewältigt? Die zweite Geschichte des Konzentrationslagers Neuengamme, 1945–1985.* Hamburg: VSA, 1987.

Burghoff, Ingrid, and Lothar Burghoff. *Nationale Mahn- und Gedenkstätte Buchenwald.* Berlin and Leipzig: VEB Tourist, 1970.

Campbell, Robert. "Rich Images Enhance Holocaust Memorial." *Boston Globe,* 25 June 1991: 56.

Chmielewski, M. "Mauzoleum Mycienstwa w Treblince." *Trybuna ludu* 332 (1960): 1.

Christoph, Horst. "Antifa mit Hrdlicka." *Profil* 48 (28 Nov. 1988): 94.

Coblentz, Gaston. "Dachau Crematorium Is Kept as Memorial." *New York Herald Tribune,* 3 March 1954.

Coffelt, Beth. "'The Holocaust' and the Art of War." *San Francisco Sunday Examiner and Chronicle Magazine,* 23 Oct. 1983: 12–15.

Council for the Preservation of Monuments to Resistance and Martyrdom. *Scenes of Fighting and Martrydom Guide: War Years in Poland, 1939–1945.* Warsaw: Sport I Turystyka, 1966.

Czaplicka, John. "The Unmasterable Past, Public Discourse, and National Identity: Alfred Hrdlicka's Monuments against War and Fascism." Paper delivered at the College Art Association meeting, New York, February 1990.

Endlich, Stephanie, and Florian von Buttlar. "Über die Schwierigkeit, sich der NS-Geschichte durch Kunst zu nähern." In *Imitationen, Nachahmung und Modell: Von der Lust am Falschen.* Basel and Frankfurt: Stroemfeld and Roter Stern, 1989.

Erhalten Zerstören Verändern: Denkmaler der DDR in Ost-Berlin—Eine dokumentarische Austellung. Berlin: Aktives Museums Faschismus und Widerstand in Berlin und der Gesellschaft für Bildende Kunst, 1990.

Fenz, Werner. "The Monument Is Invisible, the Sign Visible." *October* 48 (Spring 1989): 75–78.

Fenz, Werner, ed. *Bezugspunkte 38/88.* Graz: Steirischer Herbst, 1988.

Forgey, Benjamin. "In Search of a Delicate Balance." *Washington Post,* 23 May 1987: B1–2.

Frank, Volker. *Antifaschistische Mahnmale in der Deutschen Demokratischen Republik: Ihre künstlerische und architektonische Gestaltung.* Leipzig: Seemann, 1970.

Freed, James Ingo. "The United States Holocaust Memorial Museum." *Assemblage* 9 (1989): 59–79.

Gedenkstätte KZ-Aussenlager Sonnenallee Berlin-Neukölln: Bericht der Vorprüfung. Berlin: Senatsverwaltung für Bau- und Wohnungswesen, 1989.

Geisert, Helmut, Peter Ostendorff, and Jochen Spielmann. *Gedenken und Denkmal: Entwurfe zur Erinnerung an die Deportation und Vernichtung der jüdischen Bevölkerung Berlins.* Berlin: Berlinische Galerie, 1988.

Gerz, Jochen, and Esther Shalev-Gerz. "Das Denkmal gegen Krieg und Faschismus in Hamburg-Harburg." In Hoffmann and Ermert, *Kunst und Holocaust.*

Gibson, Michael. "Hamburg: Sinking Feelings." *ARTnews* 86 (Summer 1987): 106–07.

Gintz, Claude. " 'L'Anti-Monument' de Jochen et Esther Gerz." *Galeries Magazine* 19 (June–July 1987): 82–87, 130.

Goguel, Rudi. *Cap Arcona: Report über den Untergang der Häftlingsflötte in der Lübecker Bücht am 3. Mai 1945.* Frankfurt/Main: Roderberg, 1982.

Goldberg, G., and A. Persitz. "Monument commemoratif à Paris, tombeau du martyr juif inconnu." *L'Architecture d'aujourd'hui* 55 (July–August 1954): 20–24.

Goldberger, Paul. "A Memorial Evokes Unspeakable Events with Dignity." *New York Times,* 30 April 1989.

Golinkin, David. "Yom Hashoah: A Program of Observance." *Conservative Judaism* 37 (Summer 1984): 52–64.

———. "How Should We Commemorate the Shoah in Our Homes?" *Moment* 14 (June 1989): 30–35.

Greenberger, Robert. "The Genesis of the Holocaust Museum." *Jewish Journal,* 12 May 1989.

Haacke, Hans. "Und ihr habt doch gesiegt, 1988." *October* 48 (Spring 1989): 79–87.

Hamer, Hardt-Walther, ed. *Zum Umgang mit dem Gestapo-Gelände: Gutachten im Auftrag der Akademie der Kunste Berlin.* Berlin: Akademie der Kunste, 1988.

Hight, Jim. "Divided in Memory." *Boston Sunday Herald Magazine,* 22 April 1990: 14–20.

Hoffmann, Detlef. "Erinnerungsarbeit der 'zweiten und dritten' Generation und 'Spurensuche' in der zeitgenössischen Kunst." *Kritische Berichte* 2 (1988): 31–46.

Hoffmann, Detlef, and Karl Ermert, eds. *Kunst und Holocaust: Dokumentation einer Tagung der Evangelischen Akademie Loccum.* Loccumer Protokolle 14 (1989).

Hoheisel, Horst. "Rathaus-Platz-Wunde." In *Aschrott Brunnen: Offene Wunde der Stadtgeschichte.* Kassel: Kulturamt, 1989.

"Holocaust Memorials: How Much Is Enough?" *Reform Judaism* (Fall 1987): 8–9.

Hutt, Michael. "Alfred Hrdlicka's Umgestaltung des Hamburger Denkmals für das Infanterieregiment nr. 76." In *Unglücklich das Land, das Helden nötig hat.* Marburg: Jonas, 1990.

Koch, Heinz. *Nationale Mahn- und Gedenkstätte Buchenwald: Geschichte ihrer Entstehung.* Weimar: Buchenwald, 1988.

Koenders, Pieter. *Het Homomonument.* Trans. Eric Wulfert. Amsterdam: Stichting Homomonument, 1987.

Kolmer, Rainer. "A Holocaust Memorial in Berlin?" In *Remembering for the Future*. Oxford: Pergamon, 1988.

Lehrke, Giesela. *Gedenkstätte für die Opfer des Nationalsozialismus: Historisch-politische Bildung an Orten des Widerstandes und der Verfolgung*. Frankfurt and New York: Campus, 1988.

Lewis, Stephen. *Art out of Agony: The Holocaust Theme in Literature, Sculpture, and Film*. Toronto: CBC Enterprises, 1984.

Lishinsky, Yosef. "Yad Vashem as Art." *Ariel: A Review of Arts and Letters in Israel* 55 (1983): 14–25.

Litschke, Egon. *Nationale Mahn- und Gedenkstätte Ravensbrück: Museum*. Rostock: Ostsee-Druck, 1988.

Lopate, Philip. "Resistance to the Holocaust." *Tikkun* 4 (May–June 1989): 55–65.

Lurz, Meinhold. *Kriegerdenkmäler in Deutschland*. Heidelberg: Esprint, 1985.

McGill, Douglas C. "Making of 'Holocaust.'" *New York Times*, 10 Jan. 1986: C20.

Mai, Ekkehard, and Gisela Schmirber, eds. *Denkmal—Zeichen—Monument: Skulptur un öffentlicher Raum heute*. Munich: Prestel, 1989.

Marcuse, Harold. "Das ehemalige Konzentrationslager Dachau: Der mühevolle Weg zur Gedenkstätte, 1945–1968." *Dachauer Hefte: Studien und Dokumente zur Geschichte der nationalsozialistischen Konzentrationslager* 6 (November 1990): 182–205.

———. "West German Strategies for Commemoration." *Dimensions* 3 (1987): 13–14.

Marcuse, Harold, Frank Schimmelfennig, and Jochen Spielmann. *Steine des Anstosses: Nationalsozialismus und Zweiter Weltkrieg in Denkmalen, 1945–1985*. Hamburg: Museum für Hamburgische Geschichte, 1985.

Marszalek, Josef, and Anna Wisniewska, eds. *Majdanek*. Lublin: Krajowa Agencja Wydawnicza, 1983.

Meyerhoff, Harvey M. "Yes, the Holocaust Museum Belongs on the Mall." *Washington Post*, 18 July 1987.

Miller, Judith. *One by One by One: Facing the Holocaust*. New York: Simon and Schuster, 1990.

Milton, Sybil. *In Fitting Memory: The Art and Politics of Holocaust Memorials*. Detroit: Wayne State University Press, 1991.

Minerbi, Sergio I. "The Kidnapping of the Holocaust." *Jerusalem Post*, 25 Aug. 1989: 6.

Molotsky, Irvin. "Arbiters of Monumental Taste." *New York Times*, 8 July 1987.

Moore, Henry. *The Auschwitz Competition*. Booklet published by the State Museum of Auschwitz, 1964.

Muschamp, Herbert. "How Buildings Remember." *New Republic*, 28 Aug. 1989: 27–33.

Niemandsland: Zeitschrift zwischen den Kulturen 1 (1987). Special issue.

Noonan, Leo. "The New Holocaust Museum Has a New Idea." *Jewish Journal*, 4–10 Nov. 1989: 30.

Novak, Vaclav, et al. *Terezín*. Pamatnik Terezín and Soveroceske nakladatelstvi, 1988.

Pfefferman, Naomi. "Martyrs' Memorial: Creating the Dream." *Jewish Journal*, 28 April–4 May 1990: 22.

Plank, Karl A. "The Survivor's Return: Reflections on Memory and Place." *Judaism* 38 (Summer 1989): 263–77.

Plötzensee Memorial, Berlin. Informationszentrum Berlin, Gedenkstätte Deutscher Widerstand, 1985.

Podgarbi, Bronislaw. *Cmentarz Zydowski w Lodzi: The Jewish Cemetery in Lodz.* Warsaw: Wydawnictwo Artus, 1990.

Poplack, Alvin M. "Various Ways Jews Commemorated the Holocaust for Eternity by Permanent Memorials on Cemeteries in the Metropolitan New York Area." Ph.D. diss., Jewish Teachers Seminary, 1981.

Postal, Bernard, and Samuel H. Abramson. *The Landmarks of a People.* New York: Hill and Wang, 1962.

———. *Traveler's Guide to Jewish Landmarks of Europe.* New York: Fleet Press, 1981.

Pristin, Terry. "3 Perspectives on the Holocaust." *Los Angeles Times,* 12 June 1991: B1, 4.

Prittie, Terrence. "Dachau Revisited." *Manchester Guardian Weekly,* 16 Dec. 1954.

Puvogel, Ulrike, ed. *Gedenkstätten für die Opfer des Nationalsozialismus: Eine Dokumentation.* Bonn: Schriftenreihe der Bundeszentrale für politische Bildung, 1987.

Razumovsky, Andreas. "Wo die Toten nicht ruhen: Der Wiener Streit um Hrdlickas Mahnmal." *Frankfurter Allgemeine Zeitung,* 7 Jan. 1989.

Rieth, Adolph. *Denkmal ohne Pathos: Totenmale des zweiten Weltkrieges in Süd-Würtemberg-Hohenzollern mit einer geschichtlichen Einleitung.* Tübingen: Ernst Wasmuth, 1967.

———. *Monuments to the Victims of Tyranny.* New York: Praeger, 1968.

Rittner, Carol, and John K. Roth, *Memory Offended: The Auschwitz Convent Controversy.* New York: Praeger, 1991.

Rosen, Jonathan. "America's Holocaust." *Forward,* 12 April 1991.

Rosenblatt, Gary. "The Simon Wiesenthal Center: State-of-the-art Activism or Hollywood Hype?" *Baltimore Jewish Times,* 14 Sept. 1984: 62–74.

Rosenhaft, Eve. "The Uses of Remembrance: Some Preliminary Thoughts on the Legacy of the Communist Resistance in the GDR after 1945." Forthcoming in Leonides Hill, Francis R. Nicosia, and Lawrence D. Stokes, eds., *Opposition and Resistance to National Socialism in Germany, 1925–1945.*

Rurup, Reinhard. *Topographie des Terrors: Gestapo, S.S. und Reichssicherheitshauptamt auf dem "Prinz-Albrecht-Gelände": Eine Dokumentation.* Berlin: Willmuth Arenhövel, 1987.

Sadek, Vladimir. "The Origin of the Jewish Museum in Prague and the Tradition of Prague Jewish Studies." *Judaica Bohemiae* 24 (1988): 3–5.

Safdie, Moshe. "Holocaust Memorial." In *Jerusalem: The Future of the Past.* Boston: Houghton Mifflin, 1989. Pp. 195–98.

Schubert, Dietrich. "Alfred Hrdlickas antifaschistisches Mahnmal in Hamburg." In Mai and Schmirber, *Denkmal—Zeichen—Monument.*

Schwarberg, Gunther. *Angriffsziel Cap Arcona.* Hamburg: Stern-Buch im Verlag Gruner, 1983.

Shabekoff, Philip. "Jews Gather in Prayer at Dachau to Dedicate a Memorial for Dead." *New York Times*, 8 May 1967.

Sianko, Anna. "Quels monuments reconstruire après la destruction de Varsovie?" In *A l'Est, la mémoire retrouvée*. Paris: La Découverte, 1990.

Singer, Robert. "Ein Massenmord bedarf einer Masse von Mördern." *Jüdische Rundshau* 47 (24 Nov. 1987): 2.

Smolen, Kazimierz, ed. *KL Auschwitz*. Warsaw: Krajowa Agencja Wydawnicza, 1980.

Spector, Shmuel. "Yad Vashem." *Encyclopedia of the Holocaust*. New York: Macmillan, 1990. 4: 1681–86.

Spielmann, Jochen. "Steine des Anstosses oder Schluss-stein der Auseinandersetzung?" In Mai and Schmirber, *Denkmal—Zeichen—Monument*.

————. "Künstlerische Arbeiten als Bestandteil des kulturellen Bedachtnisses: Plädoyer für Gedenkzeichen anstelle von Denkmalen." In Hoffmann and Ermert, *Kunst und Holocaust*.

————. "Steine des Anstosses—Denkmale in der Bundesrepublik Deutschland." *Kritische Berichte* 3/1988: 5–16.

————. "Entwurfe zur Sinngebung des Sinnlosen: Zu einer Theorie des Denkmals als Manifestation des 'kulturellen Gedächtnisses': Der Wettbewerb für ein Denkmal für Auschwitz." Ph.D. diss., Freie Universität, Berlin, 1990.

Szurek, Jean-Charles. "Le Camp-musée d'Auschwitz." In *A l'Est, la mémoire retrouvée*. Paris: La Découverte, 1990.

Tagliabue, John. "A Place Where the Past Overwhelms the Present." *New York Times*, 13 Sept. 1989.

Teitelbaum, Sheldon, and Tom Waldman. "The Unorthodox Rabbi." *Los Angeles Times Magazine*, 15 July 1990: 6–11, 35–39.

Temko, Allan. "The Virtues and Flaws of the Segal Sculpture." *San Francisco Chronicle*, 8 Nov. 1984: 6.

Thompson, Vivian Alport. *A Mission in Art: Recent Holocaust Works in America*. Macon, Ga.: Mercer University Press, 1988.

Tigay, Alan M., ed. *The Jewish Traveler*. Garden City, N.Y.: Doubleday, 1987.

Tolkin, Wiktor. "Die Denkmäler in Stutthof und Majdanek." *Zeichen*, March 1988.

U.S. Holocaust Memorial Council. *Directory of Holocaust Institutions*. Washington, D.C.: U.S. Government Printing Office, 1988.

Vallee, Lillian. "This Empty Place Hurts: The Jewish Question in Recent Polish Publications." *Studium Papers*, April 1989: 60–61.

van Eck, Ludo. *Het Boek der Kampen*. Leuven: Kritak, 1979.

Volkmann, Barbara, ed. *Diskussion zum Umgang mit dem Gestapo Gelände: Dokumentation*. Berlin: Akademie der Künste, 1986.

Von Drateln, Doris. "Jochen Gerz's Visual Poetry." *Contemporanea*, September 1989: 42–47.

Warszawski, David. "The Convent and Solidarity." *Tikkun*, November–December 1989.

Webber, Jonathan. "The Future of Auschwitz: Some Personal Reflections." Oxford: Centre for Postgraduate Hebrew Studies, 1992.

Weinberg, Helen. "George Segal: Holocaust Memorial in New York." *Congress Monthly,* February 1986: 16–17.

Wenzel, Hans. *Ein Kurzer Wegweiser zu den Stätten des Gedenkens an die Zeit des Faschismus im Zentrum Wien.* Vienna: Presse und Informationsdienst der Stadt, 1988.

Werner, Gabriele. "Welche Realität meint das Reale? Zu Alfred Hrdlickas Gegendenkmal in Hamburg." *Kritische Berichte* 16 (1988): 57–67.

Will, George. "Holocaust Museum: Antidote for Innocence." *Washington Post,* 10 March 1983.

Wilson, William. "Segal: Private Visions in the Public Arena." *Los Angeles Times,* 19 Aug. 1984: 91.

Yad Vashem: The Holocaust Martyrs' and Heroes' Remembrance Authority, Jerusalem. Jerusalem: Yad Vashem Publications, 1986.

Yaffe, Richard. *Nathan Rapoport: Sculptures and Monuments.* New York: Shengold, 1980.

Young, James E. "The Biography of a Memorial Icon: Nathan Rapoport's Warsaw Ghetto Monument." *Representations* 26 (Spring 1989): 69–106.

——— . "The Counter-monument: Memory against Itself in Germany Today." *Critical Inqiry* 18 (Winter 1992): 267–96.

——— . "Israel's Memorial Landscape: *Sho'ah,* Heroism, and National Redemption." In Peter Hayes, ed. *Lessons and Legacies: The Meaning of the Holocaust in a Changing World.* Evanston: Northwestern University Press, 1991.

——— . "When a Day Remembers: A Performative History of *Yom Hashoah.*" *History and Memory* 2 (Winter 1990): 54–75.

Zachwatowicz, Jan. "The International Memorial at Auschwitz." *Poland,* January 1965: 11–13.

Zum Umgang mit dem Gestapo-Gelände. Berlin: Akademie der Künste, 1989.

Zum Umgang mit einem Erbe. Berlin: Aktives Museum Faschismus und Widerstand in Berlin, 1985.

II. Critical Literature: Theory of Public Art, Memory, and Memorials.

Adorno, Theodore W. "Valery Proust Museum." In *Prisms.* Trans. Samuel and Shierry Weber. Cambridge: MIT Press, 1981.

al-Khalil, Samir. *The Monument: Art Vulgarity and Responsibility in Iraq.* Berkeley: University of California Press, 1991.

Baczko, Bronislaw. *Les Imaginaires sociaux: Mémoires et espoirs collectifs.* Paris: Payot, 1984.

Bartlett, Frederick. *Remembering: A Study in Experimental Social Psychology.* Cambridge: Cambridge University Press, 1932.

Baudrillard, Jean. *The Evil Demon of Images.* Sidney: Power Institute Publications, 1988.

Beardsley, John. *Art in Public Places.* Washington, D.C.: Partners for Livable Places, 1981.

———. "Personal Sensibilities in Public Places." *Artforum*, Summer: 43–45.

Benjamin, Walter. *Illuminations*. Ed. Hannah Arendt. Trans. Harry Zohn. New York: Schocken, 1969.

Benson, Susan Porter, Stephen Brier, and Roy Rosenzweig, eds. *Presenting the Past: Essays on History and the Public*. Philadelphia: Temple University Press, 1986.

Berger, John. *Ways of Seeing*. London: Penguin, 1972.

———. *The Sense of Sight*. New York: Pantheon, 1985.

Berger, Peter, and Thomas Luckmann. *The Social Construction of Reality*. New York: Anchor, 1967.

Blatti, Jo, ed. *Past Meets Present: Essays about Historic Interpretation and Public Audiences*. Washington, D.C.: Smithsonian Institution Press, 1986.

Bürger, Peter. *The Theory of the Avant Garde*. Trans. Michael Shaw. Minneapolis: University of Minnesota Press, 1984.

Burgin, Victor. *The End of Art Theory: Criticism and Postmodernity*. Atlantic Highlands, N.J.: Humanities Press International, 1986.

Burke, Peter. "History as Social Memory." In *Memory*. Ed. Thomas Butler. New York: Blackwell, 1989.

Bussmann, George, ed. *Arbeit in Geschichte—Geschichte in Arbeit*. Exhibition catalogue. Berlin: NiSHEN, 1988.

Capasso, Nicholas. "Constructing the Past: Contemporary Commemorative Sculpture." *Sculpture* 9 (November–December 1990): 56–63.

Casey, Edward. *Remembering: A Phenomenological Study*. Bloomington and Indianapolis: Indiana University Press, 1987.

Clifford, James, and George E. Marcus, eds. *Writing Culture: The Poetics and Politics of Ethnography*. Berkeley: University of California Press, 1986.

Cohen, Erik. "Who Is a Tourist? A Conceptual Clarification." *Sociological Review* 22 (November 1974): 527–55.

———. "A Phenomenology of Tourist Experiences." *Sociology* 13 (May 1979): 179–201.

Collins, Jim. *Uncommon Cultures: Popular Culture and Post-Modernism*. New York and London: Routledge, 1989.

Connerton, Paul. *How Societies Remember*. Cambridge: Cambridge University Press, 1989.

Crimp, Douglas. "Serra's Public Sculpture: Redefining Site Specificity." In Rosalind Krauss, ed. *Richard Serra/Sculpture*. New York, 1986.

Culler, Jonathan. "Semiotics of Tourism." *American Journal of Semiotics* 1: 127–40.

Danto, Arthur. "The Vietnam Veterans' Memorial." *Nation*, 31 Aug. 1986: 152.

Davis, Natalie Zemon, and Randolph Starn. "Introduction [to Special Issue on Memory and Counter Memory]." *Representations* 26 (Spring 1989): 1–6.

Dehan, Emmanuel. *Shrines and Monuments in Western Jerusalem and Judea*. Tel Aviv: Emmanuel Dehan, 1986.

Doezema, Marianne, and June Hargrove. *The Public Monument and Its Audience*. Cleveland: Cleveland Institute of Art, 1977.

Donato, Eugenio. "The Museum's Furnace: Notes toward a Contextual Reading of Bouvard and Pecuchet." In Josue V. Harari, ed. *Textual Strategies: Perspectives in Post-Structuralist Criticism*. Ithaca: Cornell University Press, 1979.

Douglas, Mary. *How Institutions Think*. London: Routledge and Kegan Paul, 1986.

Eco, Umberto. "Architecture and Memory." *Via* 8: 88–94.

Elsen, Albert. *Modern European Sculpture, 1918–1945: Unknown Beings and Other Realities*. New York: Braziller, 1979.

———. *Rodin's "Thinker" and the Dilemmas of Modern Public Sculpture*. New Haven: Yale University Press, 1985.

———. "What We Have Learned about Modern Public Sculpture: Ten Propositions." *Art Journal* 48 (Winter 1989): 291–97.

Etlin, Richard A. *The Architecture of Death*. Cambridge: Harvard University Press, 1984.

Fisher, Philip. "The Future's Past." *New Literary History* 6 (Spring 1975): 587–606.

Foote, Kenneth E. "To Remember and Forget: Archives, Memory and Culture." *American Archivist* 53 (Summer 1990): 378–92.

Foster, Hal. *Recodings: Art, Spectacle, Cultural Politics*. Seattle: Bay Press, 1985.

Foster, Hal, ed. *The Anti-Aesthetic: Essays on Postmodern Culture*. Port Townsend, Wash.: Bay Press, 1983.

Foucault, Michel. "Questions on Geography." In Colin Gordon, ed. *Power/Knowledge*. New York: Pantheon, 1980.

Funkenstein, Amos. "Collective Memory and Historical Consciousness." *History and Memory* 1 (Spring–Summer 1989): 5–26.

Gaster, Theodore H. *Festivals of the Jewish Year: A Modern Interpretation and Guide*. New York: Morrow, Quill, 1978.

Genette, Gerard. *Narrative Discourse: An Essay in Method*. Ithaca: Cornell University Press, 1980.

Glassberg, David. "Monuments and Memories." *American Quarterly* 43 (March 1991): 106–14.

Greenberg, Irving. *The Jewish Way*. New York: Summit, 1988.

Griswold, Charles L. "The Vietnam Veterans Memorial and the Washington Mall: Philosophical Thoughts on Political Iconography." *Critical Inquiry* 12 (Summer 1986): 688–719.

Halbwachs, Maurice. *The Collective Memory*. Trans. Francis J. Ditter, Jr., and Vida Yazdi Ditter. New York: Harper and Row, 1980.

———. *Les Cadres sociaux de la mémoire*. Paris: Presses Universitaires de France, 1952.

Handelman, Don. *Models and Mirrors: Towards an Anthropology of Public Events*. Cambridge and New York: Cambridge University Press, 1990.

Harbison, Robert. *The Built, the Unbuilt and the Unbuildable: In Pursuit of Architectural Meaning*. Cambridge: MIT Press, 1991.

Harney, Andy Leon, ed. *Art in Public Places*. Washington, D.C., 1981.

Hess, Elizabeth. "A Tale of Two Memorials." *Art in America*, April 1985: 121–27.

Hobsbawm, Eric, and Terence Ranger, eds. *The Invention of Tradition*. Cambridge: Cambridge University Press, 1983.

Horne, Donald. *The Great Museum: The Re-Presentation of History*. London and Sydney: Pluto, 1984.

Howe, Barbara J., and Emory J. Kemp, eds. *Public History: An Introduction*. Malabar, Fla.: Robert E. Krieger, 1986.

Hudson, Kenneth. "An Unnecessary Museum." *Museum* 41 (1989): 114–16.

Hung, Wu. "Tiananmen Square: A Political History of Monuments." *Representations* 35 (Summer 1991): 84–117.

Jackson, John B., ed. *The Necessity for Ruins and Other Topics*. Amherst: University of Massachusetts Press, 1980.

Kammen, Michael. *Mystic Chords of Memory: The Transformation of Tradition in American Culture*. New York: Knopf, 1991.

Karsov, Nina, and Szymon Szechter. *Monuments Are Not Loved*. Trans. Paul Stevenson. London: Hodder and Stoughton, 1970.

Karsov, Nina, Szymon Szechter, and M. Binney, eds. *Our Past before Us: Why Do We Save It?* London: Temple, 1981.

Keyes, Charles F., and Pierre L. van den Berghe. "Tourism and Re-Created Ethnicity." *Annals of Tourism Research* 11 (1984): 343–52.

Kluxen, Wolfgang. "Denkmäler setzen—Identität stiften." In Mai and Schmirber, *Denkmal—Zeichen—Monument*.

Knapp, Steven. "Collective Memory and the Actual Past." *Representations* 26 (Spring 1989): 123–49.

Koselleck, Reinhart. *Futures Past: On the Semantics of Historical Time*. Cambridge and London: MIT Press, 1985.

Krauss, Rosalind. *The Originality of the Avant-Garde and Other Modernist Myths*. Cambridge and London: MIT Press, 1988.

Kruger, Barbara, and Phil Mariani, eds. *Remaking History*. Seattle: Bay Press, 1989.

Kubler, George. *The Shape of Time: Remarks on the History of Things*. New Haven and London: Yale University Press, 1962.

Langner, Johannes. "Denkmal und Abstraktion: Sprachregelungen der monumentalen Symbolik im 20. Jahrhundert." In Mai and Schmirber, *Denkmal—Zeichen—Monument*.

Lippard, Lucy R. *Changing: Essays in Art Criticism*. New York, 1971.

———. *Overlay: Contemporary Art and the Art of Prehistory*. New York: Pantheon, 1983.

Lipsitz, George. *Time Passages: Collective Memory and American Popular Culture*. Minneapolis: University of Minnesota Press, 1990.

Locke, Don. *Memory*. London: Macmillan, 1971.

Lowenthal, David. "Past Time, Present Place: Landscape and Memory." *Geographical Review* 65 (January 1975): 1–36.

———. *The Past Is a Foreign Country*. Cambridge: Cambridge University Press, 1985.

Lumley, Robert, ed. *The Museum Time Machine: Putting Cultures on Display.* London and New York: Routledge, 1988.

Mai, Ekkehard, and Gisela Schmirber. "Mo(nu)ment mal: Denkmal?" In Ekkehard and Schmirber, *Denkmal—Zeichen—Monument.*

Margalit, Avishai. "The Kitsch of Israel." *New York Review of Books*, 24 Nov. 1988: 23–24.

Mayo, James M. *War Memorials as Political Landscape: The American Experience and Beyond.* New York: Praeger, 1988.

Middleton, David, and Derek Edwards, eds. *Collective Remembering.* London: Sage, 1990.

Mitchell, W. J. T. *Iconology: Image, Text, Ideology.* Chicago: University of Chicago Press, 1986.

Mittig, Hans-Ernst. "Das Denkmal." In Werner Busch, ed. *Funkkolleg Kunst: Eine Geschichte der Kunst im Wandel ihrer Funktionen.* Munich: Piper-Verlag, 1987. 2: 532–58.

————. "NS-Motive in der Gegenwartskunst: Flamme empor?" In Berthold Hinz, ed. *NS-Kunst: 50 Jahre danach neue Beiträge.* Marburg: Jonas, 1989.

Mumford, Lewis. *The Culture of Cities.* New York: Harcourt, Brace, Jovanovich, 1938.

Musil, Robert. "Monuments." In *Posthumous Papers of a Living Author.* Trans. Peter Wortsman. Hygiene, Colo.: Eridanos Press, 1987.

Neff, John Hallmark. "Introduction [to Public Art]: Daring to Dream." *Critical Inquiry* 16 (Summer 1990): 857–59.

Neisser, Ulric. *Memory Observed.* Oxford: W. H. Freeman, 1982.

Nietzsche, Friedrich. *The Use and Abuse of History.* Trans. Adrian Collins. New York: Macmillan, 1985.

Nora, Pierre. "Between Memory and History: *Les Lieux de mémoire.*" Trans. Marc Roudebush. *Representations* 26 (1989): 13–25.

————. *Les Lieux de mémoire.* Vol. 1: *La République.* Paris: Gallimard, 1984.

North, Michael. "The Public as Sculpture: From Heavenly City to Mass Ornament." *Critical Inquiry* 16 (Summer 1990): 860–79.

Preziosi, Donald. *Rethinking Art History: Meditations on a Coy Science.* New Haven and London: Yale University Press, 1989.

Prost, Antoine. "Les Monuments aux morts." In Nora, *République.*

Quantrill, Malcolm. *The Environmental Memory: Man and Architecture in the Landscape of Ideas.* New York: Schocken, 1987.

Radermacher, Norbert. *Stücke für Stadt.* Catalogue from the Künstlerhaus Bethanien, Berlin, 1985.

Ragon, Michel. *The Space of Death: A Study of Funerary Architecture, Decoration, and Urbanism.* Trans. Alan Sheridan. Charlottesville: University Press of Virginia, 1983.

Rapoport, Amos. "Sacred Places, Sacred Occasions and Sacred Environments." *Architectural Design* 9–10: 75–82.

Raven, Arlene, ed. *Art in the Public Interest.* Ann Arbor: UMI Research Press, 1989.

Ricoeur, Paul. *History and Truth.* Trans. Charles A. Kelbley. Evanston: Northwestern University Press, 1965.

Rothman, Hal. *Preserving Different Pasts: The American National Monuments.* Urbana: University of Illinois Press, 1989.

Sayre, Henry M. *The Object of Performance: The American Avant-Garde since 1970.* Chicago, 1989.

Schwartz, Barry. "The Recovery of Masada: A Study in Collective Memory." *Sociological Quarterly* 27, no. 2 (1986): 147–64.

Schwartz, Barry, Yael Zerubavel, and B. N. Barnett. "The Social Context of Commemoration: A Study in Collective Memory." *Social Forces* 61 (1982): 374–402.

Scruggs, Jan C., and Joel Swerdlow. *To Heal a Nation: The Vietnam Veterans Memorial.* New York, 1985.

Springer, Peter. "Denkmal und Gegendenkmal." In Mai and Schmirber, *Denkmal— Zeichen—Monument.*

Stalker, Douglas, and Clark Glymour. "The Malignant Objects: Thoughts on Public Sculpture." *Public Interest* 66 (Winter 1982): 3–21.

Storr, Robert. " 'Tilted Arc': Enemy of the People?" In Arlene Raven, ed. *Art in the Public Interest.* Ann Arbor: University of Michigan Press, 1989.

Sturken, Marita. "The Wall, the Screen, and the Image: The Vietnam Veterans Memorial." *Representations* 35 (Summer 1991): 118–42.

Tillich, Paul. *On Art and Architecture.* Edited and translated by John Dillenberger and Jane Dillenberger. New York: Crossroad, 1981.

Toulmin, Stephen, and June Goodfield. *The Discovery of Time.* Chicago: University of Chicago Press, 1965.

Urry, John. *The Tourist Gaze: Leisure and Travel in Contemporary Societies.* London: Sage, 1990.

van Pelt, Robert Jan, and Carroll William Westfall. *Architectural Principles in the Age of Historicism.* New Haven and London: Yale University Press, 1991.

Volp, Rainer. "Zeichen der Mahnung—Zeichen sind nötig, welche Zeichen sind möglich?" In Mai and Schmirber, *Denkmal—Zeichen—Monument.*

Warren, Leon, and Roy Rosenzweig, eds. *History Museums in the United States: A Critical Assessment.* Urbana: University of Illinois Press, 1989.

Weil, Stephen E. *Rethinking the Museum and Other Meditations.* Washington, D.C.: Smithsonian Institution Press, 1990.

Wertsch, James V. "Collective Memory: Issues from a Sociohistorical Perspective." *Quarterly Newsletter of the Laboratory of Comparative Human Cognition* 9: 19–22.

Weyl, Martin. "How Do Museums Speak the Unspeakable?" *New York Times,* 11 June 1989: 38, 44.

Yates, Frances A. *The Art of Memory.* Chicago: University of Chicago Press, 1966.

Zerubavel, Yael. "New Beginning, Old Past: The Collective Memory of Pioneering in Israeli Culture." In Laurence J. Silberstein, ed. *New Perspectives on Israeli History: The Early Years of the State.* New York: New York University Press, 1990.

———. "Invented Tradition and Counter-tradition: The Social Construction of the Past in Israeli Culture." Paper presented at the Association for Jewish Studies annual meeting, December 1990.

———. "The Holiday Cycle and the Commemoration of the Past: History, Folklore and Education." In *Proceedings of the Ninth World Congress of Jewish Studies* 2 (1986): 111–18.

III. Historical, Cultural, and Other Resources

Ainsztein, Reuben. *The Warsaw Ghetto Revolt.* New York: Holocaust Library, 1979.

Améry, Jean. *At the Mind's Limits: Contemplations by a Survivor on Auschwitz and Its Realities.* Trans. Sidney Rosenfeld and Stella P. Rosenfeld. Bloomington: Indiana University Press, 1980.

Baldwin, Peter, ed. *Reworking the Past: Hitler, the Holocaust, and the Historians' Debate.* Boston: Beacon Press, 1990.

Banas, Josef. *The Scapegoats: The Exodus of the Remnants of Polish Jewry.* Trans. Tadeusz Szafar. London: Weidenfeld and Nicholson, 1979.

Barkai, Meyer. *The Fighting Ghettos.* Philadelphia: Lippincott, 1962.

Bartoszewski, Wladyslaw. *The Warsaw Ghetto: A Christian's Testimony.* Trans. Stephen G. Cappellari. Boston: Beacon Press, 1987.

Bauer, Yehuda. "Fighting the Distortions." *Jerusalem Post* International Edition, 9 Sept. 1989: 6.

———. *A History of the Holocaust.* New York and London: Franklin Watts, 1982.

Beckerman, Ruth. *Unzugehörig: Österreicher und Juden nach 1945.* Vienna: Locker, 1989.

Berenbaum, Michael. "On the Politics of Public Commemoration of the Holocaust." *Shoah,* Fall–Winter 1981–82): 6–9, 37.

———. *After Tragedy and Triumph: Modern Jewish Thought and the American Experience.* Cambridge: Cambridge University Press, 1991.

Boyarin, Jonathan. *Polish Jews in Paris: The Ethnography of Memory.* Bloomington: Indiana University Press, 1991.

———. *A Storm from Paradise: The Politics of Jewish Memory.* Minneapolis: University of Minnesota Press, 1992.

Brandys, Kazimierz. *A Question of Reality.* Trans. Isabel Barzun. London: Blond and Briggs, 1981.

Broszat, Martin. "Plädoyer für eine Historisierung des Nationalsozialismus." *Merkur* 39 (1985): 373–85.

Bunzel, John. "Austrian Identity and Anti-Semitism." *Patterns of Prejudice* 21 (Spring 1987).

Bussman, Klaus, and Kaspar Konig. *Skulptur Projekte in Münster, 1987.* Cologne, 1987.

Citron, Atay. "Pageantry and Theatre in the Service of Jewish Nationalism in the United States: 1933–1946." Ph.D. diss., New York University, 1989.

Cole, Sally J. *Legacy on Stone: Rock Art of the Colorado Plateau and Four Corners Region.* Boulder, Colo.: Johnson Books, 1990.

da Silva, Teresien, and Dineke Stam. *Sporen van de Oorlog: Ooggetuigen over plaatsen in Nederland, 1940–1945.* Amsterdam: Anne Frank Stichting, 1989.

Dawidowicz, Lucy. *The Holocaust and the Historians.* Cambridge: Harvard University Press, 1981.

Deutsch, Harold C. *The Conspiracy against Hitler in the Twilight War.* London, 1968.

Diner, Dan. "Historical Experience and Cognition: Perspectives on National Socialism." *History and Memory* 2 (Fall 1990): 84–110.

Dinur, Benzion. "Problems of Research." *Yad [V]ashem Studies* 1 (1957): 7–30.

Domansky, Elizabeth. "How to Remember What to Remember: Jenninger's Speech." Paper given at a conference at Northwestern University entitled "Lessons and Legacies of the Holocaust," November 1989.

Edelman, Marek. *The Ghetto Fighters.* New York: American Representation of the Jewish Workers' Union of Poland, 1946.

Ehrenburg, Ilya, and Vasily Grossman, eds. *The Black Book: The Ruthless Murder of Jews by German-Fascist Invaders throughout the Temporarily-Occupied Regions of the Soviet Union and in the Death Camps of Poland during the War of 1941–1945.* Trans. John Glad and James S. Levine. New York: Holocaust Library, 1981.

Elon, Amos. *The Israelis: Founders and Sons.* New York: Penguin, 1984.

Erlich, Mark. "Honoring the Past to Change the Future: Solidarity and the Warsaw Ghetto." *Tikkun* 3 (September–October 1988): 23–27.

Exenberg, Herbert. *Wien: Antifaschistischer Stadtführer.* Vienna: Wiener Bildungs-ausschuss der SPO, 1985.

Ezrahi, Sidra. "The Holocaust and the Shifting Boundaries of Art and History." *History and Memory* 1 (Fall–Winter 1989): 77–98.

———. "Revisioning the Past: The Changing Legacy of the Holocaust in Hebrew Literature." *Salmagundi,* Fall 1985–Winter 1986: 245–70.

Feig, Konnilyn G. *Hitler's Death Camps: The Sanity of Madness.* New York and London: Holmes and Meier, 1979.

Ficowski, Jerzy. "Script of a Dead Cemetery." In *A Reading of Ashes.* Translated by Keith Bosley with Krystyna Wandycz. London: Menard Press, 1981.

Forman, James. *Codename Valkyrie: Count Stauffenberg and the Plot to Kill Hitler.* New York, 1973.

Fresco, Nadine. "Remembering the Unknown." *International Review of Psycho-Analysis* 11 (1984): 411–27.

Friedländer, Albert, and Elie Wiesel. *The Six Days of Destruction: Meditations toward Hope.* Ramsey, N.J.: Paulist Press, 1988.

Friedlander, Henry. "Holocaust als Problem der politischen Bildung in den USA." In Wolfgang Scheffler and Werner Bergmann, eds., *Lerntag des Zentrums für Anti-semitismusforschung.* Berlin: Technische Universität Berlin, 1988. 5: 109–28.

Friedländer, Saul. "Die Shoah als Element in der Konstruktion israelischer Erinnerung." *Babylon* 2 (1987): 10–22.

———. "The Shoah Between Memory and History." *Jerusalem Quarterly* 53 (Winter 1990).

———. "Martin Broszat/Saul Friedländer: A Controversy about the Historicization of National Socialism." *Yad Vashem Studies* 19 (Fall 1988): 1–47. Repr. in *New German Critique* 44 (Spring–Summer 1988): 85–126.

———. "The 'Final Solution': On the Unease in Historical Interpretation." *History and Memory* 1 (Fall–Winter 1989): 61–76.

Friedländer, Saul, ed. *Probing the Limits of Representation: Nazism and the "Final Solution."* Cambridge: Harvard University Press, 1992.

Friedman, Philip, ed. *Martyrs and Fighters: The Epic of the Warsaw Ghetto.* New York: Praeger, 1954.

Friedman, Thomas. *From Beirut to Jerusalem.* New York: Farrar Straus Giroux, 1989.

Gamzu, Haim. *Ben-Zvi: A Portrait Album.* New York, 1962.

Gershon, Karen, ed. and trans. *Postscript: A Collective Account of the Lives of Jews in West Germany since the Second World War.* London: Gollancz, 1969.

Gittelman, Zvi. "History, Memory, and Politics: The Holocaust in the Soviet Union." *Holocaust and Genocide Studies* 5 (1990): 23–37.

Goldman, Nachum. "The Influence of the Holocaust on the Change in the Attitude of World Jewry to Zionism and the State of Israel." In *Holocaust and Rebirth: A Symposium.* Jerusalem: Yad Vashem, 1974.

Goldstein, Bernard. *The Stars Bear Witness.* New York: Viking, 1949.

Gross, Jan Tomasz. *Polish Society under German Occupation: The Generalgovernment, 1939–1944.* Princeton: Princeton University Press, 1979.

Grossman, David. *See Under: Love.* Trans. Betsy Rosenberg. New York: Farrar Straus Giroux, 1989.

Gutman, Yisrael. *The Jews of Warsaw: Ghetto, Underground, Revolt.* Bloomington: Indiana University Press, 1982.

Gutman, Yisrael, and Shmuel Krakowski. *Unequal Victims: Poles and Jews during World War II.* New York: Holocaust Library, 1986.

Hartman, Geoffrey H., ed. *Bitburg in Moral and Political Perspective.* Bloomington: Indiana University Press, 1986.

———. *The Shapes of Memory.* London: Blackwell, 1993.

Hayes, Peter. *Industry and Ideology: IG Farben in the Nazi Era.* New York and Cambridge: Cambridge University Press, 1987.

Hayes, Peter, ed. *Lessons and Legacies: The Meaning of the Holocaust in a Changing World.* Evanston: Northwestern University Press, 1991.

Hoffmann, Peter. *The History of the German Resistance, 1933–1945.* Cambridge, Mass., 1977.

Horowitz, Gordon J. "The Vanishing Traces." In *In the Shadow of Death: Living outside the Gates of Mauthausen.* New York: Free Press, 1990.

Irwin-Zarecka, Iwona. *Neutralizing Memory: The Jew in Contemporary Poland.* New Brunswick, N.J.: Transaction, 1989.

Kampf, Avram. *Jewish Experience in the Art of the Twentieth Century.* South Hadley, Mass.: Bergin and Garvey, 1984.

Katz, Shaul. "The Israeli Teacher-Guide: The Emergence and Perpetuation of a Role." *Annals of Tourism Research* 12 (1985): 49–72.

Kovner, Abba. *Megillot Ha'eduth.* Israel: Mossad Bialik, 1989. Krajewska, Monika. "Na Cmentarzu Cmentarza—Kazimierzu nad Visla" [Cemetery of a cemetery—Kazimierz on the Vistula]. *Nowiny-Kurier,* 3 May 1985.

Krajewski, Stanislaw. "To Be a Jew in Poland Today." Lecture and unpublished manuscript.

Krinsky, Carol Herselle. *Synagogues of Europe: Architecture, History, Meaning.* Cambridge: MIT Press, 1985.

Kubovy, Arye L. "Nissan 27—A Day of Examen of Conscience." *Yad Vashem Bulletin* 6–7 (June 1960): 2.

Kugelmass, Jack, and Jonathan Boyarin, eds. *From a Ruined Garden: The Memorial Books of Polish Jewry.* New York: Schocken, 1983.

Lamm, Maurice. *The Jewish Way in Death and Mourning.* New York: Jonathan David, 1988.

Lang, Berel. *Act and Idea in the Nazi Genocide.* Chicago: University of Chicago Press, 1990.

Lang, Berel, ed. *Writing and the Holocaust.* New York and London: Holmes and Meier, 1988.

Larkin, Margaret. *The Six Days of Yad Mordechai.* Israel: Yad Mordechai Museum, 1965.

Liebman, Charles S., and Eliezer Don-Yehiya. *Civil Religion in Israel: Traditional Judaism and Political Culture in the Jewish State.* Berkeley: University of California Press, 1983.

Littell, Marcia Sachs, ed. *Liturgies on the Holocaust.* Philadelphia: Anne Frank Institute, 1986.

Lubetkin, Zivia. *In the Days of Destruction and Revolt.* Israel: Ghetto Fighters' House, 1981.

Lukas, Richard C., ed. *Out of the Inferno: Poles Remember the Holocaust.* Lexington: University of Kentucky Press, 1989.

Maier, Charles. *The Unmasterable Past: History, Holocaust, and German National Identity.* Cambridge: Harvard University Press, 1988.

Mark, Ber. *Uprising in the Warsaw Ghetto.* New York: Schocken, 1975.

Marrus, Michael R. *The Holocaust in History.* Hanover, N.H.: University Press of New England, 1987.

Meed, Vladka. *On Both Sides of the Wall.* Israel: Beit Lohamei Hagettaot and Hakibbutz Hameuchad Publishing, 1973.

Merloo, Joost. "Delayed Mourning in Victims of Extermination Camps." In Henry Krystal, ed. *Massive Psychic Trauma.* New York: International Universities Press, 1968.

Mommsen, Hans. *The German Resistance to Hitler.* London, 1970.

Mosse, George L. *Fallen Soldiers: Reshaping the Memory of the World Wars.* New York and Oxford: Oxford University Press, 1990.

———. *The Nationalization of the Masses: Political Symbolism and Mass Movements in Germany from the Napoleonic Wars through the Third Reich.* New York: NAL and Times-Mirror, 1977.

Neuhausler, Johann. *What Was It Like in the Concentration Camp at Dachau?* Munich: R. Eimannsberger, 1974.

Niezabitowska, Malgorzata. *Remnants: The Last Jews of Poland.* Trans. William Brand and Hanna Dobosiewicz. New York: Friendly Press, 1986.

Nolte, Ernst. "Between Myth and Revisionism? The Third Reich in the Perspective of the 1980s." In H. W. Koch, ed. *Aspects of the Third Reich.* New York: St. Martin's, 1985.

Parkinson, F., ed. *Conquering the Past: Austrian Nazism Yesterday and Today.* Detroit: Wayne State University Press, 1989.

Passerini, Luisa. *Fascism in Popular Memory: The Cultural Experience of the Turin Working Class.* Trans. Robert Lumley and Jude Bloomfield. Cambridge: Cambridge University Press, 1987.

Pingel, Falk. "Erinnern oder Vergessen? Überlegungen zum Gedenken an den Widerstand und die Opfer des Nationalsozialismus." *Aus Politik und Zeitgeschichte: Beilage zur Wochenzeitung das Parlament,* 28 Feb. 1981: 14–29.

Plagemann, Volker. "Trauerarbeit: Neuere politische Monumente in Hamburg." In Bussmann. *Arbeit in Geschichte.* Pp. 33–49.

Rabinbach, Anson, and Jack Zipes, eds. *Germans and Jews since the Holocaust: The Changing Situation in West Germany.* New York and London: Holmes and Meier, 1986.

Roskies, David. *Against the Apocalypse: Responses to Catastrophe in Modern Jewish Culture.* Cambridge: Harvard University Press, 1984.

———. *Night Words: A Midrash on the Holocaust.* Washington, D.C.: B'nai B'rith Hillel Foundation, 1971.

Roskies, David, and Irving Greenberg, eds. *Holocaust Commemoration for Days of Remembrance.* Washington, D.C.: U.S. Memorial Council, 1981.

Schwarz-Bart, André. *The Last of the Just.* Trans. Stephen Becker. London: Secker and Warburg, 1961.

Senesh, Hannah. *Hannah Senesh: Her Life and Diary.* Trans. Marta Cohn. New York: Schocken, 1973.

Szonyi, David M., ed. *The Holocaust: An Annotated Bibliography and Resource Guide.* New York: Ktav, 1985.

Tate Gallery. *The Unknown Political Prisoner: International Sculpture Competiton.* London: Tate Gallery, 1953.

Tuchman, Phyllis. *George Segal.* New York: Abbeville, 1983.

Tuwim, Julian. *My, Zydzi Polscy . . . ; We, Polish Jews.* Ed. Chone Shmeruk. Jerusalem: Magnes Press, Hebrew University, 1984.

Vidal-Naquet, Pierre. *Les Juifs, la mémoire et le présent.* Paris: Maspero, 1981.

von Klemperer, Klemens. "The Legacy of the Plot to Kill Hitler." *New York Times* Op-ed page, 21 July 1990.

Wechsler, Lawrence. *The Passion of Poland: From Solidarity through the State of War.* New York: Pantheon, 1984.

Wellers, George. "Essai de détermination du nombre de morts au camp d'Auschiwtz." *Le Monde juif* 112 (1983): 127–59.

Wieviorka, Annette. *Le Procès Eichmann.* Brussels: Editions complexe, 1989.

———. *Déportation et genocide: Entre la mémoire et l'oubli.* Paris: Plon, 1992.

Wieviorka, Annette, and Itzhok Niborski. *Les Livres du souvenir: Mémoriaux juifs de Pologne.* Paris: Editions Gallimard/Julliard, 1983.

Winzen, Matthias. "The Need for Public Representation and the Burden of the German Past." *Art Journal* 48 (Winter 1989): 309–14.

Wippermann, Wolfgang. *Steinerne Zeugen: Stätten der Judenverfolgung in Berlin.* Berlin: Pädagogisches Zentrum und Verlag Albert Hentrich, 1982.

Wisse, Ruth R. "Poland without Jews." *Commentary* 66 (August 1978): 64–68.

———. "Poland's Jewish Ghosts." *Commentary* 83 (February 1987): 25–34.

Yad Vashem. *Holocaust and Rebirth: A Symposium.* Jerusalem: Yad Vashem, 1974.

Yerushalmi, Yosef Hayim. *Zakhor: Jewish History and Jewish Memory.* Seattle: University of Washington Press, 1982.

Young, James E. "Interpreting Literary Testimony: A Preface to Rereading Holocaust Diaries and Memoirs." *New Literary History* 18 (Winter 1986–87): 403–23.

———. *Writing and Rewriting the Holocaust: Narrative and the Consequences of Interpretation.* Bloomington: Indiana University Press, 1988.

Index